DATE		
NOV 14'79		

AQUINAS

Modern Studies in Philosophy is a series of anthologies presenting contemporary interpretations and evaluations of the works of major philosophers. The editors have selected articles designed to show the systematic structure of the thought of these philosophers, and to reveal the relevance of their views to the problems of current interest. These volumes are intended to be contributions to contemporary debates as well as to the history of philosophy; they not only trace the origins of many problems important to modern philosophy, but also introduce major philosophers as interlocutors in current discussions.

Modern Studies in Philosophy is prepared under the general editorship of Amelie Oksenberg Rorty, Livingston College, Rutgers University.

Anthony Kenny has been a Fellow and Tutor in Philosophy at Balliol College, Oxford since 1964. He studied at Oxford and at the Gregorian University in Rome. He translated and edited Volume 22 of the Blackfriars edition of the *Summa Theologiae*; his *Action, Emotion and Will* was published in 1963 and *The Five Ways* in 1969.

MODERN STUDIES IN PHILOSOPHY

AQUINAS:

A Collection of Critical Essays

EDITED BY ANTHONY KENNY

UNIVERSITY OF NOTRE DAME PRESS
Notre Dame, Indiana 46556

University of Notre Dame Press edition 1976

Printed by special arrangement with Doubleday & Company, Inc.

Anchor Books edition: 1969
Doubleday & Company, Inc.
Garden City, New York

Library of Congress Cataloging in Publication Data

Kenny, Anthony John Patrick, comp.
  Aquinas : a collection of critical essays.

  Reprint of the 1st ed. published by Anchor Books,
Garden City, N.Y., in series: Modern studies in
philosophy.
  Bibliography: p.
  CONTENTS: Knowles, D. The historical context of
the philosophical work of St. Thomas Aquinas.—Logic
and metaphysics: Geach, P. Form and existence.
McCabe, H. Categories. Ross, J. F. Analogy as
a rule of meaning for religious language. [etc.]
  1. Thomas Aquinas, Saint, 1225?–1274—Addresses,
essays, lectures.
 [B765.T54K43 1976]   189' .4   76-22412
ISBN 0-268-00579-6
ISBN 0-268-00580-X pbk.

CONTENTS

INTRODUCTION

As a philosopher, St. Thomas Aquinas is both over-valued and undervalued. He is overvalued by those who regard him as a unique source of philosophic truth, whose ideas can only be adapted and never superseded by later thought and discovery. He is undervalued by those who think of him as being, outside theology, no more than an erratic commentator on Aristotle. Readers within the philosophical tradition now dominant in Britain and the United States are more likely to be tempted to underrate Aquinas than to overrate him, and it is to them that I shall address myself in this Introduction.

Aquinas is, I believe, one of the dozen greatest philosophers of the western world. His philosophy of nature has been antiquated, in great part, by the swift progress of natural science since the Renaissance. His philosophy of logic has been in many respects improved upon by the work of logicians and mathematicians in the last hundred years. But his metaphysics, his philosophical theology, his philosophy of mind and his moral philosophy entitle him to rank with Plato and Aristotle, with Descartes and Leibniz, with Locke and Hume and Kant.

I do not propose to justify this opinion here. Only a systematic study of Aquinas' writings could do so: I hope that a reading of the essays in the present collection will do something to make it plausible. In this Introduction I shall suggest some reasons which have led to Aquinas' being unfairly neglected by philosophers.

The greatest single obstacle to the appreciation of Aquinas as a philosopher is undoubtedly the official respect accorded to him as a theologian, particularly within the Roman Catholic Church. This damages his reputation with philosophers in three ways.

First, the panoply of ecclesiastical approval which surrounds the *Summa Theologiae* gives some non-Catholic readers the impression that they are reading propaganda for a party line. Stomachs which feel slight nausea at the sight of an Imprimatur turn right over at the prospect of a laudatory encyclical such as Pope Leo XIII's *Aeterni Patris*.

Secondly, the extensive teaching of Thomism in Catholic institutions has resulted in the existence of a large number of Thomists whose comprehension of Aquinas does not always keep pace with their enthusiasm. To be sure, all first-rate philosophers collect second-rate followers; but Plato and Hume are not preached at street corners or boiled down into pamphlets for sale in church porches. The very existence of Thomism as a system arouses suspicion in many who doubt whether philosophy can be helpfully regarded as a set of memorizable theses which can be handed down from one generation to the next.

Thirdly, St. Thomas' reputation for orthodoxy sometimes results in his own philosophical integrity being called into question. Lord Russell, for instance, has written: "There is little of the true philosophic spirit in Aquinas. He does not, like the Platonic Socrates, set out to follow wherever the argument may lead. He is not engaged in an enquiry, the result of which it is impossible to know in advance. Before he begins to philosophize, he already knows the truth; it is declared in the Catholic faith. . . . The finding of arguments for a conclusion given in advance is not philosophy". This last remark perhaps comes oddly from a philosopher who took three hundred and sixty dense pages to offer a proof that $1 + 1 = 2$ (*Principia Mathematica* *54.43). What matters in a philosopher is surely not how he came by his conclusions, but how cogent are the arguments he presents for them. Still, many would sympathise with the spirit of Russell's remark. But it is important to remember that when official or semi-official Catholic teaching coincides with that of Aquinas it is often a case of the official teaching agreeing with Aquinas rather than Aquinas agreeing with the official teaching. St. Thomas devoted the greater part of his work, even in theology, to questions which were in his day theologically open for Catholics. The widespread Catholic admiration for Aristotle, which Russell singles out for special complaint, is manifestly the result and not the motive of Aquinas' attitude to the philosopher. In his own day he had his Aristotelianism censured by archbishops at Oxford and Paris.

It would obviously be unfair to blame Thomas for the defects of some Thomists. The more unattractive theses of neo-Thomism sometimes turn out to derive not from Aquinas but from later and lesser thinkers from Cajetan to Mercier. The fossilization suggested by the inflexible structure of scholastic manuals has little in common with the echoes of live debates in the medieval *Quaestiones Disputatae*. Canon 1366 of the code of canon law prescribed that seminarists should be taught philosophy according to the method, doctrine, and principles of the Angelic Doctor. But it would be unwise to exaggerate the effect of this canon. The enjoined study of Aquinas has not always taken the form of any actual reading of his writings. Since the Second Vatican Council the veneration accorded to Thomism as a system seems to have been considerably dissipated; and for years now a succession of distinguished medievalist philosophical scholars has taught us the difference between textbook neo-scholasticism and what Aquinas and his contemporaries themselves wrote and believed.

But even when Thomas has been firmly distinguished from Thomism, his writings present a forbidding prospect to the average Anglo-American philosopher. First, by their sheer bulk. The *Summa contra Gentiles* is only one of a score of volumes among Aquinas' works; yet by itself it is sixty thousand words longer than the whole corpus of Berkeley's philosophy.

Again, like medieval philosophers, Aquinas is an extremely technical writer, using a complicated scholastic vocabulary and discussing perennial philosophical problems within a specialised and esoteric framework of concepts. Between Boethius and Bacon there was hardly a philosopher prepared to write for amateurs and gentlemen.

Even in comparison with other medieval writers, Aquinas is difficult for a philosopher to read. For apart from his commentaries on Aristotle he wrote little explicit philosophy. Though he was uncommonly aware of the differences between philosophical and theological method, he produced much of his best philosophical work in the course of investigating theological problems. This makes it sometimes difficult to locate crucial items in his system. How could one guess in advance, for instance, that his fullest treatment of predication would occur in his discussion of the Incarnation, or that his theories about abstract ideas can be found in the quodlibetical question *Whether the number six is the creator?*

In spite of the difficulties, there are indications of an increasing interest in Aquinas among analytic philosophers. There seem to be two reasons for this, one philosophical and the other fortuitous. The unphilosophical reason is that there has been an increase in the last decades in the number of Catholic students and faculty in non-Catholic schools of philosophy in Britain and the United States. The more important reason is that the work of Wittgenstein has convinced many people that the post-Renaissance preoccupation with epistemology was in some respects a distortion of philosophy. This has removed one great barrier to the understanding of Aquinas, whose epistemological interests were comparatively slight.

In assembling this anthology I have tried to choose essays by writers whose interests and methods would be intelligible to philosophers brought up in the analytic tradition. A professional Thomist might well be surprised at the selection if he did not bear in mind the audience to which it is principally directed. While gathering material for inclusion I read many articles of impeccable scholarship and philosophical acumen which I was unable to select because they would have struck an outsider as too inbred and too disconnected with contemporary philosophical concerns. Someone compiling an anthology of articles by Thomists for Thomists would have produced an entirely different selection; but the present collection may have an interest for Thomists too, by presenting familiar ideas in an unfamiliar light and indicating what aspects of their system strike the non-Thomist as interesting and important.

I have divided the volume into four parts corresponding to the four areas in which I believe Aquinas' philosophical contribution was most significant: informal logic and metaphysics, philosophical theology, philosophy of mind, and moral philosophy. I have been fortunate in being able to include as a historical preface to the philosophical essays a paper by the former Regius Professor of Modern History in the University of Cambridge which shows how Aquinas' thought developed under the influences of the teaching of Albert, the revival of Aristotelianism, and the prevailing Augustinian theology, and how in its turn it influenced later medieval writers such as Dante and the Rhineland mystics.

In his paper "Form and Existence" Peter Geach introduces two of the key terms of Aquinas' metaphysics. He explains forms as being what predicates stand for, and links Aquinas' theories with Frege's work on numbers and concepts. He discusses also the doctrine of divine simplicity, the question whether existence is a predicate, and the real distinction between essence and existence.

Herbert McCabe, who acknowledges a debt to Geach, borrows also from Strawson the distinction between sentences and statements and sets it to work to clarify the Aristotelian-Thomist theory of Categories. He expounds the scholastic theory of predicables as a theory of five different ways in which a predicate can be appropriate to a subject, and the theory of predicaments or categories as a theory of ten different types of statement. In the course of his exposition he has a number of interesting points to make about the nature of definition, about predications of identity, and about the notion of presupposition. He connects Aquinas' theory of *entia per accidens* with Russell's theory of descriptions: *entia per accidens*, he believes, are logical constructions out of *entia per se*, which are items in one or other of the ten categories. In conclusion he has a brief discussion of the theory of analogy and shows the connection between St. Thomas' general view of language and the special question of the use of language about God.

This point is discussed at much greater length by James F. Ross, whose paper is designed to restate St. Thomas' theory of analogy in terms of modern semantic analysis. He claims that a theory fundamentally similar to Aquinas' appears to be necessary if one is to be able either to talk of God in informative language or to combine a category theory with an attempt to make true metaphysical, transcategorial statements.

Geach's paper "Nominalism", though it concerns Aquinas only in part, illuminates the relationship in his system between logic and theology. Geach attacks the theory that predication is to be understood as the attaching of a second name to what the subject of a sentence names: he shows how this theory applied in theological contexts often leads from orthodox premises to heretical conclusions. Ockham's way of dealing with this was to reject the application of logic to theology; Aquinas' approach was rather to reject the two-name theory of predication in non-theological contexts also.

The section devoted to philosophical theology

opens with Patterson Brown's paper on St. Thomas' doctrine of Necessary Being. It is often believed that St. Thomas held that everything in the world around us was contingent, and that God alone was a logically necessary, infinitely perfect being. Brown shows that in the mature thought of Aquinas there are necessary beings other than God, that "necessary being" does not mean "logically necessary being", and that a necessary being need not be an infinitely perfect being. He shows that for St. Thomas as for Aristotle "necessary" means "neither generable nor corruptible by any natural process"; and using this definition he presents an exegesis of the Third Way, the proof of God's existence from necessity and contingence.[1]

Another of the Five Ways, the proof *ex motu*, is treated in a formal and symbolic manner in the paper by Jan Salamucha. Salamucha begins with a general account of the Five Ways and an introduction to the notions of propositional calculus, set theory, and theory of relations necessary for the understanding of his formalisation. He presents a formal thesis which is capable of interpretation as "If whatever is in motion is moved by something, and if the relation of *moving* is an ordered relation, and if in the ordered field of the relation *moving* there exists a first element, then there exists an object which moves without being moved." He presents formal proofs of this thesis, and derivations of the three elements of the antecedent, and compares them with the informal proofs of their analogues in St. Thomas' argument in the *Summa contra Gentiles*. He suggests various simplifications possible in Aquinas' argument, and shows how it needs

[1] It should be noted that Guy Jalbert has shown, in his book *Necessité et contingence chez S. Thomas d'Aquin et ses prédécesseurs* (Ottawa, 1961), that in his youth Aquinas, under the influence of Avicenna, held a doctrine similar to that commonly attributed to him, but that at the time of writing the *Summa contra Gentiles* he was converted by the reading of Averroes to the different doctrine documented by Brown.

modification because of Aquinas' erroneous belief that
an infinite set must lack either a first or a last element.

Several of the Five Ways appeal to the principle
that an ascending series of causes must have a first
member. In his paper "Infinite Causal Regression"
Patterson Brown defends this principle against a number of common criticisms which, he claims, ignore
the crucial distinction between causal series which are
ordered *per se* (as when A causes B to cause C) and
those which are ordered only *per accidens* (as when
A causes B, and B causes C, but A does not cause B
to cause C). He criticises the principle himself as involving a too legalistic notion of causality which
comes close to equating it with responsibility.

Aquinas describes the relation of creatures to their
First Cause as one of total dependence. In his paper
John Deck argues that this is inconsistent with the distinction between essence and existence which Aquinas
attributes to all creatures. For the substance or essence
of a created thing to be to it "through itself", he argues, is incompatible with the total dependence of
the creature on the creator.

The paper "Divine Omniscience and Human Freedom" discusses Aquinas' treatment of the contention
that if God has always known what human beings are
going to do they cannot ever act freely. It rejects
Aquinas' solution in terms of an eternal vision copres-
ent with every moment of passing time, but suggests
an alternative way in which he might have solved the
problem he presented.

Philosophy of mind is an area which has been fruit-
fully worked in recent years by philosophers in both
the analytic and the Thomist tradition. Any attempt
to build a bridge between the two traditions in this
field must take account of St. Thomas' theory of abstraction, which is studied in the paper "Intellect and
Imagination in Aquinas". A human intellect united to
a body, Aquinas believed, consisted of two faculties,
one active and one passive. The passive intellect was

the locus of ideas, the active intellect was the power to abstract ideas from the phantasms or presentations of the imagination and senses. In opposition to any theory of innate ideas, Aquinas insisted that without the appropriate sense-experience no natural science was possible; in opposition to crude forms of empiricism he insisted that sense-experience alone was not sufficient to explain the acquisition of universal concepts and their exercise in the knowledge of necessary truths. Aquinas' theory of intellect is complicated and difficult, subtly worked out in great detail. Some of the difficulties can be removed by the patient unravelling of ambiguities in his technical terms; others seem to involve philosophical theses which it is not at all easy to accept. In particular the account of the relations between the intellect and the imagination seems to be vitiated by a misleading conception of the imagination as an interior sense.

One of the most interesting and controversial aspects of St. Thomas' philosophy of mind is his claim that it is possible to give a rigorous philosophical demonstration that the soul is immortal. His argument is presented in contemporary terms in the paper by Herbert McCabe. Aquinas believed that animals no less than men had souls, and McCabe argues that to treat the activities of particular parts of an animal as being behaviour of the whole animal is *eo ipso* to regard an animal as having a soul. But the souls of animals, according to Aquinas, were imperishable only in the trivial sense in which any form, being one of the terms used in the analysis of perishing, is imperishable. Human souls, he claimed, were imperishable in a different sense, because human beings were capable of non-bodily operations such as understanding. By his mind man is capable of understanding the nature of all bodies, and so, Aquinas argued, his mind cannot possess the nature of any corporeal thing; just as spectacles through which all colours can be discriminated cannot themselves have any colour. McCabe con-

cludes with an account of Aquinas' theory of intentionality: the mind for him is neither more nor less
than the locus of intentional being.

This theory of intentionality is criticised in the paper by Peter Sheehan. What makes the theory attrac-
tive, Sheehan says, is the breakdown of any theory
which says that the occurrence of a thought of X consists in the occurrence in the mind of some entity—a
word, or image, or symbol—which stands in some relation to X. Faced with such a breakdown, it seems at-
tractive to say that the thought of X consists in the
occurrence of X itself, or perhaps rather of the nature
of X, in an immaterial mode. But how can the nature
of a material thing occur without matter? And if the
form of a material thing occurs immaterially, how can
it be individuated? Aquinas accepted the conclusion
that only universals were directly known by the mind,
but argued that individuals could be thought of by
relating universals to mental images of particulars. But
this, Sheehan argues, involves the theory of intentionality in all the difficulties of the relational theory which
it was supposed to replace.

The final section of the volume, which is devoted
to ethics or moral philosophy, consists of two papers
only. The first, by Alan Donagan, argues that Thomist
natural law theory has much to offer contemporary
moral philosophy. Aquinas' deduction of particular
precepts is often questionable: for instance, his absolute prohibition on lying derives from the dubious
premises that the natural end of speech is to express
what is in the speaker's mind and that it is wrong to
engage voluntarily in a natural activity while prevent-
ing it from arriving at its natural end. But the general
framework of the theory is defensible, and involves
no violation of the autonomy of ethics; and Donagan
suggests a new way of deriving specific moral precepts
from the first precept of natural law, *via* the Kantian
notion that man exists as an end in himself.

Germain Grisez, in the second paper, argues that

both critics and defenders of St. Thomas are mistaken in thinking that he regards the particular precepts of the natural law as conclusions derivable from a single first principle. Aquinas' first principle is not a command to do moral good and avoid moral evil, he argues; it is rather a principle of all practical reasoning, that good is to be done and pursued and evil to be avoided, which is prescriptive but not imperative, and which refers not only to moral good and evil but to many other human values and disvalues. The basic principles of the natural law are self-evident appreciations of these values; they are not derivable from the first principle, but related to them in the way that self-evident truths of theoretical reasoning are related to the principle of non-contradiction. Aquinas, unlike the utilitarians, thought that morally good action had intrinsic worth; unlike some deontologists, he did not think it was the only thing which had intrinsic worth. The natural law as conceived by Aquinas is not only a curb on action, but a spur to action; it includes not only the good which must be done, but the non-obligatory good it would be well to do. The first principle of practical reasoning is operative in wrong evaluations as well as in correct ones, just as the principle of contradiction is operative in false judgements as well as in true ones. The principle is prescriptive and not descriptive (unlike, say, the ascription of a non-natural property of goodness to an object) but it is not imperative (it does not involve or depend on the expression of a will). The addition of will to theoretical knowledge can never make it into practical knowledge: in this Aquinas would have agreed with Hume and modern defenders of the distinction between "ought" and "is".

Grisez's paper is less like an essay in analytical philosophy, and more like an essay in professional Thomism, than the other papers in the collection. I have included it not only because of its great intrinsic interest, but because, standing at the end of the book, it could well serve as a bridge to help the reader who has persevered thus far to venture into the more orthodox Thomist literature. In the Bibliography, too, I have not been as restrictive as in the choice of papers for inclusion, but have tried to list a representative selection of studies of Aquinas from a number of different philosophical and non-philosophical viewpoints. Information about methods of citation of St. Thomas' works will be found in the Bibliography.

For suggestions about the contents of this volume I am indebted to Amelie Rorty and to John Finnis.

A.K.

THE HISTORICAL CONTEXT

OF THE PHILOSOPHICAL WORK

OF ST THOMAS AQUINAS

DAVID KNOWLES

The work (and the *Works*) of St Thomas Aquinas may be approached and considered in several different ways. The Thomist theologian, or at least the Thomist theologian of the old school, regards them as an authority, if not as a sacred book. In them he sees the origin and the basic principles of the great system of scholastic theology which he expounds and in them he expects to find the answer, or at least the way to an answer, to almost any question in philosophy or theology. Gardeil, the speculative theologian, Garrigou-Lagrange, the exponent of mystical contemplation, Maritain, the political theorist and the aesthetic critic, all go to the two *Summae* and find there the chapter and verse they require. The *Summae* are indeed a theological Harrods' where almost anything can be found if you look long enough. By these people the works of St Thomas are regarded—and quite rightly for their purpose—as a single whole and without any context. They are just the *Opera Divi Thomae*, and you may find what you want anywhere in them. Their history, their background are of no more interest to the Thomist theologian than is the history or date of Greek dictionary or a table of logarithms. They are to him as the Bible was to the Puritan.

This attitude to St Thomas was universal among scholastic theologians till, some eighty years ago, scholars, some of them also theologians, began to in-

Aquinas Society of London paper, 1958; reprinted with permission of the author, David Knowles.

vestigate the history, as distinct from the content, of
medieval thought. With them, and in particular with
one of the greatest of their number, Martin Grabmann,
began a new approach. A critical attempt was made
for the first time not only to establish in every detail
the canon of the works of Aquinas, but also to date
them and having dated them, to note the development
of thought and even the revisions and changes that
took place in the works of Aquinas as the years passed.
To Grabmann and his like there was no static system
in St Thomas' works. If we may take an analogy
from architecture, we may, in considering a cathedral
look at one—say, Salisbury—as a whole, as it is, and
examine and define its component parts: nave, tran-
septs, tower, spire, buttresses, mouldings and what
not. But we can approach it quite differently, to ask
when and by whom it was built, whether there have
been additions, how much is modern restoration and
so on. So Grabmann and the historians tell us how the
thought in the *Commentary on the Sentences* developed into that of the *Summa contra Gentiles* and
how a *quaestio* or a *quodlibet* influenced the *Summa*.
To them there is no flat Thomist system, but a mind
forever grappling with problems and advancing and
ever changing direction with the years. When one
reads some parts of Grabmann and his followers one
feels at times (though wrongly) that to use the works
of St Thomas as a repository of doctrines and demonstrations is quite impossible; that St Thomas changed
and modified his view without ceasing, and that no
one is justified in supposing that his second thoughts
are more 'Thomist' than his first, or that, had he lived
to be seventy, he would not have modified his views
again more than once. Not only is it rash to cite an
opinion without being quite sure it was not afterwards
modified, but even the decision that the last is the best
and final is a rash one. A somewhat similar process has
been at work on Plato during the past century and has
made it clear not only that Plato developed and

changed his mind again and again, but that his latest dialogues are in many ways less typically 'Platonic', and indeed criticize some of the elements in his own thought which succeeding ages have felt to be the most valuable. I am not saying that this comparison can be pressed, or that we cannot in fact find a coherent 'system' in St Thomas. I merely wish to show that the literary critic's approach to his works is different from that of the theologian.

There is yet a third approach, and it is that which I wish to develop a little in this paper. Both Garrigou-Lagrange and Grabmann are agreed in treating St Thomas' works *in vacuo* so to say—in the one case as a store-house, in the other as a living, growing, changing organism. We may, however, look upon them as merely one feature in a landscape, one link in a chain; we may consider their significance in the stream of history, before and after their composition; we may ask what they owe to the past and what, if anything, was novel or original in them. In so doing, we must forget for the time being the subsequent history of Thomism and its position in the Church of to-day.

St Thomas was born *c.* 1226 and was therefore at the receptive age of intellectual adolescence *c.* 1246–50. It is difficult for us to realize that at that time, after two centuries of scholastic activity, there was still no system or systems of philosophy taught in the schools. Theology was still, and indeed always in theory remained, a study of the Scriptures reinforced by a study of the great theological compendium of Peter the Lombard, now a century old. The preparation for this was a course in arts which was taken by those who had passed rapidly through a school course of grammar and Latin literature, and which consisted of readings and exercises in Aristotelian Logic. Till 1200 and even after that the masters of arts had no textbooks save the various logical works of Aristotle and some commentaries, ancient and recent, upon them. They did not deal, and were in fact expressly forbidden to

deal, with the great problems of philosophy such as
the existence and nature of God, the immortality of
the soul, free-will and the rest. These, so far as they
were dealt with at all, were the province of theologians. It must be remembered that until *c.* 1215 no
strictly philosophical works of Aristotle were current
in the West, and of Plato only the *Timaeus* and the
Meno, the one a long and difficult dialogue dealing
principally with cosmogony, the other putting forward, without any context, Plato's opinion that all
learning is really a remembering of experience in a
previous existence.

But from *c.* 1200 onwards the schools of the West
were receiving, in wave after wave and piece by piece,
the whole corpus of Aristotle—psychology, metaphysics, ethics, and politics. We are not concerned with the
circumstances of this invasion, or the peculiar colour
given to some of the elements of thought by their con-
tamination with Neoplatonic or Arabian opinions. For
us all that matters is that a great philosophical system,
the most complete and logical that the ancient world
had produced, was now available for study and exploi-
tation. Available—yes; but not immediately. Firstly because it came to the West piece by piece, and often
very badly translated. Secondly, because it did not
come pure, but contaminated with non-Aristotelian
elements. Thirdly, because no great philosopher—not
even Aristotle—can be grasped at first reading. The *de
Anima,* for example, and still more the *Metaphysics,*
are very tough nuts to crack, especially in a bad translation. Fourthly, because a great deal of Aristotle, especially when mingled with spurious work and accompanied by Arabian commentaries, is offensive to pious
ears. For all these reasons a period of great confusion
ensued. The artists were prohibited from lecturing on
the natural philosophy of Aristotle and were anyhow
debarred from many provinces of natural theology
and ethics. Yet they were within sight of material
enough to feed their minds for a lifetime. The old

maxim: *non est consenescendum in artibus*—'the arts school is an inn not a home'—was being outdated. The theologians, on the other hand, when they needed philosophical arguments and principles, had now a great and growing store to draw from, but they had no training behind them and no one to interpret Aristotle for them. Moreover they had all unconsciously absorbed a great deal of thought that was incompatible with Aristotle. For eight hundred years Western theology had been dominated by Augustine, and Augustine was throughout his life, in matters of philosophy and in all the No Man's Land between philosophy and theology, a Christianizing Neoplatonist. Aristotle's teaching had always been very different from Plato's; Neoplatonism was a stage further away still, and when Christianized was even more remote. For Aristotle, the philosopher of common sense and this world, knowledge comes from the mind working on experience, the visible universe is the only field of operation, the immortality of the soul is not personal, and God is needed only as a logical postulate, an ultimate linch-pin to hold the universe together. For Augustine, God and the soul alone are of interest; knowledge is an illumination of the mind in contact with the divine ideas of things; and the whole life of a Christian is a growing absorption into God. Consequently, old theologians were inevitably hostile to the cold, clear, anti-mystical thought of Aristotle, especially when this was given a pronouncedly determinist or even pantheistic twist by the Arabians. That their fears were not groundless is shown by the emergence, soon after 1250, of the movement among the artists at Paris which used to be known as Latin Averroism and which we are now asked to call radical Aristotelianism. The leader of this movement was Siger of Brabant and his aim was to extract from the works of Aristotle a complete system of philosophy which should be absolutely autonomous, i.e., it should neither ask for help nor accept warnings from Chris-

tian theology. If Aristotle said one thing, e.g., that the
world was eternal, and Christian teaching said
another, e.g., that it had been created by God, the
philosopher would make no attempt to harmonize or
to pronounce upon the contradiction—he would assert
the one as a philosopher and believe the other as a
Christian.

Quite independently, it would seem, of the Paris artists, the celebrated Dominican theologian and poly-
math, Albert, had decided to undertake the vast enter-
prise of making the whole of Aristotle usable by
means of a philosophical and theological commentary.
Albert was probably an autodidact in philosophy—
which saved him from several kinds of mistake and
prejudice—and had the greatest admiration for Aristotle. He was not, however, primarily a philosopher,
and when he wrote as a theologian he was quite ready
to go to others besides Aristotle. Thus he followed
Augustine rather than Aristotle in his treatment of the
human soul. Nevertheless, he wished Aristotle to have
fair play and no prejudice, and was outspoken enough
against those, even of his own order, who despised and
opposed what they did not really know.

Albert had the good fortune to have among his
pupils, both at Paris and Cologne, the young Thomas
Aquinas, who had been brought up on Aristotle as a
boy at Naples. Thomas had little of Albert's great
range of knowledge and interest, which made him the
fountain-head of at least three different schools of
thought; nor had he Albert's interest in individual material things—birds, plants, stars and the rest. But in
the realm of the pure intellect and in clarity of mind
he was greatly superior to Albert. Both as a pure philosopher and as a pure theologian he was unsurpassed.
He felt the need—which no theologian had hitherto
felt strongly, and which the next generation were not
to feel at all—of a system that would give principles
and axioms that could be applied all the way up, so to
say, from logic to mystical theology. To him, Aristotle

seemed, as he had seemed to Averroes, and as he still seems to many of us, to be in the main the human reason working right with no nonsense. Unlike Plato, unlike the Neoplatonists, Aristotle does not postulate beings or entities which cannot be proved or disproved; unlike Scotus and still more unlike Ockham, he does not tell us that everything is really different from, and much more complicated than, what it seems. Aristotle, once you have learnt his technique is, as has been said, the thinker who gives dazzling glimpses of the obvious. He saw the universe of being as an ordered whole, a κόσμος, and he saw visible, material, physical reality as something lower than reason and as something directed by spirit.

Aquinas took up all this into his thought, but to say that he used Aristotle as a basis, or that he 'baptized' him, is to lose the full significance of his work. Rather, we might say that he stood Aristotle's system on its head. Whereas the philosopher was primarily interested in man and his universe, and was interested neither in the human soul nor in God, whom he reduced to a postulate, almost to a mere hypothesis, as the First Mover, for Aquinas the universe is something radiating from and centred upon God, who is the infinite richness of Being compared with whom all other beings are shadows. It is the cardinal difference between Aquinas and Scotus that for the former being is a hierarchy rising from brute matter to infinity, in which only God is necessarily existent, whereas for Scotus being is simply the contrary of non-entity, and existence is a necessary condition for it. Nor is this all. Whereas Aristotle links his universe together partly as a machine and partly as a fabric of logical argument, Aquinas uses his pregnant and characteristic doctrine of analogy, by which being and all its qualities are seen to be in all that exists but in different modes, and by which even God can be described not only in purely negative terms (the so-called apophatic method) but as being the source of all being, Whose perfections are shared analogically by all his creatures. Thus even in God the Author of Nature Aquinas finds the centre and course and end of his system, but above this there is the whole realm of super-natural being, in which and through which God communicates his own way of being to rational creatures of his choice. It is by this integration of speculative theology and rational philosophy into a single system ruled and explained, at the rational level, by concepts and axioms which permeate the whole, that Aquinas created the first original philosophical system of the Christian centuries. Moreover with his presentation of a God, both transcendent and immanent, the author of Nature and Grace, the Father and Judge of all rational creatures, he could find place for much of the idealism, the other-worldliness, the preoccupation with the soul and its destiny, and the concept of our world as reflecting a higher order and based upon the divine ideas, that were the characteristic heart of Platonism. In this way, the only possible way, Aquinas went far towards making that union between the Academy and the Lyceum, between Platonic and peripatetic philosophy, that two centuries had been endeavouring to achieve. But whereas others had tried to achieve this by making the union by blending or merely juxtaposing selected elements from both, Aquinas, dominating both systems from above, transformed both into a new whole.

It was this all-embracing system, bound together by a few great principles such as the unity of substantial forms and the distinction between essence and existence, that gave contemporaries the impression of novelty or originality, and it was the rigorous order of the whole that gave them an excuse, or at least a pretext, for saying that Aquinas was substituting Arabian determinism for divine free-will. And this brings us to the other side of the watershed, to the reaction that followed St Thomas' early death. Popular writers have often supposed, and given others to understand, that Thomism became at once the reigning fashion,

and remained ever after the official system of the medieval Church. The truth is very different. Thomism
did indeed very soon become the official Dominican
doctrine, but this had the effect of uniting opponents
in attack. Moreover a series of able critical thinkers,
including even some of his own order, attacked or
developed this point and that, and put forward all
kinds of new hypotheses, so that St Thomas' work was
as it were gradually eroded rather than battered down.
Three circumstances seem chiefly to have favoured the
opponents of Thomism. One was its resemblance to
the radical Aristotelian doctrines of the Paris artists
which were condemned in 1270 and 1277. Though St
Thomas himself joined in the attack on Siger, he did
not escape inclusion in Bishop Tempier's celebrated
global condemnation of dangerous doctrines three
years after his death. This attack was directed chiefly
against his alleged determinism and against his adop-
tion of the pure Aristotelian concept of the soul as the
substantial form of the body, deriving its individuality
from matter, but the condemnation, though revoked
forty years later, had given a much wider blow to pure
philosophy and to Aristotelian metaphysics, from
which there was never a complete recovery. A second
circumstance was the strong, the permanent, appeal
of an intuitional philosophy of knowledge, whether a
purely natural intuitive process or a version of the
traditional divine illumination of the intellect. This has
always, from the days of Plato to our own, had a
powerful attraction for religious minds, who are of-
fended by Aristotelian empiricism, and the sensual
origin of knowledge; and these are unattractive also to
agnostics and pietists. Finally and perhaps most important, there was the perennial inconstancy of the
human mind, *varium et mutabile semper.* Throughout
recorded history each generation has desired to react
against its predecessor—Aristotle against Plato, Hegel
against Kant. In the natural and mechanical sciences
this can be achieved by further discoveries and better

methods; in art and speculative thought it takes the
form of conscious revolt. Certainly the thinkers of the
fourteenth century set upon the legacy of the thirteenth with little sense of its great price. William of
Ockham had many harbingers, and when he came he
found almost the whole world ready to accept his
revolutionary logic and his devastating criticism. Even
before his day prominent Dominicans, such as Durand
de S. Pourçain, had neglected or even contradicted St
Thomas' teaching, while Duns Scotus had challenged
him all along the line, pronouncing even the crucial
Thomist distinction between essence and existence as
just not true and asserting the anti-Aristotelian doctrine of an intellectual knowledge of individuals. It is
noteworthy that neither William of Ockham nor Brad-
wardine nor Fitzralph nor Wyclif treats Aquinas as
an authority whom it is rash to attack and useful to
have on one's side. They quote him just as they quote
any leading doctor of the schools, and accept or dis-
miss as they will.

Some of my readers may be wondering why Dante
has not been mentioned. Is not he, at least, an example of the universal acceptance of Thomism in Italy in
the generation after the author's death? Dante certainly knows his Aquinas and it seems to be established that he picked up his philosophy and theology
from the Dominicans at Florence. But this was in
Dante's youth, only a few years after Aquinas' death.
By the time he wrote the *Paradiso*, where he unfolds
his knowledge of speculative theology to the full, he
is by no means a pure Thomist. Rather, he stands to
St Thomas as St Thomas stood to Aristotle; he takes
him as his basis, but does not hesitate to depart from
him and to use other sources. It must not be forgotten
that in the *Paradiso* it is St Bonaventure who pro-
nounces the panegyric on St Thomas, and *vice versa*,
while it is St Thomas (of all people) who identifies
and praises the flame-like soul of Siger, standing near
himself and Bonaventure, who 'put into faultless argu-

ments his odious truths'. Dante, in other words, regards St Thomas as Etienne Gilson might regard him,
not as would, let us say, Père Garrigou-Lagrange. But
if it is true, as I think it is, that in the schools fifty years
after his death St Thomas was one of the great men of
old rather than the master and prophet of his age, it
must also be noted that he had a lasting and very important influence beyond the strictly academic circles,
not only in and through Dante, but also among the
masters and mystics of the Rhineland. At Cologne his
influence and that of Albert the Great was more lasting because less exposed to competition. Denifle, in
one of the more successful tournaments of a life so full
of knight-errantry, killed once and for all the legend
that Meister Eckhart was the grandfather of German
theology which came to full fruit in Luther. Though it
is still a matter of dispute whether Eckhart was a Neoplatonist with a smattering of Thomism or a Thomist
with a penchant for Neoplatonism, there is no doubt
that so far as Eckhart dealt with technical theology he
used the Thomist idiom. It probably says much for his
radical orthodoxy that his disciples are unimpeach-
ably orthodox (and Thomist)—John Tauler above all.
The result of this was that the great mystical school of
the Rhineland wrote and thought in the Thomist language and built up an entirely Thomist mystical theology. This was exported wherever German spiritual-
ity went. It is seen very clearly in the English *Cloud of
Unknowing* and in Walter Hilton, who follows *The
Cloud,* and it is seen still more clearly in the Spanish
Carmelites, above all in St John of the Cross. Although by his time the Thomist revival in Spain was
well under way, it was probably not so much from
Salamanca as from Tauler, directly or indirectly, that
St John derived the Thomist framework of his mystical
theology—by no means the least important part of the
Thomist legacy to modern times.

I should like to conclude this paper by returning for
a moment to two points, which have already been

briefly indicated or at least suggested. The one is, that
the achievement of St Thomas was, speaking historically, both epoch-making and culminating. In the history of medieval thought he did what no one before
him had done, and he reached heights which no one
surpassed. The other point is, that his achievement
was largely neglected by his immediate successors,
and that his thought was without influence on subsequent currents in the schools.

Let us take the second point first. Though apparently strange, it is easily comprehensible—and more so
perhaps to a historian than to a theologian. One reason, the more concrete though perhaps for that reason
the less important, can be found in contemporary
events. To us, looking back after seven centuries, St
Thomas' thorough-going Aristotelianism is perhaps
his greatest title to the esteem in which he is held as a
thinker. It raises him out of the patchwork and cross-
currents of his day and enables us to see him clearly as
a thinker and creator of a system that had to be reck-
oned with. But in his own world it was fatal to his
reputation. Thomist historians have been quick to
point out that the condemnation of 1277, in itself a
stupid mistake, was never honoured by St Thomas'
personal disciples and was formally revoked fifty years
later. All this is true, but it is also true that to men of
his day, the explicit condemnation of rationalism in
1277 was a blow to metaphysics, to natural theology
and to Aristotelianism, from which they never recov-
ered. The very real aberrations, which Etienne Tempier and the conservative theologians struck at so
hastily and clumsily, were undoubtedly a menace to
faith and morals and they were directly or indirectly
the outcome, if not the consequence, of an exclusive
devotion to philosophy, that is, to Aristotle. The con-
servatives had been proved right. This, they said, was
what philosophy led to. And the use made of Aristotle
by Marsilius of Padua thirty years later might have
seemed to justify them.

The other reason is more general and goes deeper. The human spirit, or rather perhaps, the human will and human inconstancy, loves change and novelty, above all in things of the mind. Never in the world's history has a succession of great philosophers taught the same doctrine. When a philosophy has endured, it is because it has become imbedded in an ethic, or in a political system, or in a religious tradition. Man is inconstant and avid of novelty and discovery and criticism in all things—most of all in the realm which should have been his greatest glory, the realm of pure reason, where he contemplates being *qua* being, and its Author. Here, with no stay save pure reason, he is at the mercy of his frailty and passions; he cannot see the truth; he dare not abide by what he sees. He faints in that rarified atmosphere; he asks what is truth, and denies that he can know it. The fourteenth century, like the ancient sceptics and so many modern schools of thought, fled from metaphysics to logic or to fideism; it was, indeed, a period of uncertainty and *malaise,* when the troubled pontificate of Boniface VIII was a prelude to the unhappy days of the Avignon exile. The breakdown of the metaphysicians, the distrust of abstract reasoning, the denial of all knowledge that is not intuitional and of all objects of knowledge beyond the individual thing—all this came with startling suddenness. Within a long lifetime we pass from Aquinas to Ockhamism and Nominalism.

Yet despite this St Thomas had built a monument more perdurable than bronze. The great chemist, the great physicist, even the great mathematician is surpassed and absorbed by those, even if lesser men, who come after. The great poet, the great artist, the great composer, touches a summit which may never be reached again, at least not in that mountain range. So it is with the great thinker. Pure thought and metaphysical truth—at least so some of us would hold—are not subject to change with fashions of expression or changes of psychological or scientific outlook. The human mind and its powers of reason and reflection, without which, after all, the physical universe, its vastness, its majesty and its mechanism, would exist for us no more than they do for the dog or the bird—the human mind can grasp the essence of the being that surrounds it with certainty and with clarity (within rigid limits), and transmit its findings to others.

This St Thomas did. If a personal judgment may be allowed in conclusion, it would be that the more and the longer the history of the thirteenth century is studied, the more does the thought of St Thomas, even considered merely as a historical phenomenon, appear as something more than just one tree, even if the biggest, in a row. Others, indeed, cannot be despised; they may even touch upon points that he omits and supplement or even correct him. But if one is looking for a complete system of thought in the Middle Ages, it is St Thomas or nothing. Building with material largely supplied by Aristotle he did what no other thinker of his age succeeded in doing—what none of our age has done—he gave a coherent rational account of the universe of being as known to the human mind, and gave it in a philosophical idiom which may be unfamiliar to us, but which cannot be lightly dismissed as fantastic, archaic or incomprehensible.

I

LOGIC AND METAPHYSICS

FORM AND EXISTENCE

PETER GEACH

In this paper I shall discuss what Aquinas meant by his term *esse*, or *actus essendi*, 'act of existing'. Another synonym that he uses—*quo aliquid est*, 'that by which a thing is (or: exists)'—suggests a convenient division of the subject: we can first discuss Aquinas' philosophical use of *quo*, 'that by which', and then consider which sense of *est*, which sort of existential proposition, may be relevant to Aquinas' doctrine of *esse*. But we shall see that, having got thus far, we cannot arrive at the meaning of the whole phrase, *quo aliquid est*, or the reasons for the way Aquinas uses it, simply by combining our separate considerations about *quo* and *est*.

I

Beginning with Aquinas' use of *quo* brings a great immediate advantage. The predicate *est*, 'is' or 'exists', is at least a peculiar one, and many people would deny that it is properly a predicate at all; but Aquinas uses *quo* not only with *est* but also with unexceptionable predicates. In this use, *quo* followed by a noun subject and an (ordinary) predicate is synonymous with the phrase formed by the abstract noun answering to the predicate followed by the genitive of the noun that was subject; *quo Socrates albus est* ('that by which Socrates is white') is synonymous with *albedo Socratis* ('the whiteness of Socrates') and so

From *Proceedings of the Aristotelian Society*, 1954–55, pp. 250–276, with slight stylistic changes and an extra paragraph added by the author to remove a misconceived objection. Reprinted with permission of the Editor of the Aristotelian Society; © The Aristotelian Society, 1955.

on. Either kind of phrase is thus used in order to designate what Aquinas calls Forms; to understand his use of *quo* we must examine his notion of forms, which moreover is intimately connected in other ways with his doctrine of *esse*.

For Aquinas, the real distinction between a form and the self-subsistent individual (*suppositum*) whose form it is comes out in the logical distinction between subject and predicate (Ia q. 13 art. 12; q. 85 art. 5 ad 3 um). I think this is the way to introduce his notion of form to modern philosophers. There are, however, strong prejudices against allowing that this logical distinction answers to *any* real distinction. One such obstacle is the old two-name or identity theory of predication, which flourished in the Middle Ages, and still keeps on appearing in new guises: the theory that a true predication is effected by joining different names of the same thing or things, the copula being a sign of this real identity. I shall not waste time on this logically worthless theory. Anybody who is tempted by it may try his hand at explaining in terms of it how we can fit together the three terms 'David', 'father', and 'Solomon' (which on this theory are three *names*) to form the true predication 'David is the father of Solomon'.

The futility of the two-name theory comes out clearly at the beginning of Lewis Carroll's *Game of Logic*. Lewis Carroll professes to find a difficulty over saying 'some pigs are pink'; as it stands, this suggests an impossible identity between certain things (pigs) and a certain attribute (signified by 'pink')! He seeks to remove this difficulty by expounding the proposition as meaning 'some pigs are pink pigs', where 'are' signifies real identity. But 'pink pigs' means 'pigs that are pink', and there is as much or as little difficulty about this phrase as about the predication 'pigs are pink' at which he stumbles.

If noun-phrases like 'thing that runs' can properly be regarded as names (a difficult problem of logical theory that cannot be discussed here), then it *is* possible to state the truth-condition of an affirmative predication as an identity of reference between two names; 'a man runs', let us say, is true if and only if 'man' and 'thing that runs' are two names of the same individual. Aquinas uses this way of stating truth-conditions quite often, and has in consequence been wrongly regarded as holding the two-name theory. But it is not the name 'thing that runs' that is used in the sentence 'a man runs', but the predicate 'runs' from which this name is formed; and 'runs' and 'thing that runs' are by no means synonymous; the relation between their ways of signifying in fact raises over again the same problem as the relation of subject and predicate, a problem that is thus merely shifted by expressing the truth-conditions of predication in terms of identity of reference.

Modern philosophers have pretty generally abandoned the two-name theory; at least to the extent of admitting that a logical subject and a predicate have radically different ways of signifying. But need we admit also a difference of type as regards the realities signified? Surely what distinguishes a predicate from a name is just the fact that it does not *name* anything, but is rather true or false *of* things; a true predication is one in which the predicate *is true of* what the subject *names*. Are we not blurring this distinction if we say that predicates stand for (why not, that they *name*?) a type of entity other than that which names stand for? Have not philosophers said the queerest things about the entities that predicates are supposed to stand for? No wonder; such paradoxes are bound to arise if you treat as a name what is not a name; like the paradoxes about Nobody in *Through the Looking-glass*.

But, whatever difficulties it may involve, I think we have to allow that logical predicates do stand for something, as well as being true or false *of* things. For when a question *how many* is asked and answered, we can surely ask: To what is this manyness being ascribed? And in any concrete instance we shall find that in asserting manyness we use a logically predicative word or phrase, and are ascribing manyness to what this stands for. 'How many ducks are swimming in the Chamberlain Fountain?' 'Three.' If this answer were true, there would be objects of which 'duck swimming in the Chamberlain Fountain' could truly be predicated; and my number-statement is about what this predicate stands for. You cannot say my statement ascribes a property (threeness) to a certain set of individuals—the ducks swimming in the Chamberlain Fountain. So far as I know, no ducks *are* swimming there; and it makes no difference whether there are any or not; for the sense of the question how many such ducks there are cannot depend on what the right answer to the question is. Now the answer 'three' cannot be taken as a predication about a set of ducks unless the question answered is a question about them; but the question how many such ducks there are *admits* of the answer 'o'; and noughtishness certainly is not here being taken as a property of any set of ducks. You may indeed rightly say that my proposition is about *ducks* (not: *the* ducks) swimming in the Chamberlain Fountain. The omission of the definite article is here significant. A proposition that could rightly be called 'a proposition about *the* ducks (etc.)' would have to refer (or at least profess to refer) to a certain set of ducks; but in speaking of 'a proposition about ducks (etc.)' I am not implying that the proposition mentions any individual ducks, but on the contrary that it is about what the predicate 'duck swimming in the Chamberlain Fountain' stands for.

It is only to what such a predicative expression stands for that we can even falsely ascribe manyness. It is nonsense, unintelligible, not just false, to ascribe manyness to an individual; what can be repeated is always and only a common nature. *Non enim potest in intellectum cadere pluralitas huius individui* (Ia.

q. 13 art. 9). Because, for Aquinas, forms are what answer *in rebus* to logical predicates, it is consistent for him to say that forms are as such multipliable (Ia. q. 3 art. 2 ad 3 um: q. 7 art. 1).

I cannot help being reminded here of the very similar language that we find in Frege. Frege, like Aquinas, held that there was a fundamental distinction *in rebus* answering to the logical distinction between subject and predicate—the distinction between *Gegenstand* (object) and *Begriff* (concept). (In using *Begriff* as a term for what logical predicates represent, Frege was not accepting any form of conceptualism; on the contrary, he explicitly denies that the *Begriff* is any creature of the human mind—it is, he says, 'objective'.) And for Frege the *Begriff*, and it alone, admits of repetition and manyness; an object cannot be repeated—*kommt nie widerholt vor.*

Understood in this way, the distinction between individual and form is absolutely sharp and rigid; what can sensibly be said of one becomes nonsense if we try to say it of the other. (Aquinas' 'subsistent forms' might seem to bridge the gulf; but, as we shall presently see, they do not, nor did Aquinas really think they do.) Just because of this sharp distinction, we must reject the platonic doctrine that what a predicate stands for is some single entity over against its many instances, *hen epi pollôn.* On the contrary: the common nature that the predicate 'man' (say) stands for can be indifferently one or many, and neither oneness nor manyness is a mark or note of human nature itself. This point is very clearly made by Aquinas in *De Ente et Essentia.* Again we find Frege echoing Aquinas; Frege counts oneness or manyness (as the case may be) among the properties (*Eigenschaften*) of a concept, which means that it cannot at the same time be one of the marks or notes (*Merkmalen*) of that concept. (Frege's choice of words is here unfortunate; his saying that it is an *Eigenschaft* e.g., of human nature to be found in many individuals, has led people to suppose that he regards this as a *proprium* of human nature—although so to read him makes complete nonsense of his distinction. Aquinas' saying that oneness or manyness is incidental, *accidit*, to human nature is a much clearer expression.)

The Platonic mistake about the nature of forms goes with a liberal use of what we may class together as abstract-singular expressions like 'X-ness' or 'the attribute of being X'; these expressions are not just grammatically but also logically, argumentatively handled as though they were proper names. I do not say that such abstract expressions looking like proper names should be totally banned; it would make things very difficult for philosophers. (I myself used 'human nature' in this way in the last paragraph.) But I do say that anyone who uses them ought to be ready to replace them on demand by use of the concrete predicates from which they are derived. (Thus: for 'neither oneness nor manyness is a mark of human nature itself' read 'whether there is one man or many men is irrelevant to what X must be if X is a man', or something like that.) Sometimes this replacement is stylistically better, sometimes not. But it must be possible; a sentence with an *irreducible* abstract 'proper name' in it (say: 'Redness is an eternal object') is nonsense.

All the same, Platonism of this sort is a very great temptation; and I think it is instructive to watch Frege's unsuccessful struggles against temptation in his paper *Ueber Begriff und Gegenstand* ('On Concept and Object'). I quote (*op. cit.* p. 197): 'In logical discussions one quite often needs to assert something about a concept, and to express this in the form usual for such assertions viz. to make what is asserted of the concept into the content of the grammatical predicate. Consequently, one would expect that the reference of the grammatical subject would be the concept; but the concept as such cannot play this part, in view of its predicative nature; it must first be converted into an object, or, speaking more precisely, represented by an object. We designate this object by prefixing the words "the concept": e.g.

"The concept *man* is not empty".

Here the first three words are to be regarded as a proper name'. And later on (p. 198): 'In my way of speaking, expressions like "the concept F" designate not concepts but objects'.

Of course Frege has gone astray here; he does not clear himself of the charge of having made a concept into an object just by saying that 'the concept *man*' does not stand for a concept but for an object that 'represents' a concept; no more than a writer can escape the charge of vulgarity by a parenthetical 'to use a vulgarism'. But how then are we to get into the subject of predication a direct reference to what Frege calls a concept and Aquinas calls a form? I think the solution, the way to avoid the mistake of Platonism, is that an abstract noun (or noun-phrase) referring to the form can indeed occupy the place of the subject, but cannot be the whole of the subject; the form being signified, *in recto* as Aquinas would say, by an abstract noun, we must add a mention *in obliquo* of the individual whose form it is; 'the wisdom of Socrates' and 'the redness of Socrates' nose' give us designations of forms, the spurious proper names 'wisdom' and 'redness' do not.

We must not construe 'the wisdom of Socrates' as 'wisdom, which Socrates possesses': apart from lapsing into the Platonic error of taking 'wisdom' as a singular term, we should run into notorious antinomies about the relation supposedly meant by 'possesses'. 'Of' in 'the wisdom of Socrates' does not signify a special relation, as in such phrases as 'the statue of Socrates' or 'the shield of Socrates'. The statue is *of* Socrates by being related to him in one way, the shield is *of* Socrates by being related to him in another way; but if we start saying 'and the wisdom is *of* Socrates . . .' we have already gone wrong, for logically 'the wisdom of Socrates' does not split up into 'the wisdom' and 'of Socrates' (sc. 'that wisdom which is *of* Socrates') but into 'the wisdom of . . .' and 'Socrates'. What refers to a form is 'the wisdom of . . .', not the whole phrase 'the wisdom of Socrates'; 'the wisdom of . . .' needs to be completed with a name of something that has the form, just as the predicate '. . . is wise', which also stands for this form, needs to be completed by a subject.

'Of' is a logically inseparable part of the sign 'the wisdom of . . .', indicating the need to put a name after this sign; and this need is what makes the sign suitable to express a form, since a form, as Aquinas says, is more properly termed *entis* than *ens* (Ia. q. 45 art. 4). The linguistic oddity of the division into 'the wisdom of . . .' and 'Socrates'—a division that cannot be made in Latin at all—is quite trivial and accidental; in Hebrew, for example, such a division would be perfectly natural, since 'the wisdom of Socrates' would be rendered by inflecting the word for 'wisdom' and leaving the name 'Socrates' uninflected.

It may be asked: How *can* a form be designated both by a logical predicate like '. . . is wise' *and* by an expression like 'the wisdom of . . .'? These sorts of expressions are certainly not interchangeable; but I think we can show that the difference between them is only *secundum modum significandi,* not *secundum rem significatam;* it relates to the way we are talking about a form, and makes no difference to which form we are talking about. When we want to mention a form for the sake of expressing the supposition that in a given individual that form is found, we refer to it by an expression which together with the name of that individual forms a proposition—i.e., by a logical predicate like 'is wise'. But when we want to talk directly about the form itself, to get a reference to the form into the subject-place in our proposition, then we need to refer to the form by an expression which, together with a reference *in obliquo* to that in which the form is found, will compose a complex name that can be logical sub-ject—e.g., the expression 'the wisdom of . . .'

It admittedly looks queer that a form cannot be designated either (say) by 'redness' alone or by 'the redness of Socrates' nose', but only by 'the redness of . . .' (understood to be followed by some name or other). We may help our understanding by the analo-gous case of functions in mathematics: neither the iso-lated square-root sign nor (say) '$\sqrt{25}$' designates a function, but rather the circumstance that the square-root sign is followed by some numeral or other.

This comparison of forms to functions in mathemat-ics seems to me very useful; it was suggested to me by Frege's assimilation of his *Begriffe* to mathematical functions. (Frege indeed held that *Begriffe are* a sort of functions, which can take only two values, the 'true' value and the 'false' value; I shall not try to explain here this part of his doctrine, and would emphasize that I am asserting no more than an analogy between forms and functions.) It may for instance help us to see how 'of' in 'the wisdom of Socrates' does not stand for a special relation of 'inherence in' or 'belonging to'. Somebody ignorant of mathematics might take 'the square root of 25' to mean 'that one among square roots which belongs to 25', and wonder how one num-ber can 'belong' to another; but somebody who under-stands the term 'square root' can already understand 'square root of 25' and can see that a relation of 'be-longing' does not come in. So also somebody who un-derstands the term 'wisdom', and does not Platonically misunderstand it as a proper name, already under-stands the make-up of the phrase 'wisdom of Socrates' without needing to understand the mythical relation of inherence. The term 'wisdom', like the term 'square root', of itself demands a genitive to complete its sense.

Again, in the sense of the word 'form' that we have so far used, what the phrase 'the wisdom of Socrates' designates is not a form *simpliciter;* but can legiti-mately be said to be a form *of* Socrates, a form occurring in Socrates. This too can be elucidated by our mathematical analogy. Consider the square-root function: we cannot say that the number 5 is that function or any other function: but we can say that the number 5 is that function *of* the number 25. So also the wisdom of Socrates is not a form *simpliciter* but *is* a form *of* or *in* Socrates. What designates a form is not the whole phrase 'the wisdom of Socrates', but merely 'the wisdom of . . .'—although without completion this latter phrase is senseless.

Now at this point I think Aquinas' terminology is defective. He emphatically rejects the Platonic error of taking 'wisdom' as the proper name of a form; he says, e.g., that when (pseudo-) Dionysius speaks of life *per se* and wisdom *per se,* we are not to take this authority to be meaning certain self-subsistent entities (*quasdam subsistentes res*) (Ia. q. 44 art. 3 ad 4 um). But he often uses the term 'form' for what is referred to by a phrase like *sapientia Socratis* (the wisdom of Socrates); whereas if we keep to the sense of 'form' that we have so far used, a sense that is also to be found in Aquinas, what designates a form is rather *sapientia* together with the genitive inflexion of the following noun. The syntax of Latin impedes clear statement of this point, and Aquinas could not, of course, use our mathematical analogy for elucidation.

I am here leaving myself open to the charge of developing a new doctrine of form and departing from Aquinas' own doctrine. But if we will not impute to Aquinas a slight and natural inexactness of language at this point, then his doctrine of form becomes mere inconsistency and nonsense. For 'the wisdom of Socrates' must designate something individual, something that is no more multipliable or expressible by a predicate than Socrates himself is; so if this is taken to be a typical designation of a form, the whole distinction between form and individual is undone. To keep our heads clear, we must distinguish two senses of 'form' in Aquinas—the form that is the reference of the predicate '. . . is wise' or of the phrase 'the wisdom of . . .', and the form that is the reference of a phrase like 'the wisdom of Socrates'. In the latter case I shall speak of individualized forms; individualized forms will then not be forms *simpliciter* (just as a number that is a certain function of another number is not a function *simpliciter*) and will always be referred to by the full style 'individualized forms'.

This distinction is needed in order to make Aquinas' doctrine of subsistent or separate forms logically intelligible. When Aquinas tells us that God is wisdom itself, *Deus est ipsa sapientia*, he is not meaning that God is that of which the noun 'wisdom' is a proper name; for the Platonists are wrong in thinking that there is such an object, and Aquinas says that they are wrong. But we *can* take it to mean that 'God' and 'the wisdom of God' are two names of the same thing; and this interpretation does not make Aquinas guilty of the impossible and nonsensical attempt to bridge the distinction previously expounded between form and individual, or find something intermediate. For we can significantly say that 'God' and 'the wisdom of God' and 'the power of God' are three names with the same reference; but 'the wisdom of . . .' and 'the power of . . .' have not the same reference, any more than the predicates 'wise' and 'powerful' have. *Non dicimus quod attributum potentiae sit attributum scientiae, licet dicamus quod scientia (Dei) sit potentia (Dei)* (Ia. q. 32 art. 3 ad 3 um).

This account, it may be argued, departs fatally from Aquinas' mind, in that it makes out that in 'the wisdom of God' and 'the power of God', 'the wisdom of' and 'the power of' differ in reference from the word 'God' and from one another; for this conflicts with Aquinas' teaching on the divine simplicity. But what *we* signify by 'the wisdom of' and 'the power of' is really distinct; otherwise 'the wisdom of Socrates' would coincide in reference with 'the power of Socrates'. On the other hand, what we signify by 'the wisdom of' is not, and is

not signified as being, a part or element of what we
signify by 'the wisdom of God', i.e. (according to
Aquinas) God himself. If one designation is part of
another, it does not follow that the things designated
are respectively part and whole. 'The square root of
25' is a complex designation having as parts the designations 'the square root of' and '25'; but it does not
follow (as Frege oddly inferred) that there is some
sense of 'part' in which we may suitably say that the
number 5, which is the square root of 25, has two
heterogeneous parts—the square-root function and the
number 25. Again—to get an analogy to the three
designations 'God', 'the wisdom of God', 'the power of
God'—the square and the cube are quite distinct functions, but '1' and 'the square of 1' and 'the cube of 1'
all designate the same number, and there is no distinction even in thought between the 1 that is the square
and the 1 that is the cube and the 1 that is squared
and cubed.

The supposition that x itself is that by (or in virtue
of) which x is F is certainly not logically absurd on the
face of it (as would be the supposition that x was
identical with the reference of the predicate 'F', an
individual with a form). It will be instructive to consider an example from modern philosophy in which
the assertion of identity between x and what makes x
to be F might seem plausible, and to see why such
identity must be here denied. The red-patch school
of philosophy might well wish to say that a red patch
in a sense-field neither is the red-patchiness of some
other individual (of a *suppositum*) nor yet has any
individualized forms distinct from itself. That in virtue of which the patch is red, that in virtue of which
it is *so* big, that in virtue of which it is square, is nothing other than the patch itself, which is red, *so* big,
and square.

But now let us observe our red square; after a short
time it begins a gradual change, and the outer region
of the square becomes green, while an inner region

remains red and is circular in shape. Are we then to say 'The red was square and larger, and has become circular and smaller', or rather 'The square was all red and has become partly green'? Plainly we may say either—or rather *both*. But now the individual red and the individual square appear as distinct individual things, each with its own distinct persisting identity; there is no third individual, the red square; *rubrum et quadratum non est ens.* I do not mean, of course, that there cannot be a red square *object;* but then the persistent identity of this object will not consist in any simple sensible character like redness or squareness. It is because the philosophers' red square is supposed to have no characteristics except a few simple sensible ones that it falls to pieces under examination; for to each such character there answers a distinct individual reality, an individualized form—an individual extension, colour, shape, etc.—and though these are united in one *suppositum x* as the redness of *x*, the squareness of *x*, etc., they are not all one thing, the red patch; the red patch has no identity of its own, *non est vere unum nec vere ens.*

These examples of individualized forms may be objectionable to some people as factitious philosophical examples. But a wave, for example, is an identifiable individual that can move locally (although Professor Prichard *knew* that it was nonsense to say so); and this is certainly an individualized form—it is that by which a certain body of water is in a certain shape over part of its surface.

II

The expression 'that by which the individual *x* is (or: exists)' is senseless unless there is a sense in which 'is' or 'exists' is properly predicable of individuals. Now many modern philosophers would deny that there is such a sense: 'exists' is not a predicate! This maxim is often glibly and thoughtlessly used, but it has a serious use; it is an attempt to resolve the paradox of reference that arises over the denial of existence. For we *can* significantly and truly deny existence; indeed I should hold that there is no sense of 'exists' for which we do not get significant and true denials of existence. (Some philosophers have thought otherwise—that for a certain sense of the verb 'to be' 'A is' or 'As are' is a form of proposition that is always true; even dragons *are*, even round squares *are*, in this sense! But at any rate to a discussion of Aquinas this supposed sense is irrelevant; we may stick to the everyday senses of 'to be' or 'to exist' for which existence *can* be truly denied.) How is such denial possible? It might look as though 'A is not' or 'A does not exist' were never true; for if it were, the subject-term 'A' would fail to have reference, and so no predication would have been made at all, let alone a true predication.

We can get out of this difficulty by denying that in 'A is not' or 'A does not exist' the verb 'is' or 'exists' is a logical predicate. For since 'subject' and 'predicate' are correlatives, this is tantamount to denying that the grammatical subject 'A' is a logical subject. And from this again it follows that the proposition 'A does not exist' is not really about what the subject 'A' ostensibly stands for; so in asserting the proposition we do not fall into the absurdity of using 'A' as though it stood for something and then in effect denying that it does so.

But though saying that 'exists' or 'is' is not a genuine logical predicate of individuals would thus resolve the paradox of non-existence, this does not prove that it is not, sometimes at least, a genuine logical predicate; for the paradox might be resoluble some other way. Moreover, it is not enough to say that in 'A does not exist' 'A' cannot be the genuine subject of predication, unless at the same time we can bring out the real logical role of 'A'—the real logical nature of existential propositions.

I think it is a great mistake to treat all existential propositions as having the same logical status. I am not here concerned with the familiar thesis that existence is an analogical notion—that questions of existence are different according to what it is whose existence is in question, a God, an historical character, an animal species, a sub-atomic particle . . . Quite apart from these differences, we have to recognise three different kinds of existential proposition even about the same kind of things—e.g., about the existence of living creatures. The difference perhaps comes out best when we take negative propositions as our examples.

A. There is no such thing as Cerberus; Cerberus does not exist, is not real.

B. There is no such thing as a dragon; dragons do not exist.

C. Joseph is not and Simeon is not.

The A proposition that I gave as an example might typically be used to comfort a child who had been frightened by hearing Greek myths and thought Cerberus would come and bite him. 'Cerberus', we might say 'doesn't exist (is not real) like Rover'. Here we are not pointing out any trait that Cerberus has and Rover lacks; for it would be nonsense to speak of the trait of *being what there is such a thing as,* and more nonsense to say that some things (e.g., Rover) have this trait, while other things (e.g., Cerberus) lack it, and are thus things that there is no such thing as. Logically our proposition is about a difference not between two dogs, Cerberus and Rover, but between the uses of two words 'Cerberus' and 'Rover'. The word 'Rover' is seriously used to refer to something and does in fact so refer; the word 'Cerberus' is a term that we only make believe has reference.

Since 'Cerberus does not exist' and 'Rover does exist' have not (as they seem to have) the names of two dogs as their logical subjects—since we are not here *using* 'Cerberus' and 'Rover' as names, but talking *about* their use—it is appropriate to say that in A propositions 'exists' or 'is real' is not a predicate, not even of the word 'Cerberus'. To show the real force of the parent's reassuring 'Cerberus does not exist', and how it is about the word 'Cerberus', we cannot content ourselves with writing '(The word) "Cerberus" does not exist', but must completely recast the sentence, say as follows: 'When I said "Cerberus" in that story, I was only pretending to use it as a name'.

As regards the B proposition 'there is no such thing as a dragon' or 'dragons do not exist', it is equally clear that this cannot be referring to an attribute of *being what there is such a thing as,* which cows have and dragons lack. But there is also a great difference between A and B propositions. In the A proposition we have an ostensible use of a proper name; in the B proposition we have a descriptive, predicable expression like 'cow' or 'dragon'—what Frege would have called a *Begriffswort* (concept-word).

The difference between A and B propositions may perhaps come out better if I shift to another pair of examples. A certain astronomer claimed to have identified an intra-Mercurian planet, which he christened 'Vulcan'. His claim was not substantiated; and a modern astronomer would accordingly say 'Vulcan did not exist' (an A proposition); he would also say 'So far as we know, an intra-Mercurian planet does not exist' (a B proposition). Now the force of the A proposition is to deprecate the premature introduction of the term 'Vulcan' into astronomical discourse; but in the B proposition the astronomer does not deprecate the use of the term 'intra-Mercurian planet', but himself uses that term to make a scientific remark. He is not, however, using the term as a name, as a subject of predication, but as a logical predicate. 'There is no intra-Mercurian planet' means 'nothing at all is an intra-Mercurian planet'. (Similarly, the affirmative B proposition 'there is a hairless cat' means 'something or other is a hairless cat'.) Now the use of a logical predicate in general does not commit you to allowing that there is something it applies to; it does so commit you if you make an affirmative assertion with that as the predicate, but not if, e.g., you use the predicate negatively or in the antecedent or consequent of a hypothetical. So saying 'nothing whatever is an intra-Mercurian planet' does not commit you to allowing that there is after all such a planet.

The importance of B propositions is that the question whether there is *a* so-and-so, what Aquinas calls the question *an est?* has to be answered with an affirmative or negative B propositions. Aquinas realised the logical peculiarity of B propositions: that the B proposition 'an F exists' does not attribute actuality to an F, but F-ness to something or other; e.g., 'there is evil' does not mean 'evil has actual existence' but 'some things have defects' (Ia. q. 48 art. 2 ad 2 um). And let us not think this is so because of some peculiarity of the term 'evil'; Aquinas speaks of the question *an est?* quite generally in the place I have cited, and says that the 'existence' involved in a true affirmative answer to it consists in the truth of an affirmative predication (*compositio*). This is exactly right, for 'an F exists' is true if and only if 'F' is truly predicable of something or other. Moreover, the same logical status is expressly ascribed to 'God exists', or 'there is a God' (Ia. q. 3 art. 4 ad 2 um); and Aquinas expressly denies that this proposition relates to what *he* calls God's *esse* or *actus essendi*. (This most important negative indication as to how we must understand the term *esse* has often been overlooked.) In 'God exists' we are not predicating something of God, but predicating the term 'God' itself; 'God exists' means 'something or other is God'. When we see this, we can steer our way safely through all the shoals of the seventeenth-century ontological argument. (Though it is commonly called by the same name, I think Anselm's argument is essentially different; I shall not here discuss it.)

It is important that for Aquinas 'God' is a descriptive, predicable, term (*nomen naturae*—Frege's *Begriffswort*) and not a logically proper name. Only because of this can the question whether there is one God or many make sense; just as the question whether there is one sun or many makes sense only if 'sun' is used to mean 'heavenly body of such-and-such a nature', not if it is a proper name of *this* heavenly body (Ia. q. 13 art. 9). Only because of this can the heathen say his idol is God and the Christian contradict him and both be using 'God' in the same sense; if 'God' were a proper name, it would be a logically impossible, not a lying, wicked, act, to predicate it of stocks and stones (Ia. q. 13 art. 10).

This may seem to raise difficulties about another view of Aquinas I have discussed—that 'God' in the context of the phrases 'the power of God' and 'the wisdom of God' has the same reference with either of these phrases, namely God himself. If 'God' is a predicative expression, how can it significantly stand in place of a proper name like 'Socrates', after 'the wisdom of' or 'the power of'? I think it is enough to reply that 'God' in *such* contexts, or indeed in subject position before 'is wise' or 'is powerful', has the force of a definite description—'the one and only God'; whatever our theory of descriptions may be, it will have to yield the result that a definite description can significantly take the place of a proper name, as subject of a proposition or again after a phrase like 'the wisdom of'.

We now come on to C propositions like 'Joseph is not and Simeon is not'. It would be quite absurd to say that Jacob in uttering these words was not talking about Joseph and Simeon but about the use of their names. Of course he was talking about his sons; he was expressing a fear that something had happened to them, that they were dead. We have here a sense of 'is' or 'exists' that seems to me to be certainly a genuine predicate of individuals; the sense of 'exist' in which one says that an individual came to exist, still exists, no longer exists, etc.; the sense of 'to be' in which God says of himself 'I am who *am*' (i.e. 'I am he who *is*'), or in which Homer spoke of the Gods who ever are, *aien eontes*. Now why should one suspect that this cannot be a genuine predicate of individuals? The fact that in A and B propositions the verb 'exist' or 'be' is not such a genuine predicate tells us nothing about C propositions.

Moreover, we cannot argue that if the C proposition '*x* is not' is true, then the subject term '*x*' no longer has anything to refer to and therefore no predication has been made. As Wittgenstein says (*Philosophische Untersuchungen* 1§40): 'That is to confound the reference (*Bedeutung*) of the name with the bearer of the name. When Mr. N.N. dies, we say that the bearer of the name dies, not that the reference dies. And it would be nonsensical to say that; for if the name ceased to have reference, it would make nonsense to say "Mr. N.N. is dead"'. To put the same thing another way: The reference of a name admits of no time qualification; names are tenseless. Octavian was not known as 'Augustus' till quite late in his career; but once the name was in established use with that reference, it could be used by anybody at any time, in relation to any stage of Octavian's career (e.g. in answering the question 'Where was Augustus born?') and regardless of whether Octavian was alive or dead. So negative C propositions can raise no paradoxes of reference—and in showing this we had no need to deny that in them 'is' or 'exists' is a genuine predicate.

Now it is *this* sense of 'is' or 'exists', the one found in C propositions, that is relevant to Aquinas' term *esse*. This interpretation, I maintain, alone makes coherent sense of all that Aquinas says about *esse*.

It is worth noticing that as regards living beings 'to be' (in the C sense) has the same reference as 'to live', *vivere viventibus est esse* (Ia. q. 18 art. 2). This may confirm us against sophistical attempts to show that the verb 'to be' in this sense is not a genuine predicate of individuals. 'Poor Fred was alive and is dead', how could one argue that this is not a genuine predication about poor Fred? and what difference does it make if we say instead 'poor Fred *was,* and *is not*'?

Some people may not easily see the difference between 'God exists' (sense B) and 'God is' (sense C). But in the contradictories the difference is apparent. 'God is not' (sense C) would have to be construed like 'Joseph is not'; it would then suitably express the supposition that perhaps the world was made by an old superannuated God who has since died (a suggestion of Hume's). This is quite different from the Atheist's 'there is no God' (sense B).

One would indeed wish to say that everlasting existence is part of the concept of a God; of Hume's senile creator one would wish to say that since he is dead now he never was God when he was alive. But saying this does not commit us to the fallacy of the Ontological Argument. It belongs to the concept of a phoenix that it should never die by accident and should ward off old age with a bath of flames at regular intervals; so a dead phoenix is a contradiction in terms. But this does not mean that there must be a live phoenix. If there is a God, then he lives forever; but we cannot determine from this whether there is a God.

Existence in sense C is, according to Aquinas, always existence in respect of some form: *quodlibet esse est secundum formam aliquam* (Ia. q. 5 art. 5 ad 3 um). For it is in this sense of 'exist' that we say a thing goes on existing; and for a thing to continue to exist is for it to be the same X over a period of time, when 'X' represents some *Begriffswort;* and this in turn means the persistence in an individual of the form expressed by the predicable expression 'X'. Thus, a man continues to exist in that the baby, the youth, and the grown man are *the same man;* and this means the persistence in some individual of the form, *Begriff,* that answers to the *Begriffswort* 'man'.

III

Having explained the construction of the phrase
'that by which . . .', and the relevant sense of 'is', we
consider what is meant by phrases of the form 'that
by which *x is*', '*x*' being replaced by a name of an individual. Now it is the fundamental doctrine of Aquinas, repeatedly stated, that except when *x* is God, *x*
is never identical with that by which *x is*. This doctrine
is, I think intelligible in the light of our previous enquiry; but it is a most surprising doctrine. Why should
we, how can we, distinguish between an individualised form and that by which the individualised form
is? e.g. between the redness of Socrates' nose and that
by which the redness of Socrates' nose *is*, goes on existing? We find in Aquinas himself remarks which
might suggest the view that *esse* is an inseparable and
only conceptually distinct aspect of the individualised
form itself. '*Esse* of itself goes with a form, for form is
actuality' (*Esse autem per se convenit formae, quae
est actus*) (Ia. q. 75 art. 6); 'For any given thing,
that *by* which it exists is its form' (*unumquodque
formaliter est per formam suam*) (IIIa. q. 2 art. 5 ad 3
um).

All the same, I think there are good reasons for accepting the real distinction between an individualised
form and the corresponding *esse*. The most important
and most general reason is stated succinctly but
clearly by Aquinas himself. If *x* is F and *y* is F, then
in respect of F-ness *x* and *y* are so far alike; the F-ness
of *x* will indeed be a different individualised form
from the F-ness of *y*, but they will be, as F-nesses,
alike. But when *x is* and *y* also *is*, the *esse* of *x* and the
esse of *y* are in general different as such. (Ia. q. 3
art. 5: *Tertio* . . .) Now this marks an unbridgeable
distinction between *esse* and any form F-ness whatsoever. And the distinction between the references of
the expressions 'that by which—*is*' and 'that by which

—is F' will not vanish even if the *esse* of God and
(say) the wisdom of God are identical; no more than
'the square of' and 'the cube of' have the same reference because 1 is both the square and the cube of 1.

A modern philosopher will often challenge philosophical assertions with the question: As opposed to
what? This is a legitimate move; as Aquinas says,
knowing the truth of an assertion is tantamount to
knowing the falsehood of its contradictory opposite
(Ia. q. 58 art. 4 ad 2 um). Well then, as opposed to
what does one say that in general the *esse* of *x* and
the *esse* of *y* are as such distinct? In the fairy-tale, all
the human members of the family and the family cat
shared a single life, that is, a single *esse* (*vivere
viventibus est esse*); and when the betrothed of the
youngest daughter took a pot-shot at the cat, its
death was the death of the whole family. In actual
families, animality is common to all the members of
the family, including the cat, but *esse* is not, and so
killing the cat has no such consequence. So, although
for a man or cat to go on existing is precisely the continued existence of his animality, that is, the persistence of a certain individualised form in continuously
renewed matter: nevertheless we must recognise a
real distinction between his animality and his *esse*.

A second reason appeals to the nature of intensive
magnitude. It may be that *x* is F and *y* is F, and that
they have the same specific F-ness, but yet the F-ness
of *x* is more intense than that of *y*. Moreover, the
F-ness of *x* may become more or less intense; and increase of F-ness plainly resembles a thing's coming to
be F, whereas a decrease of F-ness resembles a thing's
altogether ceasing to be F. Now difference between
x and *y* as regards intensity of F-ness is not difference
precisely as regards F-ness (especially as we may suppose *x* and *y* to have the same specific F-ness); it is
rather, I wish to say, difference as regards the existence of F-ness—the F-ness of *x* exists more than the
F-ness of *y*. So also a change in mere intensity is a

change as regards existence; increase in the intensity of x's F-ness resembles the coming to be of x's F-ness, both being additions of existence; decrease in the intensity of x's F-ness resembles the ceasing of x's F-ness, both being subtractions of existence. Here again, there is a real distinction between the F-ness of x and the *esse* of this individualised form; while the F-ness as such remains unchanged, its existence may vary in degree.

(I have deliberately stated this argument in a schematic way, in order to avoid irrelevant controversy about my choice of an example. It is not so easy as it looks to find an unexceptionable case of difference or change in mere intensity, without any difference or change in quality: Aquinas' favourite example, heat, would land us in many difficulties. So far as I can see, *sound* is a good example. A louder and a softer sound may be qualitatively identical; and a sudden increase of loudness resembles a sound's suddenly starting, a sudden decrease of loudness its suddenly stopping.)

A third reason is found in considering the nature of thought. How remarkable that if there can (logically) be an X, there can also be a thought of an X! What is this relation *being a thought of*, which can have anything whatsoever as its term—even non-existent things like dragons? And how can there be an activity whose whole nature consists in its having this relation to something—to 'something' possibly non-existent?

Now Aquinas' account of thought denies that its nature consists wholly in relation to something outside itself. When Plato thinks of redness, what exists in Plato is not a certain *relation* to redness or red things, but *is* redness, is an individual occurrence of the very same form of which another individual occurrence is the redness of this rose. But how then is it that this rose is red but not Plato's mind? Because the *mode* of occurrence of redness—not the redness that occurs—is unlike; the redness in Plato's mind *is*, exists, in a different way (*esse intentionale*) from the redness in this rose (which has *esse naturale*). We thus understand the intimate connexion of thought and its object. There is, as Aquinas often says, *likeness* (*similitudo*) between them. We also now understand the odd-seeming fact that there can be a thought of anything that there can be. Existence makes no difference to, and can impose no restriction on, the nature of that which exists; if it is possible that there should be F-ness at all, then it is possible alike that there should be F-ness occurring with *esse naturale* (a real live cow, say) and that there should be F-ness occurring with *esse intentionale* (a thought of a cow). The whole basis of this account is that the individual F-ness is really distinct from its *esse, naturale* or *intentionale* as the case may be.

To get this doctrine of Aquinas' properly straightened out in our minds we must realise that Aquinas is not saying e.g. that the cow in the meadow leads a double life and has another *esse* in my mind; or that I, when I think of the cow, become somehow identical with the cow. These kinds of talk (derived, I should guess, from taking too seriously the notorious trick expression 'in the mind') are expressly rejected by Aquinas. 'A stone is *not* in the mind (*anima*), it is the likeness (*species*) of a stone that is there . . . the similitude of a thing thought of (*intellectae*) is a form in the understanding' (Ia. q. 85 art. 2). There is one individualised form in the stone, and another individualised form in the mind of the man who thinks of it; these individualised forms are both occurrences of the same form, but differ in their manner of *esse;* neither the stone nor its individualised form is to be found in my mind.

Even when one angel thinks of another, what is in the knower is an individualised form differing from the individualised form that is in (or rather, for Aquinas, is identical with) the angel who is known, although both are occurrences of the very same form. On Aquinas' view, the difference (say) between Michael's thought of Gabriel and Gabriel himself, like the difference between my thought of a cow and the cow in the meadow, consists in one and the same form's occurring in Michael (or me) with *esse intentionale*, in Gabriel (or the cow) with *esse naturale;* and this involves the existence of two individualised forms (Ia. q. 56 art. 2 ad 3 um). It should be noticed in regard to the last citation that the difference between *esse naturale* and *esse intentionale* can occur even when there is no question of matter; angels, for Aquinas, have no sort of matter in their make-up, but the difference still holds good in their case.

I have had to be brief and leave out many important topics: in particular, the difference between the nature or essence and the (substantial) form of a material thing; the sense in which the human soul is the 'form' of the human body; the conception of *materia prima;* the question whether angels are 'forms' (sc. individualised forms.) Even so I could not make this paper easy going, nor avoid what many people would call hairsplitting distinctions. But all serious philosophy *is* difficult; and as for hairsplitting,

> A Hair perhaps divides the False and True,
> Yes; and a single Alif were the clue—
> Could you but find it—to the Treasure-house
> And peradventure to THE MASTER too.

CATEGORIES

HERBERT MC CABE

Some people hold that there is only one kind of genuine statement which can properly be said to be true
or false. They say that apparent statements which are
not of this kind are in fact not statements but persuasive utterances intended not to convey truth but to
encourage the listener to adopt a particular attitude
or policy in living; among such pseudo-statements are
usually included ethical and theological doctrines. I
think that these people are mistaken but it is not my
purpose here to vindicate the statement-making character of ethical and theological language. What I propose to argue is that there are not one but many
different types of statement. By this I do not simply
mean that there are many different types of sentence
or many different ways of formulating truths, but that
the word 'statement' has to be used in several irreducibly different senses and cannot be treated as a
univocal term. This I take to be Aristotle's and St
Thomas' theory of the Categories. If this theory is correct the way is at least open to an intellectualist ethics
and theology; it will at any rate not be possible to say
that because a statement is not a factual one it is neither true nor false.

1. Meaning and Grammatical Function.

People often say nowadays that the meaning of a
word is the way in which it is used. When they say
this they are usually concerned to reject the naive
opinion that the meaning of a word is something that

Dominican Studies, Vol. VII, 1954, pp. 147–179. Reprinted
with the permission of the author and the Editor of *New
Blackfriars*.

the word stands for, that, as Professor Ryle has put it, every word is related to something which is its meaning in the way that the name 'Fido' is related to the dog Fido.[1] Wittgenstein characterizes such a naive theory as follows: 'The individual words in a language name objects—sentences are combinations of such names. In this picture of language we find the roots of the following idea: Every word has a meaning. The meaning is correlated with the word. It is the object for which the word stands.'[2] In this essay I am taking it for granted that such a view is inadequate. What I want to do is to examine the alternative opinion that the meaning of a word is given by giving the rules for its use.

I think there is an important difference between explaining to a foreigner the difference in English between 'horse' and 'pony' on the one hand and between 'horse' and 'from' on the other. Doubtless in both cases we would be explaining rules of the English language but there would be such different kinds of rules involved that this general account of what we had been doing would not be very helpful. When all is said and done there remains some sense in saying that Peter's French grammar is quite good but his vocabulary is not very large. Doubtless in increasing his French vocabulary Peter will be learning rules of the French language but not the same sort of rules as he learned when he was acquiring his grammatical skill.

Any artificial formalization of a living language is rightly suspect nowadays, but for the sake of clarity I am going to codify the distinction I have referred to by distinguishing between the grammatical function of a word and its meaning. What grammarians used to call 'Parts of Speech' is a rough classification of words according to their grammatical functions. I shall say that two words have different grammatical func-

[1] Review of Carnap's *Meaning and Necessity* in *Philosophy*, Jan. 1949.
[2] *Philosophical Investigations* (Oxford 1953), Part I, 1.

tions when a well-formed expression containing one of the words ceases to be a well-formed expression when the other word is substituted for the first. Thus, for example, 'The table laughed heartily' remains a well-formed expression if we substitute 'chair' for 'table' but not if we substitute 'therefore' for 'table'. Thus, in this case at least, 'table' and 'therefore' have different grammatical functions.

I want to suggest that we do not normally inquire about the difference in *meaning* between two words unless they have the same grammatical function. Generally speaking learning the meaning of words is a matter of extending your vocabulary and not of mastering your grammar. In some of its common uses the word 'to' differs in meaning from the word 'towards', but we would not, I think, normally say that there was a difference in *meaning* between 'towards' and 'federation'. Similarly 'rarely', 'often', 'sometimes', 'not' and 'almost' can form a group with one grammatical function within which there are differences of meaning and so can 'cabbage', 'antelope', 'sky-scraper' and 'postman'; but the differences of meaning in one group are of a quite different sort from those in the other, and the difference between a word in one group and a word in the other is only a difference of meaning in a very extended and artificial sense of that word.

One of the reasons why we say that there is a difference in meaning between 'bread' and 'jam' but are reluctant to say that there is a difference in meaning between 'bread' and 'because' is that in English we speak not only of the meaning of words but also of the meaning of sentences. The use of 'meaning' as applied to sentences is closely related to its use as applied in a restricted way to words of one grammatical function, but not so closely related to its use as applied indiscriminately. If I have a sentence with a certain meaning and I change one of its words for another word of different meaning but with the same grammatical function I shall get a new sentence which will either have a new meaning or, perhaps, will be a piece of nonsense, but if I change one of its words for a word of different grammatical function I shall not have a sentence at all. Thus if I start with 'The boy was playing with a piece of string', I can substitute for 'boy' a word of the same grammatical function but different meaning. As a result I may get, for example, 'The kitten was playing with a piece of string' (which has a new meaning) or perhaps 'The window was playing with a piece of string' (which is nonsense but is still a perfectly good sentence). But if I substitute a word which differs not merely in meaning but in grammatical function, too, for example 'occasionally', I shall get 'The occasionally was playing with a piece of string' (which is not just nonsense, it is not a sentence at all).

It is most important to recognize that there is a great difference between an expression which is a sentence but nonsense and one which is not a sentence at all. In the first place nonsense sentences can be and are used as part of the language, we use them for telling fairy stories, for example. In the second place we can give reasons why a nonsense sentence does not make sense—'Windows can't play with string'—but very often we cannot give a reason why a string of words does not make sense; there is no reason why it should.

To avoid confusion I shall henceforth not speak of sentences as meaningful or unmeaningful, I shall instead say that they make sense (are sensible) or do not make sense (are nonsense); I shall keep the word 'meaning' for words and phrases and I shall not speak of a difference in meaning between words or phrases of different grammatical functions. I shall use the word 'expression' for any word or group of words. A sentence is an expression that is well-formed in accordance with the grammar of the language. Just as a sentence is an expression in which the constituent expressions are rightly ordered in accordance with their grammatical functions, so a sensible sentence is one in which the constituent expressions are rightly ordered in accordance with their meanings. We can sometimes criticize malformed expressions with remarks like 'It hasn't got a main verb', we criticize nonsense sentences with remarks like 'Walruses can't really talk'.

I am now going to examine the relationship between the sense of indicative sentences and the meaning of the expressions which function as subjects in these sentences. This is, of course, but one small problem out of many similar ones but I choose it for special consideration firstly because it is interesting in itself and secondly because it involves questions that philosophers in Europe have been thinking about for a very long time. If we cannot be right in a small matter where we have the successes and failures of a long tradition to learn from, there is no point in pontificating in general terms about Meaning and Truth.

2. *Criteria of Nonsense.* (*a*) *The Principle of Verification.*

It will be well to begin by noting the difference between the general view I am taking of sense *versus* nonsense and the view, which used to be common amongst some logical positivists, that the sense of a proposition is the way of showing whether it is true or false. According to this Principle of Verification a sentence makes sense if it expresses a true or false proposition, otherwise it does not make sense. In opposition to this doctrine I am taking the view which is fairly common amongst contemporary philosophers that the question of whether or not a sentence makes sense is a question about the ordering of its constituent expressions in accordance with their meaning, and has nothing to do with truth and falsity. I think that the logical positivists were mistaken in supposing that truth or falsity attached to something called a 'proposition' which a sentence expresses. The word 'proposition' is useful for expressing the relationship between different languages, as when we say that 'Je me trouve à Paris' in French expresses the same proposition as does 'I am in Paris' in English, but it simply will not do to say that the proposition expressed by 'I am in Paris' is true or false any more than one can say that the sentence expressing it is true or false. The quite unmysterious reason for this is that when I am in Paris I may use the French or English sentence which expresses this proposition and will thus say something that is true, but when I am not in Paris I may use exactly the same sentence expressing exactly the same proposition and thus say something that is false. Truth and falsity belong not to propositions or sentences as such but to particular uses of sentences. One can no more describe a sentence or proposition by saying that it is true than one can describe a pair of shoes by saying that George wore them on Tuesday; certainly if he wore them they would at least be a pair that would fit him and this would characterize them to some extent, but they would fit him whether he wore them or not. Just as a pair of shoes can be black size nines with rubber soles even in a country where nobody ever wears shoes, so a sentence can make sense even at a time or in a place in which there is no occasion when it is used for saying something true or false. To take the classical example, 'The present king of France is wise' makes perfect sense even though to-day it cannot be used for saying anything true or false because there is no king of France to talk about truly or falsely. The sense of the sentence is exactly the same as it was in the seventeenth century when there was a king of France; it retains this sense even though nowadays there is no way of showing that what it expresses is true or false.[3]

[3] This point is made very clearly by Mr Strawson ('On Referring'. *Mind*, N.S.235, July 1950, p. 320). From this article

3. *Criteria of Nonsense.* (*b*) *Appropriateness—The
   Predicables.*

It seems clear, then, that when we ask whether 'The
king of France is wise' makes sense, we are *not* asking
whether the proposition it expresses can be verified; I
want to suggest as an alternative to this view that one
of the things we *are* asking is whether the meanings
of the subject 'The king of France' and of the predicate
'. . . is wise' are such that they are appropriate to each
other. We are asking, among other things, whether
the sentence is or is not like 'The king of France is an
exact multiple of three' or 'The breadknife was snor-
ing unusually loudly' in which the predicate is not
appropriate to the subject.

The notion of the appropriateness of a predicate to
a subject is not a simple one, for there are many ways
in which predicates can be appropriate. Professor Ryle
has recently protested rightly against the 'undiscrimi-
nating employment of smother expressions like "Quality", "Property", "Predicate", "Attribute", "Characteristic" . . .' to cover anything which is said about a
thing.[4] He attributes this to the hold which Aristotelian logic had upon seventeenth and eighteenth-
century thinkers among others. This is scarcely fair to
the Aristotelian tradition which in fact contained a
definite, if rudimentary, theory of the different ways

and from his *Introduction to Logical Theory* (London 1952)
I have borrowed the terminology of 'Referring' and 'Statement'.
My general indebtedness to Mr Strawson's writings will be obvious though I hasten to absolve him of any responsibility for
the theory of Substance that I am putting forward.

[4] *Dilemmas* (Cambridge, 1954), p. 85. This is perhaps a suitable point to note that Professor Ryle's use of 'Category' (e.g.
ibid., p. 9 and in the phrase 'category mistake'—*Concept of
Mind,* p. 16, etc.) seems to me quite different from the Aristotelian usage. Broadly speaking his categories have to do with different types of words in sentences whereas Aristotle's categories
have to do, as I shall suggest, with the distinction of types of
statements.

in which a predicate can function. The Aristotelians distinguished five different things that can be covered by the smother expression 'Predicate'; these were called the five *Predicabilia* or *Universalia* and they were: *Genus, Differentia, Definitio, Proprium,* and *Accidens.* These five represent five different ways in which a predicate can be appropriate to a subject, five ways, that is, in which an indicative sentence can make sense. It seems unlikely that this can stand as an exhaustive or final treatment of appropriateness, but I propose to work for the moment within this traditional framework since there seem to be no modern developments of the theory. (I think that the simple bipartite division, which used to be fashionable, into factual and tautological propositions represents a crude retrogression rather than a development of the Aristotelian theory.)

It is difficult to define precisely the sense of each of the five predicables without first seeing their relation to each other, so I propose to begin with a fairly vague account of the predicable of *Accidens.* For a scholastic philosopher the first temptation to be resisted is that of confusing the predicable *Accidens* with the predicamental or categorical *Accidens.* The categories, as we shall see, are not a classification of predicates in their relation to subjects, they have nothing to do directly with the ways in which *sentences* make sense; they are a classification of certain types of true or false *statements* that sensible sentences can be used to make. The statement that a certain (categorical) accident belongs to a substance may often be made by means of a sentence in which the predicate is appropriate to the subject not as a (predicable) accident but, for example, as a *proprium.* For example, 'George can think' and 'George is pink' are sentences in which the predicates are appropriate to the subject in different ways, that is, they make sense in different ways, but both may be used for attributing an accident (in the categorical sense) to George. Conversely

'George is happy' and 'George is on my left' are the same from the point of view of the predicables but the statements they can be used to make are categorically different. To ask, as scholastics sometimes do, whether such and such is a predicable or a categorical accident is to muddle up two different kinds of question; it is like asking, 'Does the Equator pass through Kenya, or is it merely a geographical fiction?'

In order to avoid this sort of confusion I shall not use the word 'accident' in the sense of predicable accident. Instead I shall call a sentence in which the predicate is appropriate to the subject in the way peculiar to a predicable accident a 'factual sentence'. I shall keep the word 'accident' for use in connection with the distinction of different types of statement. Any introduction of technical vocabulary necessarily produces a distortion of everyday speech, and it is worth while drawing attention to some of the distortions that have been produced here. Notice in the first place that ' "p" is a factual sentence' is not equivalent to ' "p" is a fact' or to 'It is a fact that p'. I am simply going to rule out sentences like ' "p" is a fact' because they would be hopelessly misleading. As for 'It is a fact that p', I shall interpret this as saying two things: (*a*) that 'p' is a factual sentence, and (*b*) that the sentence is being used to make a true statement. Thus a statement made by a sentence of the form 'It is a fact that p' would be false if either 'p' were not a factual sentence or the statement that 'p' was used to make were false. Thus the statements made by 'It is a fact that God exists' and by 'it is a fact that London is smaller than Wigan' will both be false, but for different reasons, the latter because London is bigger than Wigan and the former because 'God exists' is not a factual sentence. 'God exists' is not a factual sentence because the way in which '. . . exists' is appropriate to 'God' is not the way in which the predicate of a factual sentence is appropriate to its subject.

After these preliminaries we are in a position to give

some account of what a factual sentence is. First of all I want to explain by examples the term 'contrary predicate'. The predicates '. . . doesn't hunt beetles in the cellar' and '. . . is rather tall for his age' are the contrary predicates respectively of the predicates '. . . hunts beetles in the cellar' and '. . . is not taller than average for his age'. I can only explain this fairly simple notion by means of examples because a living language is too fluid to be governed by rigid rules for the formation of contrary predicates. All that can be said as a general rule is that in the case of a predicate P, the contrary predicate of P is one which when attached to a subject yields a sentence which could be used to make a statement by which we would deny the statement made by the sentence in which P is attached to the same subject. We can then say, as a first approximation, that a sentence is a factual sentence when the predicate is appropriate to the subject in such a way that the contrary predicate would be equally appropriate. Thus sentences such as 'I came here on Tuesday', 'My kangaroo is hungry', 'Peter bought a new car', 'The litmus has turned red', are factual sentences and the corresponding sentences with contrary predicates—'I did not come here on Tuesday', 'My kangaroo is not hungry', etc.—are also factual sentences. In such sentences the meaning of the subject is in no sense a reason for preferring any predicate to its contrary and if a factual sentence makes sense with a certain predicate it will necessarily make sense with the contrary predicate.

4. The meaning of the subject and restriction of the predicate range.

I now want to suggest that there is an important sense in which the meaning of a word which functions grammatically as the subject of an indicative sentence is given by giving the types of predicates (and their contraries) that can be attached to it to yield factual sentences that make sense. It is because of the meaning of 'window' that we think there is something odd about the question, 'Was the window playing with a piece of string?' The question looks like the question, 'Was the kitten playing with a piece of string?' but we recognize that the answer 'No' would not have the same force in the two cases. We think that the question about the window is a bit like the catch question, 'Have you stopped cheating at poker?' which carries with it the perhaps unjustified presupposition that you have been cheating in the past. The question about the window seems in the same way to carry with it the unjustified presupposition that the window might have been playing with string. But this is not peculiar to the question about the window, for the question about the kitten carries with it the same sort of presupposition but in this case we do not notice it because it is justified and it does not seem queer. I am not suggesting that all questions are like 'Have you stopped cheating at poker?' For that question is peculiar in that it presupposes a *fact* about you, the fact, namely, that you have been cheating at poker, whereas what is common to all questions is that they presuppose not an extra *fact* but that the sentence expressing the fact makes sense. They presuppose, that is to say, that the meaning of the subject is such that the predicate in question and its contrary (a question offers a choice between the two) fall within the restricted range of predicates that can sensibly be attached to the subject.

It is clear that some subjects such as 'My black pencil' will exercise two sorts of restriction over the range of predicates that can be attached to them. It is one sort of restriction that excludes both the predicates '. . . is not hungry' and '. . . is hungry', and another sort that excludes '. . . is not black' but does not exclude '. . . is black'. The reason why '. . . is not black' is inappropriate is that in calling something 'My black pencil' you have already begged the question about its blackness, you have incorporated into your naming a presupposition of fact about the pencil which is incompatible with its not being black. A question about a black pencil already presupposes a *fact* (much as the question 'Have you stopped cheating at poker?' presupposes a fact) as well as presupposing a certain predicate range within which the answer must fall. Thus in learning the meaning of 'My black pencil' you are learning not merely a rule but also certain particular exceptions to the rule. In accordance with the first sort of restriction you learn that to the subject in question you may not sensibly attach any predicates other than '. . . is P' and '. . . is not P', '. . . is Q' and '. . . is not Q', '. . . is R' and '. . . is not R', etc. In accordance with the second sort of restriction you learn that you may not attach '. . . is not Q'.

5. *Rules of meaning that have no exceptions—Definable words.*

The next step in this theory that the meaning of a subject expression is given by giving an account of the predicates that can appropriately be attached to it, is to examine the possibility that we might have subject expressions which, unlike 'My black pencil', exercise only the first sort of restriction over their predicate range. To learn the meaning of such expressions would be to learn rules of appropriateness to which there were no particular exceptions. I want to suggest that we might use as names expressions which do not incorporate any presuppositions of fact about what they are naming. To illustrate what I mean I shall take the classical example of the noun-phrase 'human being'. The meaning of this expression I shall take to be given purely and simply by giving the types of predicate that can be attached to it. This is part of what is meant by the Aristotelian who says that it is possible to *define* a human being and who goes on to say that a human being is a rational animal. To say that a human

being is an animal is not, for the Aristotelian, to state
any facts about human beings or to describe human
beings in any way; it is to say that it makes sense to
speak of human beings as hungry or not hungry, as
trying to climb on the table or not so trying, as in pain
or not in pain, as being young or growing old. Similarly to say that a human being is rational is not to
say that human beings are understanding anything or
thinking about anything; it is to say that it makes sense
to say of them that they are guilty or not guilty, seeing
or failing to see the point of an argument, making or
not making decisions, clever or stupid, unscrupulous
or charitable. When Whitehead emended the traditional definition to 'Man is an animal intermittently
liable to fits of rationality', he was saying not less but
more than the Aristotelian says. As far as his definition
goes the Aristotelian is not claiming that any human
being can think or is liable to think, but only that it
would not be nonsensical to say that he has been
thinking. Of course, as Aristotle is at pains to point
out[5] having said that a human being is a rational animal there remains a great deal more to be said. There
remains the investigation of what is involved in being
a rational animal. We have to discover empirically
just what is the logical behaviour of the predicates
authorized by the definition; we have to find out how
we use words like 'sees', 'feels', 'hungers', 'wants' and
'dislikes'. The definition at first roughly circumscribes
what I think Wittgenstein would call a 'language
game'. It remains for us to discover in detail how it is
played. In learning the internal economy of the game
we become more precise about its boundaries and we
may well find that our original definition needs to be
modified or understood in a new way. It is important
to recognize, however, that since a definition is not a
collection of facts or a description, no empirical discoveries can make it logically necessary to modify our

[5] *De Anima*, 1.1, 402b, 15 *et. seq.*

definition. Nevertheless we do modify our definitions and we do regard some language games as better than others. Part of the theory of substance is an attempt to explain what we are saying when we say this. There is nothing to prevent us from deciding arbitrarily upon a language in which such and such factual sentences will make sense and such and such others will not. Thus, for example, Malebranche decided that 'My dog is in pain' did not make sense (and used to beat his dog every day to proclaim his faith in this). His position was not that 'My dog is in pain' always makes a false statement because 'My dog is not in pain' always makes a true one but that both these sentences are nonsensical like 'My telephone is in pain' or 'My dog is in mortal sin' or 'My dog is not in mortal sin'. Clearly, if we happen to disagree with Malebranche we cannot simply adduce facts to discredit him since the argument turns precisely on what is to count as a factual sentence; nevertheless most people do think that his definition of a dog is an incorrect one because they do want to be able to say that dogs are in pain or not in pain. This is the sort of case that St Thomas is thinking of when he says:

> 'Si quis ergo assignet definitionem per quam non deveniatur in cognitionem accidentium rei definitae, illa definitio non est realis sed remota et dialectica.'[6]

The position that I am going to maintain is that to assert concerning something that its essence has such and such a definition is to assert something that claims to be true. But for the moment we must return to meaning of 'human being'.

As has been said, when an Aristotelian says that a human being is an animal he is not asserting that a

[6] *Comm. in De Anima*, Lect. 1, n. 15. ['If a definition is given which will not lead to a knowledge of the accidents of the thing defined, this is no real definition but an abstract and dialectical one.']

human being has certain characteristics or that he is recognizable in this or that way, but only that it makes sense to assert or deny that he has these characteristics or ways of being recognized. 'George is an animal' might, though I think misleadingly, be described as a second order predication as compared with 'George is hungry'. 'George is an animal' gives a reason why 'George is hungry' and 'George is not hungry' make sense. It establishes a language game in which these sentences have a part to play. It is not a factual sentence and its predicate cannot be synonymous with or the contrary of any predicate in a factual sentence whose subject is 'George'. When we say that it is a fact that George is hungry, we are not expressing but *making use of* our knowledge that George is an animal. That George is an animal is not part of what is asserted or denied by the statement that he is hungry. If we say that George is hungry and so George must be an animal we are making use of an odd kind of implication which is quite unlike the kind we make use of when we say that George is free, white and twenty-one and so he must be white; it is more like saying that this piece has put the king in check so it must be a chessman.

'George is an animal' makes sense in a different way from a factual sentence: the latter makes sense if the predicate does not fall outside the range of predicates in factual sentences authorized by the meaning of the subject term, the former states (partially) what the meaning of the subject term is. In traditional terminology the predicate '. . . is an animal' is predicated 'in eo quod quid'; the predication belongs in the predicable of *genus* and not of *accidens*. The sentence may be used for stating *what* the thing referred to by the subject is. Among the five predicables three are of this kind. The Aristotelian tradition distinguishes the ways in which 'George is an animal', 'George is rational' and 'George is a rational animal' make sense, and these three ways are respectively the predicables of *genus*, *differentia*, and *definitio* (the latter is sometimes mis-leadingly called '*species*'). For the present it must suffice to say that the difference between these three is that a sentence in which the predicate is appropriate to the subject as a *definitio* completely circumscribes the meaning of the subject, while the other two do so only partially and their ways of being partial are quite distinct. All three, however, yield sentences which can be used to say *what something is*, rather than what it is like or what has happened to it or what it has done or will do, etc. I have not discussed and shall not be able to discuss the predicable of *proprium* although it is of great importance in the Aristotelian theory. It has to do with complications which can, I think, for the moment be ignored.

6. The 'Facts about the World or else Rules of Language' theory.

At this point, if not a good deal earlier, the reader will have come to suspect that all I am doing is making rather heavy weather over a simple distinction that has become almost a platitude among contemporary philosophers: the distinction between facts about things and rules of language. A great many people would admit that there is an important distinction between sentences like 'George is an animal' and sentences like 'George is hungry', and they would make the distinction as follows. 'George is hungry' can be used to state a fact about George, whereas 'George is an animal', although it looks as if it could be used to talk about George, is in fact used to talk about the word 'George'. It is used to say that the word 'George' has such a meaning that a certain range of predicates such as '. . . is hungry' or '. . . is not ill' can be attached to it to make sense. Such people would say that 'George is hungry' is used to state a fact about the world, while 'George is an animal' is used to state a rule of language, and some of them would call the

latter sentence a 'tautology' and would prefer to say
that it is used to express or show a rule of language
than to say that it is used to state such a rule. These
people would point out that the truth or falsity of
the statement made by 'George is hungry' depends
upon some contingent events in the world, so that we
cannot say that it is true or false without examining
the world around us empirically, whereas the truth or
falsity of the statement (if any) made by 'George is
an animal' depends not on any contingent events in
the world but on the constitution of the language
which we have constructed to talk about the world.
These people frequently say that sentences like
'George is an animal' cannot be used to convey information about the world. Sometimes they regard
such sentences as expressing an attitude or a policy towards George on the part of the man using the sentence.

This is a very simplified account of a set of opinions
which is fairly common among contemporary philosophers and I want to agree with a great deal of what
these people say. I think that one of the things that
they want to insist on is that if you are simply telling
someone about the meaning of a word you are not
giving him the kind of information you would be giving him if you told him that there was a horse in the
bathroom. I think this is clearly true. But the view
does seem to rest on the assumption that since when
you assert that 'George is an animal' you are not stating a fact about the world, then you must be stating
or expressing nothing but a rule of language. This I
find unsatisfactory. In the first place I cannot see that
there are any facts about the world. I do not see that
any obvious sense can be given to the statement that a
sentence such as 'The water has come to the boil' can
be used to make a statement about, or state a fact
about, *the world.* To me it seems that it is used to state
something about some water, and that it can be so
used because first of all it makes sense; and it makes

sense because 'The water' has a meaning such that
'. . . has come to the boil' can be appropriately attached to it. I do not know what the meaning of 'The
world' is, or (what is the same thing) how we could
decide what it makes sense, or does not make sense,
to say about it. Of course 'The world' has a perfectly
ordinary meaning when we distinguish it from e.g.
'The sun' or 'The stars' or 'Europe', but clearly this is
not what these philosophers mean by it when they
say that some sentences can make statements about
the world. In the second place I think that if you say
that 'George is an animal' is a tautology you may be
overlooking what I think is an important difference
between the sense in which 'The old grey mare is old'
is a tautology and the sense in which 'George is an
animal' is a tautology, but I shall not discuss this point
at present.

I think that underlying a great deal of what some
people say about facts and tautologies, or what some
people used to say about what were called 'truths of
fact' and 'truths of reason', is the unexamined presupposition that there exist side by side a World full
of things or decorated with facts, and a Language full
of words or decorated with sentences, and that part
of the philosopher's job is to sort out what belongs to
the World and what belongs to Language. It is a little
like what the Aristotelians used to accuse the Platonists of believing in, an extra world governed by logic
and meaning set over against the ordinary world with
no government to speak of. In such a set up explaining
the meaning of a word is like explaining the proper
moves of a pawn in chess without explaining that people play chess and try to win. It is possible to do this
but there is always the danger that the learner will
come across the word 'winning' and ask what sort of
move is a winning move. (Just as a man might ask:
What sort of a sentence is a true sentence? What sort
of a name is a proper name? or What sort of a description is a definite description?) The teacher will then

patiently explain that a winning move is not a sort of move and that he cannot explain what winning is in the terms in which he has been explaining the game. The learner is then liable to ask why the teacher has restricted himself to this way of explaining the game, and whether there might not be more to be said about moving a pawn than an account of the rules according to which it is moved. Not that in explaining the rules one can say more in the sense of telling the learner that on some occasion Capablanca moved his pawn to a particular square, but that in explaining them one is also in some sense explaining why people move pawns at all. In a rather similar way when we say that George is an animal we may sometimes be doing more than giving the rules for the use of 'George', not in the sense of telling anybody any particular facts about George but rather in the sense of pointing out that statements of fact can be made about George, that there is, so to speak, some point in having sensible sentences with 'George' as subject.

In other words one cannot complete the job of describing a Language and then pause, turn round to look at the World and add some additional information about the correspondence between the two. Rather the world permeates all of one's definitions of some parts of language, some definitions are worldly definitions. One does not say in the first place that 'chair' is used in such and such a way and then add as a further fact that it names something in the world (what in the world is *something?*). Some of one's definitions are like explanations of the moves of chess, in which the whole explanation is permeated by and presupposes the notion of playing the game and trying to win, but others, like the explanation of 'chimera' are like explanations of the rules of a game which nobody plays or wins or enjoys. There is not much point in having a set of sensible sentences beginning 'The chimera is . . .' because nobody will ever want to use these to make true or false statements, for there are not any chimeras to make statements about. It is the latter type of explanation rather than the former that needs to be accounted for on the face of it, and the contrast between the two induces us to try to explain what makes a game a real game, just as the contrast between what we do when we define 'chimera' and what we do when we define 'human being' leads us to talk about being. The only difference seems to be that there are human beings but no chimeras. As St Thomas says:

'Si non sit aliqua res cuius essentiam definitio significet *nihil differt* definitio a ratione exponente significationem alicuius nominis.'[7]

7. *The Aristotelian alternative—Different types of statement.*

The alternative that the Aristotelian offers to the theory I have discussed above is that 'George is an

[7] *Comm. in* 11. *Post. Anal.* Cap. VII, Lect. 6. ['If there is no thing to have its essence signified by a definition, then the definition is no different from the explanation of the meaning of a term'] I find it interesting that when Wittgenstein asks himself what after all is a *game?* What is it that is common to all games in virtue of which we call them games? his answer has a great deal in common with that of Aristotle and St Thomas when they ask themselves what after all is being? What is it that is common to all beings in virtue of which we say that they are? Wittgenstein points out that there is nothing common, what we have is:
'a complicated network of similarities overlapping and crisscrossing sometimes overall similarities, sometimes similarities of detail.'
He compares the concept of game to that of number:
'we extend our concept of number as in spinning a thread we twist fibre on fibre. And the strength of the thread does not reside in the fact that some one thread runs through its whole length, but in the overlapping of many fibres.'
(*Philosophical Investigations*, 1, 66 and 67.)
Similarly St Thomas points out that there is nothing common to all beings, *Ens non est genus*, and his theory of the general use of the word 'being' is the well-known and often misinterpreted theory of analogy which, however, I cannot discuss at this point.

animal' and 'George is hungry' do not differ in that
the former expresses a rule of language while only the
latter can be used to make a statement about George,
but that both of them can be used to make statements
about George; the difference is a difference in the
type of statement that they can be used to make. The
view that I have been criticizing seems to be that
while there may be different types of sentence by
which statements may be made about things, there is
only one type of statement; and since sentences of the
type of 'George is an animal' cannot be used to make
this type of statement they cannot be used to make
statements at all. The view that I am proposing is
that there are different types of statement as well as
different types of sentence, that there are in fact at
least ten different types of statement. I am further
going to suggest that these several types of statement
are related to one another in a variety of different
ways but that there is no common formula which they
all exemplify in virtue of which they are all called
statements. This is what I take to be Aristotle's and St
Thomas' theory of the Categories or Praedicamenta.

My strongest reason for preferring this theory to
that of the Fact/Language-Rule philosophers is that
the latter after explaining that sentences like 'George
is an animal' merely show the place of 'George' in
some language, seem to be left with peculiar insoluble
problems about the word 'exists'. They find difficulty in
saying what is meant by 'George' being the *name* of
something, for they have carefully and accurately
demonstrated that the question of whether or not
'George' is the name of anything has nothing to do
with its meaning. For example Mr J. L. Evans says
with perfect truth:

> 'The obvious alternative to the Relational Theory of
> meaning (and one which is gradually supplanting
> it) is to admit that in considering the question of
> meaning no reference need be made to any extra-
> linguistic facts. This must apply to all words, expres-

sions and sentences and no favourites such as logically proper names must be granted exemption. On this theory the meaning of a word is simply the rules which govern its use, and to ask for its meaning is to ask for the rules.'[8]

There remains then the question: What are we saying when we say that George exists? When we say this we are certainly not stating an extra-linguistic *fact*; that George exists cannot be a fact about George; but neither are we giving additional rules for the proper use of 'George' in the English language.

Some people think that any puzzles we have about the word 'exists' are our own fault, because there is no need to have the word in our language. They think that we can get on very well without it and that the puzzles that it generates all arise from the hopeless attempt to treat it as though it had a useful function. In particular they think that it can never appropriately be used as a predicate attached to a singular subject. I want to show that, on the contrary, this word has a definite part to play in a philosopher's language. More precisely I want to show that we need *some* expression which expresses something about things which is neither a fact about them nor a rule for the linguistic use of their names. I shall show this by an examination of the difference between sentences that do and sentences that do not make statements. This is St Thomas' line of approach to the question of *esse*, for him it is in the *judicium*, the act of stating something truly or falsely, the second operation of the intellect, that we are concerned with *esse*

Prima quidem operatio respicit ipsam naturam rei . . . Secunda vero operatio respicit ipsum esse rei.[9]

[8] 'On Meaning and Verification' *Mind* 245, Jan. 1953, p. 9.
[9] *In Boet. De Trinitate.* Q. 5, Art. 3. [The first operation concerns the very nature of a thing, the second operation concerns the very *esse* of a thing.]

8. *Referring and Existence. (a) Subject and predicate.*

If we say 'The old man was not a plumber' we have
a factual sentence that makes sense, but we cannot
claim to be saying something that is true, or even
something that is false, unless we are using this sentence to say something about an old man. Simply considered as a sentence it is neither true nor false. It is
only when we use it on this or that occasion to talk
about this or that old man that we can be right or
wrong. To use Mr Strawson's terminology,[10] the sentence becomes a true or false *statement* only when its
subject 'The old man' is being used to *refer* to something. The second part of the sentence, the predicate
'. . . was not a plumber', on the other hand is not being used to refer, nor is its constituent phrase 'a
plumber' being used to refer. We might ask, 'Which
old man isn't a plumber?' but it would be stupid to
ask, 'Which plumber isn't he?' This doctrine of the
different functions of subject and predicate in a
statement-making sentence is a favourite one of St
Thomas', he comes back to it again and again, usually
in such terms as these:

> 'Terminus in subiecto positus tenetur materialiter,
> idest pro supposito; positus vero in praedicato tene-
> tur formaliter, idest pro natura significata.'[11]
> 'An expression functioning as a subject is taken *ma-*

[10] *Op. cit.*
[11] *Summa Theol.* III. 16. 7 ad 4. See also: I. 13. 12. c; I. 16.
2. c; I. 31. 3 ad 2; III. 16. 9. c; III. 17. 1 ad 3; Met. 9, Lect.
11, n. 1898; 3 Sent. 7. 1. 1. c. This extremely important doctrine has been strangely neglected by thomists. The only good
account of it that I know is an invaluable article by Mr P.
Geach, 'Subjects and Predicates', *Mind* 236, Oct. 1950. Those
interested in St Thomas' theory of language will notice that I
am taking this distinction (*tenetur* materialiter et formaliter) to
be different from the distinction made in e.g. *De Potentia,* 9. 4.
c between formal and material *signification.* And, of course,
for an expression to be taken materially is not the same as for
it to have material *supposition.*

terially to stand for something, but when it functions as predicate it is taken *formally* to signify a nature.'

9. (*b*) *Referring and Identity.*

St Thomas, however, did not think that this was invariably the case. He notes an exception which is of peculiar interest; it is worth turning aside to consider it since it helps to clarify the notion of referring. In the Commentary on the Sentences he notes that in the case of a sentence of the form '*x* is *y*' where '*x*' and '*y*' are both substantives, it may happen that '*y*' is taken *materialiter*, as a referring word, instead of *formaliter*. This case he calls a 'praedicatio per identitatem' as distinct from the common 'praedicatio per informationem' which is more properly a predication.[12] Thus in a predication *per informationem* as, for example, 'George is very stupid', you are saying that what is referred to by 'George' is very stupid. But in a predication *per identitatem* as, for example, 'George is Mr Smith', the substantive 'Mr Smith' in the predicate is taken materially in the same way as the subject expression 'George', and so you are saying that what is referred to by 'George' is also referred to by 'Mr Smith'. Thus, for St Thomas, a statement of identity, *unlike* other kinds of statement, asserts that two referring expressions refer to the same thing. This view of identity seems to be the same as that of Wittgenstein in the *Tractatus:*

'"a is identical with b" means that the sign "a" is replaceable by the sign "b".'

and

'Identity of the object I express by identity of the

[12] 3 Sent. 5. Exp. Text. Substantiva (as opposed to adiectiva) significant non tantum formam sed etiam suppositum formae, unde possunt praedicari ratione utriusque; et quando praedicantur ratione suppositi dicitur praedicatio per identitatem, quando autem ratione formae dicitur praedicatio per denominationem sive informationem, et haec est magis proprie praedicatio quia termini in praedicato tenentur formaliter . . .

sign and not by means of the sign of identity. Difference of objects by difference of the signs.'[13]

Lord Russell had defined identity as follows:

'X and y are identical when every predicative function satisfied by x is also satisfied by y.'[14]

In the *Tractatus* Wittgenstein objected:

'Russell's definition of '=' won't do, because according to it one cannot say that two objects have all their properties in common. (Even if this proposition is never true it is nevertheless *significant*.)[15]

This view clearly depends on the belief that one can say 'x is not y' significantly as a pure *praedicatio per (non) identitatem* without *eo ipso* attributing any difference of properties to x and y. It is interesting that Carnap, for example, notices Wittgenstein's objection and brushes it aside:

'This objection is dismissed as soon as all properties are understood as including those of position.'[16]

It seems clear that, for Carnap, to refer to a thing is the same as to assign to it a certain *position*. For him the properties of what he calls 'position' seem to have a mystical significance akin to that of the primary qualities for Locke. I am not very sure what Carnap does mean by 'position' but I take it that, whatever extensions are made to the ordinary use of the term, only concrete things can have position. One of the important differences between referring to something and assigning a position to it is that we seem to be able to refer by means of abstract nouns as easily as by means of concrete ones. When I say that the preva-

[13] *Tractatus Logico-Philosophicus* (London 1951), 4.241 and 5.53.
[14] *Principia Mathematica*, p. 168, cf. 13.01.
[15] *Tractatus*, 5.5302.
[16] *Logical Syntax of Language*, p. 50.

lence of divorce is a sign of the instability of modern life, I do seem to be referring to either the prevalence of divorce or the instability of modern life, but it is not easy to see how either of these could be assigned a position. It is only by tinkering with the statement in a rather dubious way that one can make it appear equivalent to a statement or set of statements about concrete individuals with positions.[17] As Mr Strawson puts it, the theory of referring 'does not put any limits on the sorts of things that can be referred to. It puts no premium on concreteness.'[18] In fact referring cannot be the same as assigning a position even though pointing in a certain direction is a common way of referring to individuals, for in assigning a position we are either simply adding further predicates to the subject or else we are stating that what is named by the subject has a certain position. In the former case our sentence is no more a statement than it was before the additional predicates were added—we still need to presuppose that the subject refers—in the latter case we have included the presupposition of reference in the statement of position. Thus the sentence 'The whale is travelling rather fast' does not become a statement simply because it is expanded to 'That whale over there beside the lighthouse, near the seagull, is travelling rather fast'. Both of these are simply sentences and only become statements when it is presupposed that their subjects refer to something. It is very important to see that the referring character of the subject is not part of what is asserted by a statement. When I assert that George is hungry I am not asserting

[17] I do not mean to suggest that there could be a statement about divorce unless there were individuals who were divorced. For we can only make statements about what exists, and divorce cannot exist except as the divorce of some people. Nevertheless the statement is about the divorce and not about the people, and it is the divorce that is referred to. St Thomas makes this point very clearly against Avicenna, *Comm. in Met.*, V, Lect. 9, n. 894.

[18] *Introduction to Logical Theory*, p. 145.

that 'George' has reference, I am presupposing it; because unless I am presupposing it I will not have said
anything true or false, I will merely have enunciated
a sentence.

10. *The Presuppositions of Existence and of Definition.*

For convenience I am going to use the word 'real'
in the following sense: When an expression 'S' that
functions as subject in a sentence has reference I am
going to say that S is real. This is merely a device for
avoiding circumlocutions. (I am going to suggest later
that 'S is real' is *not* used in the same way as 'S exists'
for if the latter is to be used in a technical Aristotelian
sense the two will only be the same for certain kinds
of substitution for 'S'.) When I assert that George is
hungry, I presuppose, but do not (in the ordinary
sense of the word) *imply* that George is real. If I said,
'George is hungry so he must be real', I would not be
making use of the sort of implication that I would be
using if I said 'George is free, white and twenty-one
so he must be white'. I have used this example before
in a different context; part of the Aristotelian theory of
statements is that these two contexts are not so very
different. I said before (Sect. 5) that the assertion that
George is an animal is presupposed by but not part of
what is asserted by the assertion that George is hungry. I am now saying that the assertion that *George is
real* is presupposed by but not part of what is asserted
by the assertion that George is hungry. Let us, for the
moment, call sentences like 'George is an animal' definitional sentences, and sentences like 'George is real'
referential sentences. The central doctrine of the Aristotelian theory is that in the case of certain subject
expressions (of which, as it happens, 'George' is *not*
one) what is asserted by means of the referential sentence is the same as what is asserted by means of the
definitional sentence. Such subject expressions are the
proper subjects of the predicate '. . . exists', they are,

in St Thomas' language, names of *entia per se,* and *entia per se* are either substances or qualities or quantities, etc., all other subject expressions are the names of *entia per accidens;* of this we shall see much more later.

The classical example of a subject expression of this special kind is 'The human being'. According to the Aristotelian what is asserted by saying 'The human being is real' (or, by saying ' "The human being" has reference') is the same as what is asserted by saying 'The human being is a rational animal', and hence by the rule just given 'The human being is real' is the same as 'The human being exists'. Thus just as when the factual sentence 'The human being is white' is used to make a statement, we assert concerning the human being that he is white; so when the definitional sentence 'The human being is a rational animal' is used to make a statement, we assert concerning the human being that it exists and nothing more. Of course it is by no means necessary that a definitional sentence should be used to make a statement; no sentence is, as such, a statement. When it is not used to make a statement it is neither true nor false but merely expresses a rule of language that has been decided upon. But if we do ask, 'Is it *true* that a human being is a rational animal?' we can only be asking if there is a human being, just as if we ask, 'Is it *true* that a knight moves like this?' we can only be asking if there are games of chess. The difference between a definitional sentence used as a rule of language and used as a statement of existence, is not that any reference is made to any extra-linguistic *fact,* for the existence of a cow is not a fact about the cow nor a fact about anything else, unless it is a fact about some unintelligible metaphysical entity called 'The World' or 'Reality' or whatever.

The difference between such rather special subject expressions as 'The human being' and the vast majority of subject expressions in the English language is that when we construct a sentence which can be used to express the rules of language for 'The human being' we can also use this sentence as a statement to assert that the human being exists and nothing more, whereas with nearly all other subject expressions this is not so. To know that something is a human being is purely and simply to know *what* it is, but to know, for example, that something is a postman is not simply to know *what* it is, but also to know some facts about it, that it is employed to deliver letters, etc. Thus the sentence giving the rules for the use of 'The postman' is (let us say) 'The postman is the human being that delivers letters'. But if we use this sentence as a statement we do not merely state the existence of something but also the extra-linguistic *fact* that it delivers letters. The postman could continue to exist if this became no longer a fact, if he retired or got another job, but he could not continue to exist if he ceased to be a human being. To say that he is a human being is to give, so to say, the minimum determination that he must have in order to be at all.

If I say 'The postman is insane' you might answer, 'Yes, that's true, though as a matter of fact he isn't the postman really, he's my uncle wearing the postman's uniform.' But you could not sensibly reply: 'Yes, that's true, though as a matter of fact it isn't the postman really, it's a statue dressed up in the postman's uniform' because it does not make sense to say that a statue is or is not insane. Still less could you sensibly repy: 'Well that's only partly true because it isn't really the postman at all; I don't know what it is but it's some x' for you have absolutely no notion whether 'x' is a subject to which '. . . is insane' can be appropriately attached. Nevertheless there have been logicians who have cheerfully offered, 'There is an x such that x is a postman and x is insane' as an equivalent of 'A postman is insane'. According to the Aristotelian, the least that is required in order that 'A postman is insane' should be a statement (i.e. both a sentence that makes sense and one the subject of which has reference) is that 'A postman' should refer to something of which it makes sense to say that it is insane or not insane, but there is no need that it should refer to something that is a postman. Thus the Aristotelian would say that 'A postman is insane' might be re-written as 'A human being (who delivers letters) is insane'. The clause in brackets represents a factual presupposition incorporated into the subject expression which may turn out to be mistaken without damaging the original statement unduly. But if you say, 'An x (who is a human being who delivers letters) is insane', the clause in brackets is absolutely essential to understanding the sentence, for without knowing that x is a human being you could not know that it made sense to say that x is insane. 'X' is a variable and a variable is not a very, very general name; it is a labelled blank space. As Aristotle and St Thomas point out at laborious length, the condition for '—— is walking and —— is white' to make a statement is not merely that some subject expressions should be put in the two spaces, nor in order to assert that the walking thing is white is it sufficient to note that the *same* subject expression should be put in the two spaces; we must put in a subject expression of a definite meaning, a subject expression to which both '. . . is walking' and '. . . is white' are appropriate. 'The walking (thing)', as Aristotle puts it, 'walks and is white in virtue of something else besides'. Before anything can walk or be white or both, it must be something of a definite kind (the kind of thing that can walk or be white); and to say that this is *what it is* is to make the same assertion as we make when we say that it exists.

11. *Entia per accidens and Entia per se. (a) Entia per accidens as Logical Constructions.*

The distinction between subjects such as 'The human being' and subjects such as 'The postman' is the

distinction I mentioned before (Sect. 4) between subjects the meaning of which exerts only one kind of
restriction over the predicates that can be attached to
them to yield factual sentences that make sense, and
those the meaning of which exerts two kinds of restriction. It is the distinction between meanings that are
given by simple rules and those that are given by
rules with particular exceptions. 'The postman is an
exact multiple of three' is excluded by the first kind of
restriction (which also excludes 'The postman is *not*
an exact multiple of three') whereas 'The postman is
not employed to deliver letters' is excluded by the
second (which does not exclude 'The postman *is* employed to deliver letters'). Expressions like 'The human being' only exercise the first sort of restriction.
St Thomas' way of distinguishing the two kinds of
subject is to say that a postman is an *ens per accidens*
whereas a human being is an *ens per se.*

Scholastic philosophers who have some familiarity
with St Thomas' terminology should beware of the
temptation to confuse *ens per accidens* with *ens acci-
dentale;* the distinction between *ens per se* and *ens per
accidens* is *not* the distinction between substance and
accident, accidents are *entia per se* just as truly as
substances are; St Thomas is very insistent that the
categories are a classification of *entia per se.* The difference between substance and accident is not that
only substances are properly said to exist (*ens per se*)
while accidents are only said to exist *per accidens,*
but that while both are properly said to exist, the
predicate '. . . exists' is used analogically of them; it is
said *per prius* of substances and *per posterius* of accidents. This point can be put by saying that whereas
all statement-making sentences whose subjects are
names of *entia per accidens* can be shown to be equivalent to statement-making sentences whose subjects
are names of *entia per se,* it is not true that statements
about accidents can be thus reduced to statements
about substances. Nothing but sheer ignorance could

lead to the belief that St Thomas' theory of substance is the theory that all statements are analysable into statements about substances, or the even more fantastic belief that St Thomas, noticing that a lot of Latin sentences contained a subject and a predicate, thought that the subject ought to stand for a substance and the predicate for a quantity, quality, relation, etc.[19]

One way of putting St Thomas' theory would be to say that an *ens per accidens* is a logical construction out of *entia per se*.[20] Thus, Mr A. J. Ayer once wrote:

> 'The assertion that tables are logical constructions out of sense contents . . . is tantamount to saying that sentences which contain the symbol "table" . . . can all be translated into sentences of the same language which do not contain that symbol, not any of its synonyms, but do contain certain symbols that stand for sense contents.'[21]

If for 'sense contents' you substitute '*entia per se*', and if you give a charitable interpretation to 'stands for', you get a fair account of St Thomas' theory of *entia per accidens*. Thus 'A postman was insane' can be translated to 'A human being was employed to deliver letters and he was insane'. This kind of translation can be carried further since both insanity and being employed to deliver letters are still *entia per accidens*, and an empirical investigation of the ways in which we use 'insane' and 'employed to deliver letters' will enable us to expand the sentence into one containing only expressions that stand for the *entia per se* of which these are logical constructions. To make such a

[19] To see the absurdity of this it is sufficient to read a passage (e.g. 1 Sent. 22. 1. 1 ad 3) where St Thomas carefully distinguishes the grammarian's use of 'substantia' in e.g. 'nomen significat substantia cum qualitate' from the logician's use when *substantia* is the name of one of the ten categories.

[20] I owe this suggestion, like so much else in this article, to Fr Columba Ryan, O.P.

[21] *Language Truth and Logic* (London 1949), pp. 63–64.

translation is not, of course, to produce a preferable way of saying that the postman was insane; it will be cumbersome, stilted and less readily intelligible; its only advantage will be that it exhibits unambiguously the way in which it makes sense.

12. (*b*) *Entia per accidens are described; entia per se are defined.*

It is impossible in a short article to enter into the complications which arise from the circumstance that in any language actually in use there are practically no words for *entia per se*. This is simply because, as St Thomas repeatedly points out, we name things according to their outstanding characteristics, according to the properties that interest us and which we find useful for recognizing things in the ordinary course of events. For practical purposes we are not usually interested in what things are but only in how they affect us or how we may use them. Generally speaking our names are abbreviated descriptions rather than abbreviated definitions; a description of a horse tells us what we may expect to find when we examine a horse, a definition merely tells us what the horse must be in order to be at all, it tells us what it would make sense to say that we have found or not found. The same definition is compatible with two descriptions which differ on every point, it is only incompatible with two descriptions which have not got the same points.

The descriptional character of our names gives them a certain looseness of application that Professor Waismann has called 'open texture'.[22] We can never, as Locke saw, come to the end of describing a material object; there is always something further that might be said. A descriptional name never completely circumscribes the thing named; we are perpetually confronted by the possibility of the thing developing a

---

[22] '*Verifiability*'. In the collection *Logic and Language*. Edit. Antony Flew (Oxford, 1952), p. 117.

new property. Must we then find a new word for it? or must we expand the sense of the old word? The answers to these questions are, of course, largely a matter of linguistic convenience. The so-called theory of Substance which seeks to regulate the answer by finding a stable core of essential characteristics which may not be changed without changing the name, surrounded by a penumbra of less essential characteristics which can be dispensed with, should be sufficiently discredited by now. The interesting thing however is that the question necessarily arises. It is in principle impossible to construct descriptional names which correspond to things: there must be constant shifts of meaning and adjustments in order to maintain a working approximation. There is nothing regrettable about this; it just happens to be how every practicable language works. The reason for it is that no description or enumeration of characteristics expresses what it is for a thing to be; things do not come into being in virtue of having this or that characteristic nor cease to be in virtue of losing it. Things are not facts nor collections of facts, they are the topics of a certain range of facts. To say that a factual sentence makes a true statement is not the same as saying that what is named by the subject exists, for what is named by the subject would be real (or—if it is an *ens per se*—would exist) if the statement were false. What exists is a topic of disagreement. A description gives you one side of the possible disagreement—the majority opinion; a definition simply tells you what the disagreement is about.

Thus it is in the definition that St Thomas finds the point of contact between language and things; definitions are incorrigible, they are not adjusted to meet new facts because they do not assert or deny facts, they are merely rejected if we are compelled to state new facts outside their range. From the point of view of language the *definition* founds a language game; these and these things may be asserted or denied.

From the point of view of things the *essence,* what
the thing is, founds an object of experience; these and
these things may or may not be the case. No accumulation of facts about a thing is equivalent to what the
thing is, just as no accumulation of sensible sentences
whose subject is 'S' is equivalent to the meaning of 'S'.

Notice that if my interpretation of him is correct it
is through the search for the definition, the linguistic
expression of *ens* that St Thomas approaches the
question of *esse,* or the proper use of '. . . exists', and
not *vice versa.* It does not seem to be his view that we
all start off by knowing what 'exists' means in virtue
of our empirical experience, the experience, as people
say, of the concrete existential chair. Whether or not I
am here differing from those contemporary thomists
who like to speak of the 'existentialism of St Thomas'
I do not know, for I am never certain of what exactly
they mean by this.

13. Types of entia per se—The Categories.

In a certain sense it is misleading to say that St
Thomas has a theory of substance. He has a theory of
Praedicamenta or Categories only one of which is the
category of substance. The ten categories represent a
classification of definables, or *entia per se,* according
to the ways in which they exist; or, what is the same
thing, it is a classification of statements according to
the ways in which they are statements.[23] It is clear that
there are different kinds of statement since the statement which results from predicating the definition (or
part of the definition) of something, which simply asserts the existence of what I have called a 'topic of
disagreement', is irreducibly different from any statement or statements made by factual sentences on one

---

[23] *Comm. in Met.* V, Lect. 9, n. 890. 'Oportet quod ens con-
trahatur ad diversa genera secundum diversum modum praedicandi qui consequitur diversum modum essendi . . . et propter
hoc ea in quae dividitur ens primo dicuntur 'praedicamenta'
quia distinguuntur secundum diversum modum praedicandi.'

or other side of the disagreement. When I say that a man is a rational animal (a statement in the category of substance) I merely assert his existence, or announce that a certain range of factual sentences will be statement-making sentences; when I assert that he is pink I state a fact about him but I do not by that statement announce his existence. It is true that the factual statement (which is in the category of quality) does presuppose—in a special sense of presuppose—the statement in the category of substance, but this is not part of what it asserts. Thus (supposing for present purposes that being pink, or pinkness, unlike e.g. being a trump or a centre-forward, were an *ens per se*) to attribute pinkness to something is to make a statement in a different sense of 'statement' from making a statement by attributing humanity or rational-animality to something. This is what is meant by saying that pinkness belongs to one category (quality) and humanity to another (substance); pinkness exists in one way and humanity in another.

Some people would be doubtful of the propriety of saying that pinkness exists at all, on the grounds that it is an abstraction whereas only concrete things exist; but in this they are, I think, the victims of a muddle. Properly speaking, 'concrete' and 'abstract' are grammarian's adjectives qualifying nouns and not things; things are neither concrete nor abstract. In St Thomas' terminology the difference between concreteness and abstractness is not one of 'res significata' but of 'modus significandi'. The peculiarity of a quality, such as pinkness, is not that it exists, or subsists, or fails to exist, *abstractly*, but that 'pinkness' can only refer to an existent quality which is the pinkness of some substance, for there cannot *be* pinkness which is not something's pinkness. This is what is meant by saying that pinkness can only exist in a substance. This is not like saying that fish can only exist in the water, for the whole of what it is to be pinkness is the being pink of something, an accident is a being 'cuius *esse* est inesse'.

14. Transcendental Words.

Thus, in distinguishing the categories St Thomas is distinguishing ten ways of existing or ten senses of the word 'exists', and correspondingly, ten senses of the words 'true' and 'statement' and hence of 'thing', 'something', 'topic of disagreement', etc. A great deal of his metaphysical writing is concerned with an analysis of the behaviour of words of this kind which he calls 'transcendental words' because they transcend the categories and belong to them all. To say that something is white or four feet tall or upside down is to attribute something to it in one or other of the accidental categories, to say that it is a human being is to state something about it in the category of substance, to say that it is a quality or a relation or a place or a time is also to make a statement about it in the category of substance ('Whiteness is a quality' makes a statement in the category of substance, for it says— partially—*what* whiteness is), but to say of it that it *exists* or is *something* or that there are *statements* about it which are true or false, is not to make a statement in any determinate category. We cannot assign any simple meaning to transcendental words because this would be to restrict their application to a particular category; in fact their meanings change according to the category in which they are applied. In the metaphysics of St Thomas there are no such questions as 'What is existence?' or 'What is truth?' or 'What are statements ultimately about?' We can, of course, explain the meaning of one transcendental word in terms of others; we can say, for instance, that a statement is true when it states what is so; but 'is so' suffers the same shifts in meaning as do 'statement' and 'true'. This means that there can be no rules for the translation of all statements into a single universal language

about a single reality called 'the world', that there can
be no all-comprehensive Principle of Verification, but
only many principles according to the many senses of
'verification'. There is no one kind of reality that we
'ought' to talk about, but many which are real in different senses.

15. *The Theory of Analogy.*

Once we have eliminated the metaphysical pipe-
dream of discovering the Nature of Truth, etc., we can
begin to enquire how it is that we do use the same
transcendental words in different contexts although
their meaning changes from one context to another.
It is in answer to this that St Thomas first develops his
theory of analogy. I have, of course, no intention of
dealing with this theory here but it may be useful to
notice its beginnings in the theory of categories. St
Thomas asks how it is that the same predicate can be
used in all ten categories and he notes that although
there can be no form, or way of being, common to
things in any two categories (since the categories are
precisely different ways of being) the nine accidental
categories have at least, and at most, this in common
that they are all dependent (each in its own way—in
nine different senses of 'dependent') on substance. No
statement in a category of accident can be true (or
false) unless a statement in the category of substance
is true; or, to put it in terms of another transcendental,
a quantity cannot *be* which is not the quantity of some
substance, and a quality cannot *be* which is not the
quality of some substance. This is what he means by
saying that 'exists' (and the rest of the transcendental
words) are used *per prius* of substance and *per posterius* of accidents because of their dependence on substance. It means one thing for a quality to exist and
another thing for a quantity to exist, but each use of
'exist' is related in some way to the use of 'exist' in
which we speak of a substance existing. St Thomas

illustrates this by comparison with the fairly common linguistic phenomenon of the transferred epithet. We speak of a healthy man as having a healthy complexion and living on good healthy food, and in such cases the adjective 'healthy' is used *per prius* of the man and *per posterius* of the complexion and the food. There is nothing common to the complexion and the food in virtue of which we call them both healthy, except that in each case the healthiness depends in some way on the healthiness of the man; healthy food is the sort of food that makes men healthy, a healthy complexion is the sort of complexion that healthy men have. In the same way there is nothing in common between a quality and a relation in virtue of which we say that they both exist except that in each case the existence depends in some way on the existence of a substance. There is of course much more to be said about the theory of analogy and the peculiar behaviour of transcendental words; I have only said this much here in order to make a transition between the discussion of St Thomas' general view of language and things which I have attempted here and the special question of the use of language about God.

ANALOGY AS A RULE OF MEANING

FOR RELIGIOUS LANGUAGE

JAMES F. ROSS

In this paper I am attempting to restate the analogy theory of St. Thomas Aquinas in terms of modern semantic analysis. I am restating it because its general outline is little known and because its vast significance for present-day philosophers concerned with problems of religious language is little understood.

In addition to its deserved philosophical interest, the theory has additional historical value as an example of a very common solution to the problem of informative theological language offered throughout the thirteenth century in Western philosophy. It is essentially a reply to the question: "Can you show that theological statements are meaningful?" A. N. Prior has remarked: "The real intellectual difficulty of the believer or would-be believer is not the problem of proof but the problem of meaning."[1] It is worth noting that the same question was hotly and subtly discussed by most of the medieval writers and the most common conclusion was that a theory of analogy was required. Most recent writers in philosophical theology have made some reference to the theory of analogy current in medieval times, and almost universally these writers have judged it hopeless. As will appear in the course

---

International Philosophical Quarterly, Vol. 1, 1961, pp. 468–502. Reprinted with permission of the author and the Editors of *International Philosophical Quarterly.*

[1] This is the utterance of Logician in the conversation reported in "Can Religion Be Discussed?," *New Essays in Philosophical Theology,* ed. A. Flew and A. MacIntyre (New York: Macmillan, 1955), p. 3.

of this paper, authors like Flew and MacKinnon,[2] Farrer,[3] and Mascall[4] have offered interpretations of the analogy doctrine considerably different from the one I shall propose. I consider their interpretations as seriously deficient and misleading, and I shall endeavor to show implicitly[5] both how little they understood the complexity of the doctrine and how much more penetrating a language theory the analogy rules constitute than most modern writers have supposed.

St. Thomas Aquinas actually formulated four distinct but complementary analogy rules. In this paper I am concerned to analyze only the two most important of these, although the other two rules are stated in the list of definitions given below. This paper is divided into three main parts, the first two sections being summaries of the 'exhibition analyses' by which the two rules in which we are interested are formulated. The third section is a brief sketch of how these rules were employed to solve the problems of informative discourse about God.

Before undertaking the analysis of analogy rules, I must make the following additional points of introduction:

[2] A. Flew and D. M. MacKinnon, "Creation," in *New Essays in Philosophical Theology.*

[3] A. M. Farrer, *Finite and Infinite* (Westminster: Dacre Press, 1943), *passim.*

[4] E. L. Mascall, *Existence and Analogy* (London: Longmans, 1949), *passim.* The chief problem is that Mascall follows Pénido, Cajetan, John of St. Thomas, Garrigou-Lagrange, and many other writers in interpreting the proportionality analogy on the model of a simple mathematical proportionality, with the result that analogy as a theory of *inference* (not employed by St. Thomas) is confused with analogy as a theory of *meaning.* This kind of pseudo-mathematical talk, represented by formulas like "life of cabbage: essence of cabbage = life of elephant: essence of elephant"—even if one does not take the '=' literally —is inimical to the whole objective of St. Thomas, which was to make the meaningfulness of religious language obvious and clear from its very similarity to the way we talk in everyday life.

[5] Lack of space will prevent an explicit critique of each of the above-mentioned interpretations.

1. The two rules of analogy herein discussed are concerned with the comparative meaning of two or more instances of the same term used as predicate in two or more statements of the form a) "X is T" and b) "Y is T."

2. As a result, we must distinguish between the *technical* sense of 'analogy' which we shall use and at least one other ordinary language sense of 'analogy.'

When the word 'analogous' occurs in ordinary language, there is usually a context of comparison: "Spanish is analogous to Portuguese"; "The navigator of a ship and the ruler of a state are analogous"; etc. *Things* are said to be analogous if they have common characteristics or similar relations. And the term 'analogy' is often taken as a synonym of 'similar' or 'similarity.'

We are not speaking of the analogy of things in this paper; we are speaking of the analogy of *terms*. And 'being analogous' will signify a semantical property of a term in several of its instances. Which semantical property? The property of conforming in its employment to one of the analogy rules stated below. Hence, the analogy theory of St. Thomas is concerned with the similarity of *meaning* of instances of the same term —not directly with the similarity of things. Of course, Aquinas argues that similarity of meaning is connected with the similarity of the things signified by the terms in question; but that comes much later and is not part of the meaning-theory itself.

3. St. Thomas' analogy rules are the results of a language analysis and are designed to solve specific language problems. The first of these is this: Aquinas, for theological reasons, was committed to accepting the traditional Christian language about God which is found in the liturgy and in the traditional catechetical instruction given children and converts, as being accurate, informative and true. This was 'ordinary language' and was to be accepted as being applicable to God. But Aquinas has undertaken to solve the follow-

ing problem: How could he show that this language (all of the terms, expressions and employments of which are learned from human experience) can be applied, without such equivocation as would render invalid all argument, to God, an entity which is so different from the objects of experience as to be 'inexperienceable' in any of the ways common to ordinary human experience? Although the analogy theory I am treating as a whole was actually formulated piecemeal as problems arose over the applicability of 'experience' predicates to God, the object of the whole theory is to preserve the literal sense of ordinary beliefs about God.

The second specific language problem St. Thomas was trying to solve is as follows: He accepted the Aristotelian theory of the categories as a classification of predicates such that entities denoted by the predicates in a given category, say 'substance,' were all those things denoted by all the terms in that category used *univocally.* As a result, transcategorial statements cannot have univocal predicates. An example of a transcategorial statement is: "Both trees and numbers exist"—where 'trees' belongs to the category of substance and 'numbers' to quantity. Aquinas would remark that the whole statement given is elliptical for two statements in which the predicate 'exists' occurs twice and is used analogously. Hence, the theory of analogy was required to justify the meaningfulness of transcategorial statements. And, since metaphysical statements were by their very generality transcategorial, the theory of analogy was required as a justification of the metaphysician's claim to be uttering meaningful discourse.

4. The following are the definitions employed in this study:[6]

---

[6] It should be noted that the definitions beginning with Roman numeral I are derived in common from (and are not entirely attributed to either) St. Thomas and C. I. Lewis, *Knowledge and Valuation* (La Salle: Open Court, 1946).

DEFINITIONS

General Conditions: 1. (a) and (b) stand for sentences
2. All definitions are for (a) and (b) in a language 'l.'

Def. I-1: *Verbal Symbol*:
  " 'S' is a verbal symbol":
  if 'S' is a recognizable pattern of marks or of sounds used for the purpose of expression and communication. (What is regarded as the same pattern in difficult instances is partly a matter of physical similarity, and partly a matter of conventional understanding.) Two marks or two sounds having the same recognizable pattern are two instances of the same symbol, not two different symbols.

Def. I-2: *Linguistic Expression*:
  " 'L' is a linguistic expression":
  if 'L' is a verbal symbol (S), and if S is associated with a fixed meaning either by convention or stipulation.

Def. I-3: *Same Expression*:
  " 'L' in sentence (a) and 'L' in sentence (b) are the same expression":
  if 'L' in (a) and 'L' in (b) are instances of the same symbol, and if the two instances are not totally equivocal.

Def. I-4: *Word*:
  " 'W' is a word":
  if 'W' is a linguistic expression.

Def. I-5: *Same Word*:
  " 'W' in sentence (a) and 'W' in sentence (b) are the same word":
  if 'W' in (a) and (b) respectively is a linguistic expression, and if (*according to Def. I-1*) 'W' in (a)

and 'W' in (b) are numerical instances of the same verbal symbol. *Note*: 'W' in (a) and 'W' in (b) can be the same word without being the same expression.

Def. I-6: Term:
    " 'T' is a term":
    if 'T' is a word capable of naming or applying to a thing or things. *Note*: All terms are words, but not all words are terms.

Def. I-7: Same Term:
    " 'T' in (a) and 'T' in (b) are the same term":
    if in each case 'T' is a term and if 'T' in (a) and in (b) is the same word. *Note*: Sometimes 'T' in (a) and 'T' in (b) will be the same word *and* the same expression (*Def. I-3*), and sometimes the same word but *not* the same expression. When 'T' in (a) and 'T' in (b) are the same term, they are "instances of term T." This is a departure from the practice of C. I. Lewis in *Knowledge and Valuation*, but it conforms to the practice of the Scholastics whom I am explaining, and using Lewis' definitions would require two parallel sets of definitions which would constantly require correlation.

Def. I-8: Same Term and Same Expression:
    " 'T' in (a) and 'T' in (b) are the same term and the same expression":
    if (1) 'T' in (a) and 'T' in (b) are the same word; and (2) if 'T' in (a) and 'T' in (b) are the same expression.

Def. I-9: Same Meaning of Same Term:
    " 'T' in (a) and 'T' in (b) have the same meaning":
    if (1) 'T' in (a) and 'T' in (b) are instances of the term 'T,' i.e. are the same term; and (2) 'T' in (a) and in (b) is used univocally (*Def. I-12*).

Def. I-10: Signification:
    "Term 'T' signifies F" if:
    F is one of the properties which it is both necessary

and sufficient for a thing to have in order to be denoted by 'T.'

Def. I - 11: Intention:
The intention of term 'T' is the conjunction of all other terms each of which must be applicable to anything to which the term 'T' is correctly applicable.

Def. I - 12: Univocity:
a) "Term 'T' is used univocally in (a) and (b)":
if 'T' in (a) signifies the same property as 'T' in (b).
b) "Term 'T' is used univocally in (a) and (b)": if there is a one to one correspondence of the same terms in the intention of 'T' in (a) and of 'T' in (b).

Def. I - 13: Equivocity:
"Term 'T' is used equivocally in (a) and (b)":
if 'T' in (a) and 'T' in (b) are not univocal.

Def. I - 14: Total Equivocation:
"Term 'T' is totally equivocal in (a) and (b)":
if there is no property which is included both in the signification of 'T' in (a) and in the signification of 'T' in (b).

Def. I - 15: Partial Equivocation:
"Term 'T' is partially equivocal in (a) and (b)":

The definitions beginning with Roman numerals II, III, and IV are derived from St. Thomas. Definitions *II*-1 and *IV*-7 are the two additional analogy rules which will not be explained in this paper.

It should also be remembered that the names given these four analogy rules were not coined by Aquinas but were applied by Thomas De Vio (Cardinal Cajetan) in his work *On the Analogy of Names,* trans. by Bushenski and Koren (Pittsburgh: Duquesne Univ. Press, 1953). It should be added that the interpretation of the analogy theory presented in this article coincides in the main with that put forward by Cajetan, not merely by election, but by selection, in that the writer thinks it appropriate both on exegetical grounds with regard to St. Thomas and on systematic grounds as part of the systematic equipment needed for a solution of the contemporary question of the meaningfulness of religious utterances.

if 'T' in (a) and 'T' in (b) are used equivocally, but not totally equivocally.

Def. II - 1: Analogy of Inequality:
"Term 'T' is analogous by inequality in (a) and (b)":
 if 1. 'T' in (a) and 'T' in (b) are instances of the same term.
  2. 'T' in (a) and 'T' in (b) are univocal by *Def. I - 12.*
  3. The property F, signified by 'T' in (a) and (b) is either:
   1) not physically congruent, in the one case being a nonseparable part of the subject, and in the other, all of the subject; or
   2) different in degree according to some standard; or
   3) possessed by the subject in (a) in a different mode (necessity, contingency, etc.) from the subject in (b).

Def. III - 1: Analogy of Attribution:
"Term 'T' is analogous by attribution in (a) and (b)":
 if 1. 'T' occurs as predicate in two or more indicative sentences: (a) "F is T" and (b) "G is T."
  2. 'T' in (a) signifies a property T of F.
  3. 'T' in (b) signifies a relation of G to F where G is either a cause of F's having property T or is in some respect an effect or affected causally by F's having property T.

Def. IV - 1: Sameness of Res Significata:
"The *res significata* of 'T' is the same in (a) and (b)":
 if 1. there are given at least two sentences (a) and (b) in which there is respectively a predicate term 'T.'
  2. 'T' in (a) and 'T' in (b) are instances of the same term.

3. 'T' signifies property T of X in (a) and T of Y in (b).

4. all the terms of the intention of 'T' in (a) which specify the class of things to which property T belongs, occur in the intention of 'T' in (b).

Def. IV - 2: Difference of Modus Significandi:
"The *modus significandi* of 'T' is different in (a) and (b)";
  if 1, 2, 3, and 4 of *Def. IV - 1* hold.

5. for any thing Z, having the property T implies that Z can perform either actions (A) 1, 2, 3, - n; or (B) 2, 3, 4, - n and not 1; or (C) 3, 4, - n and not 1 and 2; or....; or n....

6. the intention of 'T' in sentence (a) and in (b) is determined by the intention of the subject term 'X' or 'Y' in such a way that only one of the alternative groups of actions is signified.

7. the terms of the intention of 'T' in (a) which specify which of the alternates (A), (B) or (C) is performed, are not the same as the terms in the intention of 'T' in (b) which, consequently, specify a different alternative.

Def. IV - 3: Similar:
"A is similar to B":
  if 1. A and B are terms, things, properties, relations, or anything of any kind or kinds.

2. A and B are in some respect or respects identical.

3. A and B and the identical respect or respects are not numerically identical.

Def. IV - 4: Proportional Similarity:
"ATx and BTy are proportionally similar":
  if 1. A and B are things, x and y are properties, actions, etc.

2. there is a term 'T' which signifies the two instances of relation T.

3. ATx and BTy are proportions: i.e., A is related to x by T and B is related to y by T.

4. 'T' when used in the statement "ATx is proportionally similar to BTy" is not univocal.

5. T in ATx and in BTy is not numerically identical.

6. T in ATx and T in BTy are similar.

Def. IV - 5: Analogy of Proper Proportionality:
"Term 'T' is used analogously by proper proportionality in (a) and (b)":

if 1. 'T' occurs as predicate in two or more sentences of the form (a) "A is (or has) T," and (b) "B is (or has) T," where 'B' and 'A' denote individual things A and B.

2. 'T' signifies a relation T which holds between x (where x is a property, action, event, relation, etc.) and A; and between y (property, action, relation, etc.) and B.

3. ATx and BTy are proportionally similar.

Def. IV - 6: Similarity of Relations:
"Relation R is similar to relation R¹":

if 1. both are relations;

2. they have common formal properties with respect to either a formal or merely linguistic set of axioms, the latter not being explicitly formulated in ordinary language.

Def. IV - 7: Analogy of Improper Proportionality:
"Term 'T' is analogous by improper proportionality in (a) and (b)":

if A) alternative 1:

1. 'T' is used as a predicate in a sentence (a) of the form "F is T."

2. the denotation of 'T' is a class of objects Z having as members individuals w, y, z, according to the ordinary rule for its employment.

3. F is not a member of Z.

4. between F and the members of Z there is a pro-

portional similarity with respect to relations R and R¹ and the characteristic behavior or other properties of F and the members of Z.

5. 'T' is used as a predicate of F to call attention to the similar relations of F and the elements of Z.

6. 'T' is equivocal with respect to its occurrence in (a) and in sentences where it denotes members of Z.

B) alternative 2:

1. 'T' is used as predicate in two indicative sentences of the form (a) "x is T" and (b) "y is T," where 'x' and 'y' denote x and y, individual things.

2. term 'T' is used as predicate of 'x' with respect to a language rule R which determines the intention of 'T' and x has the property signified by 'T.'

3. 'T' cannot be used as predicate of 'y' because y does not have the property signified by 'T.'

4. in terms of R, sentence (b) is incorrect.

5. 'T' is equivocal with respect to (a) and (b).

6. there is a similarity between a relation of x to its characteristics and the relation of y to its characteristics.

7. 'T' is used of y to call attention to the similarity.

5. In the sections of this paper where I summarize two of the exhibition analyses by which Aquinas developed the language rules of Analogy of Attribution, *Def. III-1*, and Proper Proportionality, *Def. VI-5*, there is a basic presumption that the cases of ordinary language which are taken for examination are in fact cases of *informative* language. And the rules which result are supposed to be recipes by which St. Thomas can construct other parallel uses of language which will also be informative. These statements generated according to these rules will be applicable in arguments about God and in metaphysical contexts without further justification as to their meaningfulness, provided that St. Thomas' analysis of ordinary language has in fact produced the rules according to

which the ordinary language employment of certain
terms is rendered meaningful.

6. There is no direct argument for any philosophical point in what follows. But I suggest that the analogy theory herein discussed does offer evidence for
the following two claims:

a) If one wishes to talk of God in informative language (that is, the language of literal assertion) and
to employ the language of Christian tradition (the
Creeds, etc.) one must have an analogy theory something like that herein explained.

b) If one wishes to maintain that there are any exclusive categories (in Aristotle's sense) of things in the
world and at the same time supposes that there can
be any universally true metaphysical statements, he
must have a meaning-theory fundamentally similar to
the proportionality theory of St. Thomas.

ANALOGY OF ATTRIBUTION

The first of the analogy rules is called the rule of
'attribution.' We are concerned here with sets of two
statements of the form a) "F is T" and b) "G is T."
We shall take two examples of such pairs of statements:

(1) a) Fido is healthy.
    b) Fido's bark is *healthy.*
(2) a) John is brilliant.
    b) John's work is brilliant.

The first of these pairs is roughly the example used
by St. Thomas. The other is contributed to push his
analysis a little further than he did in his own desul-
tory discussions of attribution. It might be useful to
keep in mind that I am following St. Thomas' line of
thought up to *Def. III*-1 and its corollaries.

In his analysis of attribution, St. Thomas wishes to
discuss the cases where a term occurs as the predicate
of two statements with different subjects, only *one* of
which subjects, by the usual rules governing the em-

ployment of predicate terms to signify properties of the subject, could have the property signified by the predicate term.

It is easy to see what Aquinas means from his example.[7] Suppose we have two statements: (a) "The dog is healthy" and (b) "His bark is healthy." It is clear from conventional linguistic practice that both employments of the term are informative and proper in ordinary discourse. St. Thomas believed the property of "being healthy" to be compatible only with animals and plants as such, and he concludes rightly that at least part of what is signified by the term 'healthy' in both these cases is numerically the same: the one state of affairs of the whole dog.[8] In other words, the term 'healthy' in sentence (b) does not signify some property numerically *different* from what 'healthy' signifies in sentence (a); it does not signify a numerically *different instance* of health. Presuming that the 'bark' in (b) belongs to the dog in (a), then the health in (b) is one and the same as the health in (a).

He says that the predicates of some sentences signify properties which *inhere* in what is denoted by the grammatical subject, e.g., sentence (a); and the predicates in *other* sentences, like (b), do not signify properties all of which *inhere* in the subject of that sentence, but rather partially specify that the subject of that sentence is related to the subject of that other sentence in which the same predicate does signify a property *inherent* in the subject. (I am using 'subject' to stand for 'what is *denoted* by the grammatical subject.') The predicate term in (b) *partially* specifies

---

[7] *De Veritate*, q. 2, a. 11, c. This example occurs frequently in St. Thomas' passages on analogy. Some representative passages are: *De Veritate*, q. 1, a. 4, c. ad finem; *In IV Metaph.*, lect. 1, n. 537; *Sum. Theol.*, I, q. 16, a. 6; *C. Gent.*, I, 34; *I Sent.*, d. 19, q. 5, a. 2, ad 11.

[8] Cf. *In IV Metaph.*, lect. 1, n. 539; *In XI Metaph.*, lect. 3, n. 2196; I, q. 16, a. 6, c.

the relation of the secondary subject of (b) to the primary subject because the predicate term in such a
sentence usually only tells us which of the properties
of the primary subject we should look to if we wish
to figure out the relation of the secondary subject to
the primary subject.[9] The other conditions which I
shall cite for analogy of attribution will further specify
the *kinds* of relations that may obtain between primary and secondary subjects. In any given use of ordinary language, reflection is expected to disclose the
particular kind of relation which obtains. But when
constructing philosophical instances of analogy of attribution, the philosopher will have to show the two
subjects to be related in one or the other of the ways
known from the forthcoming ordinary language exhibition to justify such uses of terms.

Before discussing the kinds of relations which are
found to obtain in ordinary language instances, and
before investigating the possibility and usefulness of
philosophical constructions, it may be helpful to consider the following question. Given the sentences (a)
and (b), above, and given that part of what is signified by 'healthy' in (b) is numerically the same as that
property signified by 'healthy' in (a), and given further that there is only one health which is inherent in
the dog, does sentence (b) say anything about the
dog's *bark* or not? That is, sentences in general pur-
port to say something about what the subject denotes
(they do *not* say what the subject denotes, but
only something about what the subject denotes). If
'healthy' signifies a property of the dog, one might
conclude that then the sentence (b) says nothing
about the *bark.* However, Aquinas notes that if (b) is
to function as sentences usually do, it will in fact say
something about the dog's bark. St. Thomas' move was
to say: "The sentence (b) says the dog's bark is re-

[9] Cf. *De Veritate*, q. 21, a. 4, ad 2; *In XI Metaph.*, lect. 3, n.
2196; John of St. Thomas, *Logica*, II, 13, 3 (Reiser edition,
Turin, 1930, p. 484).

lated to the dog's health in a certain one of the specified kinds of ways in which a predicate of the 'dog'
can be used of its 'bark' or of 'medicine.'" This move
is later found to be equivalent to saying: "Sentence
(b) is a short-hand for the statement: 'The dog's bark
is a sign that the dog is healthy.'" What is *said* is
that the bark performs a signifying service with respect to the presence of an inhering property 'health'
in the dog. In summary, this analysis, so far, proposes
that the statement (b) tells us *that* and *how* the subject either actually or potentially functions (i.e., is related) with respect to a certain property belonging
to another subject. Most of the traditional Thomists,
Cajetan and John of St. Thomas and many neo-
Thomists, have expressly interpreted the 'designation'
of the analogous term with respect to the secondary
subject (secondary analogate) to be merely 'extrinsic,' merely designating accidental (fortuitous, even
though constant) relations.[10] However, these writers
cautiously add that this does not *exclude* the "presence of the analogous property in the secondary
analogates, although imperfectly." What they could
mean by this is obscure and the fact that they place
their emphasis on the extrinsic relations which they

[10] In this connection one should consider: Hampus Lyttkens,
The Analogy between God and the World (Uppsala Universitets
Arsskrift, 1953); G. M. Manser, *Das Wesen des Thomismus*, 3
aufl. (Freiburg i. Schw.: Paulusverlag, 1949) p. 447; M. T.-L.
Pénido, *Le rôle de l'analogie en théologie dogmatique* (Paris:
Vrin, 1931), p. 34; K. Feckes, *Die Analogie in unserem Gotte-
serkennen* (Münster: Albertus-Magnus-Akademie zu Köln, Band
II, Heft 3, 1928), p. 158. Also: J. Ramirez, "De Analogia secun-
dum doctrinam aristotelico-thomisticam," *La Ciencia Tomista*,
XXIV (1921), 243; A. Goergen, *Kardinal Cajetans Lehre von
der Analogie* (München, 1938), pp. 68, 80; J. Maritain, *Degrees
of Knowledge* (2d. ed.; New York: Scribner, 1959), p. 418;
R. Garrigou-Lagrange, *God: His Existence and Nature* (St.
Louis: Herder, 1936), II, 207; G. B. Phelan, *Saint Thomas and
Analogy* (Milwaukee: Marquette Univ. Press, 1948), p. 37;
J. Le Rohellec, "De fundamento metaphysico analogiae," *Divus
Thomas* XXIX (1926), 81–87.

say are 'designated' is the point I wish to emphasize. As far as I can see, what they are saying is exactly the analysis given above: that the sentence (b) tells us *that* and *how* the secondary subject either actually or potentially functions with respect to a certain property (signified by the predicate term) belonging to the primary subject in (a). For the authors mentioned, then, the initial conditions for an analogy of attribution are of two kinds: (1) The term is used at least once (in the two sentences under consideration) to signify a property inherent in a subject. (2) The term is used on other occasions of subjects which do not actually possess the property but are related in specified ways to the things which do have the property.

Many interpreters have claimed that the sentence containing the secondary use of an analogous term of this kind does not say anything about the nature or properties of its subject in itself, but only states facts about the relation of the subject to the primary subject with respect to the property signified by the analogous term. Contrary to this commonly accepted interpretation, I shall attempt to show that these secondary sentences *do* say something about the nature of the subject, even though it be very little and indirectly. A person who says "That's a healthy bark your dog's got" is saying something about the dog, to be sure, but he is also saying something about the bark.[11] And when I tell you "This food is healthful," I am not *only* telling you something about the *relation* of the food to your health; I am telling you something about the food, which is additional to its relation as cause of health. It is true that you would not know very much about the food if you did not know what properties food would have to have in order to be healthful. But if you did, it would be legitimate for you to conclude

[11] Cf: I, q. 13, a. 2, ad 2; ad 3; I, q. 13, a. 6, c.; *De Potentia*, q. 7, a. 5.

that this food has those properties (or at least that I believed it had these properties); and thus I would have told you something about the food.

Another example: When we say that a student's work is brilliant, we are not only saying something about the fact that this work is a sign of the brilliance of the student who wrote it, we are saying something about the work itself. Even though the term 'brilliant' appears to be applied primarily to students who can and habitually do produce work of a given quality, saying "The work is brilliant" tells a person who has some information about the standards for being called 'brilliant' and the kind of work brilliant people produce, something about the work produced.

However, this brings up a further problem. For the sake of an example, I assumed that the *primary* sense of 'brilliant' was the instance of the term signifying the intellectual prowess and creativity of the student and that the secondary sense has its application to the work produced. Actually, in re-examining certain terms functioning analogously it is sometimes difficult to say which is the primary instance of the term, although it is clear that the two instances are different but related.

Aquinas, preparing for philosophical employment of analogy, offers a rule for deciding which instance is primary. He distinguishes between the order of things and the order of knowledge. In effect, he says that the use of the term which is supposed by the other uses of the same term is the primary one, the one which *must be known first* in order to use the term of the other cases.[12] Thus, it seems that to be correct in calling a student 'brilliant' we must have evidence of the high quality of his work, and since the potentiality of producing high quality work is what is meant by 'brilliant' when applied to the student, just the oppo-

[12] See *C. Gent.*, I, 34. Many writers have accepted this rule as a means of distinguishing the analogates; see Goergen, *op. cit.*, p. 16; Manser, *op. cit.*, p. 450.

site of my previous assumption is the case: the primary sense of the term on Aquinas' rule is to signify 'high quality work' although the more frequent use of the term may be to signify a person's capacity for producing such work.

Aquinas points out that the order of things may be different from the order of knowledge. There can be times when the order of things is neither the same as the order of knowledge nor as the order of applying the terms which follows it. Our example of 'brilliant' is a case in point. As a matter of fact, the student must have certain powers before he can produce high quality work; this is a causal and logical priority. But we do not *know* his powers until he has produced some high quality work; this is a psychological priority. Hence, we *describe* his powers in terms of the quality of his work, although he works in terms of his powers.

It is this fact which Aquinas cites as part of one of the arguments to show that we can 'name' God from His effects, because even though we *know* God from His effects, the properties of the effects are derived from the powers of God. St. Thomas says:

> Sometimes, indeed, that which is prior in nature is secondary regarding knowledge, and then among the analogues there is not the same order both regarding the things and the order of the term: thus the power of healing which is in medicines is naturally prior to the health which is in the animal, as cause to effect; *but because we know that power through its effect, we also name it from its effect.* And thus it happens that 'healthful' is prior in order of nature, but the animal is called 'healthy' with priority in the order of naming.[13]

[13] *C. Gent.*, I, 34. This argument is useful only if enough similarity has already been demonstrated between God and other things to justify a statement that a causal relation holds. It is this distinction which Hampus Lyttkens, *op. cit.*, p. 283, seizes upon to justify some statements about God. This position is similar to that of Sylvester of Ferrara. Even if there is such

So far, the exposition of analogy of attribution has shown Aquinas to be exhibiting the following points about the function of certain words in ordinary language which are called 'analogous by attribution':

1. The 'analogy of attribution' is concerned with the comparative functions of two instances of the same term occurring as predicate in two sentences, one primary, the other secondary.

2. A term analogous in this way is used in at least one instance in a sentence as predicate where all the properties it signifies do not belong to the subject, but where it signifies a relation of that subject to another subject possessing the property normally signified by the term and related *via* that property.

3. These predicate terms always have a primary use where in some indicative sentence they signify a property inherent in the subject and have this property as their *definitive* property.

4. Irrespective of the fact that these secondary sentences do not signify a specific property of the entity denoted by the subject, they do give information about the properties of the subject.

5. The property signified by an analogous term in its primary and secondary occurrences is numerically one. That is, there is only one property of 'health' which belongs to the dog, and the secondary sentence does *not* say it belongs to the bark.

The several other points so far made regarding (1) the kind of analysis Aquinas was doing, (2) the uses to which he would put the analysis, (3) the fact that the Thomists do not make much use of analogy of attribution in natural theology, and (4) the fact that there is a rule for deciding which of the terms, in doubtful cases, will be considered the primary one, are all points necessary in the exposition; however, they are not part of the special information necessary for the analysis which will be developed.

---

an analogy, it cannot be the basic one, for it supposes true statements about God.

Let us consider the other properties of analogy of attribution.

6. "The primary analogate is put into the definition of the others with respect to the analogous name."[14] St. Thomas says:

> It is necessary in all cases where terms are used analogously of several things, that they are all used with respect to one; and thus, that one use must be contained in the definition of all. And since the notion which the term signifies is its definition, as is said in the *Fourth Book of the Metaphysics*, it is necessary that that term be used primarily of that which is supposed in the definition of the others, and secondarily of the others, in the order by which they approach more or less to the primary term: thus 'healthy' which is used of 'animal' is part of the definition of 'healthy' which is used of 'medicine', which is called healthy in as much as it causes health in the animal; and of the definition of 'healthy' which is used of 'urine', which is called 'healthy' in as much as it is a sign of the health of the animal.[15]

Suppose we take 'healthy' as used in the sentence (a) "My dog is healthy" to be defined as follows: "X is healthy" equals by definition: "X has a certain organic state characterized by properties a, b, c, ...n." We are not concerned that the assertion 'X is healthy' is defeasible even though all the properties are present. By hypothesis, let us suppose it can be and is defined by a finite list of properties and degrees of properties. If we are going to define the term 'healthy' in the following sentences, we shall have to appeal to the definitions already given of 'healthy' in the sentence (a) above.

(b) "My dog's bark is healthy."

(c) "His pills and dog-food are healthy."

[14] Cajetan, *De. Nom. Anal.*, Ch. 2, par. 14.
[15] I, q. 13, a. 6, c.

Sentence (b) can only mean something like this: "My dog's bark has those qualities which are signs to me that the dog is 'healthy' that is, has the organic state characterized by a, b, c, ...n." Hence, I take it that Aquinas' point is clear: In all cases where a term is used as a predicate to attribute a relation to a subject with respect to a property possessed by a different subject, and where the term used normally signifies that property of the other subject, the definition of the term in its primary sense is part of the definition of the term in its secondary sense.[16]

Aquinas does not try to rule out the possibility that two different people might disagree about which is the primary sense of the analogous term, nor does he deny that they might even disagree about when to use the term because of that. Suppose that someone has been reared only hearing the word 'healthy' applied when a dog's or man's voice was loud and clear. The term 'healthy' might thus be associated with the meaning of 'loud and clear voice.' When I say to him that the dog or man is healthy, he interprets this to mean 'capable of a loud and clear vocal utterance.' Thus his conception of the significance of both sentences (a) and (b) is different from mine. Another person might learn that the term 'healthy' usually follows another set of rules which also reverse the relative priority of the 'senses' of the analogous term. But neither event, his learning to apply the word by a different convention,

16 This point is made repeatedly and emphatically by St. Thomas. For example: I, q. 13, a. 10 corpus; I, q. 13, a. 6; III, q. 60, a. 1: "Omnia quae habent ordinem ad unum aliquid, licet diversimode, ab illo denominari possunt...sic igitur sacramentum potest aliquid dici vel quia in se habet aliquam sanctitatem occultam, et secundum hoc sacramentum idem est quod sacrum secretum, vel quia habet aliquem ordinem ad hanc sanctitatem, vel causae, vel signi, vel secundum quamcumque aliam habitudinem." Also I, q. 15, a. 6: "Quando aliquid praedicatur univoce de multis, illud in quolibet eorum secundum propriam rationem invenitur...quando aliquid dicitur analogice de multis, illud invenitur secundum propriam rationem in uno eorum tantum a quo alia denominantur."

nor his reversing the convention, would be an exception to the rule presupposed by Aquinas, which could be formulated thus:

> In any case where a term is neither univocal nor totally equivocal but occurs in several instances as predicate of indicative sentences, the meaning it has in at least one instance (supposing that we have at hand at least one each of every kind of instance in which the word can be used according to the conventional rules for its employment) must be entirely included in the meaning it has in every other instance.

In fact, on the definitions given of univocity and total equivocity, the rule is a tautology. Cajetan,[17] Pénido,[18] Aquinas,[19] and Aristotle[20] (at least as Cajetan interprets him) all seem to imply that the secondary analogate can only be related to the primary analogate as efficient, final, material, or exemplary cause (which they extend to equal: sign and symptom). When we say that a man is charitable, Cajetan would say we are showing that he is dispositionally (at least) the efficient cause of charitable acts; when we say a given kind of action is charitable, we are saying that its performance is usually a sign of a charitable act. It functions as a sign because it is usually an effect of charity. Thus Aquinas' rule for analogy of attribution contains a provision that the secondary uses of the term will signify a causal relation of their subject to the normal subject of the property. By this he means that the subject of the secondary sentence must denote something which is either cause or effect (in the wide, Aristotelian sense of the four causes) of the property signified by the primary

[17] *De Nom. Anal.*, Ch. 2, par. 9.
[18] Pénido, *op. cit.*, p. 33.
[19] *De Principiis Naturae*, Ch. 6.
[20] *In IV Metaph.*, 2, 1003 a 34 ff.

occurrence of the term, as belonging to the primary subject.

7. Hence, this is the seventh characteristic: The secondary analogate in its definition, in addition to the definitions of the term in its primary instance, will also contain a phrase specifying a causal relation to the signification of the primary term.

8. The eighth characteristic of this kind of analogy is that the "term does not have one definite meaning common to all its partial modes."[21] There is nothing about the term itself as it occurs in various sentences which tells us that it is not being used 'denominatively,' to signify its definitive property as inherent in the subject; nor is there anything about the form of sentences which tells us that the term is not being used to signify its definitive property of the subject. When we formulate (1) 'The dog is healthy' and (2) 'The bark is healthy,' they are both of the same form: X is F and Y is F. That the term 'F' has not the same meaning in both sentences is only known from the 'logical rules of ordinary language.'[22] Sometimes we are not sure whether a term indicates only a property of its subject or a relation to a property of another subject, as was shown by the example of 'brilliant' when applied to the student and his work. However, Cajetan's point is clear enough. The term cannot possibly have exactly the same meaning in all its instances if we include as part of its *meaning* in some instances the *relationship* of the definitive property to the subject.

Some Scotists have said that what is analogous is not the property term but the copula. "The dog *is* healthy" means: The dog has the property 'healthy'; "The bark *is* healthy" means: The bark is related to the health of the dog. But Aquinas' supposition seems to be recom-

---

[21] Cajetan, *De Nom. Anal.*, Ch. 2, par. 15. This is equivalent to the claim that the term is partially equivocal on our definitions.

[22] This is not a phrase mentioned as one used by St. Thomas.

mended by its simplicity and by the fact that relevant questions and answers about the dog's bark being healthy would indicate that in ordinary discourse the speaker realizes he doesn't mean by 'healthy' exactly the same thing in both cases.

The analysis which St. Thomas suggests for the statement "Term 'T' is analogous by attribution in (a) and (b)" is as follows:

Def. III - 1: Analogy of Attribution:
"Term 'T' is analogous by attribution in (a) and (b)" if:

1. 'T' occurs as predicate in two or more indicative sentences: (a) "F is T" and (b) "G is T."

2. 'T' in (a) signifies a property T of F.

3. 'T' in (b) signifies a relation of G to F where G is either a cause of F's having property T or is in some respect an effect or affected causally by F's having property T.

The following propositions are implied by the definition and are corollaries:

1. There is only one (numerically) instance of the property T of 'T' in (a) and it belongs to subject F.

2. The term 'T' in sentence (b) cannot be defined unless the entire definition of the term 'T' in sentence (a) is made part of its definition; and still the definition will not be complete, because part of the intention must be a specification of the causal relation of G to F.

3. The term 'T' does not have the same intention in both of its instances in (a) and (b): i.e., the term 'T' is not formally univocal, *Def. I*-12; nor is it totally equivocal.

Terms are said to be analogous by attribution not because they attribute a property to subjects which logically cannot have that property, but because the sentences in which they are used in their secondary meanings ascribe a causal relation of their subjects to the thing having that property, and at the same time imply that the subject of the secondary sentence has whatever properties, relations, and dispositions are necessary in order to be related in that way to the subject of the primary analogate (the term used in its primary sense).

ANALOGY OF PROPER PROPORTIONALITY

In looking at the language analysis by which this rule for Analogy of Proper Proportionality is generated, we are concerned with pairs of statements of the following forms:

1. a) "A is (or has) T."
   b) "B is (or has) T."
2. a) "ATx"
   b) "BTy"

And the supposition is that statements of the first form which fit the rule we are developing (*Def. IV*-5) are reducible in principle to statements of the second form. This supposition is not an integral part of the theory; and it seems to have independent justification. Examples of each form are:

1. a) Fido has knowledge of his dog house.
   b) Plato has knowledge of philosophy.
   or
   a) Fido is the cause of his barking.
   b) Plato is the cause of his actions.
2. a) Fido knows his dog house.
   b) Plato knows philosophy.
   or
   a) Fido caused the barking.
   b) Plato caused the murderous shot.

1. Let us take it as given, by inspection of the examples, that the *predicates* 'knows' and 'causes' *are not univocal in* (*a*) *and* (*b*) *of each set*. This is *the first characteristic* of the language rule. Later paragraphs will justify this presumption, if it should be in doubt here.

2. *The second characteristic is that there are at least two instances of the property signified by 'T.'*

On this condition rests the first and most important difference between Analogy of Proportionality and Attribution. In the latter case, there is numerically only one instance of the definitive property signified by both instances of the analogous term, whereas in this case there must be one instance of the property for each instance of the term as predicate of a sentence with a different subject.

A problem raised by this requirement can be phrased thus: if the term is equivocal, then the intention (or connotation) of the term must differ in its various instances; i.e., a sentence affirming and denying a term 'T' of the same subject would be contradictory if the intention of the term was identical in each instance; and the term would not be equivocal by *Def. I*-13. If the intention of the term differs, then a criterion must be given of how far the intention of the term can vary in two instances of the term before a different property is signified. For if different properties are signified by a term in two of its instances, then the second condition of the analogy of proper proportionality is either unsatisfied or ambiguous. The second condition states, briefly, that the two things denoted by the term 'T' must have the property signified by 'T' and that the first condition must still be preserved: that the term is equivocal. On the assumption that 'T' is equivocal, one might say, "Yes, the things denoted do have the property signified in each case, but the properties are not the same." And if "Term 'T' in its instances signifies the same property" equals by definition "Term 'T' in its instances has the same intention," then either the term is univocal or the second condition is unsatisfiable. Hence, we must demand some analysis from St. Thomas which will allow a term to be univocal in signification (*Def. I*-12-a) while being equivocal in not conforming to the rule for univocity in intention (*Def. I*-12-b).

St. Thomas claims to offer such an analysis; for he held the theory that the intention (*intentio*) of a term specifies not only the kind of property signified but the *way* the property is signified.[23] And hence, "signification" has two senses: the *res significata* and the *modus significandi*. It was part of his theory that the linguistic rules which govern the use of a term, and thereby determine its intention, make into elements of the intention of a term those terms which specify the *modus significandi* (which I shall explain shortly). To our objection that when we define a term we cite the terms characteristic of its intention and we never find a term indicating the mode of signification, Aquinas would reply that most of our predicates signify in the *same* mode of signification, and that for ordinary purposes it is not necessary to make such a distinction. Furthermore, it is only a logical technique for one to distinguish between what is signified and how it is signified, because in every actual instance of discourse about the world of experience the mode of signification corresponds to the *mode of existence* which the property has,[24] and, consequently, is implicit in the rule which governs the employment of a term. In the *Commentary on the First Book of Sentences*, Aquinas says:

> Although every perfection which belongs to creatures is taken by exemplary causality from God, as from a principle having unified in itself all perfections, no creature can receive that perfection according to the same mode by which it is in God. So, the creature fails to be a perfect representation

[23] We are assuming that the sentences (a) and (b) are true, that the subjects are not numerically identical, and that the sentences say the subjects have a certain property. I am still using 'subject' in the private sense stipulated in Part I, where it refers to *what is denoted by the grammatical subject*.

[24] St. Thomas seems to assume this: *C. Gent.*, II, Ch. 98; I, q. 19, a. 4; q. 75, a. 5. I am using 'element' to signify terms which make up the intention of another term.

of the exemplar because of the different mode in which the perfections are received. And because of that (difference in the mode of receiving) there is a scale, as it were, among creatures according to which some creatures receive from God more and higher perfections and participate in His perfections more fully. And because of this there are two aspects of the terms to consider: the thing [*rem* which equals 'what *kind* of thing'] signified and the mode of being signified. Therefore we must consider that when we, who know God only from creatures, employ a term, we always fall short of a representation of God with respect to the 'mode of being signified': because the term signifies the divine perfections through the mode by which they are participated in by creatures.

If, however, we consider *what* is signified by the term, what the term is used to signify, we find that some terms are used primarily to signify the perfections exemplified in God alone, not being concerned with any mode in their signification; and that some terms are said to signify a perfection received according to a given mode of participation; for example, all knowing is an imitation of divine knowing, and all knowledge of divine knowledge. Therefore, the term 'sense' is used to signify knowing through that mode by which knowledge is materially received through the power of the conjoined organ. But the term 'knowledge' does not signify a particular mode of participating in its principal signification. Hence, it must be said that all those terms which are used to signify a perfection absolutely are properly used of God, and primarily are used of Him with respect to what is signified, even though not with respect to the mode of signification, such as 'wisdom,' 'goodness,' 'essence,' and others of this type.[25]

---

[25] *I Sent.*, d. 22, q. 1, a. 2 corpus.

I have used this passage to illustrate two things: (1) that Aquinas understands a difference between what is signified (the kind of property signified) and what kinds of conditions are supposed as surrounding what is signified, even though both are signified simultaneously by any term given its use in a determinate context; and (2) that Aquinas has two different uses of the phrase '*modus significandi*' which function in entirely different ways. First, there is the sense in which 'knowledge' as used of a man and of a dog is understood to be different, not in what is meant by 'knowledge,' but in what *kind* of knowledge is possible. Since 'knowing' is a property which admits of degrees according to the ability of the person, and of kinds according to the nature of the thing which knows, in the two sentences (a) "Fido knows his dog house" and (b) "Plato knows philosophy," the term 'knows' is different not as to *what* is signified but as to which *kind* of knowledge is signified. To avoid possible confusion, I point out that St. Thomas did not believe that sentence (a) is an anthropomorphic or metaphorical description of the dog's actions. He merely claimed that words like 'knowing,' 'wise,' 'good' are vague with respect to classes of activity included in the signification of the term. He says the intention of 'knows' is proportionally the same in sentence (a) and (b), but the mode in which the property is possessed makes entirely different the kinds of action which can be performed.

This allows the Thomist to construct a hierarchy of 'powers' or 'perfections' on the Neoplatonic assumption that (1) being a man is better than being an animal and an animal better than a plant, etc.; and (2) any other beings which know or will in a simpler (less complex), freer way and act more accurately to satisfy their desires are higher on the scale of perfection in beings. Those properties which belong to several levels

of the hierarchy[26] and which are named by a single
term are said to be named by an analogous term. Thus
in Thomist terms the foundation of this kind of analogy is the unequal and different-in-kind participation
of different natures in the same property according to
differing modes of being determined by their natures.[27]

Divine knowing, human knowing, and animal knowing are all 'knowing,' but one is not the other; yet the
term 'knowing' (apart from any particular sentence)
is neutral with respect to the three modes of knowing.
An obvious objection is this: if the term 'knowing' is
neutral with respect to the three various modes, then
why is the term not univocal? St. Thomas' answer is
that terms are univocal or equivocal by comparison of
their use in sentences, and 'knowing' as used in a sentence with 'dog' for a subject and in another sentence
with 'man' for a subject is not univocal, even though he
would admit we may form a meta-language term
'knowing' which is neutral with respect to all object-
language senses of 'know'; but then the meta-language
sense of knowing will not be univocal with *any* object-
language sense.

In considering this example, we must remember
that St. Thomas' conception of knowing is considerably different from contemporary notions. He assumes
(1) that the man is more than quantitatively different
from the dog; he is *essentially* different; (2) the *possessio formae alterius ut alterius*, which constitutes
knowing, is fundamentally known as a human activity
involving abstraction and it is the mode of 'abstrac-

[26] The term 'hierarchy' itself is analogous for St. Thomas in
the statements about the hierarchy of things under God. I, q.
108, a. 1, c. He offers a definition in q. 108, a. 2, c. and *II Sent.*
d. 9, q. 1, a. 1, where it is obvious that this term is itself used
analogously by proper proportionality. This is further evidence
of the crucial nature of this language for St. Thomas' philosophy
and theology.

[27] Cf. I, q. 75, a. 5, ad 1; *C. Gent.*, III, Ch. 92.

tion' which is 'cancelled out' as inapplicable when 'knowing' is used in sentences about animals.

If, in attempting to criticize the Thomist claim that there is a foundation for the analogy of the term 'knowing' in the unequal and disparate participations of things in the powers of knowing, we were to suggest that we could formulate three *different* concepts of knowing and terms for each, one for humans, animals, and God, St. Thomas would reply that the properties signified would have in common something which is the basis for an analogous term. (It is here that analogy becomes a theory about things, or at least supposes one.) For example, Aquinas could formulate a vague concept which would include the three concepts of knowing, as I said. To do this, let us accept Aquinas' technical and admittedly recondite partial definition of 'knowing' as the *possessio formae alterius ut alterius,* "the possession of the form of another as belonging to another." For St. Thomas, however, this is not a complete definition, for he wishes to add the phrase: 'according to one's natural mode of possession.' So, 'knowing' is "the possession of the form of another as belonging to another according to one's natural mode of possession." This concept is neutral with respect to the concepts of knowing. But it is not on the same level as the other three notions. It is a meta-language notion which includes the other three and which signifies all three equally and alternatively. In the sentences (a) "Sense knowing is the possession of the form of another as belonging to another according to one's natural mode of possession" and "Divine knowing is the possession etc.," the phrase "possession of the form etc." serves as a univocal term. It is a predicate in sentences about predicates of sentences used earlier as examples; hence, it is a predicate in meta-language sentences. But the fact that we can form a term in a meta-language whose intention will include the intentions of terms occurring in object-language statements and which are analogous, does not make the analogous terms univocal. In fact, the only reason our constructed term can include the intentions of the analogous terms is that we *constructed* it to signify the intentions of the analogous terms; and the only time it actually includes the intentions of the other terms is when it occurs in a meta-language sentence.

From this discussion, it should be clear why St. Thomas could say, "What is 'knowing' for a man is not what is 'knowing' for a dog, although both are properly called 'knowing.'"[28] There are some instances of terms used as predicates where they signify not only what property is possessed but *what kind of possession* the property is had by.

Moreover, the language rules which govern the employment of terms like 'knowing' make the intention of the term (which has a section of its intention that, if imagined in C. I. Lewis' terms, *Def. I*-12, is a conjunction of other terms) contain some *conjoined disjunctions* of terms. When a term like 'knows' is used in a given sentence (b), a context is established which concels out the inapplicable elements of the intention of 'knows' in (a), thus making the intention fixed in the sentence as a conjunction of terms. Aquinas would say that the elements cancelled out are the inapplicable modes of possession; i.e., from the intention of 'knowing' in the sentence "Fido knows his dog house" there are cancelled out of the intention any terms like 'abstractly,' 'by deduction,' 'by induction,' etc.[29]

The second sense of the phrase *'modus significandi'*

---

[28] The general assumption upon which this is based is stated by St. Thomas: *I Sent.*, d. 38, q. 1, a. 2: "Unumquodque autem est in aliquo per modum ipsius, et non per modum sui."

[29] St. Thomas' analysis of meaning offers a clear sense of 'contextual' meaning. That is: The contextual meaning of two instances of the same term is different if the difference in context is a sufficient condition for the claim that the two instances of the term differ in intention. 'Contextual meaning' might be thus defined in terms of the effect of the context upon the intention of terms therein.

refers to elements of the intention of a term which are derived from the *way we learn the term.*[30] For, Aquinas says, many people do not understand the difference between the way a dog knows and the way a human knows (in fact, it is almost impossible to specify), chiefly because we apply 'knowing' to dogs, having recognized the similarity of their actions to ours. Hence, for these people, in the connotation of the term 'knowing' there are elements which are appropriate only to humans; and most times, even when they are consciously ruled out when the term is used in sentences about animals, they are not replaced by anything definite.[31] That is, within the intention of the term applied to animals there is no term which specifies *how* the dog knows. This point is of considerable importance for Aquinas in his discussion of language about God. If the intentions of terms have as elements terms which express the mode by which the property signified by the term is possessed, and if all the modes of possession are determined by the nature of the thing which has the property, then the terms of our experience-language, if applied directly to God, would signify a way of having the property which is no more compatible with the nature of God than the elements of the intention of 'knowing' which make it signify 'knowing as humans know' would be compatible with the nature of the dog.

But if the sentence in which the term is used establishes for a person who understands the nature of the subject the context which 'rules in' or 'rules out' certain elements of the intention of a term, then some elements will not be common to the intention of the term 'knows' in the sentences (a) "God knows" and (b) "A man knows." And St. Thomas' rule is: the na-

[30] *De Potentia,* q. 9, a. 3, ad 1; I, q. 13, a. 8; *C. Gent.,* I, Ch. 30; *I Sent.,* d. 22, q. 1, a. 2.

[31] This is, of course, an interpretation of St. Thomas. I am not assuming that present day philosophers would discuss various meanings of 'knowing' in this way.

ture of the thing denoted by the logical subject determines the modal elements of the intention of predicates which are applied to the subject.

This analysis has supplied the elements of Aquinas' answer to the problem proposed earlier: namely, if the analogous term signifies two different properties, it should be called 'equivocal'; but Aquinas' second condition for analogy of proper proportionality is that the two things must have the property signified by the analogous term. Yet if the term signifies two instances of the same property, then there seems to be no reason why it should be called 'equivocal,' for it will be univocal on our definition of univocity *I*-12-a and not univocal on *Def. I*-12-b. However, in terms of *Def. I*-11: *Intention,* Aquinas would thus say that, in brief, the term is used univocally if it has the same intention in each instance, and the intention in two instances is the same if all elements of the intention in one instance are common to the intention of the term in the other. But he holds that the 'mode of signification' is part of the intention of the term (wherever a mode of *possession* is relevant). Thus, if the 'mode of signifying' is different, the intention of the term is different even though the property signified be the same; and hence the term is equivocal (*Def. I*-13). And, he would argue, there are cases where a term is univocal in signification but equivocal in intention, just because there are *modes* of signification.

Although I have indicated that St. Thomas does not believe it possible to separate, more than logically and artificially, the *res significata* from the *modus significandi,* the example of 'knowing' is some help in understanding what he means. The *res significata* is what is common to all activities which we can call 'knowing.' But what we call 'knowing' admits of kinds and of degrees. There is no instance of knowing which is not one kind or another, and both the kind, 'sense' or 'abstract,' and the metaphysical mode, 'finite' or 'infinite', are part of the meaning of 'knowing' in any synthetic statement in which it occurs. This is what is meant by *modus significandi.*

St. Thomas' two statements that the *modus significandi* differs and that the *res significata* is the same when some terms are applied to God can be defined as follows:

Def. IV - 1: Sameness of Res Significata:
"The *res significata* of 'T' is the same":

if 1. There are given at least two sentences (a) and (b) in which there is respectively a predicate term 'T'.

2. 'T' in (a) and 'T' in (b) are instances of the same term.

3. 'T' signifies property T of X in (a) and T of Y in (b).

4. All the terms of the intention of 'T' in (a) which specify the class of things to which property T belongs, occur in the intention of 'T' in (b).

Def. IV - 2: Difference of Modus Significandi:
"The *modus significandi* of 'T' is different":

if 1, 2, 3, and 4 of *Def. IV - 1* hold.

5. For any thing Z, having the property T implies that Z can perform either actions (A) 1, 2, 3, - n; or (B) 2, 3, 4, - n and not 1; or (C) 3, 4, - n and not 1 and 2; or......; or n.....

6. The intention of 'T' in sentence (a) and in (b) is determined by the intention of the subject term 'X' or 'Y' in such a way that only one of the alternative groups of actions is signified.

7. The terms of the intention of 'T' in (a) which specify which of the alternates (A), (B) or (C) is performed, are not the same as the terms in the intention of 'T' in (b) which, consequently, specify a different alternative.

Thus, St. Thomas could hold that a term which differs in *modus significandi* but is the same in *res significata* is equivocal, even though all things denoted by the term will have the same property signified.

That there is at least one such term is evident from the example given: "knowing," provided we accept at least provisionally Aquinas' analysis of the nature of knowing.

One would be inclined to seek an easy formulation of the analogy of proper proportionality in terms of the points so far explained by saying that terms are analogous by proper proportionality if they differ in their respective instances in *modus significandi* but not with respect to *res significata.* However, this is *not* what Aquinas meant by analogy of proper proportionality. *This is merely the reason why certain terms cannot be used of God and creatures univocally and it is St. Thomas' explanation of how a term can in two instances signify the same property and yet be equivocal.* St. Thomas has merely explained how the first and second conditions of this analogy can be rendered compatible. He has yet to exhibit the other conditions of this analogy.

3. *The third characteristic* of terms analogous by proportionality is that there must be a proportional similarity between what is denoted by 'T' in (a) and what is denoted by 'T' in (b).

I shall briefly explain what Aquinas meant by *similarity,* secondly what he meant by *proportion,* and thirdly, what he meant by *proportional similarity.*

a) *Similarity*: Aquinas has four senses of 'similarity'; since the explanation of these notions is not possible under the circumstances of this paper, let us, instead, take a very general definition of 'similarity' as being sufficient for our purposes. "Two things are similar if they are in some respect or respects identical but never numerically identical." The 'respect or respects' can be and must be specified, says Thomas, wherever a factual proposition "This A is similar to that B" is analysed. This very general definition is what I have given as *Def. IV*-3.

b) *Proportion*: For Aquinas the term 'proportion' (not *proportionality,* now) is a synonym of 'relation.'

And a proportion obtains between A and X where a *relation* obtains between A and X. Note: I stipulate that 'property' is a one place predicate in object-language sentences; 'relation' is a two or more place predicate.

c) *Proportionality*: When Aquinas says: "A proportionality holds between A and B," he means: There is a *similarity in the proportions* (or relations) of A and B. That is, a relation R obtains between A and some property, thing or event, X, and a relation R^1 obtains between B and some property, thing or event, Y, and R and R^1 are similar.

Hence, a proportional similarity obtains between any two things, A and B, which have similar relations to some property, event, or thing. So, Aquinas would say that a proportional similarity obtains between *Plato* and *Fido* because the relations signified by 'knowing' which obtain between Fido and his dog house and Plato and his philosophy are similar (that is, in its two instances the relation signified by the term 'knows' has some common properties or relations.)

Since the term 'knows' denotes both Fido and Plato, St. Thomas has formulated his third characteristic of the analogy as follows: there must be a proportional similarity between what is denoted by 'T' in (a) and 'T' in (b).

4) Turning now to *Definitions IV-4, Proportional Similarity,* and *IV-5, Analogy of Proper Proportionality,* we observe that the latter is formulated in terms of the former. A term is analogous by proper portionality if it signifies in both its instances relations of the respective subjects and if the subjects, in regard to these relations, are proportionally similar.

And the subjects are proportionally similar if there exist entities, relations, properties or events such that ATx and BTy are true or could be true, and term 'T' used to refer to the two instances of T would not be univocal, and the relations T of ATx and BTy are similar.

5) *Similarity of Relations.*

For the analogy of proportionality rule to be fully established, it must be possible to apply the definition of *proportional similarity* to things and to decide whether or not two things are *in fact* proportionally similar. But to do this, we need a criterion for *similarity of relations.* That is, it is a necessary condition of this analogy that the things denoted by the predicate be proportionally similar and it is a necessary condition of proportional similarity that the *relations* of the things be similar. Hence to apply the rule confidently in crucial cases we should need a criterion of similarity of relations.

Now, St. Thomas had not the slightest doubt that with regard to most ordinary language uses of terms like 'knows,' 'exists,' etc., in senses which fulfill this rule of analogy (like the two paradigm sentences: (a) "Plato knows philosophy" and (b) "Fido knows his dog house"), the reason the term was extended to its analogical use about dogs by human convention in the first place was that men had *recognized* the similarity in the relations. And later, in talking about God, Aquinas points out that if one can establish that God has certain relations to the world (from empirical premises) then it will follow from the general form of language that the relations are similar to relations of our experience.

Taking account of what Bochenski has proposed[32] and of what Aquinas seems to have had in mind, I suggest the following definition (*IV*-6) of Similarity of Relations:

Def. IV - 6: *Similarity of Relations:*
    "Relation R is similar to relation R¹":
    if 1. Both are relations.

[32] I. M. Bochenski, "On Analogy," *The Thomist,* XI (1948), 424–447.

2. They have common formal properties with respect to either a formal or merely linguistic set of axioms, the latter not being explicitly formulated in ordinary language, or, they have a common property.

The difficulties with this criterion of similarity are obvious; Bochenski's proposed criterion says relations are similar if they have common formal properties, i.e., common syntactical and semantical properties. This is obviously not a thought which St. Thomas might have had. Furthermore, while this offers some hope for a more careful development of the analogy theory, it means that a great deal of analysis would have to be done to see if the relations attributed to God do have common properties with relations in the world of experience. Such a criterion supposes a more extensive formalized language than seems practicable. The second alternative, the proposal that the relations have common properties with respect to linguistic axioms which are presupposed by implicit language rules governing the employment of the analogous term, is very similar to St. Thomas' assumption that if the relations are sufficiently similar we will recognize that fact and use the same term to signify the two relations. I am not really sure what such language rules would be like.

This deficiency in the analogy theory is serious, because it is so difficult to imagine a set of rules under which the necessary conditions for analogy of proper proportionality (that the relations be similar) could be determined to have been fulfilled. Yet, it would be an *ad ignorantiam* error to argue that no such criterion is possible. However, let us go on to see how this theory is applied to language about God. For I think it will be found that the difficulty I have just mentioned is not so prominent when the rule is used in practice, although it is clear that a fully accurate and adequate analogy theory will have to contain a practicable criterion of similarity of relations.

APPLICATION OF THE ANALOGY RULES
TO LANGUAGE ABOUT GOD

1. Aquinas argues that he needs a theory of analogy
for language about God because:

a) If the predicate terms in G-statements (statements with 'God' or a synonym as the subject) are
totally equivocal with respect to the occurrences of
the same predicate terms in E-statements (with any
object of ordinary, direct or indirect experience as
subject), then all arguments with an E-statement in
the premises and a G-statement as the conclusion will
be invalid, committing the fallacy of equivocation;
and all G-statements will be meaningless because none
of human experience will count either as evidence for
or as explications of those statements.

b) If the predicates of G-statements are *univocal* with respect to instances of the same predicates
in E-statements, then God will be anthropomorphic,
since all predicates we have are derived from experience and are primarily used of limited or finite things.
And it was a basic thesis among the medievals that our
descriptive categories of the world are of 'the world-
as-experienced,' are homocentric. The term 'finite' or
'dependent' refers for Thomas to a mode of existence,
and he holds that the context of all our language supposes that part of the meaning of the predicate terms
is the *mode* of existence of the entity to which the
property is attributed. I made this point earlier in distinguishing the *modus significandi* from the *res significata*. He insists that if you do not make such a
distinction of kind from mode, you will not be describing the Christian God, the transcendent God.
Furthermore, he also argues that if God is to have such
properties as self-existence and omnipotence, He must
be a significantly different[33] kind of thing from any-

[33] I have said here 'significantly different' because Aquinas is
not committed to the absurd notion that God is entirely different

thing in our experience. So, the predicates attributed to Him cannot be univocal with any E-statement occurrences of the same terms.[34]

2. As a result, the terms in G-statements must be partially equivocal with respect to the same terms in E-statements. St. Thomas claims that he can show as a matter of empirical fact that if we use these analogy rules we can explain the way these predicates in G-statements are related to ordinary E-sentence occurrences of the same terms; *and,* moreover, if we do explain the theological language this way, we shall (1) preserve the transcendence of God; (2) preserve the intelligibility of theological language; (3) make sense of the claim that human experience can furnish some evidence for the truth of the theological beliefs. For, God will be *at most* proportionally similar to the world. That is, God's *operations* will have properties in common with some operations, like causing, which are internal to the world. And we will *name*[35] God from his operations (in a way to be described). So, while all our natural knowledge of God's properties will be by inference from His operations, what we do attribute to God will not be grossly anthropomorphic and will not be arrived at by invalid arguments. How,

from creatures. In fact, the analogy theory is designed to permit expression in language of the similarity between God and creatures while protecting our discourse from a claim that God is directly similar to creatures.

[34] In effect, Aquinas admits both contemporary philosophical points: (a) if G-statement predicates are equivocal with respect to all E-statement occurrences of those predicates, then all G-statements are meaningless to us who have understanding only of the terms in our E-statement language; and (b) if the G-statement predicates are univocal with a representative set of instances of those predicates in E-statements, then our statements about God will be, in most cases, obviously false and in the remainder, misleading.

[35] 'Name' here is a verb which Aquinas used to cover both the description of God in terms of common nouns: 'creator,' 'designer,' etc. and to cover the process of attribution: "God is merciful," etc.

in outline, this application of the analogy rules is carried out, I shall now describe.

1. Aquinas believes that he can show that between the world described in E-statements, the world of experience, and some entity not part of that world there obtain several relations: (1) 'being moved by'; (2) 'being efficiently caused by'; (3) 'being conserved in existence by'; (4) 'being excelled by'; (5) 'being designed by' (each relation is established by one of the five existential arguments).[36]

2. A term which signifies these relations, (let us take only one, for consideration, say, 'being caused by') can not be used in exactly the same way as it is used in a sentence like this: "My black eye was caused by John." For this latter is an E-statement and the fundamental assumption is that God won't have any properties or relations in the same way as any of His creatures. (This assumption is outside the purview of our analysis; let us take it as a supposition that all theologians would accept it.)

So, the argument is: God is at most proportionally similar to John (that is, is not *directly* similar) because the relation 'being caused by' is similar (but not identical) in the statements of the form (a) wCg and (b)

---

[36] The application of the analogy theory will require the demonstration (logically prior) of the existence of a relation (say, 'being caused by') between the objects of experience and some one entity not otherwise specified. The reason we choose to call the relationship 'being caused by' is that the kind of evidence at hand is exactly the kind of evidence present when we call the relationship between my black eye and my antagonist one of 'being caused by.' It is true that the well-known difficulties against the traditional arguments for the existence of a First Cause, etc., may make the application of the analogy rules suspect. But, one can for the sake of the discussion either imagine that new evidence has been found that there exists an entity which is First Cause, or one can take it as a matter of religious faith that such a Creator exists. We are now concerned with the sense of these statements ("A First Cause exists" or "A Creator exists") which will be analyzed by the application of the analogy rules.

bCj.[37] And the term 'being caused by' is analogous by proportionality because in its two occurrences it is used equivocally but not totally equivocally. The reason why we cannot replace *this* term ('being caused by') with a univocal term is that in (a) the 'mode of signification' which is proper to 'C' in (b) has been cancelled out; and because we don't know the characteristics of the *mode of possession* by which God has His properties, we can't fill in the part of the signification which is cancelled out.

So, the term 'being caused by,' while having all elements of its intention present which are necessary to distinguish 'being caused by' from any other relation, *still* does not have present the positive elements (elements not made up of negations of finite modes) by which to distinguish the divine mode of being from the finite mode. And yet, even if these latter modal elements *were* present, the term would still be equivocal because the modal elements of 'C' in (a) and 'C' in (b) would be different.

3. All natural knowledge of God consists basically in showing that certain relationships with possible worlds actually obtain between things that exist and God.[38]

4. These relation terms, which are thus analogous by proper proportionality with instances of the same terms in statements about the world, are then transferred into *names* of the other relatum, 'God.' This transference of relation terms into names follows the rule of Analogy of Attribution, since you can call a person by the names of his actions, because he is the cause of his actions. Thus we call a man who smokes, a 'smoker,' and a man who judges, Judge, and a man

[37] Where "wCg" means "The world is caused by God" and "bCj" means "The blackeye is caused by John."

[38] The term 'God' is a shorthand for the definite description which would result from a combination of all the properties shown to be attributable to one unique being with some (psychologically prior) property such as 'First Cause' or 'Creator.'

who designs, a 'designer.' And transforming the name of an effect to become a name of the cause is an instance of analogy of attribution.[39] So, the entity X which has the relation 'being mediate or immediate cause' of all other entities and events is called 'First Cause.'

5. Next, utilizing the fact that secondary employments of terms analogous by attribution still tell us something about the subject, St. Thomas proceeds to determine what properties God would have to have if He is the Cause, the Judge, the Conserver, etc. Thus He arrives at properties like: intelligence, free will, simplicity, etc. But *these* terms can all be turned into 'relation predicates' and shown to be analogous by proportionality with respect to ordinary language oc-

---

[39] It may be argued that where morphological changes occur, such as from 'smoke' to 'smoker,' there is no one term which is used according to the rule of analogy of attribution, and hence no linguistic analogy. Instead there is a case of a broader 'conceptual' process called *denomination*, where the meaning of the one term is *derivative* from the meaning of the other. In every such case, however, a new term could be coined which would fulfill the functions of both the original and derivative terms and which would have its diverse functions related according to the rule of analogy of attribution.

Hence, while the analogy of attribution involved here is not actually linguistic (since there is no one term to fulfill the rules), it is highly probable that the conceptual operations which preceded the development of the differing terms were the same as those involved in any linguistic analogy of attribution. This is supported by the fact that in every such case it is possible, by coining a new term, to construct such an analogy. Perhaps a more common case of naming a cause in terms of its effects is this: the sensed quality *red* has the same name as the property (physical dispositional) *red*; for the redness of things is their disposition to cause us to have the sensations called 'red.' Thus I would argue (cf. also *De Veritate*, q. 21, a. 4, ad 2) that wherever there is extrinsic denomination, there is analogy of attribution. This would, of course, render a large part of our knowledge of the world knowledge through analogy of attribution; but I think this is exactly what St. Thomas would have held.

currences of the same terms—occurrences which are psychologically prior.

6. Hence, all statements about God employ terms which are analogous by proper proportionality with respect to psychologically prior instances of the same terms in ordinary experience-describing statements. Thus analogy of proper proportionality is the general form of language about God.

In a word, Aquinas supposes that there are two basic sets of statements made in discussing the existence and nature of God. (A) The statements which assert that some relation 'R' obtains between entities of a certain kind (the things of the world) and some entity not a member of that kind. (B) The statements which employ cognate forms of the relation term 'R' as common nouns or adjectives to either name or describe the entity. An example of (A) is: "Every thing which has really distinct properties is causally dependent upon some entity which does not have distinct properties; and there are some entities which have distinct properties." An example of (B) is: "There exists a First Cause." It is immediately obvious that statements of set (B) logically presuppose both the truth and meaningfulness of statements of set (A). How set (B) is derived from (A) is described in the next section (7). The relation terms that occur in sentences of set (A) are said to be analogous by proper proportionality with ordinary language occurrences of the same term, or suppose statements where terms are employed in a manner according to that analogy rule.

7. Some statements about God employ terms which, in addition to being used analogously by proportionality with respect to E-statements, are also used analogously by attribution with respect to other, and logically prior G-statements. That is, the statement "The world is caused by God" is logically prior to "God is the First Cause." The statements which attribute common names to God employ predicates analogous by

attribution with respect to instances of the same predicates occurring in statements asserting that certain relations obtain between the world and God. Thus, to say "God is the artificer, the designer, the Judge," etc., is to employ as a common name a term which by both logical and psychological priority is employed in a statement which says "The world is made, planned, and judged by God."

In summary, having ruled out univocal language about God, Aquinas claims that his analogy rules offer a way of taking ordinary language literally in orthodox claims about God. Furthermore, he claims that he cannot be accused of accepting an inadequate kind of language about God, for no other language is *possible* given the Christian assumption that God is transcendent and different in kind from all other things.

Perhaps the sense of the claim I made at the outset, but did not directly support, is now clearer: if one wishes to render philosophically plausible the claim of most orthodox Christians that their traditional descriptive statements about God are both literally meaningful and true, one must employ an analogy theory fundamentally similar to that of St. Thomas; and, I might add, the existence of such a theory as that of Aquinas, even with its substantial defects, renders quite plausible the belief of many Christians that their theological utterances are indeed literally meaningful. It seems that the whole question of whether or not explicit rules can be developed to give a criterion for the meaningfulness of religious statements must be re-opened and re-examined in the light of the substantial progress that can be made toward such rules with a properly understood and developed theory of analogy.

NOMINALISM[1]

PETER GEACH

Although this is not just one more piece on 'the problem of universals', I need not make much apology for my title. I shall not make much of the fact that some leading exponents of the theory I shall be attacking, like Buridan, Ockham and Hobbes, have commonly been called Nominalists: what is much more important is that this theory is a theory attaching a preeminent importance to names, and that its mistake, as I shall argue, lies precisely in attempting to resolve problems in terms of names and what they name, in cases where actually we need to consider some other logical category than that of names.

The theory I want to attack is the two-name theory of predication: namely, that in an affirmative predication the subject is a name and so is the predicate, and the predication is true if and only if the subject-name and the predicate-name stand for the same thing or things. On this view, the simplest form of predication will be the traditional 'SiP', 'Some S is P', which will come out true just in the case where there is something named 'S' and also named 'P'. It is an interesting fact that the two-name theory has recently had a great revival in Poland, under the odd name of 'ontology'; and in one way of axiomatizing ontology, 'SiP' is

From *Sophia,* Vol. 3, 1964, pp. 3–14. Reprinted with permission of the author and the editors of *Sophia.*

[1] This paper was originally read to a gathering of Catholic priests; and it accordingly assumed throughout that Catholic dogmas are in fact true—not because this assumption could not reasonably be disputed, but because no one in the original audience was going to dispute it. It is hoped, however, that a discussion of the relation between logic and dogma from this point of view may be of some interest for those who do not share the author's faith.

taken as the primitive form of proposition, though this particular form of presentation is not essential. In any event the distinction between subject and predicate is of no particular logical significance if both are names; the unimportance of the distinction is specially clear if we take 'SiP', which is simply convertible to 'PiS', as the simplest form of proposition.

The origins of the two-name theory may fairly be traced back to Aristotle; Aristotle was Logic's Adam, and his doctrine of terms was Adam's Fall, with ruinous consequences for his posterity. In his days of original justice, Aristotle had held quite a different view, which we find in the *De Interpretatione*. Here, the very simplest form of predication contains not two names, but a name and a verb; and names and verbs are assigned essentially different characteristics. A name is always tenseless (*aneu chronou*); a verb is, or may be, tensed. A name is a possible logical subject; a verb is essentially predicative (*aei ton kath heterou legomenon semeion*). A predication may be negated by negating the verb, never by negating the name that is the logical subject. Both names and verbs, however, are supposed to be syntactically simple—to contain no significant parts of which logic need take account. This theory and terminology may be found in all essentials in Plato's *Sophist*; and I see no reason to doubt that in his state of original justice Aristotle would have accepted what Plato there explicitly says —that you cannot get a predication by combining two names or two verbs, but only by combining a name and a verb.

Except in one particular, I believe this *De Interpretatione* theory to have been thoroughly sound. The point to which I must demur is the requirement that verbs should be syntactically simple. Aristotle's corresponding requirement about names is entirely reasonable: complex names are a chimerical category. For the role of a name is simply to stand for the thing named; and then a name must signify its bearer directly, and not *via* other signs in the language, as any complex sign would have to do. But there is no reason at all why the predicative part of a proposition should be syntactically simple; what you say about a named object may have to be very complex. It looks as though when he wrote *De Interpretatione* Aristotle had a programme of analysing complex propositions as molecular combinations of atomic, one-name one-verb, propositions. He must, however, have soon satisfied himself that this programme would not work out.

In the *Prior Analytics* we get a different and irreconcilable story. The simplest form of proposition is still the subject-predicate form; but we find no mention of the distinction between name and verb. Instead, a proposition may be split up into two terms (*horoi*); in the proposition, one will be subject and the other predicate, but neither is essentially predicative; the very same term that in one proposition is a predicate may, without any change of meaning, be a subject in another proposition. The requirement of syntactical simplicity is altogether dropped. The schematic letters in a syllogism 'If A applies to every B and B applies to every C, then A applies to every C' need not be interpreted by single words nor even by expressions that are grammatically noun-phrases: to use Aristotle's own example we may take 'There is one science of any contraries' as an instance of the schema 'A applies to any B', taking 'B' to mean '(pair of) contraries' and 'A' to mean 'there being one science of them', and here the interpretation of 'A' is neither a single word nor a noun-phrase.

The doctrine of terms appears to me to be one of the worst disasters in the history of logic. It was a *felix culpa* in that it probably helped Aristotle to grasp the idea of a general logical form expressible with schematic letters—without this idea formal logic could hardly exist—and also in that it freed him from the mistaken restriction of "verbs" or predicates to syntactically simple words. But the price to be paid was heavy: by dropping the requirement of syntactical simplicity for names as well, the distinctive notion of a name became obscured; and the distinctive notion of a predicate became still more obscured, by dropping the requirement that a "verb" should be *essentially* predicative, and requiring that any predicate could in some other proposition be a subject; I am convinced, on the contrary, that the class of "terms" which can be indifferently subjects and predicates is in fact empty.

Aristotle's false doctrine of terms made it easy to commit a further confusion: to confuse the relation of a name to what it names with the relation of a predicate to what it applies to or is truly predicable of. Aristotle, I think, never expressly made this identification. If we do make it, we fall into the two-name theory almost at once. For if we waive some details, not of present concern, about the quantifiers 'every' and 'some', we may say that the truth of an affirmative predication consists in the predicate's being true of, or applying to, what the subject names: if now we confound the relation of applying to with the relation of naming, we get the two-name theory, that truth consists in having a subject-term and a predicate-term that name the same thing. And then, since a predicate that is not a noun-phrase (or at least an adjective!) does not look much like a name, we get the requirement, explicitly rejected by Aristotle, that a proposition must come in the guise of two such name-like terms joined by a part of the verb "to be"—otherwise it is logically not properly dressed. A further development along this line is the idea that tense must be shoved onto one of the terms, not left in the copula: e.g. 'Peter will be a sinner' is to be turned into 'Peter is a future sinner'. I shall not discuss this development, which is not found in the medieval formulations of the two-name theory.

I have elaborated elsewhere an attack on the Aristotelian doctrine of terms, and its sequel the two-name theory of predication, from the point of view of a formal logician. My task here is rather different: I shall argue that the two-name theory leads inevitably to grave distortions of Catholic dogma, and is therefore not a relatively harmless speculative error. Since I have found some manuals of logic used in courses of philosophy for seminarians to be heavily infected with the errors of the two-name theory, the importance of the matter is obvious.

My manner of refuting the two-name theory will be to show that arguments that would be valid by the two-name theory lead from true premises to false and heretical conclusions; particularly in relation to the dogmas of the Trinity and the Incarnation. This shows that the arguments in question are logically invalid, and therefore that the two-name theory is false. A refutation of this form does not, indeed, show just what is wrong with the two-name theory, but it does show that it is wrong, and wrong in an area where error is particularly to be avoided; and this may stimulate people to look out for fallacies in the theory that might otherwise go unsuspected.

While nobody is going to say that an argument with true premises and a heretical conclusion is logically valid, I am not sure that everyone would infer that such an argument must contain an ordinary logical fallacy, which we can detect and expose if only we are clever enough. If all the arguments against a mystery of faith can be cleared up, then surely, people may object, the mystery ceases to be a mystery. This objection is confused. What I am maintaining is that for each single argument against faith there is a refutation, in terms of ordinary logic; not that there is some one general technique for refuting all arguments against faith, or even all arguments against a particular dogma of faith. I do not claim that we can prove, or even clearly see, that the propositions expressing mysteries of faith are consistent. Modern logicians like Church and Gödel have shown what a severe requirement the demand for a general consistency proof is:

as regards many theories, the demand is demonstrably unreasonable. And as regards the doctrine of the Trinity in particular we can see that a demand for a consistency proof could never be satisfied. For the propositions expressing this dogma, relating as they do to the inner life of God without bringing in any actual or possible creatures, cannot be only possibly true; if they are possibly true, they are necessarily true. So a proof that the doctrine is consistent would be a proof of its truth, which is certainly impossible. What I do claim about this and every other dogma is that in any given proof that an adversary sets up against it there is some fallacy to be found if one is sharp enough: *manifestum est probationes quae contra fidem inducuntur non esse demonstrationes sed solubilia argumenta.*

The exponent of the two-name theory whom I am going to study in some detail is William of Ockham: I have chosen him because he is so consequent and clear in following out the theory's implications. We shall see that in the end he avoids open heresy only by the most arbitrary means: as regards the Trinity, by declaring the ordinary laws of logic inapplicable; as regards the Incarnation, by an unacceptable redefinition of the term 'man'.

The logical strain that the doctrine of the Trinity puts upon the two-name theory does not come about merely from the mysteriousness of the doctrine. Any doctrine in which relative terms essentially occur is bound to strain the two-name theory. It is clear in the first place that on a two-name theory there can be no relations—no *res* answering specially to relative terms. For take a proposition affirming a relation, like 'The cat is on the mat': if the word 'on' answers to something *in rebus,* a relation, then clearly this *res* is neither named by 'cat' nor by 'mat', and these terms do not name the same thing as one another; so we have an affirmative proposition whose truth is not accounted for by the two-name theory. It is thus natural that Ockham should deny the existence of relations:

there are only relative terms, and these are names of
the things related, e.g. 'father' or 'father of Solomon'
would be a name of David. This, of course, raises new
problems. What sort of term is 'of Solomon'? We can
hardly say that in 'pater Salomonis' two names of
David are put in opposition, for then how would 'pater
Salomonis, Isai filius' differ from 'pater Isai, Salomonis
filius'? Should we not have, each time, the same four
names of David stuck together? Ockham in fact is content to say that a relative term is one that e.g. a
genitive congruously goes with; he does not explain
the mode of significance of the genitive.

I shall not pursue this, but go straight on to the
special Trinitarian puzzles. Rejecting as he does the
idea of relations *in rebus*, Ockham cannot remove the
appearance of contradiction that arises if we say that
one single simple thing is each and all of three distinct
things. Aquinas can and does say that the term *'res'*,
'thing', is a transcendental or category-jumping term,
which applies both to *res absolutae*, non-relative realities, and to relations. The Blessed Trinity is one *res*
or three *res* according as we are speaking of *res
absolutae* or of relations. We do not find ourselves
forced to say that one single and simple *res absoluta*
is at the same time three *res absolutae*—these are only
three distinct *relations*. This is not, of course, the end
of puzzles: we now have to ask how and in what sense
a *res absoluta* can "be" a relation. But if Aquinas is
still in check, Ockham has already been checkmated;
and this he himself recognizes in effect. The line he
takes is this: certain arguments about the Persons of
the Trinity are invalid, although other arguments of
the same logical form are valid; the only decision procedure we can apply is to see whether the premises
and the contradictory of the conclusion are all guaran-
teed true by some text of Scripture or decision of
the Church—or, Ockham adds, by some "evident syllogism" from premises of this kind! Ostensibly valid
syllogisms not thus ruled out by authority are "uni-

versally valid"; so we need not worry about applying the rules of logic, such as the *dictum de omni,* in the domain of creatures, where the Church does not require us to believe one thing is each and all of three different things; but syllogisms about the Divine Persons are subject to ecclesiastical censorship.

The difficulties about the Trinity arose over relative terms; the difficulties about the Incarnation arise, for one thing, over abstract terms, like 'humanity' or 'human nature'. It will not, however, be necessary for the moment to discuss either the general difficulties of abstract terms or the special difficulties of the term 'nature' in the theology of the Incarnation; for we can show up the predicament of the two-name theory by shifting to another mode of expression. Instead of saying 'Christ's human nature was passible, his divine nature impassible', we may say 'Christ as man was passible, Christ as God is impassible': and so in other cases. But the feasibility of this depends as Aquinas pointed out, on taking seriously the distinction of subject and predicate. The term after 'as' occurs predicatively—'Christ as man' means 'Christ in so far as he is a man'; if we take the subject-predicate distinction seriously, we may therefore distinguish between what is predicable with truth of the subject 'the man Christ' and what is predicable of 'Christ as man'. Such distinctions are indispensable in the theology of the Incarnation. For example, 'Christ as man is God' is false, and 'Christ as man began to exist' is true; but on the contrary 'The man Christ is God' is true, and 'The man Christ began to exist' is false.[2] But for a two-name theory no distinction like this can make sense. A term like 'man' or 'God', in subject or predicate position, is just a name, and is a name of the same thing in either position. There can be no distinction between what is true of Christ as man and what is true of the man Christ. Ockham has indeed a logical theory of this re-

[2] *Summa Theologiae, III,* q. 16 a. 5.

duplicative construction 'A qua B is C', but one of no use for present concerns: for he expounds the form by a conjunction 'A is B, and A is C, and every B is C, and if anything is B it is C'. This form of exposition is surprisingly redundant—both 'A is C' and 'every B is C' are superfluous given the other clauses—but anyhow it is useless for present purposes, since it would give e.g. 'if anyone is a man, he is sinless' as part of what is meant by 'Christ as man is sinless'.

Ockham's view as to the logical character of propositions about the Incarnation is obscured by a sort of logical thimble-rigging with the terms 'man', 'humanity', and *'suppositum'*. The term 'humanity' as used by Ockham has only the outward guise of an abstract noun: it is no more a genuine abstract noun than 'Majesty'—the humanity of Socrates just is Socrates, as the King's Majesty just is the King. A humanity is a concrete thing consisting of body and soul; the humanity which is Socrates could be assumed by a divine person and go on existing, and the humanity which now is sustained by the Son of God could be laid down by him and go on existing. We can indeed say that Christ is a man and Christ's humanity is not a man: this is because the definition of the term 'man', *exprimens quid nominis,* is a disjunction—'either a humanity or a *suppositum* sustaining a humanity'. The first half of this disjunction applies to any man other than Christ; the second half, to Christ alone, since an ordinary man is a humanity, and is not a *suppositum* sustaining a humanity, because he does not sustain himself. And thus if the humanity that is Socrates were assumed by the divine *suppositum* that is the Son of God, it would by definition no longer be a man; and the humanity now sustained by Christ is not a man but would forthwith and *eo ipso* become a man if Christ merely laid it down.

The meaning of Ockham's doctrine may escape us because he talks in a way familiar to us of Christ's assuming or sustaining or laying down his humanity (the last expression has of course no actual application except for the *triduum mortis*). But when we talk this way, if we know what we are doing, we are using 'humanity' with these verbs the way that a proper abstract noun is used; as when we speak of a man's assuming or sustaining or laying down a mayoralty. It would be manifest nonsense to say that the mayoralty a man assumes could go on existing after he had laid it down and would then forthwith and *eo ipso* be a Lord Mayor. Of course the cases are not the same; but the difference between them arises because of the category-difference between the concrete terms 'Lord Mayor' and 'man', not because in its relation to the corresponding concrete term 'mayoralty' is any different from 'humanity'. If Ockham were using 'humanity' as a proper abstract noun, what he says would be as much nonsense as my nonsense about a mayoralty becoming a Lord Mayor. It is pretty clear, though, that in fact his doctrine is not nonsense but thinly disguised Nestorian heresy. Ockham thinks, as the Nestorians thought, that what was assumed to some sort of union with the Word of God was a human creature existing independently of such union. He merely writes 'humanitas' where an outspoken Nestorian would write 'homo'; this no more alters the force of his propositions than writing 'the King's Majesty' instead of 'the King'. And though he can claim that his definition of 'homo' makes it unequivocally true of Christ and other men, this too is a mere subterfuge; for Christ is not *verus homo* as we are, if 'homo' applies to him and us only because one half of the disjunctive definition applies to him and the other half to us. Moreover, this definition of 'homo' would certainly not have been in the mind of any Latin-speaking contemporary of Christ; so on Ockham's showing Pilate will have erred in saying 'Ecce Homo', since what Pilate meant by 'homo' will not on Ockham's showing have been true of Christ.

I think the sort of troubles which arise for Ockham

are inevitable for any consequent thinker who holds the two-name theory. Medieval two-name theorists are in general liable to say about some abstract logical rule, 'Haec regula habet instantiam (i.e. has a counter-example) in mysterio SS Trinitatis/Incarnationis'. To my mind, the need to say such a thing about the rule simply shows that the rule is wrongly formulated and that we must try for an unexceptionable reformulation of it. And this reformulation must not contain a saving-clause that actually cites the theological cases as ones to which the rule shall be inapplicable; that would be contrary to the nature of logical science—no particular terms of first intention, whether theological or geological or what you will, can come in for special mention in logical rules; a logical rule must contain only syncategorematic words and second-intention terms. There is a confusion about the way that logic is *de secundis intentionibus* which I ought perhaps to mention here: one sometimes encounters it in print—I have read a cleric's attempt to rule out of court a logical objection to the IIIa Via, on the score that St. Thomas was thinking on an ontological level and not on the second-intention level of abstract logic. Suppose a man gave a narrative of his past life that was not only implausible but positively inconsistent, it would not lie in his mouth to reject a protest against his inconsistency, on the score that he had been talking on the ontological level of action and not on the second-intention level at which there arise questions of inconsistency between propositions. This would be mere impertinence; it is no less impertinent to reject logical criticism of an argument on the score that the argument itself is not *de secundis intentionibus*. And the similar objection that one cannot infer the invalidity of an argument-form from the material truth of premises and falsity of conclusion in some instance of the form is equally not to be listened to.

All the same, it can never be the case that the *only* way to refute an incorrect logical rule is to cite a concrete counter-example from theology, i.e. a theological argument of the suspected form with true premises and a false conclusion. Even if, having our eye on the theological counter-example, we framed our rule so as to avoid trouble over the example without expressly bringing theological terms into the rule: even so the position would be unsatisfactory, and an unbeliever could be excused for suspecting that logic had been bent *ad hoc* to meet the needs of theology. It is a tasteless and dubious procedure on Ockham's part when he cites *only* theological counter-examples to some invalid syllogistic forms. The procedure is all the more objectionable because some of Ockham's alleged theological truths are in fact Nestorian heresies; but it would be objectionable anyhow. A theological counter-example shows that a form of argument is invalid; but it does not show why it is invalid; and the same of course would hold about a counter-example from geology or botany or physics.

To make the role of counter-examples clear, let us consider Aristotle's use of them in the *Prior Analytics*. His invariable way of refuting an invalid syllogistic form is to find a set of three concrete first-intention terms which he thinks make the premises true and the conclusion false. For example, he refutes the form 'If no C is B and some B is not A some C is A' by the counter-example that 'no swan is a horse' and 'some horse is not white' are true, but 'some swan is not white' is false. Unfortunately, 'some swan is not white' is true, so the refutation fails in this instance; and is it not unworthy of logic to have to worry about black swans' turning up, even if they never do?

Saccheri ingeniously overcame this difficulty by constructing for each invalid mood a counter-example belonging to logic itself and using only second-intention terms. Thus, the invalidity of the mood *AEO* in the first figure is shown by the following example of the mood: "Any instance of *Barbara* is valid; no instance of AEO in the first figure is an instance of

Barbara; ergo, some instance of AEO in the first figure is invalid". If this instance of AEO in the first figure is valid, we cannot infer that AEO in the first figure is a valid form; for though a valid form cannot have invalid instances, an invalid form may well have some valid instances (ones that are also instances of some other, valid form). We can on the contrary say that if this particular instance of this AEO form is valid, then, since its premises are true, its conclusion is true, namely that not every instance of this form is valid; and thus AEO in the first figure will be an invalid form. If, on the other hand, this instance of AEO in the first figure is invalid, then obviously the form AEO in the first figure is invalid.

Saccheri's procedure, brilliantly original and thoroughly sound as it is, is by no means necessary to remove the defect of Aristotle's refutation method. We may for example convince ourselves by a Lewis Carroll diagram of the general possibility that there should be terms A, B, C, such that 'No C is B' and 'Some B is not A' are true and 'Some C is A' is false: this method does not require any actual interpretation of the letters, not even one using second-intention terms.

When we prove that a logical form is invalid by citing an actual instance, using first-intention terms, in which it fails, this may be a perfectly logical proof in the sense of being a valid argument with true premises; but for all that it will not be the sort of proof for a logical result that a logician ought to put in a logic book, for qua logician he ought not to appeal to the actual truth of premises, nor to the actual falsehood of a conclusion, containing first-intention terms. The thesis that a logical form is invalid is certainly true if some instance of that form has true premises and a false conclusion; but this logical thesis does not itself specially relate to one or other instance of the invalid form; and if we know a form to be invalid, it can only be our lack of ingenuity that makes us fail to find a counter-example to it outside a specific subject-matter, since logic applies to all subject-matters alike.

Let me sum up the three theses for which I have just been arguing.

I. If an argument has true premises and a heretical conclusion, then a logical rule that would make it out formally valid is simply a bad bit of logic.

II. A correct statement of a logical rule will not be vitiated by a theological counter-example; nor, in order to avoid this, will it expressly advert to theological propositions.

III. Whenever a logical form is shown to be invalid by a theological counter-example, we could if we were clever enough construct a non-theological counter-example.

To meet these requirements, it is clear that a lot of hard work in logic will have to be done. Some indications of the lines on which we should work are to be found in Aquinas. He was not much interested in formal logic for its own sake, as many medieval philosophers were; he never bothered to finish his commentary on the *De Interpretatione* (and what there is of his commentary is of little intrinsic interest, apart from the passage on future contingents) and he never commented on the *Prior Analytics* at all. But in the practice of theological argument he was well aware of the need for having sharp logical tools and a good stock of them; and some of the logical distinctions he finds it necessary to draw, in e.g. his treatises on the Trinity and the Incarnation, are of an importance that could hardly be exaggerated.

First, Aquinas explicitly rejects the two-name theory of predication and truth. Subject and predicate terms have different roles: a subject relates to a *suppositum,* a predicate to a form or nature, and the truth of an affirmative predication consists in con-formity—the form that exists intentionally in the mind, signified by the predicate, answers to the form in the thing (*in-*

dicat rem ita se habere sicut est forma quam de re apprehendit). Taking the subject-predicate distinction seriously gets him over shoals on which two-name theorists like Ockham came to grief: e.g. he is readily able to distinguish pairs like 'Christ came to be a man' (true) and 'The man Christ came to be' (false) or 'Christ in so far as he is a man is a creature' (true) and 'The man Christ is a creature' (false). For 'man' in subject position is a name—here, in apposition to the name 'Christ', it is a name of the eternal *suppositum*; 'man' in predicate position relates rather to the nature by which Christ is a man. Two-name theorists treat this distinction as an idle one at their peril. Nor need one resort to theological examples to bring out the point. With regard to 'Christ became a man' one may be tempted to ask 'which man?'; but the nonsensicality of this sort of question is glaringly apparent in the parallel case of 'The present Prime Minister only recently became Prime Minister'. It would be nonsense to ask which Prime Minister he became; even though it happens to be true that he only recently became Sir Alec Douglas-Home, this is not giving a name of the Prime Minister that the Earl of Home became. In 'became Prime Minister' the noun is not used to name a Prime Minister but to refer to that which formally constitutes someone Prime Minister.

Ockham's attempt to bring 'becomes' propositions within the scope of the two-name theory is a desperate one. He begins by expanding 'Socrates became a philosopher' into 'First of all Socrates was not a philosopher and then he was a philosopher': fair enough. But then he says that of this expanded form the first clause is true because of all the contemporary philosophers that Socrates wasn't, and the second half because of the philosopher that he eventually was, namely Socrates; and this is manifest nonsense.

Another point where the two-name theory is at fault is over the thesis that if two terms apply to the same thing, then as logical subjects they admit of the same predications. A two-name theorist is committed to this thesis by his view of truth. Aquinas states this thesis (Ia, q. 40, art. 1, 3) but only to reject it. What can be truly predicated depends not only on what the subject-term signifies but also on the *modus significandi* of the subject-term. In view of the many headaches that the nominalist principle about identity has caused in modern logic, a modern logician need not be so confident of its truth as to be sure Aquinas was wrong to reject it. Aquinas here attaches particular importance to the distinction between concrete and abstract terms, even *in divinis* when there is no question of any real distinction between God and Deity, or between the Father and his paternity; for example, predicates expressing acts like begetting or creating can be truly attached only to concrete terms as logical subjects.

There are various other important logical distinctions emphasized by Aquinas, for which there is no room in the two-name theory: for example, the distinction between substantival and adjectival terms. But I hope I have said enough to show how important it is for theology to have a subtle and complex logic of terms; learning a bad, crude doctrine in the logic course may make things easy for the time, but will assuredly lead to confusion and darkness later on in dogmatic theology.

II

NATURAL THEOLOGY

ST. THOMAS' DOCTRINE

OF NECESSARY BEING

PATTERSON BROWN

The purpose of this paper is to clear up several long-standing misinterpretations of St. Thomas Aquinas' views on necessary being.[1] I shall begin by quoting from the works of several reputable philosophers who claim to be expounding and/or criticizing St. Thomas' theory of necessary and contingent existence, but who appear to have misunderstood his writings on this topic. For example, J.J.C. Smart offers the following summary and demolition of what he takes to be Aquinas' so-called cosmological argument:

> Everything in the world around us is *contingent.*
> That is, with regard to any particular thing, it is
> quite conceivable that it might not have existed.
> . . . For a really satisfying explanation of why any-
> thing contingent (such as you or me or this table)
> exists you must eventually begin with something
> which is not itself contingent, that is, with some-
> thing of which we cannot say that it might not have
> existed, that is we must begin with a necessary be-
> ing. So the first part of the argument boils down to
> this. *If anything exists an absolutely necessary being
> must exist. Something exists. Therefore an abso-
> lutely necessary being must exist.*

The Philosophical Review, Vol. LXXIII, 1964, pp. 76–90. Reprinted with the permission of the author and of *The Philosophical Review.*

[1] I am indebted to Mr. P. T. Geach for suggesting to me the general interpretation of St. Thomas' thought which I have attempted to follow out in this essay. My thanks are also due to Professor William E. Kennick for a number of helpful suggestions concerning an earlier version of this paper.

   The second part of the argument is to prove that
a necessarily existing being must be an infinitely
perfect being, that is, God. . . .
   The cosmological argument is radically unsound.
. . . For the first stage of the argument purports to
argue to the existence of a necessary being. And
by "a necessary being" the cosmological argument
means "a *logically* necessary being," i.e. "a being
whose non-existence is inconceivable in the sort of
way that a triangle's having four sides is inconceivable." The trouble is, however, that the concept of a
logically necessary being is a self-contradictory concept. . . . The demand that the existence of God
should be *logically* necessary is thus a self-contradictory one. . . . We reject the cosmological argument, then, because it rests on a thorough absurdity.[2]

As I hope to show, the following assumptions which
Smart has here made are groundless, albeit widely
shared: that St. Thomas thought that everything in
the world around us is or must be contingent; that
Aquinas held that a necessary being must be an infinitely perfect being; and that by "necessary being"
Aquinas meant "logically necessary being." Similar
misconceptions are evident in P. Edwards' exposition:

   This is the third of the five ways of Aquinas. . . .
   All around us we perceive contingent beings. This
   includes all physical objects and also all human
   minds. In calling them "contingent" we mean that
   they might not have existed. . . . To say that there
   is a necessary being is to say that it would be a self-
   contradiction to deny its existence.[3]

   [2] "The Existence of God," *Church Quarterly Review* (1955);
reprinted by A. Flew and A. MacIntyre (eds.), *New Essays in
Philosophical Theology* (New York, 1955), pp. 35–39.
   [3] Editor's Introduction to section entitled "The Existence of
God" by A. Pap and P. Edwards (eds.), *A Modern Introduction*

Again, we may quote R. W. Hepburn's account:

> St. Thomas' Third Way—the argument about "might-not-have-beens"—uses . . . the concepts of "contingency" and "necessity." The contingent is what happens to exist, but need not have existed: necessary being is being that *has* to exist, that cannot *not* exist. . . . We could rephrase the Argument in this way: "The proposition 'God exists' is necessary." That is, it would be contradictory to deny God's existence.[4]

And C. B. Martin is in the same muddle:

> St. Thomas claims that . . . since something does now exist, there must exist a Being for whom it is not possible for it not to exist. . . . The difficulty with [this claim] is . . . that it suggests that God's existence is logically necesssary. That is, it suggests that it does not make sense to say that it is possible that God should not exist. But, surely, we can *understand* what it would be like for God not to exist. What we can understand is a possibility.[5]

As a final example, we may note that Father Copleston has ascribed to the Angelic Doctor the view that "there can be but one necessary being."[6]

A large number of commentators have, like Smart, interpreted the first part of Aquinas' Third Way according to the following schema:

(1) If anything exists, then there must exist a logically necessary being.

(2) Something exists.

to *Philosophy* (Glencoe, 1957), p. 455. I have omitted Edwards' actual statement of what he takes to be Aquinas' argument, as it follows the same lines as Smart's delineation.

[4] *Christianity and Paradox* (London, 1958), p. 171. Hepburn goes on to consider another interpretation of "necessary" which bears greater resemblance to St. Thomas' doctrine.

[5] *Religious Belief* (Ithaca, N. Y., 1959), pp. 151–152.

[6] *A History of Philosophy* (London, 1959), ii, 363.

(3) Therefore: there must exist a logically necessary being.

St. Thomas would have to have been rather artless to defend such an argument. For the most obvious point about it is that the two premises are entirely superfluous. That is to say, if God's existence is supposed to be *logically* necessary, then surely the conclusion will stand on its own. Step (3), in short, itself constitutes the rationalistic version of the ontological argument. So, if this interpretation of Aquinas' demonstration were correct, the Third Way would really be an *a priori* proof merely masquerading as *a posteriori* (cf. n. 42, *infra*).

The foregoing shows a complete misunderstanding of St. Thomas' thought, however. For, to begin with, he writes about necessary beings *other* than God so often in his works that it is hard to imagine how anyone who bothered to check could overlook the point. The most obvious passage on this matter is in the last part of the Third Way itself:

> Therefore, not all beings are merely possible, but there must exist something the existence of which is necessary. But every necessary thing either has its necessity caused by another or not. Now it is impossible to go on to infinity in necessary things which have their necessity caused by another. . . . Therefore we cannot but admit the existence of some being having of itself its own necessity, and not receiving it from another. This all men speak of as God.[7]

This, the very passage which Smart and the others are claiming to expound and discuss, both admits the possibility of a *plurality* of necessary beings, and also explicitly states that a being's necessity can be *caused* by another being. This latter point, one would have thought, conclusively rules out the possibility that by

[7] *Summa Theologica* (hereafter *S.T.*), I, Q. 2, Art. 3.

"necessary being" Aquinas meant "being whose existence is logically necessary." For it would be naive to think that there could be an efficient cause for what is logically necessary. And St. Thomas' admission that there might in principle be many necessary beings should lead one to doubt whether he thought that "*x* exists necessarily" entails "*x* is an infinitely perfect being; that is, God"—Kant to the contrary notwithstanding.

Now we find the following, rather unambiguous, assertion in the *Summa Theologica*: "there are many necessary things in existence."[8] Again, Aquinas speaks of "those necessary things that are created."[9] Further, he mentions "all that is in things created by God, whether it be contingent or necessary."[10] Nor does St. Thomas fail to particularize: "heavenly bodies, with their movements and dispositions, are necessary beings";[11] "in the heavenly bodies, the substantial being . . . is unchangeable";[12] "the heavenly bodies . . . are incorruptible."[13] Further: "the intellectual principle which we call the human soul is incorruptible";[14] "of all creatures, the rational creature chiefly is ordained for the good of the universe, being *per se* incorruptible."[15] Further: "matter . . . is incorruptible, since it is the subject of generation and corruption."[16] And lastly: "it must necessarily be maintained that the angels are incorruptible of their own nature";[17] "the

[8] S.T., I, Q. 44, Art. 1, Obj. 2 (although the passage quoted actually occurs in an Objection, St. Thomas' Reply implicitly accepts its truth); see also Q. 19, Art. 8 and Q. 22, Art. 4.
[9] S.T., I-II, Q. 93, Art. 4, Reply Obj. 3.
[10] S.T., I-II, Q. 93, Art. 4.
[11] S.T., I, Q. 115, Art. 6, Obj. 1 (again, the Reply does not dispute the quoted statement).
[12] S.T., I, Q. 10, Art. 5; cf. also Q. 66, Art. 2.
[13] S.T., I, Q. 75, Art. 6.
[14] *Ibid.*
[15] S.T., I, Q. 23, Art. 7.
[16] S.T., I, Q. 104, Art. 4.
[17] S.T., I, Q. 50, Art. 5.

angels . . . have, as regards their nature, an unchangeable being";[18] "in the form itself [of an angel] there is
no potency to non-being; and so such creatures are
immutable and invariable as regards their being."[19]
It is quite certain, therefore, that St. Thomas held that
celestial bodies, human souls, prime matter, and
angels are one and all necessary beings. And so he
clearly did not think that God alone exists necessarily.

The foregoing implies, as I previously hinted, that
Kant was entirely wrong in his contention that the
cosmological argument subsumes the ontological argument—at least if he intended this polemic to weigh
against St. Thomas. The following well-known passage
from the *Critique of Pure Reason* is simply not germane to Aquinas' natural theology:

> The cosmological proof uses . . . experience only
> for a single step in the argument, namely, to con-
> clude the existence of a necessary being. What
> properties this being must have, the empirical
> premise cannot tell us. . . . If I say, the concept of
> the *ens realissimum* is a concept, and indeed the
> only concept, which is appropriate and adequate to
> necessary existence, I must also admit that neces-
> sary existence can be inferred from this concept.
> Thus the so-called cosmological proof really owes
> any cogency which it may have to the ontological
> proof from mere concepts.[20]

It cannot have been St. Thomas' opinion, at any rate,
that the concept of the *ens realissimum* or *perfectissimum* is the only concept which is proper to necessary existence. For he obviously did not hold that
those necessary beings which are God's creatures are
themselves most real or perfect beings. Kant's celebrated refutation is completely off the mark.

In the light of what has been said, it cannot reason-

[18] *S.T.*, I, Q. 10, Art. 5.
[19] *S.T.*, I, Q. 9, Art. 2.
[20] A606–607, B634–635.

ably be thought that Aquinas considered that a necessary being is one which cannot not-exist. For he of course opined that everything but God is a creature of God; "everything, that in any way is, is from God."[21] And this implies that some necessary things—namely, all of them save God—are created. Some people have held, writes Aquinas, that

> what is necessary has no cause. But [St. Thomas replies] this is manifestly false. . . . There are some necessary things which have a cause of their necessity. But the reason why an efficient cause is required is not merely because the effect can not-be, but because the effect would not be if the cause were not.[22]

So St. Thomas quite openly asserts that necessary things can not-exist, and moreover can have a cause of their (necessary) being. This is just faithful Aristotelianism, since the Philosopher had written that "some things owe their necessity to something other than themselves; others do not, but are themselves the source of necessity in other things."[23] Accordingly, Aquinas states that "to create belongs to God alone; and hence whatever can be caused only by creation [*ex nihilo*] is caused by God alone—viz., all those things which are not subject to generation and corruption."[24] But all creatures, necessary and contingent, began to exist a finite time ago; "God is the Creator of the world in such a way that the world began to be."[25] So the necessary creatures not only can not-be, but in addition they have not everlastingly been. Therefore, it cannot possibly have been St. Thomas' view that "*x* exists necessarily" is equivalent to "it is logically impossible that *x* should not

[21] *S.T.*, I, Q. 44, Art. 1.
[22] *S.T.*, I, Q. 44, Art. 1, Reply Obj. 2.
[23] *Metaphysica*, bk. V, ch. 5.
[24] *S.T.*, I, Q. 47, Art. 1.
[25] *S.T.*, I, Q. 46, Art. 2.

exist." This is stated with clarity by Aquinas in his reply to Aristotle's argument[26] that the presence of necessary beings in the world proves that the world never began to exist:

> Whatever has the power always to be, from the fact of that power cannot sometimes be and sometimes not-be. However, before it received that power [from its creator], it did not exist. Hence this argument [of Aristotle's] . . . does not prove absolutely that incorruptible beings never began to be; it proves that they did not begin according to the natural process by which generable and corruptible beings begin to be.[27]

We must conclude, then, that Aquinas did not hold either that everything in the natural world is contingent, or that a necessary being is one which cannot possibly not-exist, or that any being which is necessary must be the *ens realissimum* or *perfectissimum*.

If it be demonstrated that St. Thomas did not understand by "necessary existence" what he is commonly thought to have understood, then it is incumbent upon me to explain what he did mean by that phrase. And our previous quotations suggest that Aquinas meant by the term "necessary," as applied to beings, that they be neither generable nor corruptible.[28] That is to say, a necessary being is defined as one which cannot come into existence via conglomeration, construction, or (re)formation, and which cannot pass out of existence via deterioration, destruction, or deformation. This notion is obviously derived from Aristotle (see *De Caelo*, Bk. I, Chs. 9–12; *De Generatione et Corruptione*, Bk. II, Ch. 11; *Metaphysica*, Bk. II, Ch. 2,

[26] *De Caelo*, bk. I, ch. 12.
[27] *S.T.*, I, Q. 46, Art. 1, Reply Obj. 2.
[28] It must be borne in mind that "necessary" was for St. Thomas an alethic modality *de re*, not *de dicto*; by "*x* necessarily exists" he did not mean "$N(x$ exists)." Cf. G. H. von Wright, *An Essay in Modal Logic* (Amsterdam, 1951).

Bk. V, Ch. 5, Bk. VI, Chs. 1–4, and Bk. XII, Chs. 1–10). In short, for both Aristotle and Aquinas, *a necessary being is one which cannot undergo any essential change* in any of the ways permitted by the Aristotelian theories of matter and form, potentiality and actuality, and simplicity and complexity. So, as we have already seen (notes 23 and 26), Aristotle thought that a necessary being can have a cause but nonetheless cannot possibly come into or pass out of existence, since to do either would involve a change in the above-mentioned sense. And St. Thomas followed Aristotle in holding that a necessary being could not begin or cease existing by any "natural" process allowed by the Aristotelian physics; but Aquinas added that such beings can come into existence via creation *ex nihilo,* as well as pass out of existence via total annihilation.[29] A necessary being, then, is one which cannot undergo any essential alteration—though all of them but God can undergo accidental change (cf. n. 33).

With regard to the angels, for instance, St. Thomas says the following:

> It must necessarily be maintained that the angels are incorruptible of their own nature. The reason for this is that nothing is corrupted except by the separation of its form from matter. Hence, since an angel is a subsisting form [without any matter], . . . it is impossible for its substance to be corruptible. . . . Therefore, the angel's immateriality is the reason why it is incorruptible by its own nature. . . .
>
> There is a kind of necessary thing which has a cause of its necessity. Hence it is not repugnant to a *necessary or incorruptible being* [my italics] to depend for its being on another as its cause. Therefore, when it is said that all things, even the angels, would lapse into nothing, unless preserved by

[29] See nn. 24 and 27, and *S.T.,* I, Qs. 44–46, 65–66, and 104, as well as Q. 50, Art. 5, Q. 61, Art. 1, and Q. 90, Art. 2.

God, this does not mean that there is any principle of corruption in the angels, but that the being of the angels is dependent upon God as its cause. For a thing is not said to be corruptible because God can reduce it to non-being, by withdrawing His act of preservation; but because it has some principle of corruption within itself, or some contrariety, or at least the potentiality of matter.[30]

For St. Thomas, then, "*x* exists necessarily" entails each of the following propositions: "*x* can undergo no substantial change," "*x* is a subsisting being," *x* is neither generable nor corruptible," and "*x* can come into existence only via creation *ex nihilo,* and can pass from existence only via total annihilation"—none of which, it should be noted, entails "there is an *x.*" Aristotle's doctrine was the same, except that he had not allowed for creation or annihilation:

In its most proper use the predicate "indestructible" is given because it is impossible that the thing should be destroyed, i.e. exist at one time and not at another [subsequent time]. And "ungenerated" also involves impossibility when used for that which cannot be generated, in such fashion that, while formerly it was not, later it is.

What is "of necessity" coincides with what is "always," since that which "must be" cannot possibly "not-be." Hence a thing is eternal if its "being" is necessary: and if it is eternal, its "being" is necessary.[31]

These two quotations show that the Philosopher held that necessary beings are those whose existence is neither generable nor corruptible by any natural proc-

---

[30] *S.T.*, I, Q. 50, Art. 5 and Reply Obj. 3; cf. also Q. 66, Art. 2 and Q. 75, Art. 6, where Aquinas gives parallel arguments for the necessity of celestial bodies and human souls.

[31] *De Caelo,* bk. I, ch. 11; *De Generatione et Corruptione,* bk. II, ch. 11.

ess. All that Aquinas added to this was the notion of a *super*natural beginning or ceasing to be, namely by the creation or annihilation of a necessary thing's entire being, effected by another being.

The distinction between the necessity of God and the necessity of angels, prime matter, souls, or celestial bodies is simply that the latter are all created by God —who is defined for the purposes of St. Thomas' natural theology as the uncreated creator (Aquinas says that his purpose is to demonstrate concerning God "whether He exists, and . . . what must necessarily belong to Him, *as the first cause of all things*").[32] Thus, St. Thomas writes:

> God alone is altogether immutable, whereas every creature is in some way mutable. We must observe . . . that a mutable thing can be so called in two ways: by a power in itself, and by a power possessed by another. For all creatures, before they existed, were possible, not by any created power, since no creature is eternal, but by the divine power alone, inasmuch as God could bring them into being. . . . Therefore, as it was in the Creator's power to produce them before they existed in themselves, so likewise it is in the Creator's power, when they exist in themselves, to bring them to nothing. In this way, therefore, by the power of another—namely, of God —they are mutable, inasmuch as they were producible from nothing by Him, and are by Him reducible from being to non-being.
>
> If, however, a thing is called mutable by a power existing in it[self], in this way also every creature is in some regard mutable. . . . In every creature there is a potentiality to change: either as regards subsantial being, as in the case of corruptible things; or as regards being in place only, as in the case of the celestial bodies; or as regards the order to their end, and the application of their powers to

[32] *S.T.*, I, Q. 12, Art. 12 (my italics).

divers objects, as is the case with the angels; and universally all creatures generally are mutable by the power of the Creator, in Whose power is their being and non-being. Hence, since God is mutable in none of these ways [i.e. neither in Himself (whether essentially or accidentally), nor by the power of another], it belongs to Him alone to be altogether immutable.[33]

The corresponding passage from Aristotle reads as follows:

If something is moved it is capable of being otherwise than as it is. Therefore if [as in the case of the heavenly bodies] its actuality is the primary form of spatial motion [i.e. circular motion], then in so far as it is subject to change, in *this* respect it is capable of being otherwise—in place, even if not in substance. But since there is something which moves [others] while itself unmoved, existing actually, this can in no way be otherwise than as it is. . . . The first mover, then, exists of necessity. . . . [It] cannot be otherwise, but can only exist in a single way.[34]

According to St. Thomas, therefore, there are three sorts of beings. (1) *Contingent beings*: these are non-subsisting; that is, generable and corruptible, as well as mutable in various inessential ways. (2) *Necessary creatures*: these are subsisting beings; that is, ungenerable and incorruptible, but yet are mutable in various ways which do not pertain to their essential being, and in addition they are created *ex nihilo* by another, who could therefore annihilate them. And (3) the *uncreated necessary being*: he is ungenerable and incorruptible, and thus subsists, but is not mutable in any inessential way either; moreover, he is *un*created and therefore cannot be annihilated. Thus God is, as it were, underivatively necessary, whereas

[33] S.T., I, Q. 9, Art. 2; see also Q. 104, *passim.*
[34] *Metaphysica*, bk. XII, ch. 7.

the other necessary beings were created as such by God. And, of course, God also created the contingent creatures—although, "just as accidents and forms and other non-subsisting things are to be said to co-exist rather than to exist, so they ought to be called *con-created* rather than *created* things. . . . Properly speaking, it is subsisting beings [alone] which are created."[35] So all things can come into and pass from existence except God, who is defined as the first being —from which it follows, Aquinas claims, that he is ungenerable, incorruptible, nonannihilable, and entirely immutable.

Let us now return to the first half of the Third Way, in which St. Thomas tries to demonstrate that if anything exists, then at least one necessary being exists:

> We find in nature [some] things that are possible to be and not to be, since they are found to be generated and to be corrupted; and consequently, it is possible for them to be and not to be. But it is impossible for these always to exist, for that which can not-be at some time is not. Therefore, if everything can not-be, then at one time there was nothing [left] in existence. Now, if this were true, even now there would be nothing in existence, because that which does not exist begins to exist only through [the agency of] something already existing. Therefore, if at one time nothing was in existence, it would have been impossible for anything [subsequently] to have begun to exist; and thus even now nothing would be in existence—which is absurd. Therefore, not all beings are merely possible [or contingent], but there must exist something [i.e., at least one thing] the existence of which is necessary [and so forth].[36]

I think that St. Thomas' reasoning here can be para-

[35] *S.T.*, I, Q. 45, Art. 4.
[36] *S.T.*, I, Q. 2, Art. 3.

phrased as follows. Some (but not all) of the things
that we find around us in the world are seen to be
either generating or perishing, and are thus shown to
be inherently corruptible. Thus, mountains are thrust
up only to erode away, animals are born only to grow
old and die whereupon their bodies decompose, clouds
gather and disperse, metal is hammmmered into one or
another shape but subsequently rusts and disinte-
grates, and so on. This is really the crux of the Third
Way, but unfortunately it is very often misunderstood.
The point is not that contingent beings in principle
can not-be; rather it is that they have a built-in *process*
of corruption, an actual *progress* toward non-being. A
typical misconstruction of this point, for example, has
been made by C. B. Martin, who writes that "it is hard
to see how St. Thomas came to assert" that "if a thing
is possible to be and not to be, then at some time that
thing is not."[37] What Aquinas was in fact contending
was that when we see certain things in the world actually being generated, surviving awhile, and finally
succumbing to deterioration, we thereby know that
such things are naturally corruptible or contingent.
And anything which is inherently corruptible must
in fact corrupt, and thus eventually cease to exist.
Again, part of the source is Aristotle:

> It is impossible that the destructible should not at
> some time be destroyed. For otherwise it will al-
> ways be at once destructible and in actuality in-
> destructible, so that it will be at the same time ca-
> pable of always existing and of not always existing.
> Thus the destructible is at some time actually de-
> stroyed.[38]

But now, the Third Way continues, if there existed
only such inherently deteriorating things, then obviously the day would come in which each contingent

[37] *Op. cit.*, p. 151.
[38] *De Caelo*, bk. I, ch. 12.

thing had completed its own built-in process of corruption; and so on that day nothing would remain in existence. Thus, to take a simple analogy, if clocks ceased existing as soon as they ran down, then the time would come when there were no clocks left—unless we also hypothesize some being continually to wind them and/or make new clocks. Similarly, a modern-day St. Thomas might argue, if the Second Law of Thermodynamics is true, then the time must arrive in which entropy is maximal and all energy dispersed. Moreover, if past time be infinite (which, Aquinas says, it would have to be if there were no Creator, since the world cannot have come into existence without a cause),[39] then this day of universal decay and death would already have arrived; for in an infinite amount of time all the individual processes of corruption would have been completed. Now, if indeed this had ever come to pass in the history of the world—namely, that nothing at all existed—then there would still be nothing in being at the present time. Things cannot just have begun to exist again without some cause; so that there can have been no fresh beginning, as it were. But there are obviously many things currently in existence which have thus not utterly corrupted. We must therefore conclude that our earlier premise was wrong; there do not exist *only* inherently deteriorating, contingent things. There must in fact exist some being or beings which by their nature do not progress toward nonexistence. And so, as a preliminary conclusion, Aquinas feels forced to postulate at least one necessary being, that is, at least one being which has no inherent propensity to corrupt. Such a necessary being could then continually cause new corruptible things to come into being as the older ones died off. And indeed, we do find some necessary things in the world around us—for example, human souls, the heavenly bodies, and prime matter (a con-

[39] Cf. *S.T.*, I, Q. 46, *passim*.

temporary St. Thomas might suggest, in place of the
latter pair, the subatomic particles and/or energy
quanta, which are necessary in the Aristotelian sense).

Now, the Third Way continues, not all of the incorruptible beings need be creators; but at least one of
them must be, as otherwise the continually renewed
supply of deteriorating and expiring things cannot be
accounted for. Some of the necessary beings, then, may
themselves be created (cf. n. 22); and we know that
at least one of them must be a creator. The question
now arises: can there be an infinite regress of these
subsisting beings, each having been created by
another? Aquinas' answer to this is no. I pick up the
quotation of the Third Way at the point where we left
it earlier:

> Therefore, not all beings are merely possible, but
> there must exist something [i.e. at least one thing]
> the existence of which is necessary. But every neces-
> sary thing either has its necessity caused by an-
> other, or not. Now it is impossible to go on [re-
> gressing] to infinity in necessary things which have
> their necessity caused by another, as has been
> proved already [in the Second Way] in regard to
> efficient causes. Therefore we cannot but admit the
> existence of some being having of itself its own ne-
> cessity, and not receiving it from another, but rather
> causing in others their necessity. This all men speak
> of as God.[40]

At first sight, the suggestion of uniqueness in the next-
to-last sentence here seems to be a *non sequitur*, since
it has not been demonstrated that there is *only* one
uncreated necessary being. St. Thomas goes on to try
to prove this point, however (I, Q. 3, Arts. 3 and 4,
Q. 11, Art. 3, Q. 44, Art. 1, and Q. 45, Art. 5). So perhaps the disputed sentence could be restated in the
following way: "Therefore we cannot but admit the

[40] *S.T.*, I, Q. 2, Art. 3.

existence of at least one being having of itself its own necessity, not receiving it from another, and which may cause in others their necessity." This seems especially likely in light of the fact that, in the first sentence of the above quotation, Aquinas uses "something" to mean "at least one thing," as we previously noted. It is thus plausible to believe that, in the next-to-last sentence, he employs "some being" to mean "at least one being." Admittedly, this interpretation is *prima facie* difficult to square with the concluding sentence of the demonstration: "This all men speak of as God." I can only suggest that St. Thomas was, in the last two sentences of his Third Way, tacitly presupposing his own subsequent proof regarding uniqueness. Otherwise, I cannot understand why he should have felt obliged to offer that proof at all.

The gist of Aquinas' uniqueness argument, in short, is that the concept "uncreated creator" involves the notion of an identity of *suppositum*, essence, and being; and this triple identity, in turn, involves the notion of uniqueness. A first being's *suppositum* and essence must be identical because a creator must as such be a form without matter, and forms are individuated of themselves. And to add that a first being's existence is the same as its *suppositum-cum-*essence is just to say that it exists of itself, that is, is uncreated. The mistake is often made of thinking that St. Thomas' doctrine of identical essence and being is the same as his doctrine of necessary existence; but this is emphatically not so. Only a being which is both necessary and also uncreated is supposed by Aquinas to have an identity of essence and being. This crucial aspect of the Angelic Doctor's thought comes out in statements like "God alone is Being by virtue of His own essence (since His essence is His being), whereas every creature has being by participation, so that its essence is not its being."[41] In other words, to be a creature (to exist "by participation") is to owe one's existence to another being; whereas to be uncreated (to exist "of oneself") is to own one's own existence, to have it as part of one's own essence. So the identity of God's essence and being by no means implies that he actually exists, but only that his existence would be underived. After all, Aquinas explicitly rejected the idea of basing an ontological argument on the unity of God's essence and being.[42] Since "x is both necessary and uncreated" entails "the *suppositum* of x is identical with the essence of x," it follows that all beings which are both necessary and uncreated must share one and the same *suppositum*—which is to say, must be the same individual. And so, St. Thomas concludes, there can in principle be only one first being, that is, only one God.

My purpose in this essay has been merely to delineate St. Thomas' doctrine of necessary being, and not to criticize it. There are, I think, some very severe difficulties in the Aristotelian notion of necessary existence, as well as in Aquinas' employment of this concept in his natural theology. But we cannot intelligently discuss these issues until we are clear on what the doctrine really was. I hope that this essay has made a step toward that understanding.

[42] See the third argument which he entertains in the *Summa contra Gentiles,* I, ch. 10, together with his reply in ch. 11.

Addendum, 1968: I urge the reader to consult Thomas' *Summa contra Gentiles,* Bk. II Ch. 30, "How Absolute Necessity can exist in created things" (Garden City, N.Y.: Doubleday Image Book, 1956, pp. 85ff.) for an especially clear delineation of Aquinas' views on the question of necessary being.

THE PROOF *EX MOTU*

FOR THE EXISTENCE OF GOD:

LOGICAL ANALYSIS

OF ST. THOMAS' ARGUMENTS

JAN SALAMUCHA

My main reason for considering this subject may seem rather paradoxical. I shall discuss it because I do not know how to deal with it in the framework of traditional logic.

For a long time now I have accepted the view that the so-called traditional logic is unsatisfactory and insufficient for the precise presentation of scientific problems, unless they are restricted to relatively simple ones. Mathematical logic, although it is a comparatively young science, provides us with many new and subtle tools for exact thinking. To reject them is to adopt the attitude of one who stubbornly insists on traveling by stagecoach, though having at his disposal a train or an airplane.[1]

However, although I hold this opinion, it does not

New Scholasticism, Vol. XXXII, 1958, pp. 334–372. Reprinted with permission of the American Catholic Philosophical Association. Translated by Tadeusz Gierymski and Marian Heitzman, of the College of St. Thomas, St. Paul, Minn.

[1] At present I am not the only one in the scholastic camp who holds such an opinion. A similar view was expressed by Fr. Bochenski, O.P. during the last International Thomistic Congress in Prague: ". . . il me parait clair aujourd'hui, bien que j'ai nié autrefois, que la logistique est de nos jours la seule logique formelle scientifique de la deduction. Pour se convaincre qu'il en est ainsi, il suffit de comparer les traités de logistique avec les oeuvres des logiciens de l'ancienne école; ils traitent beaucoup plus des problèmes et d'une manière de beaucoup supérieure à celle des anciens. Surtout au point de vue de la rigeur dans la démonstration la chose est plus qu'évidente."

necessarily follow that I enthusiastically endorse all the views of mathematical logicians.

Too conservative an attitude in logic is particularly dangerous in the philosophical field—much more dangerous than in the other fields of scientific research, for reasons which I will not elaborate here. It results in philosophical activity dropping to such a low level that the philosophers themselves become incapable of realizing it. Philosophy then ceases to be a science; it becomes a *Dichtung,* and what is even worse, this *Dichtung* is so poor that even literary critics refuse to take it seriously. Modern philosophy provides many examples of such deterioration.

Anybody with an inclination for strict reasoning will be struck by the vigor and freshness of the works of the principal medieval philosophers, especially after he has compared them with the turgid writings of many contemporary philosophers.

The great philosophers of the past did not rely exclusively on those weak logical tools left to them by their predecessors. The very problems themselves and their own scientific genius forced them to build rational constructions which went far beyond those of their own time.

Many a time, when I investigated the arguments of Aristotle or St. Thomas, I was unable to reduce them to syllogistic forms. Neither am I able to fit the classical proof for the existence of God given by St. Thomas, and known as the argument *ex motu,* into the syllogistic form or into any other schema of traditional logic.

Because of its subtle and complicated structure, this proof presents very interesting material for the logician. If, in addition, one remembers how poor were the logical tools which St. Thomas had at his disposal, this proof must be recognized as a beautiful pearl in the scientific work of the Angelic Doctor.

Dr. I. M. Bochenski, O.P., Kraków, "La métaphysique et la logique moderne," *Sbornik Mezinarodnich Tomistickych Konferenci, v Praze,* 1932, (Olomouc 1933) 154.

I want my analysis of the proof to be a modest contribution to the laudatory hymn sung by so many distinguished scholars in honor of this great pioneer of Christian philosophical and theological thought.

A General Discussion of the Topic

St. Thomas Aquinas formulated five proofs for the existence of God. Commonly known by the name of "*quinque viae*," they are individually referred to as the proofs *ex motu, ex causalitate, ex contingentia mundi, ex finalitate,* and *ex gradibus perfectionis.* St. Thomas presents all five proofs in the *Summa Theologiae,* I, q. 2, a. 3. In the *Summa contra Gentiles,* I, c. 13, he gives two proofs *ex motu,* one *ex causalitate,* one *ex gradibus perfectionis* and one *ex finalitate;* the proof *ex contingentia mundi* is omitted.

The second proof *ex motu* given in the *Summa contra Gentiles,* is connected with that of *ex contingentia mundi.* For this reason, St. Thomas himself is not satisfied with this proof and closed it with the remark, *Praedictos autem processus duo videntur infirmare.* . . . He then gives explanations stressing the weak points of the proof. It is possible that later this second proof *ex motu* was reformulated, elaborated and presented in the *Summa Theologiae* as the proof *ex contingentia.*[2]

The first proof *ex motu* presented in the *Summa contra Gentiles* is repeated in the *Summa Theologiae* in an abbreviated form; more precisely, it is abbreviated in such a way that it forms a part of the same proof offered in the *Summa contra Gentiles.* I shall submit to logical analysis the first proof *ex motu* given in the *Summa contra Gentiles.*

In the *Summa Theologiae* St. Thomas gives no indication as to the sources of his proofs. In the *Summa contra Gentiles* he refers to Aristotle in both proofs *ex motu,* in the proof *ex causalitate* and *ex gradibus*

[2] *Summa Theologiae* is chronologically posterior to the *Summa contra Gentiles.*

perfectionis; in the proof *ex finalitate* he refers to St. John Damascene and to Averroes.[3] It seems, also, that in the formulation of these proofs, St. Thomas was dependent on St. Augustine, Avicenna and Moses Maimonides.[4] However, in this paper I shall completely disregard the problem of historical sources, and will deal exclusively with the analysis of the argument as given by St. Thomas.

In Christian philosophy, the *quinque viae* of St. Thomas are the principal proofs for the existence of God. In addition to these there is a modern variation of the proof *ex motu,* the "entropic proof," based on the principles of thermodynamics. The different variants of the ontological argument, which still reappear in the writings of some authors, have already been duly refuted by St. Thomas. Although they may have a great psychological value, the so-called moral proofs lack the cogency of strict formal proof.

For these reasons my paper is not merely of an historical nature, particularly in view of the fact that St. Thomas himself considers the proof *ex motu* to be stronger than the others; for him this is the *prima et manifestior via* (1. q. 2. a. 3.). A detailed analysis of the logical structure of the proof will disclose all the suppositions on which it is based and will bring a better understanding of its value and cogency.

A Discussion of the Logical Tools Used in this Paper

I have already said that I am unable to work out the logical analysis of St. Thomas' argument within the framework of traditional logic. Such an analysis requires acquaintance with certain concepts from the calculus of propositions, the theory of relations, and the set theory, as well as a knowledge of the theory of quantifiers. Since I want my paper to be intelligible to

[3] St. Thomas calls Averroes simply by the name of "Commentator."

[4] Cf. F. Ueberweg *Die patristische und scholastische Philosophie* (Berlin, 1928) p. 437.

anyone who is accustomed to abstract thinking, even though he knows none of these theories, I shall explain briefly the concepts used in this paper.

I shall use symbols when reconstructing various parts of St. Thomas' argument because they make it, (1) shorter and clearer (2) free from ambiguity (3) free from stylistic distortions.

I shall use the notation of *Principia Mathematica* of Russell and Whitehead, as it seems to me to be the best one, introducing only very slight changes.[5]

The following concepts are taken from the propositional calculus. Expressed symbolically they will be used invariably throughout this paper.

1. The concept of the logical sum, called also the alternation:

$$p \lor q$$
read: p or q

2. The concept of the logical product:
$$p \cdot q$$
read: p and q

3. The concept of negation:
$$\sim p$$
read: it is not true that p

4. The concept of implication:
$$p \supset q$$
read: if p then q

5. The concept of logical equivalence:
$$p \equiv q$$
read: p is equivalent to q

[5] Although I borrow much from logician Bertrand Russell, this does not imply that I agree with his nominalistic attitude in logic and his materialistic or positivistic tendencies in philosophy. With traditional logic as a common basis, various philosophical systems, no matter how harmonious or disharmonious, could develop equally well. I think that the situation is similar when mathematical logic is the foundation. There is only this difference here, the responsibility is greater.

All these concepts are functors of arguments, the arguments being either propositions or propositional variables.

I stress that: (1) "logical sum," as used here, is true if at least one of its components is true, or if they are both true. (2) "logical product" is true only if both factors are true. (3) "negation" refers to the whole sentence, not to a part of it only. (4) "implication" means that $p \supset q$ is equivalent to $\sim p \vee q$. (5) equivalence is equal to reciprocal implication, i.e., $p \equiv q$ means the same as $p \supset q$ and $q \supset p$.

I use two quantifiers: general and particular.

The general quantifier:

$$[x].\chi(x)$$
read: for all x: χ for x.

The particular quantifier:

$$[\exists x].\chi(x)$$
read: for some x: χ for x or: there is such an x that χ for x or: there exists such an x that χ for x.

It is necessary to digress slightly at this point and to consider the concept of existence since this concept will occur frequently in the following pages.

Scholastic philosophy divides all things (*entia*) into two fundamental groups: real things (*entia realia*) and non-real things (*entia rationis*). A real thing is that which is independent of our cognition and thinking and one on which our cognition and thinking depend. A non-real thing is that which is dependent on our cognition and thinking. In this terminology, the expression: "x exists" means: "x is a real object."

Contemporary philosophers avoid such fundamental divisions; at most, they take note of only certain groups of objects, speaking of physical, psychical, logico-mathematical objects. Hence the notion of existence for them bristles with a variety of meanings.

The poorest in content is the logico-mathematical concept of existence. The positive condition of such an existence is the introduction of a certain object by definition; the negative condition is that of noncontradiction. In this sense, "*x* exists" means: "*x* is introduced by a definition, and *x* is noncontradictory." Something exists physically if it has all the properties characterizing every physical object; something exists psychically if it possesses all the properties of psychical objects, etc. Mathematical logicians assume that the particular quantifier has an existential import. It is evident that this existential import of the particular quantifier varies according to the variance of the existence concept itself, and only the context shows precisely which kind of existence is meant in a given case.

I mentioned previously that I shall use the dot as the symbol of the logical product. Also, following Russell and Whitehead, I shall use dots instead of parentheses to indicate the scope of constants. The following explanation will show the reader how to understand the function of dots.

Principal rules:

(1) Dots put immediately before or after symbols of implication, equivalence, alternation, definitional equality, or immediately after the quantifier, are used instead of parentheses. Dots appearing elsewhere are signs of the logical product.

(2) A greater number of dots has greater scope. However, in order to avoid an excessive number of dots, we divide all cases in which dots are used into three groups:

I. Dots appearing with the signs of implication, equivalence, alternation, definitional equality.
II. Dots appearing after quantifiers.
III. Dots appearing as symbols of the logical product.

Group I is stronger than groups II and III; group II is stronger than group III. Dots appearing at any place, range beyond all sets of dots composed of a lesser number of dots or composed of the same number of dots but belonging to the weaker group. Their scope ends either with the greater number of dots, or with the same number of dots, but belonging to the stronger group or with the end of the expression.

Now I shall mention a few indispensable facts about the theory of relations and the set theory. I shall not enter into any intricate discussion of the concept of relation, but shall take my examples from everyday life.

If x is the father of y, we say that x is in a certain relation to y or that between x and y occurs the relation of fatherhood. If x is the husband of y, then again between x and y occurs a certain relation—matrimonial relation.

We shall denote the fact that between x and y occurs a certain relation in the following way:

$$x \; R \; y$$

If a certain relation R_1 is given, we shall call the field of this relation, the class of all objects among which this relation occurs; I shall denote the field of a given relation by the sign:

$$C'R_1$$

In the examples given above, the class of all fathers and sons (i. e., in this case, the class of all male humans, since every male human, even if he is not somebody's father, is at least somebody's son) is the field of the first relation. The class of all husbands and wives (i. e., the class of all married men and women) is the field of the second relation.

I shall indicate the fact that x belongs to the field of a given relation R, i. e., that it is an element of this field, as follows:

$$x \in C'R$$

The precise definition of this abbreviation is:

Df. 1. $[x, R] \therefore x \in C'R . = : [\exists t] : tRx . \vee . xRt$[6]

The field of a given relation may be a finite or an infinite class.

The concept of infinity was rather vague in the old logic and old mathematics. With the development of the set theory the notion of infinity became much more precise. Today, following Dedekind, we call a set infinite if it is similar to its proper part.[7] If we take, for example, two such sets, as the set of all positive integers

$$1, 2, 3, 4 \cdots$$

and the set of all even positive integers

$$2, 4, 6, 8 \cdots$$

we see that the first set is similar to the second set although the second set is the proper part of the first set. This is due to the fact that, using the one-one relation: $y = 2x$, we can assign some element of the second set to every element of the first set. Therefore, the set of all positive integers is an infinite set.

Some relations are such that they introduce order into their field, i. e., every element of their field has its designated position among the other elements. Thus, for example, the relation "greater than" in the class of real numbers, orders that class. For, of any two different real numbers that we take, one is always

---

[6] In writing definitions I shall connect the *definiens* with the *definiendum* by the sign of equality and put the *definiendum* on the left side of the sign of equality, and the *definiens* on the right. It should be noted that when discussing the concept of the field of relation, I deliberately omitted the problem of the theory of types or semantic categories connected with it, because in this paper we shall deal only with relations whose elements of the domain and counterdomain belong to the same type.

[7] In my use of the expression "proper part" I follow the theorists of the set theory who use the expression "part" as meaning that every object is a part of itself but not a proper part of itself. The notion of proper part implies the existence of a remainder; x is the proper part of y if, and only if, x is contained in y, but y is not contained in x.

greater than the other; and the relation "greater than" decides which of the two has priority over the other. On the other hand, the relation of fatherhood does not order its field because it does not decide whether, for example, the father of x has priority over the father of y or vice versa; a priority might occur here only for some additional reasons.

Relations which order their fields are called ordering relations. I shall denote an ordering relation R_1 in the following way:

$$K(R_1)$$

The field of an ordering relation is called an ordered set.

A relation R_1 is an ordering relation if, and only if, it is: (1) irreflexive, (2) transitive, (3) connected.

A relation R_1 is irreflexive if, and only if, the following condition is satisfied:

$$[x, y] : xR_1y \, . \supset . \, x \neq y^8$$

E. g., the relation of equality is in every respect a reflexive relation because every object is equal to itself. But the relation of fatherhood is an irreflexive relation because nobody is his own father. It should be noted that an irreflexive relation must not be confused with a non-reflexive relation; e. g., on the assumption that not everyone loves himself, the relation: "x loves y" is neither reflexive nor irreflexive.

A relation R_1 is transitive if, and only if, the following condition is satisfied:

$$[x, y, z] : xR_1y \, . \, yR_1z \, . \supset . \, xR_1z$$

---

[8] "$x \neq y$" means: "x is not identical with y." In accordance with this definition describing the ordering relation, I say that only sets composed of at least two elements can be ordered. I am completely omitting the mathematical precise formulations which make possible an ordering of those sets which only contain one element. I am doing it for the following reasons: (1) in connection with St. Thomas' pluralistic conception of the universe, we will deal in this paper only with sets which contain at least two elements; (2) in my opinion, the need for ordering a set, containing one element only, occurs exclusively in the field of mathematics.

E. g., the relation of consanguinity in the direct line is a transitive relation because, if x is a kinsman of y in the direct line and y is a kinsman of z in the direct line, then x is a kinsman of z in the direct line; on the other hand, the relation of fatherhood is an intransitive relation.

It should be noted that, from the fact that a relation is non-transitive, it does not follow that it is intransitive. E. g., on the assumption that it is not true that "friends of our friends are our friends," the relation: "x is a friend of y," is neither a transitive nor an intransitive relation.

A relation R_1 is connected if, and only if, it satisfies the following condition:

$$[x,y] \therefore x \in C'R_1 . y \in C'R_1 . x \neq y . \supset : xR_1y . \lor . yR_1x$$

E. g., the relation "greater than" is a connected relation in the class of real numbers because, for any two different real numbers x and y, there occurs the relation $x < y$ or $y < x$; on the other hand, the matrimonial relation is not a connected relation.

The exact definition of an ordering relation is the following:

Df. 2. $[R] :: K(R) . = \therefore [x,y] : xRy . \supset . x \neq y \therefore$
$[x,y,z] : xRy . yRz . \supset . xRz \therefore [x,y] \therefore x \in C'R . y \in C'R .$
$x \neq y . \supset : xRy . \lor . yRx$

From the fact that a given relation is an ordering relation it follows that it is an asymmetrical relation.

The relation R_1 is asymmetrical if, and only if, the following condition is satisfied:

$$[x,y] : xR_1y . \supset . \sim (yR_1x)$$

E. g., the relation of fatherhood is an asymmetrical relation because nobody is father of his own father. On the other hand, the relation: "x is the brother of y" is not an asymmetrical relation, because in some cases y is also the brother of x, although it could be x's sister.

The negation of asymmetry together with transitivity gives as a result the negation of irreflexiveness: for if

$$[\exists x, y] . xRy . yRx$$

and if also transitivity occurs, then we have *xRx*. This means that, if a relation is an ordering relation, then it is an asymmetrical relation.

It makes sense to speak of a first or last element only in connection with an ordered set. In the case of a non-ordered set the notion of a first or last element has no meaning at all. Formerly, when all concepts of infinity were vague, there was a common opinion that an ordered infinite set could not have both a first and a last element, that it must be open at least from one side; hence it was argued, for example, that, if a certain ordered set had a first and a last element, it was a finite set.

In the light of contemporary mathematical research on infinity, this opinion appears to be erroneous. E. g., the class of all real numbers, included within the limits of $1 \leq x \leq 2$, and ordered in such a way that every following element is greater than the preceding one, is an infinite set although it has a first and last element.

Here I end the description of the logical tools and also my introductory remarks. Without such a lengthy introduction, marginal explanations would have had to be given continuously in the course of the logical analysis itself; this would have spoiled the compactness and clarity of the argument.

The Reconstruction of the Basic Proof

St. Thomas does not present his proof *ex motu* in the form of an inference, but in the form of a proof *modo geometrico*. After giving the basic proof, he proves the validity of the assumptions appearing in it. This basic proof is contained in the text of St. Thomas beginning with the sentence, *Omne quod movetur ab alio movetur,* and ending with the sentence, . . . *ergo necesse est ponere aliquod primum movens immobile.*

The following abbreviations will be used throughout this paper:

1. A constant functor "ϕ" meaning: "is in motion"; so, for example "$\phi(x)$" means "x is in motion."[9]

[9] "Motion" in St. Thomas' usage is an equivocal term. Although the logical sequence of a strict proof is independent of the meaning of the terms used, this meaning is decisive for the contents of the theses appearing in the proof; therefore, it is epistemologically important for the following reasons: (1) the contents of the assumptions, and consequently their acceptance and affirmation, is dependent upon the meaning of the respective terms; (2) Also, the contents of the conclusion, and consequently its cognitive value, depend upon the meaning of the respective terms. Therefore, I think that the concept of motion which appears in the proof should be more accurately discussed, at least in a note.

Following St. Thomas, scholastics use the term "motion" (*motus*) as a synonym of the term "change" (*mutatio*), and they give the classification of change presented in the following diagram.

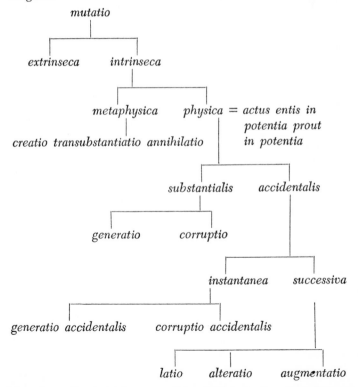

Moreover, they use the term "change" in such a broad sense

2. A constant relation "*R*" meaning "moves"; e. g., "*x R y*" means: "*x* moves *y*."

I have reconstructed the basic proof of St. Thomas in the following way and denoted it with the letter "T."

T. $[x]: \phi(x) . \supset . [\exists t] . tRx \therefore K(R) :: [\exists y] \therefore$
$y \in C'R \therefore [u] : u \in C'R . u \neq y . \supset . yRu ::$
$\supset \therefore [\exists v] \therefore \sim (\phi(v)) \therefore$
$[u] : u \in C'R . u \neq v . \supset . vRu$

Explanation of thesis T: thesis T is a conditional proposition; the antecedent is composed of three factors; the consequent is composed of two factors bound by one particular quantifier.

The factors of the antecedent:

1. $[x]: \phi(x) . \supset . [\exists t] . tRx$ means: "for every *x*, if *x* is in motion, then there is a *t* such that *t* moves *x*";

_____

that it comprises, in addition to all the kinds of change mentioned above, purely psychic activities (*intelligere et velle*).

Which motion does St. Thomas have in mind in his proof? As an example, he mentions local motion: *Patet autem sensu aliquid moveri, utputa solem.* In the second digression, inserted in the argument (from words: *Sciendum autem quod Plato . . . , loc. cit.*) he mentions explicitly that here he excludes purely psychic activities (*intelligere et velle*) from the extension of the concept of motion. Scholastics use the concept of motion in the reconstruction of the proof *ex motu* in such a sense that it comprises all kinds of change indicated in the diagram presented above, with the sole exception of external changes (cf. e. g., J. Gredt, O. S. B., *Elementa Philosophiae Aristotelico-Thomisticae* (Fribourg im B., 1926) II, p. 790.

However, I have serious reasons for believing that St. Thomas uses in his proof a concept of motion limited to physical motion only: (1) He assumes that if something is in motion, it is a body (cf. the following text: *Oportet etiam ipsum (scil. quod movetur) divisibile esse et habere partes, cum omne quod movetur sit divisibile. . . . Si in motoribus et motis proceditur in infinitum, oportet omnia huiusmodi infinita corpora esse, quia omne quod movetur est divisibile et corpus . . . , loc. cit.* (2) He refers to the Aristotelian definition of motion: *actus existentis in potentia secundum quod huiusmodi. . . .*

for greater convenience, I shall denote this factor by "$f1$."

2. "$K(R)$" means: "the relation of moving is an ordered relation"; for convenience, I shall denote this factor by "$f2$."

3. $[\exists y] \therefore y \in C'R \therefore [u] : u \in C'R . u \neq y . \supset . yRu$
On the assumption that the relation R is an ordering relation, this factor means: "in the ordered field of the relation R there exists the first element." I shall denote this factor by "$f3$."

The consequent means: there exists an object which is not in motion and which moves everything which is in motion. If all factors of the antecedent are accepted as true, then the consequent too has to be accepted as true if the thesis T is a true thesis.

Thesis T is a true thesis. In my proof of it I shall denote the principal steps by Arabic numerals in round brackets, placed before the thesis. The numbers and letters in square brackets placed after the theses will indicate the basis from which the given thesis has been deduced.

To avoid repetition of the same antecedent, I shall write down a given antecedent once, and underneath it I shall deduce, one by one, the consequents I need. I shall denote the consequents by Greek letters in round brackets placed before the given consequent. The thesis, denoted by a given number, is composed of the antecedent, written immediately after this number, and of the last consequent. I shall use this symbolic method throughout the entire paper.

Dem.:

$(1) \quad [x] : \phi(x) . \supset . [\exists t] . tRx : \supset : \qquad$ [Assumption]

$(\alpha) \quad [x] : [t] . \sim (tRx) . \supset . \sim (\phi(x))$
$\qquad\qquad\qquad\qquad\qquad$ [Transposition[10]]

---

[10] If from p follows q, then from non-q follows non-p: $p \supset q . \supset . \sim q \supset \sim p$.

(2) $K(R) . \supset \therefore$ [Assumption]
   $[y, u] \therefore$

 (α) $yRu . \supset . \sim (uRy)$:
                         [Df. 2; asymmetry of relation R]
 (β) $u \in C'R . u \neq y . yRu . \supset . \sim (uRy)$ [α]

(3) $K(R) :: [\exists y] \therefore y \in C'R \therefore [u] : u \in C'R . u \neq v .$
                        $. \supset . yRu :.: \supset \therefore$ [Assumption]
             $[\exists v] \therefore$

            $[u] : u \in C'R . u \neq v . \supset .$
 (α) $vRu .$ $[v/y^{11}]$
 (β) $\sim (uRv) .$ $[\alpha, 2]$
 (γ) $\sim (uRv) . vRu$ $[\beta, \alpha]$

(4) $K(R) :: [\exists y] \therefore y \in C'R \therefore [u] : u \in C'R .$
                 $. u \neq y . \supset . yRu :.: \supset \therefore$ [Assumption]
 (α) $[\exists v] \therefore [u] : u \in C'R . u \neq v . \supset . \sim (uRv) \therefore$
                   $[u] : u \in C'R . u \neq v . \supset . vRu$ $[3^{12}]$

(5) $[u, v] : \sim (u \in C'R) . \supset . \sim (uRv)$ [Df. 1]
(6) $K(R) . \supset : [u, v] : u = v . \supset . \sim (uRv)$ [Df. 2]
(7) $K(R) :: [\exists y] \therefore y \in C'R \therefore [u] : u \in C'R .$
                 $. u \neq y . \supset . yRu :.: \supset \therefore$ [Assumption]
 (α) $[\exists v] \therefore [u] . \sim (uRv) \therefore [u] : u \in C'R .$
                      $. u \neq v . \supset . vRu$ $[4, 5, 6^{13}]$

(8) $[x] : \phi(x) . \supset . [\exists t] . tRx \therefore K(R) :: [\exists y] \therefore$
     $y \in C'R \therefore [u] : u \in C'R . u \neq y . \supset . yRu :: \supset \therefore$
                               [Assumption]

 (α) $[\exists v] \therefore \sim (\phi(v)) \therefore$
        $[u] : u \in C'R . u \neq v . \supset . vRu$ $[7, 1]$

(8) is equiform with the thesis T; in this way the proof is complete.

---

[11] The consequent is the repetition of the second factor of the antecedent—a repetition which has been weakened by the elimination of one factor and changed by the substitution of "v" for "y".

[12] If p implies q and r, then p implies q and p implies r: $p \supset q . r : \supset : p \supset q . p \supset r$.

[13] This transition is made in accordance with the following thesis of the propositional calculus: $\sim p \supset q : r \supset . s \supset q : p . \sim s \supset q : \supset . r \supset q$.

Comparison of Thesis T with the Text of St. Thomas

St. Thomas does not formulate the thesis T as precisely as I did; also we shall not find in his text anything similar to my proof of the validity of thesis T; St. Thomas assumes his analogon of thesis T as a thesis which is evident without proof.

What are the differences between thesis T and the text of St. Thomas? As far as the consequent is concerned, the differences are linguistic only; St. Thomas expresses the conclusion as follows: ". . . *ergo necesse est ponere aliquod movens immobile.*" Differences in the formulation of the antecedent are rather great. The first factor is given explicitly by St. Thomas but in a stronger form; and when expressed in symbolic language it reads as follows:

$$T_1 \quad [x] : \phi(x) . \supset . [\exists t] . tRx . t \neq x$$

In my reconstruction I weakened the first factor for two reasons: (1) In its weaker form, when taken together with the other factors of the antecedent of the thesis T, it constitutes a sufficient reason for the consequent. (2) From the first and the second factor of the antecedent of thesis T the thesis T_1 follows:

Dem.:

$$(1) \quad K(R) . \supset : [x,y] : xRy . \supset . x \neq y \qquad [\text{Df. } 2^{14}]$$
$$(2) \quad K(R) \therefore [x] : \phi(x) \supset . [\exists t] . tRx \therefore \supset : [x] : \\ : \phi(x) . \supset . [\exists t] . tRx . t \neq x \quad [1]$$

The second factor is not mentioned explicitly in the basic proof; it can only be conjectured. St. Thomas mentions it explicitly only at the end of his argument, when he is proving the validity of the third factor; and obviously, he does not give any definition of an ordering relation.

In his basic proof, St. Thomas gives a very different formulation to the third factor of the antecedent of

---

[14] Irreflexiveness of the relation R.

thesis T. This formulation is connected with an introduction of an additional factor, which does not appear
in T. Moreover, St. Thomas introduces *explicite* a certain empirical factor: "*Patet autem sensu aliquid
moveri utputa solem. . . .*" Expressed in precise symbolic language this factor reads:

$$[\exists z] . \phi(z)$$

It is stipulated that the truth of this expression is verified empirically. Taking into account the first factor of
the antecedent of T, one can conclude that z, in the
above expression, is an element of the field of the relation R.

St. Thomas formulates the third factor of the basic
proof as follows: the set of elements, preceding the
element z in the ordered field of the relation R, cannot
be an infinite ordered set but only a finite ordered set,
and as such possesses a first element.

In the further course of his argument, St. Thomas
gives three reasons for the validity of his third factor.
The existence of the first element in the field of the
relation R is stated clearly and explicitly in the second
and third reasons, which are logically simple; but the
problem of finiteness or infinity of this field is not mentioned. The first reason is a rather complicated proof
per reductionem ad absurdum. This proof in an abbreviated form runs as follows: if there is no first element in the field of the relation R, then nonsense follows; therefore, there is a first element in the field of
the relation R.

Here it would seem possible to connect the above
reasoning with the argumentation of the basic proof
by the following additional stipulation; if there exists
a first element in the ordered field of the relation R,
then the sector of the field of the relation R, contained
between the empirical element z and the first element
of the set, is not an infinite set. In this way the truth
of the third factor, which is given as the negation of
infinity, would be proved.

In the first proof *ex motu* of the *Summa Theologiae*

(I. q. 2. a. 3), the following transition is directly used: *Hic autem non est procedere in infinitum, quia sic non esset aliquod primum movens. . . .*

All these arguments of St. Thomas involve the belief that, if an ordered set is infinite, then it is non-limited at least from one side, i. e., it has no first element or no last one. This belief is quite understandable in view of the old notion of infinity which was then generally accepted: *infinitum est id, quod limitem non habet.* However, according to the contemporary mathematical theories of infinity, this belief is erroneous since (as I mentioned before), the theory of sets contains ordered infinite sets which have a first and a last element.

Mathematical theories of infinity are still beset with various difficulties, rooted in the very foundations of mathematics; hence, in my opinion, one cannot transfer the results of these examinations into the realm of reality without some qualifications. On the other hand, however, we must not disregard them as though they were simply non-existent. The imposing edifice of science is being built through collective effort, and workers from various fields ought to help each other as well as take into account their respective achievements. Thus, in the present stage of science I cannot accept as correct the statement that, if an ordered set is infinite, then it is non-limited at least from one side.

In view of what has been said, two interpretations of the text of St. Thomas are possible:

1. We can assume that the third factor in the antecedent of T states that the ordered set of antecedents of z is finite. On this assumption this factor would be stronger than the factor concerning the existence of the first element, since, if an ordered set is finite, it has the first as well as the last element, and would consequently also be a sufficient factor. But then the long arguments of St. Thomas concerning the truth of this third factor, would become irrelevant.

2. We can connect the basic proof with the long

argument of St. Thomas concerning the truth of the third factor; but then we will have to assume the third factor in its weaker form, *viz.*, as asserting the existence of the first element.[15]

I have chosen the second interpretation because it is closer to St. Thomas' thinking; but there are additional reasons for preferring it. St. Thomas maintained that it is impossible to prove philosophically that the duration of the world is finite. The possibility of an infinite series of moved movers is often associated with the possibility of an infinite duration of the world, although, evidently, it does not follow from it. Hence, the second interpretation harmonizes better with the possibility of the eternal duration of the world. In addition, the proof is stronger under the second interpretation, for then it is *a fortiori* valid for the finite series. It is for these reasons that the third factor acquired in my reconstruction the form which it possesses in T.

In T, I completely omitted the empirical factor: $[\exists z] . \phi(z)$ because in my formulation, it is logically unnecessary, since the remaining factors are a sufficient reason for the consequent. Even so, this factor still plays a great role, though a logically secondary one: for it indicates that the field of the relation R is something real, and not merely a logical construction. Consequently the element v, the existence of which is asserted in the consequent, exists not only in the logico-mathematical sense, but is a real object. Briefly, in my formulation of T, the empirical factor of St. Thomas is equivalent to the postulate of reality of the field of the relation R.

[15] There is still a third possibility; to make additional, and even possibly fruitful assumptions concerning the type of order of the relation R, e. g. that every section of the field of the relation R determines a leap; then the section of the field contained between any two determined elements, is a finite set. However, it seems to me, that this would be an unnecessary increase in the number of assumptions and therefore I disregard this possibility.

Are all the factors of the antecedent of the thesis T necessary? The proof of thesis T shows at the same time that the antecedent of T constitutes a sufficient reason for the consequent, i. e., that all the factors contained in the antecedent of T suffice to make the assertion of the consequent possible.

Now, however, we have to consider the question whether all those factors are necessary for our implication to obtain? Perhaps some of them could be omitted altogether, or be given a weaker formulation.

Factors one and three constitute a premise of our proof and it is easy to show that both of them are necessary.

Factors two and three alone are not a sufficient reason for the consequent, for functor "ϕ" which appears in the consequent, does not appear in any of them; it appears only in the first factor.

The indispensability of the third factor, in addition to the other two, can be shown in the following way:

Let us consider a class of positive integers ordered according to the relation "greater than" . . . 4, 3, 2, 1. If "$\phi(x)$" means: x is a positive integer, and "xRy" means: x is greater than y, then the first and second factors of the antecedent of T will be satisfied, but the consequent will not be satisfied, since the third factor of the antecedent is not.

On the other hand, the second factor is included in our proof only as a premise for the asymmetrical and irreflexive character of R.

When the relation is an ordering one, it is also asymmetrical, but not vice versa. The assumption that the relation R is an ordering one, is stronger than the hypothesis that it is asymmetrical.[16]

It can be shown that the replacement of the second factor of the antecedent of T by the assumption of the asymmetrical character of R is sufficient to prove the consequent.

---

[16] Being irreflexive follows from its being asymmetrical.

Let us suppose that copies of Raphael's "Madonna di Foligno" were made. Let "$\phi(x)$" mean: x is a copy of the "Madonna di Foligno," and let "xRy" mean: x is an original of y.

Then both the first and the third factor of the antecedent of T are satisfied; R is asymmetrical and—although the relation R is not an ordering one, for it is neither connected nor transitive—the consequent of T will also be true.

If one adopts the minimalistic position of many contemporary mathematical logicians who limit the assumption by a number of arbitrary requirements without paying any attention to their intuitive character, one would have to postulate only the asymmetricity of the relation R in the antecedent of T; it would be unnecessary for it to be an ordering one as well. But then the third factor would lose the intuitive character of the first element and the entire antecedent of T would become less evident.

St. Thomas, in order to secure greater self-evidence, gives up the postulates of logical minimalism.[17]

The Proofs of the Irreflexiveness of Relation R

Having presented the basic proof, St. Thomas concerns himself with the proof of T_1:

$$T_1 \quad [x] : \phi(x) . \supset . [\exists t] . tRx . t \neq x$$

This is a strengthened first factor of the antecedent of T.

He presents us with three proofs for it: *Proof No. 1.* It is found in the text between the words: *Primo sic: Si aliquid movet . . .* and *. . . necesse est ergo omne quod movetur ab alio moveri.*

Here St. Thomas introduces certain new assumptions, involving a new conception of the proper part.

[17] I want to point out that if in our proof we not only disregard the transitiveness and reflexiveness of R, but explicitly deny them, which step would of course be a much stronger one, then such a position would involve some form of occasionalism, not unlike that of Moses Maimonides or Malebranche, or something akin to the *harmoniae praestabilitae* of Leibniz.

He does not formulate a definition of it. This notion could be defined without any special difficulty; but as it would require a prolonged discussion, I shall, following St. Thomas, use this notion without defining it, relying more or less, upon the sense given to it in common parlance.[18]

In order to shorten the reasoning, I shall introduce only one new abbreviation, a constant functor of one argument, "M," with a subscript at the bottom; "$M_x(a)$" means: "a is a proper part of x."

Assumption 1.1 $[x] : \phi(x) . \supset . [\exists a, b] . M_x(a) .$
$. M_x(b)$

Assumption 1.2 $[x] :: [\exists ab] \therefore M_x(a) . M_x(b) \therefore$
$\sim (\phi(a)) . \phi(b) . \lor : \sim (\phi(a)) . \supset .$
$. \sim (\phi(b)) \therefore \supset . \sim (xRx)$

Assumption 1.3 $[x] : \phi(x) . \supset . [\exists t] . tRx$[19]

Dem.:
(1) $[x] :\because \phi(x) . xRx . \supset ::$
$[\exists a, b] ::$
(α) $M_x(a) . M_x(b) \therefore$ [1.1]
(β) $M_x(a) . M_x(b) : \sim (\phi(a)) . \phi(b) . \lor .$
$. \phi(a) . \lor . \sim (\phi(b)) ::$ $[\alpha^{20}]$
(γ) $M_x(a) . M_x(b) \therefore \sim (\phi(a)) . \phi(b) . \lor :$
$: \sim (\phi(a)) . \supset . \sim (\phi(b))$ $[\beta]$

[18] In connection with the notation of a proper part, I would like to mention that a logical theory of relations between things and their proper parts can be found in the Mereology of S. Leśniewski, an exhaustive exposition of which is found in "O podstawach matematyki" (On the Foundations of Mathematics), *Przeglad Filozoficzny*, XXX (1927) 164–206, XXXI (1928) 261–291, XXXII (1929) 60–101, XXXIII (1930) 77–105, XXXIV (1931) 142–170.

[19] This assumption is equiform with the first factor of *T*; it is not formulated explicitly by St. Thomas in his proof, but it appears as a premise in it. Throughout the proof we find the conviction that if anything moves, then either it moves itself, or it is being moved by something else.

[20] β differs from α in that the consequent is strengthened by a certain substitution of the law of excluded middle; this transition proceeds according to the following thesis of the calculus of propositions: $p \supset .\therefore q \supset v . \supset : q \supset v . p$.

$$(2) \quad [x] : \phi(x) . xRx . \supset . \sim \{ [\exists ab] \mathinner{.\,.} M_x(a) .$$
$$. M_x(b) \mathinner{.\,.} \sim (\phi(a)) . \phi(b) . \vee : \sim$$
$$(\phi(a)) . \supset . \sim (\phi(b)) \} \qquad [1.2]$$

$$(3) \quad [x] : \phi(x) . \supset .$$

(α)	$\sim (xRx).$	$[1, 2^{20a}]$
(β)	$[\exists t] . tRx . \sim (xRx).$	$[1.3, \alpha]$
(γ)	$[\exists t] . tRx . t \neq x$	$[\beta^{21}]$

In this way T_1 is proved.

It is necessary however, to make the following remarks:

1. T_1 and the third factor of the antecedent of T without the second factor, are not a sufficient reason for the consequent of T.

We can show this by the following example: Let "$\phi(x)$" mean: x is a member of John Doe's family; "xRy": x has the same name as y. Assuming that there are at least two people in the John Doe family, that one and only one family bears that name, and that at the time in question all the members of that family are males born into it plus their wives, sons and unmarried daughters, thesis T_1 will be satisfied on the basis of the above interpretation. The third factor of the antecedent of T will also be confirmed, but the consequent of T will not.

2. Thesis T_1 follows from the first and second factors of thesis T.[22]

Thus, the transformation of the first factor of the

[20a] If any proposition implies two contradictory propositions then it is false; that transition takes place according to the following thesis of the calculus of propositions: $p . q . \supset r: p . q . \supset \sim r: \supset . p \supset \sim q.$

[21] This transformation is justified not only on the basis of Leibniz's notion of identity (*identitas indiscernibilium*): $[x, y] : x = y . \equiv . [\phi] . \phi(x) \equiv \phi(y)$ but also according to other and more rigorous notions of identity.

[22] Cf. page 189.

antecedent of T into T_1 without changing the other factors, constitutes an unnecessary strengthening of the antecedent. On the other hand, the replacement of the first factor in the antecedent of T by T_1 with the omission of the second factor, will result in the antecedent not being a sufficient reason for the consequent.

In the argument of St. Thomas reformulated symbolically, the first factor of T appears as assumption 1.3. Thus the sole result of the entire argument is that the first factor is strengthened to become T_1.

In the form quoted, therefore, this argument is not connected with thesis T and is completely unnecessary.

We must admit, however, that it contains some sound intuitions. The inexactness arises out of the inadequacy of the logical tools employed by St. Thomas. Namely, if to the assumptions 1.1 and 1.2 we add still another, and a very intuitive one, the entire argument becomes easily transformable into a proof of the irreflexive character of the relation R.

Assumption 1.4 $[x, y] : xRy . \supset . \phi(y)$

Let us retain all the steps of the previous reasoning up to and including 3α:

(4) $[x, y] : xRy . \supset .$

$\quad (\alpha) \qquad\qquad\qquad \sim (yRy) . \qquad\qquad\qquad [1.4, 3\alpha]$

$\quad (\beta) \qquad\qquad\qquad xRy . \sim (yRy) . \qquad\qquad [\alpha]$

$\quad (\gamma) \qquad\qquad\qquad x \neq y \qquad\qquad\qquad\qquad [\beta]$

In this way we obtain the proof of the irreflexiveness of the relation R.

With the help of assumptions: 1.1, 1.2 and 1.4, it is possible to weaken the second factor of the antecedent of T. Acceptance of these three assumptions enables us to replace the second factor of the antecedent of T by the assumption that the relation R is connected and transitive.

Some Remarks Concerning
the Newly Introduced Assumptions

Although the assumptions 1.1 and 1.4 are sufficiently certain intuitively, especially if we keep in
mind that the motion spoken of is a physical one, the
assumption 1.2 lacks evidence, although it is quite
thought provoking.[23]

A weaker premise would be more intuitively evident:

$$[x] \therefore [\exists a, b] : M_x(a) . M_x(b) : \sim (\phi(a)) .$$
$$. \phi(b) . \vee . \phi(a) . \sim (\phi(b)) : \supset . \sim (xRx)$$

or more briefly:

$$[x] : [\exists a, b] . M_x(a) . M_x(b) . \sim (\phi(a) \equiv$$
$$\phi(b)) . \supset . \sim (xRx)$$

But if I add this new and weaker assumption to 1.1
and 1.4, I am no longer able on their strength alone
to prove the irreflexiveness of the relation R.

Proof No. 2.

This proof is contained in the text between the
words: *Secundo probat per inductionem sic. . . .*
Ergo omne quod movetur ab alio movetur.

Logically it is a very simple proof; it possesses an
empirical character and I shall simply call it an empirical proof.

[23] This assumption can be expressed in a much simpler way,
although then it loses much of its thought provoking character.
The antecedent of the assumption 1.2 consists of three factors,
bound by a particular quantifier. The third factor is a substitution instance of the law of excluded middle, and according to
the thesis of the propositional calculus, $q . p \vee \sim p: \supset r \therefore$
$\equiv . q \supset r$ may be omitted in a system which accepts the law of
excluded middle. The first and second factor postulate the existence of two proper parts in the same object x, but from the
existence of one proper part the existence of at least another
proper part follows automatically. A converse implication is also
obvious. Thus the assumption 1.2 is inferentially equivalent to:
$[x] : [\exists a]. M_x(a) . \supset . \sim (xRx)$. What is more, a may also be
imported into the universal quantifier as a result of which we
get the assumption: $[x, a] : M_x(a) . \supset . \sim (xRx)$.

Following Aristotle, St. Thomas classifies motion:

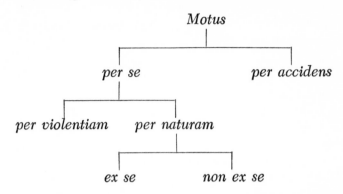

Then briefly, either analytically or empirically, he shows that if anything moves, it is moved by something else.

The conclusion is not quite clear, but it seems to be rather T_1 and not the thesis about the irreflexiveness of R.

This reasoning, the weakest logically, is reductive in character. Its cogency depends on the classification being complete and the empirical interpretations being correct.

Proof No. 3.

It is contained in the text of St. Thomas between the words: *Tertio probat sic . . . et sic nihil movet seipsum.*

I shall introduce some new abbreviations: Let "xA_Sy" mean: in respect to S, x is *in actu* in relation to y; "xP_Sy"—in respect to S, x is *in potentia* in relation to y.

Assumption 2.1 $[x, y, S] : xA_Sy . \supset . \sim (xP_Sy)$

Assumption 2.2 $[x, y] : \phi(x) . yRx . \supset . xP_Ry$

Assumption 2.3 $[x, y] : \phi(x) . yRx . \supset . yA_Rx$

Assumption 2.4 $[x] : \phi(x) . \supset . [\exists t] . tRx$[24]

---

[24] This assumption is not fully formulated by St. Thomas, but not unlike the first proof, it is used as a premise in the proof.

Dem.:

(1) $[x, y] : xA_R y . \supset . \sim (xP_R y)$ [2.1]

(2) $[x, y] : \phi(x) . yRx . \supset . xP_R y . yA_R x$ [2.2, 2.3]

(3) $[x] : \phi(x) . xRx . \supset .$

 (α) $xP_R x . xA_R x$ [2]

 (β) $\sim (xA_R x . \supset . \sim (xP_R x))[\alpha]$

(4) $[x] : xA_R x . \supset . \sim (xP_R x)$ [1]

(5) $[x] \therefore \phi(x) . xRx . \supset : xA_R x . \supset . \sim (xP_R x)$ [4.2⁵]

(6) $[x] : \phi(x) . \supset . \sim (xRx)$ [5, 3²⁶]

(7) $[x] : \phi(x) . \supset . [\exists t] . tRx . \sim (xRx)$ [2.4, 6]

(8) $[x] : \phi(x) . \supset . [\exists t] . tRx . t \neq x$ [7]

All the remarks I made about the first proof, except those referring exclusively to the assumptions involved in it, are applicable here.

I would like to stress that it is this proof alone that we find repeated in the *Summa Theologiae*.

If we omit the empirical proof, then the result of the remaining two which apparently refer to thesis T_1, may be summarized as follows: The set of assumptions 1.1, 1.2, 1.4, or the set of assumptions 2.1, 2.2, 2.3, and 1.4²⁷ eliminates the postulate of the irreflexiveness of the relation R from the second factor of the antecedent of T.

The Proofs for the Existence
of the First Element in the Ordered Field
of the Relation R

St. Thomas now proves that in the ordered field of the relation R there must be a first element. He presents us with three proofs.

---

²⁵ A true proposition follows from any proposition.

²⁶ If two contradictory propositions follow from some proposition, that proposition is false.

²⁷ The set of assumptions: 2.1, 2.2, 2.3, 1.4, may be easily simplified. According to the postulate 1.4, from xRy follows $\phi(y)$, hence we may omit the first factor of the antecedent in 2.2 and 2.3.

The first proof is contained in the text between the words:

Quarum prima talis est: Si in motoribus et motis proceditur in infinitum. . . . Et sic unum infinitum movebitur tempore finito quod est impossibile, ut probatur sexto Physicorum. The reasoning has the form of a *reductio ad absurdum*. I shall introduce new abbreviations: Let "$\sigma(x)$" mean: x is a body,[28] "$\phi_{t_1}(x)$"—t_1 is the time which x is in motion; "t" with a subscript is a temporal variable; "$F(t_1)$"—t_1 is a finite time interval.

St. Thomas introduces the following new assumptions:

3. 1 $[x] : \phi(x) . \supset . \sigma(x)$
3. 2 $[x] : \sigma(x) . \phi(x) . \supset . [\exists t_1] . \phi_{t_1}(x)$
3. 3 $[x, t_2] : \sigma(x) . \supset : \phi_{t_2}(x) \, F(t_2)$
3. 4 $[x, y, t_1, t_2] : xRy . \phi_{t_1}(x) . \phi_{t_2}(y) . \supset . t_1 = t_2$

The following thesis is provisionally accepted in the reasoning and then rejected on account of its paradoxical consequences:

$$\text{Tp} \quad [x, y] : xRy \supset . \phi(x) . \phi(y)$$

We must make the following remarks about Tp.

1. In order to connect the reasoning *per reductionem ad absurdum* with the problem of the existence of the first element in the field of R, it is necessary that from the negation of Tp which at the most may be adjoined to some asserted theses, the existence of the first element in the field of relation R should follow.

2. Thesis Tp does not mean the same as the negation of the existence of the first element in the field of the relation R; it is obvious even from the fact that in Tp we have a functor "ϕ" which does not appear in the thesis asserting the existence of the first element.

3. The assumptions: 3.1, 3.2, 3.3, and 3.4 cannot serve as a link between Tp and the question of the existence of the first element in the field of R, for in

---

[28] St. Thomas characterizes a body as something divisible.

each of them we find some mutually irreducible functors and variables which do not appear either in Tp or in the thesis asserting the existence of the first element in the field of R.

4. To connect Tp with the problem of the existence of the first element we may, at the most, use the first and second factor of the antecedent of T, since they are already asserted.

Thus, from Tp and the first and second factor of the antecedent of T follows the negation of the existence of the first element in the field of R.

Dem.:

(1) $[x, y] : yRx . \supset . \phi(y) . \phi(x)$ [Tp $y/x, x/y$]
(2) $[x, y] \therefore xRy . \lor . yRx : \supset . \phi(x) . \phi(y)$ [Tp, 1]
(3) $[x] \therefore x \in C'R . \supset :$
$$[\exists t] :$$
(α) $tRx . \lor . xRt :$ [Df. 1]
(β) $\phi(x) . \phi(t) .$ [$\alpha, 2$]
(γ) $\phi(x) .$ [β]
$$[\exists u] .$$
(δ) $uRx .$ [γ, f1]
(ϵ) $u \in C'R . u \neq x . \sim (xRu)$
                                    [δ, Df. 1, f2[29]]

(3) is equivalent to the negation of the first element in the field of R.

But from the fact that from Tp, f1 and f2 follows the negation of f3, it does not follow at all that Tp follows from f1 and f2 and the negation of f3. I shall prove it in the following way:

Let us consider a class of integral numbers, positive and negative, zero being included, which is ordered by a relation "greater than": $x > y$:
            $\ldots$ 4, 3, 2, 1, 0, −1, −2, −3, $\ldots$
Let "$\phi(x)$" mean: x is a positive integer; "xRy"—: x is greater than y. f1 and f2 will be confirmed by this interpretation and there is not a first element in such

---

[29] Irreflexiveness and asymmetry of the relation R.

a set, but the thesis Tp will not be true, for, e. g., $-1 > -2$, and it is not true that -1 and -2 are positive integers.

I would also like to add that we shall not be able to get Tp from $f1$ and $f2$ and the assumption about the field of R being infinite; the assumption about the ordered set being infinite is weaker than the negation of the first element in an ordered set. From the denial of the existence of the first element in an ordered set it follows that the set in question is infinite, but not vice versa.

In order to connect the above argumentation *per reductionem ad absurdum* with the question of the existence of the first element in the field of the relation R, we must make use of some new assumption.

It is enough to strengthen the first factor of the assumption of T by adding to it, as a new assumption, its converse, thus making an equivalence out of it.

In order to supplement the reasoning of St. Thomas, I should add this assumption, as it suits the context best.[30]

Assumption 3.5 $[x] : [\exists t] . tRx . \supset . \phi(x)$

Now, from $f2$, negation of $f3$, and 3.5 we can deduce Tp.

Dem.:

(1) $[x.y] : xRy . \supset . x \,\epsilon\, C^{\iota}R . y \,\epsilon\, C^{\iota}R$ [Df. 1]

(2) $\sim \{[\exists y] \,\dot{.}\, y \,\epsilon\, C^{\iota}R \,\dot{.}\, [u] : u \,\epsilon\, C^{\iota}R . u \neq y .$
           $. \supset . yRu \} . \supset : [y] : y \,\epsilon\, C^{\iota}R . \supset .$
      $[\exists u] .$

     (α) $u \,\epsilon\, C^{\iota}R . u \neq y . \sim (yRu) .$[31]

     (β) $uRy .$ [α, Df. 2[32]]

     (γ) $\phi(y) .$ [β, 3.5]

     (δ) $[x,y] : xRy . \supset . \phi(x) . \phi(y)$ [1, γ]

---

[30] In the arguments formulated in colloquial language, such assumptions easily slip in unnoticed. This assumption is deductively equivalent to 1.4.

[31] The consequent is equivalent to the antecedent.

[32] It is a question of the connectivity of R.

From the assumptions: 3.1, 3.2, 3.3, 3.4, thesis Tp and the second factor of the antecedent of T, follow certain consequences, which according to St. Thomas are unacceptable.

Dem.:

(1)　$[x, y] \therefore xRy . \lor . yRx : \supset . \phi(x) . \phi(y)$　　　[Tp]

(2)　$[x] :: x \epsilon C'R . \supset . \therefore$

　　　　　　　　　　$[\exists z] . \therefore$

　　(α)　　　　　　　$zRx . \lor . xRz :$　　　[Df. 1]

　　(β)　　　　　　　$\phi(z) . \phi(x) .$　　　$[\alpha, 1]$

　　(γ)　　　　　　　$\phi(x)$　　　　　(β)

(3)　$[x] : x \epsilon C'R . \supset . \sigma(x)$　　　　　[2, 3.1]

(4)　$[x] : x \epsilon C'R . \supset . \sigma(x) . \phi(x)$　　　[3, 2]

(5)　$[x] : x \epsilon C'R . \supset . [\exists t_1] . \phi_{t_1}(x)$　　　[4, 3.2]

(6)　$[x] \therefore x \epsilon C'R . \supset : [t_2] : \phi_{t_2}(x) . \supset .$

　　　　　　　　　　　　　　$. F(t_2)$　[3, 3.3]

(7)　$[x] \therefore x \epsilon C'R . \supset : [\exists t_1] . \phi_{t_1}(x) . F(t_1)$　　[5, 6]

(8)　$[x, y, 't_1, t_2] \therefore xRy . \lor . yRx : \phi_{t_1}(x) .$

　　　　　　　　　　$. \phi_{t_2}(y) . \supset . t_1 = t_2$　[3.4]

(9)　$[x, y, t_1, t_2] : x \epsilon C'R . y \epsilon C'R . x \neq y .$

　　　　　$. \phi_{t_1}(x) . \phi_{t_2}(y) . \supset . t_1 = t_2$　[Df. 2,[33] 8]

In (7) we assert that each element of the field of R moves in time and that the duration of that motion is a finite time interval. In (9) we assert that all the elements of this set move simultaneously. To measure the time during which all the elements are in motion it is sufficient therefore, to measure only one of the elements, (according to (7) it will be a finite time).

In (3) we assert that every element is a body. Thus,

---

[33] It is the question of the connectivity of R. Thesis (9) would be more correct from the logical point of view if the factor: $x \neq y$ was omitted from the antecedent; on the basis of some conceptions of identity (Leibniz's *identitas indiscernibilium*) this can be done easily. I shall not do so for the following reasons: 1) Thesis (9) is quite sufficient for the further deductions. 2) I do not wish to introduce rather difficult problems of identity without being forced to do so, especially as here we have to deal with a temporal factor as well which would bring in various relativistic complications.

if an ordered set of bodies which are in motion and move others is infinite, then that infinite and ordered set of bodies moves in a finite time.

This is impossible, however, on account of the following assumptions:

Assumption 3.6. An infinite body—or even an infinite set of bodies which might be said to form one body *per continuationem* or *per contiguationem*—can not be moving in a finite time interval.

Assumption 3.7. Bodies cannot act at a distance.[34]

From 3.7 it follows that a class of bodies which are in motion and make others move, forms one body at least *per contiguationem*.

From the assumption: 3.7 and 3.6 we got the following thesis:

A. An infinite and ordered set of bodies which are in motion and make others move does not move in a finite interval of time.

From f_1, f_2 and Tp it follows that the ordered field of the relation R has no first element. It is therefore an infinite set.[35] From the assumptions 3.1, 3.2, 3.3, 3.4 together with f_2 and Tp it follows that each element of the field of R is a body.

Thus we get the following thesis:

B. An infinite and ordered set of bodies which are in motion and make others move, moves in a finite interval of time.

B and A are inconsistent. Accepting 3.6 and 3.7, St. Thomas asserts thesis A and rejects thesis B. Acceptance of 3.1, 3.2, 3.3, 3.4, f_1, f_2 and rejection of thesis B necessitates rejection of Tp. Tp follows from 3.5, f_2 and negation of f_3.[36] Rejection of Tp and acceptance of 3.5 and f_2 necessitates rejection of the negation of f_3, i. e., we must assert that in the ordered field of R there is a first element.

This is the subtle and complicated form of the first

[34] This empirical assumption is explicitly formulated by St. Thomas, who makes use of Aristotle's physics here.

[35] Cf. pp. 203–5.

[36] Cf. p. 204.

proof for the existence of the first element in the field of the relation *R*.

The Second and Third Proofs

In addition St. Thomas gives two reasons for the existence of the first element in the field of the relation *R*. They are contained in the text of St. Thomas; the first between the words: *secunda ratio ad idem probandum talis est . . .* and *et sic nihil movebitur in mundo;* the second between the words: *Tertia probatio in idem reddit . . .* and *ergo nihil movebitur.* These are theses borrowed from Aristotelian *Physics.* The conclusion we seek follows from them directly with the help of some slight logical transformations.

Reason 1. In the set of bodies which move and are moved, and are ordered in such a way that each element is in the relation *R* to the following ones, no body can move unless the first element exists among them.

Reason 2. The dependent movers (*moventes instrumentaliter*) can operate only if there is at least one independent mover (*movens principaliter*).

St. Thomas makes it quite explicit that the relation *R* is an ordering one. Of all the three proofs for the existence of the first element in the field of the relation *R*, only the second reason is quoted in the *Summa Theologiae.* With this ends the argument of St. Thomas for the existence of God based upon the phenomenon and concept of motion.[37]

[37] In the argument *ex motu* of St. Thomas, we find these two digressions. The first, occasioned by the first proof of the irreflexiveness of the relation *R*, is contained in the text between the words *Hoc obviat huic rationi . . .* and *Si homo est asinus, est irrationalis.* This digression is logically interesting. St. Thomas emphasizes here that the conditional statement may be true even when the antecedent is false. It is still a far cry from the concept of material implication. It is rather the case of such substitution instances of formal implication which make the an-

Analysis of the Conclusion

The consequent of thesis T asserts the existence of an object which: (1) is not in motion itself; (2) moves every object which is in motion. Since the real existence of the field of the relation *R* is postulated we also assert real existence of that object in the conclusion. However, the uniqueness of that object is not proved. Consequently, all that the conclusion states is that there is at least one such object. It is possible however to deduce from the antecedent of thesis T that only one such object exists. As it goes well beyond the reasoning of St. Thomas, this proof of uniqueness will only be sketched here. Let us assume that there are two different first elements in the co-ordinated field of the relation *R*, say, objects A and B.

If object A is the first element, then

(1) $\qquad [x] : x \epsilon C^{\prime}R . x \neq A . \supset . ARx$

If object B is the first element too, then:

(2) $\qquad [x] : x \epsilon C^{\prime}R . x \neq B . \supset . BRx$

Since both A and B belong to the field of *R* by definition and are not identical, then on account of the connexity of *R* we have:

(3) $\qquad ARB . \vee . BRA$

If it is the case that *BRA* obtains then it cannot be *ARB*. Consequently (1) must be false. The assumption that there are at least two different first elements in the co-ordinated field of the relation *R* leads to a contradiction. Thus there can only be one such object. In the argument *ex motu* we do not postulate that the field of *R* is finite; the argument is valid even if we assume that the field of *R* is infinite. In the light

---

tecedent false. The second digression occasioned by the third proof of the irreflexiveness of the relation *R* is contained in the text between the words: *Sciendum autem quod Plato . . .* and *quod omnino sit immobile secundum Aristotelem*. Here the difference between the Platonic and the Aristotelian concept of motion is indicated.

of this argumentation, it might seem that the world is an ordered set of objects which are in motion and move others, and God is the first element of this unique series. But such a conception of the world is not very plausible.

It would be more plausible to conceive of the universe as consisting of a set of series of objects which are in motion and move others. To continue this topological simile, we should say that those series run along straight and curved lines, and cross each other at various points. They all begin at one point which is God, *Motor Immobilis.*[38]

Then any one of these series can serve as a basis for the argument *ex motu;* it will be designated then more or less univocally (on account of the criss-crossing of those series) by an empirical factor introduced into the reasoning in some form or other.

Summary of the Assumptions

I shall now give a summary of the assumptions involved in the Thomistic proof *ex motu,* omitting those of a general logical nature. The empirical proof of the irreflexiveness of the relation R will also be omitted.

1. $[x] : \phi(x) . \supset . [\exists t] . tRx$
2. $[x, y, z] : xRy . yRz . \supset . xRz$
3. $[x, y] \therefore x \in C'R . y \in C'R . x \neq y . \supset : xRy .$
$$. \vee . yRx$$

A or B[39]

A: 1.1 $[x] : \phi(x) . \supset . [\exists a, b] . M_x(a) . M_x(b)$

---

[38] With such a conception of the world the argument *ex motu* does not entitle us to assert the uniqueness of the First Mover; the proof indicated above shows only that in every coordinated series of bodies which are in motion and impart it to others, there is only one first element; from this it does not follow that all the first elements of the various series are identical. The question would have to be settled along different lines, cf. *Summa cont. Gent.,* I, 42 and *Summa Theol.,* I, 11, 3.

[39] Sets of assumptions accepted alternately are designated by capital Latin letters.

1.2 $[x] \therefore [\exists a, b] : M_x(a) . M_x(b) :$
$$: \sim (\phi(a)) . \phi(b) . \vee .$$
$$. \sim (\phi(a)) . \supset . \sim (\phi(b)) :$$
$$: \supset . \sim (xRx)$$

1.4 $[x, y] : xRy . \supset . \phi(y)$

B: 2.1 $[x, y, S] : xA_S y . \supset . \sim (xP_S y)$

2.2 $[x, y] : \phi(x) . yRx . \supset . xP_R y$

2.3 $[x, y] : \phi(x) . yRx . \supset . yA_R x$

2.4 $[x, y] : xRy . \supset . \phi(y)$

C or D or E

C: 3.1 $[x] : \phi(x) . \supset . \sigma(x)$

3.2 $[x] : \sigma(x) . \phi(x) . \supset . [\exists t_1] . \phi_{t_1}(x)$

3.3 $[x] : \sigma(x) . \supset . [t_2] . \phi_{t_2}(x) . \supset . F(t_2)$

3.4 $[x, y, t_1, t_2] : xRy . \phi_{t_1}(x) . \phi_{t_2}(y) . \supset . t_1 = t_2$

3.5 $[x] : [\exists t] . tRx . \supset . \phi(x)$

3.6   An infinite body, and even an infinite set of bodies which form one body *per continuationem* or *per contiguationem,* cannot move in a finite interval of time.

3.7   Bodies cannot act at a distance.[40]

D: In a set of bodies which are in motion and impart motion to others, co-ordinated together in such a way that each element is in the relation R to the following ones, no body can be in motion if the first element does not exist.

E: Dependent movers (*moventes instrumentaliter*) can act only when there is at least one independent mover (*movens principaliter*).

For those readers who are not too familiar with the symbolic notation, the symbolic formulae are expressed below in ordinary language.

1.   If anything moves, then there is a mover which imparts motion to it.

2.   Relation R is a transitive relation.

3.   Relation R is a connective relation.

---

[40] *Actio in distans* is excluded.

A:1.1 If something is in motion, then it consists of proper parts.

1.2 If in any object x are found two proper parts a and b, such that: 1) a is not in motion and b is in motion, or 2) if a is not in motion, then b is not in motion, then it is not true that object x makes itself move.

1.4 If an object y is moved by another object x, then object y is in motion.

B:2.1 If some object x is, under a certain aspect, *in actu* in relation to some object y, then it is not the case that the same object x may be under the same respect, *in potentia* in relation to the same object y.

2.2 If an object x is in motion and is moved by an object y, then as regards this motion, x is *in potentia* in relation to y.

2.3 If an object x is in motion and moved by an object y, then as regards this motion y is *in actu* in relation to x.

C:3.1 If an object x is in motion, then this object x is a body.

3.2 If some material object is in motion, then a certain time interval is the measure of the continuance of this movement.

3.3 If a material object is in motion, then the measure of the continuance of the motion of this object is a finite time interval.

3.4 The time during which a mover is in motion is identical with the time during which an object moved is in motion.

3.5 If for an object x there is an object t, such that t makes x move, then x is in motion.

The assumptions enumerated above could be simplified without difficulty. As I merely wanted to reconstruct this argument, without making it be more cogent, I did not introduce these simplifications. Also, I wished to avoid depriving the argument of St. Thomas of its intuitiveness and evidency and thus distort its character. Now, however, I feel obliged to remark that the following simplifications are logically unavoidable.

1.   In 1.1, one of the factors within the scope of the existential quantifier in the consequent can be omitted, since the second factor is deducible from the definition of a proper part.

2.   Assumption 1.2 as I already remarked in footnote 23 is inferentially equivalent to:

$$[x, a] : M_x(a) . \supset . \sim (xRx)$$

3.   3.5 is inferentially equivalent to 1.4.

4.   Because of 1.4, the first factor of the antecedent in 2.2 and 2.3 may be omitted, according to the thesis:

$$p \supset q . \supset \therefore q . p . \supset r : \equiv . p \supset r$$

5.   Because of 3.1, the first factor of the antecedent in 3.2 may be omitted for the same reason as above.

The following words of St. Thomas seem sufficient to justify my new approach to this traditional problem: . . . *quamvis scientia divina sit prima omnium scientiarum, naturaliter tamen quoad nos aliae scientiae sunt priores. Unde dicit Avicenna in princ. suae Meta: 'Ordo illius scientiae est ut addiscatur post scientias naturales, in quibus sunt determinata, quibus ista scientia utitur. . . .' Similiter etiam post mathematicam. Indiget enim haec scientia ad cognitionem substantiarum separatarum cognoscere numerum et ordinem orbium celestium, quod non est possibile sine astrologia, ad quam tota mathematica praeexigitur.* (*In Boetii de Trin.* V, 1.)[41]

On account of our contemporary knowledge some slight changes of terminology and modifications in reasons would be required in the above text.

---

[41] [Although divine science is the first of all sciences, other sciences are by nature prior with regard to us. And so Avicenna says at the beginning of his Metaphysics: "Order demands that this science be learned after the natural sciences since it makes use of conclusions determined in them. . . ." Likewise it must be learned after mathematics; for in order to know the separate substances this science needs to know the number and arrangement of the heavenly spheres, which is impossible without astronomy which presupposes the whole of mathematics.]

INFINITE CAUSAL REGRESSION

PATTERSON BROWN

> The whole modern conception of the world is founded
> on the illusion that the so-called laws of nature are the
> explanations of natural phenomena. Thus people today
> stop at the laws of nature, treating them as something
> inviolable, just as God and Fate were treated in past
> ages. And in fact both are right and both wrong:
> though the view of the ancients is clearer in so far as
> they have a clear and acknowledged terminus, while
> the modern system tries to make it look as if *everything*
> were explained.
>
> WITTGENSTEIN, *Tractatus*, 6.371-6.372

Arguments concerning the possibility of an infinite
regress of causes have always played a crucial role in
metaphysics and in natural theology. And of course
this issue was once important in the sciences as well,
namely in Aristotelianism. Indeed, the most influential
reasons which have been adduced by philosophers
and theologians against infinite causal regressions—as,
for example, St. Thomas' well-known Five Ways—
arose directly and explicitly out of Aristotelian scientific considerations; they are meta-physical proofs,
that is, proofs which are supposed to follow on
theorizations in physical science. The gist of them is
that, if there were an infinite regress of causes, then
no adequate scientific explanation would be possible,
and observed phenomena would thus be unintelligible—which consequence is absurd. In this paper I
shall attempt to delineate the medieval elaboration of
this argument, as given by such men as Avicenna,
Averroes, Maimonides, Aquinas, and Duns Scotus.

The Philosophical Review, Vol. LXXV, 1966, pp. 510–525.
Reprinted with the permission of the author and the editors of
The Philosophical Review.

I

The *locus classicus* of the scholastic discussion was the following passage from Aristotle's *Metaphysics*, wherein he claims that a so-called ascending series of any of his four types of cause must have a first member:

> One thing [cannot] proceed from another, as from matter, *ad infinitum*, . . . nor can the sources of movement form an endless series. . . . Similarly the final causes cannot go on *ad infinitum*. . . . And the case of the essence [that is, of formal causes] is similar. For in the case of intermediates, which have a last term and a term prior to them, the prior must be the cause of the later terms. For if we had to say which of the three is the cause, we should say the first; surely not the last, for the final term is the cause of none; nor even the intermediate, for it is the cause only of one. (It makes no difference whether there is one intermediate or more, nor whether they are finite or infinite in number.) But of series which are infinite in this way, . . . all the parts down to that now present are alike intermediates; so that if there is no first there is no cause at all.[1]

Early in the eleventh century, Avicenna drew a distinction, as Aristotle had not, between the causality of a *mover* and that of a *maker*.[2] The latter was then called an "efficient" or "agent" cause, and Aristotle's same line of reasoning was directed against there being an infinite regress of such causes of being (see,

[1] 994a2-19. All quotations from Aristotle will be from R. Mc-Keon (ed.), *The Basic Works of Aristotle* (New York, 1941). "Ascent" in a causal series was defined as proceeding from effect to cause, while "descent" meant proceeding from cause to effect.

[2] Cf. E. Gilson, *History of Christian Philosophy in the Middle Ages* (New York, 1955), pp. 210–212.

for example, Aquinas' Second Way). There was, then, one basic argument which the medieval Aristotelians held to demonstrate that neither efficient, moving, formal, final, nor material causal series can regress infinitely.

It is perhaps commonplace nowadays to assume that the Aristotelian schoolmen were unconditionally opposed to beginningless series, or at least to beginningless causal series. Thus we find W. I. Matson laconically stating that the "contention is defensible only if it is logically impossible for a series to have no first member, . . . such as the series of all negative integers."[3] This criticism is clearly ineffectual against the Aristotelians, none of whom wished to deny that some series—for example, mathematical ones—may have no termini. After all, consider Aristotle's own definition of an infinite quantity: "A quantity is infinite if it is such that we can always take a part outside what has already been taken."[4] The application of this to the series of negative integers is self-evident. As John Hick has realized, however, the claim was in fact limited to causal series: "Aquinas excludes the possibility of an infinite regress of causes, and so concludes that there must be a first cause, which we call God."[5] Even Hick's remark, however, must be considerably qualified if we are to reach any understanding of the argument, for it was only some among causal series which were held to require a first member. In the course of proving that the world might in principle be everlasting, St. Thomas wrote:

> In efficient causes it is impossible to proceed to infinity *per se.* Thus, there cannot be an infinite number of causes that are *per se* required for a certain

[3] *The Existence of God* (Ithaca, N.Y., 1965), p. 59.

[4] *Physics,* 207a8. See also Aquinas, *Summa Theologica,* ed. by A. C. Pegis (New York, 1945), I, Q. 7, Art. 4, Obj. 1 and Reply (hereafter referred to as *ST*).

[5] *Philosophy of Religion* (Englewood Cliffs, N.J., 1963), p. 20.

effect; for instance, that a stone be moved by a stick, the stick by the hand, and so on to infinity. But it is not impossible to proceed to infinity *accidentally* as regards efficient causes. . . . [It is, for example,] accidental to this particular man as generator to be generated by another man; for he generates as a man, and not as the son of another man. For all men generating hold one grade in the order of efficient causes—viz., the grade of a particular generator. Hence it is not impossible for a man to be generated by man to infinity.[6]

The claim is, then, that causal regresses like a's being begotten by b, b's being begotten by c, and so forth, can go on to infinity, whereas causal regresses like z's being moved by y, y's being moved by x, and so forth, cannot. So not only did the Aristotelians admit the possibility of infinite regresses in general (like -1, -2, -3, and so forth, and even—as we shall see—today, yesterday, day before yesterday, and so forth), but they also admitted the possibility of certain infinite *causal* regresses.

It is important to note that it is the composite causal series, and not the individual constituent causes, which Aquinas is contrasting as either *per se* or *per accidens* in the above quotation. Aristotle had of course differentiated between essential and accidental causes, meaning by the latter an accidental attribute of an essential cause;[7] but that is not the distinction to which St. Thomas is here alluding. This is confirmed by Duns Scotus' comment in his presentation of the argument:

It is one thing to speak of incidental causes (*causae*

[6] *ST*, I, Q. 46, Art. 2, Reply Obj. 7.
[7] Cf. *Physics*, 195a27 ff., 196b24-29, and 224a21-36, as well as *Metaphysics*, 1013b29. In St. Thomas' words, "If A is the cause of B *per se*, whatever is accidental to A is the accidental cause of B"—*Summa contra Gentiles* (Garden City, N.Y., 1955), III, ch. 14 (hereafter referred to as *SCG*).

per accidens) as contrasted with those which are intended by their nature to produce a certain effect (*causae per se*). It is quite another to speak of causes which are ordered to one another essentially or of themselves (*per se*) and those which are ordered only accidentally (*per accidens*).[8]

There is, then, a difference between essential and accidental *causes* on the one hand, and essential and accidental *ordering* of causes on the other. Moreover, it is the latter distinction which is supposed to be germane to the impossibility of certain infinite causal regressions; infinite causal regression *per accidens* is said to be possible, while infinite causal regression *per se* is said to be impossible. Scotus fortunately tells us in some detail what was understood by the crucial contrast:

> *Per se* or essentially ordered causes differ from accidentally ordered causes. . . . In essentially ordered causes, the second depends upon the first precisely in its act of causation. In accidentally ordered causes this is not the case, although the second may depend upon the first for its existence, or in some other way. Thus a son depends upon his father for existence but is not dependent upon him in exercising his own causality [that is, in himself begetting a son], since he can act just as well whether his father be living or dead.[9]

[8] *Opus Oxoniense,* I, Dist. II, Q. 1, as found in A. Wolter (ed.), *Duns Scotus: Philosophical Writings* (Edinburgh, 1962), p. 40.

[9] *Ibid.,* pp. 40–41. From this fundamental criterion Scotus then claims to derive two more: that in essentially ordered causes each step must be to a new order of cause, and that a series of *per se* ordered causes must be instantaneous. See also the selection from Scotus' *Tractatus De Primo Principio,* ch. iii, included in A. Freemantle, *The Age of Belief* (New York, 1955), pp. 189 ff. I gather that this analysis of variously ordered series originated with Avicenna, in Bk. VI of his *Metaphysics,* but no copy of that important work has been available to me.

I shall now quote what is perhaps the best scholastic statement of the Aristotelian argument against an infinite regress of essentially ordered causes, as found in Aquinas' *Summa contra Gentiles*:

> In an ordered series of movers and things moved (this is a series in which one is moved by another according to an order), it is necessarily the fact that, when the first mover is removed or ceases to move, no other mover will move [another] or be [itself] moved. For the first mover is the cause of motion for all the others. But, if there are movers and things moved following an order to infinity, there will be no first mover, but all would be as intermediate movers. . . . [Now] that which moves [another] as an instrumental cause cannot [so] move unless there be a principal moving cause. But, if we proceed to infinity among movers and things moved, all movers will be as instrumental causes, because they will be moved movers and there will be nothing as a principal mover. Therefore, nothing will be moved [which consequence is patently false].[10]

II

Before going on to consider this argument in any detail, let us first repudiate perhaps the three most common criticisms of it. The first of these[11] takes off from statements like the following, found in St. Thomas' Second Way: "To take away the cause is to take away the effect. Therefore, if there be no first cause among efficient causes, there will be no ultimate, nor any intermediate, cause."[12] This passage may

[10] I, ch. xiii; cf. *ST*, I, Q. 2, Art. 3, First Way. See also Averroes' version in his *Tahafut Al-Tahafut* (London, 1954), I, the Fourth Discussion.

[11] It may be found, e.g., in Paul Edwards' introduction to the section entitled "The Existence of God," in P. Edwards & A. Pap (eds.), *A Modern Introduction to Philosophy* (Glencoe, Ill., 1957), pp. 450–451.

[12] *ST*, I, Q. 2, Art. 3, Second Way.

seem to contain an equivocation on "taking away the first cause." It is certainly true that, in any causal sequence, to take away any of the earlier causes—in the sense of removing it from the chain altogether—would break the progression; and this would then preclude any of the subsequent members of the series from coming about at all. But if, with regard to any such catena, we take away any first cause—in the sense of denying that any member is first, that is, uncaused—we do not thereby remove any of the links from the causal chain; the progression is not broken, and so the later members are not precluded. In the hand-stick-stone case, for example, we must differentiate between taking away the stick, and denying that the stick is an uncaused cause of the stone's motion. We might thus think that the Aristotelian rejection of an infinite regress of causes rests on an equivocation between "taking away any first cause" (that is, denying that any cause is first) and "taking away one of the causes" (that is, removing one of the members from the causal series).

Even if we could believe that this glaring fallacy could have gone undetected for two millennia, however, it will hardly do as an objection to the argument. For the above-mentioned polemic cannot account for the distinction between essentially and accidentally ordered causal regresses. If Jacob or Isaac or Abraham *vel cetera* had not copulated, this would in fact have precluded Joseph's existence—just as taking away the motion of the stick or the hand would in fact have resulted in the stone's not moving. In both cases a statement of the effect materially implies a statement of all the string of causes (although in neither instance is there a strict implication; the stone could equally well be caused to move by a hand or a foot, just as Joseph could equally well be descended from Adam or a baboon). It seems highly unlikely that Aristotle and the others would have equivocated in contending that there must be a first mover, and yet have avoided exactly the same type of fallacy in admitting that there need not be a first ancestor.

The second standard criticism of the argument is voiced, for example, by Hick, in his retort that time may never have begun. "The weakness of the argument as Aquinas states it," he writes, "lies in the difficulty (which he himself elsewhere acknowledges) of excluding as impossible an endless regress of events requiring no beginning."[13] A similar point is made by W. T. Blackstone, who objects that "it is perfectly conceivable that time has no beginning, and that every event was preceded by an earlier event."[14] Such comments simply cannot be reconciled with the texts. For of course the Aristotelians notoriously held that causal efficacy must be instantaneous rather than chronological. Aristotle says that "the motion of the moved and the motion of the movent must proceed simultaneously (for the movent is causing motion and the moved is being moved simultaneously)."[15] St. Thomas concurs: "It is clear that when a thing moves because it is moved, the mover and the mobile object are moved simultaneously. For example, if the hand by its own motion moves a staff, the hand and the staff are moved simultaneously."[16] After all, it was only on these grounds that Aristotle could argue both for a First Cause and for the perpetuity of the world.[17] This also explains why Aquinas held it to be of no theological concern that we cannot demonstrate

[13] *Op. cit.*, p. 21; the clause in parentheses is footnoted by Hick: *ST*, I, Q. 46, Art. 2, and *SCG*, II, ch. xxxviii.

[14] *The Problem of Religious Knowledge* (Englewood Cliffs, N.J., 1963), p. 164.

[15] *Physics*, 242a23-26.

[16] *Commentary on Aristotle's "Physics"* (New Haven, 1963), Bk. VIII, lec. 2, #892 (hereafter referred to as *On Physics*). Cf. n. 9, *supra*, for Scotus' parallel claim.

[17] Cf. *Physics*, 250b11 ff. and 256a4 ff. Some critics have gone so far as explicitly to claim that Aristotle contradicted himself here; see, e.g., S. van Den Bergh's introduction to Averroes, *op. cit.*, I, xvi.

whether or not the world had a beginning in time (leaving it a matter to be settled by revelation alone).[18] The requirement for a Prime Cause is, he thought, the same in either case, since causal chains are necessarily confined to one instant. This same doctrine was later defended by Descartes when he wrote that "all the moments of [the world's] duration are [causally] independent the one from the other";[19] for, he held, "any motion involves a kind of circulation of matter all moving simultaneously."[20]

The third commonplace objection is found, for example, in the following remark by C. J. F. Williams:

> The flaw in this argument is its use of the term *moventia secunda* in an attempt to prove the impossibility of an infinite series of causes. For not until we know that such a series is impossible can we know that all movers are properly described as either "a first mover" or as "second movers." This, however, is precisely what the argument assumes.[21]

The gravamen of this criticism is, I gather, that to designate anything as a second (intermediate, instrumental, dependent) mover must involve a *petitio principii*, since "second mover" just means "mover dependent for its efficacy on an unmoved mover." This, however, is simply not what the Aristotelians understood by "second mover"; this phrase meant merely "mover dependent for its efficacy on another," with no question-begging stipulation that this other be itself unmoved. In Aquinas' words, "everything which both

[18] *ST*, I, Q. 46, *passim*.
[19] Letter to Chanut, quoted by F. Copleston, *History of Philosophy* (London, 1960), IV, 134.
[20] *Principles of Philosophy*, Pt. T. II, xxxix, as found in G. E. M. Anscombe and P. T. Geach (eds.), *Descartes: Philosophical Writings* (Edinburgh, 1954), p. 217; cf. all of pp. 213–219. For a similar doctrine, cp. Aristotle, *Physics*, 214a25-32, 217a10-19, 242a23, and 267a21-b9.
[21] "*Hic autem* . . . (St. Thomas Aquinas)," *Mind*, LXIX (1960), 403.

moves [another] and is moved [by yet another] has the nature of an instrument."[22] Thus, if the hand pushes a stick, the stick in turn pushes a stone, and the stone in turn pushes a clod, then the stone is called an "intermediate" mover just because it depends on the stick for its efficacy; what makes the stick move, and *a fortiori* whether there is an infinite regress of movers, is entirely irrelevant to the classification of the stone as a second mover. There is therefore no begging of the issue in the very introduction of the phrase "second mover."

III

It is evident that we cannot hope to understand the argument against infinite causal regresses without first getting straight on the supposedly critical contrast between causal series ordered *per se* and those ordered *per accidens*. So let us examine the previously quoted explanation by Scotus that "in essentially ordered series, the second [that is, the posterior] depends upon the first [the prior] precisely in its act of causation." I assume that the entire argument would be laid bare if we fully understood this criterion and its application to the two paradigm cases, propulsion and genealogy.

The criterion delineated by Scotus seems straightforward enough; it is simply that each member of an essential series (except of course the first and last *if* there be such) is causally dependent upon its predecessor for its own causal efficacy regarding its successor. The members are each intermediate (secondary, instrumental, dependent) in the sense discussed above. In an accidental series, however, each member is not dependent upon its predecessor for its own causal efficacy—though it may be dependent in some other regard. Thus a causal series is *per se* ordered if and only if it is throughout of the form: w's being F causes x to be G, x's being G causes y to be H, y's

[22] *On Physics*, Bk. VIII, lec. 9, #1044.

being H causes z to be I, . . . (here $F\hat{x}$, $G\hat{x}$, $H\hat{x}$, and $I\hat{x}$ may be identical or differing functions). A causal series is ordered *per accidens,* however, if and only if it is throughout of the form: w's being F causes x to be G, x's being H causes y to be I, y's being J causes z to be K, . . . (here $G\hat{x} \neq H\hat{x}$ and $I\hat{x} \neq J\hat{x}$, but otherwise $F\hat{x}$, $G\hat{x}$, $H\hat{x}$, $I\hat{x}$, $J\hat{x}$, and $K\hat{x}$ may be identical or differing functions). In other words, the two functions of each individual variable must be identical in the essential case, but must differ in the accidental case.

Consider the paradigm case where one's hand pushes a stick which in turn pushes a stone. This causal series is *per se* because it is the same function of the stick (namely, its locomotion) which both is caused by the movement of the hand and causes the movement of the stone. Again, a series where the fire heats the pot and the pot in turn heats the stew, causing it to boil, is also essentially ordered; for the warmth of the pot is both caused by the warmth of the fire and cause of the warmth of the stew, while the warmth of the stew is both caused by the warmth of the pot and cause of the stew's boiling.

On the other hand, consider the paradigm case of Abraham's begetting Isaac, who in turn begets Jacob. Here the series is accidentally ordered because that function of Isaac (namely, his copulating) which causes Jacob's birth is not caused by Abraham's copulation; the latter results in Isaac's *birth,* whereas it is Isaac's *copulation* which causes Jacob to be born. Genealogical series like the following are thus *per accidens*: Abraham's copulation causes Isaac's birth, Isaac's copulation causes Jacob's birth, Jacob's copulation causes Joseph's birth. Each member has one attribute qua effect (being born) and quite another attribute qua cause (copulating).

Now Aristotle and his followers held as a critically important thesis that the constituent relations in an essentially ordered series are *transitive*. This is, I suggest, the point of Aristotle's statement that "everything that is moved is moved by the movent that is further back in the series as well as by that which immediately moves it."[23] If, to use the standard example, the hand propels the stick and the stick in turn propels the stone, then the hand propels the stone by means of the stick. Again, if the fire heats the pot, which heats the stew, which causes the stew to boil, then the fire causes the stew to boil. St. Thomas makes this point in the following passage:

> If that which was given as moved locally is moved by the nearest mover which is increased, and that again is moved by something which is altered, and that again is moved by something which is moved in place, then that which is moved with respect to place will be moved more by the first thing which is moved with respect to place than by the second thing which is altered or by the third thing which is increased.[24]

Here we have an undisguised claim that "x moves y" is a transitive causal relation.

The Aristotelians claimed such transitivity not only for "x moves y" (moving causation), but also for "x creates y" (Avicennian efficient causation), "y is made out of x" (material causation), "x is the form of y" (formal causation), and "x is the goal of y" (final causation). Maimonides writes:

> A cause must . . . be sought for each of the four divisions of causes. When we have found for any existing thing those four causes which are in immediate connexion with it, we find for these again causes, and for these again other causes, and so on until we arrive at the first causes. E.g., a certain production has its *agens*, this *agens* has again its *agens*, and so on and on until at last we arrive at a

[23] *Physics*, 257a10-12.
[24] *On Physics*, Bk. VIII, lec. 9, #1047.

first *agens,* which is the true *agens* throughout all the intervening links. If the letter *aleph* be moved by *bet, bet* by *gimel, gimel* by *dalet,* and *dalet* by *hé*—and as the series does not extend to infinity, let us stop at *hé*—there is no doubt that the *hé* moves [each of] the letters *aleph, bet, gimel,* and *dalet,* and we say correctly that the *aleph* is moved by *hé.* In that sense everything occurring in the universe, although indirectly produced by certain nearer causes, is ascribed to the Creator. . . . [By parity of reasoning] we arrive at length at that form which is necessary for the existence of all intermediate forms, which are the causes of the present [that is, last] form. That form to which the forms of all existing things are traced is God. . . . The same argument holds good in reference to all final causes.[25]

So, in an essentially ordered series of any type of cause, each member is supposed to be the cause of all those which follow on it, owing to the transitivity of the relations involved. And then, of course, if there is or must be a first member of such series, the transitivity would make it natural to say that the first member was the ultimate cause of every one of the others.

It might be questioned whether these various causal relations are really always transitive. We may suspect that a careful examination of the ordinary uses of, for example, "x moves y" would show it sometimes to be used transitively and sometimes not. But such a discovery would, I think, be irrelevant to the argument, because Aristotle and the others are employing these causal relation statements in refined ways. It can simply be stipulated that "x moves y" and the others be invariably transitive within the Aristotelian scientific model. Nor would this be to use those expressions in ways greatly different from their employment in ordi-

[25] *The Guide for the Perplexed* (New York, 1956), I, ch. lxix.

nary language, for they are commonly—even if perhaps not universally—used transitively.

As a counterpart of the foregoing, the Aristotelians held that the constituent relations in an accidentally ordered causal series are *intransitive*. Thus, regarding the paradigm case of "*x* begets *y*," if Abraham begets Isaac, who in turn begets Jacob, then Abraham clearly does not beget Jacob.

IV

Why was an infinite regress thought to be impossible in essentially ordered series, but not in accidentally ordered ones? It has been widely believed that it was the purported simultaneity in the former case which was held to be decisive.[26] Some of Aquinas' statements in particular might seem to support this interpretation; at one place, for instance, he says:

> It is impossible to proceed to infinity in the order of efficient causes which act together at the same time, because in that case the effect would have to depend on an infinite number of actions simultaneously existing. And such cases are essentially infinite, because their infinity is required for the effect caused by them. On the other hand, in the sphere of non-simultaneously acting causes, it is not . . . impossible to proceed to infinity. And the infinity here is accidental to the causes; thus it is accidental to Socrates' father that he is another man's son or not. But it is not accidental to the stick, in moving the stone, that it be moved by the hand; for the stick moves [the stone] just so far as it is moved [by the hand].[27]

[26] E.g., by Ockham; see his *Quaestiones in lib. I Physicorum,* Qs. 132–136, included in P. Boehner (ed.), *Ockham: Philosophical Writings* (Edinburgh, 1957), pp. 115–125.

[27] *SCG,* II, ch. xxxviii; see *ST,* I, Q. 7, Arts. 3 & 4.

The gist of this argument would seem to be that an instantaneous causal series would have to be essentially ordered, and furthermore that all *per se* ordered series must have a first member. But this is not at all to claim that essentially ordered series must have a beginning just because they are instantaneous; on the contrary, the contention is that instantaneous series must have a beginning just because they are always *per se* ordered. Whatever it is, therefore, that requires essentially ordered causal series to have a first term, we know that it is not their (purported) simultaneity. For example, the argument was not that an infinite series of essentially ordered causes, being instantaneous, would involve an impossible concurrent infinity, whereas an infinite series of accidentally ordered causes, being chronological, would not involve this absurd consequence. For Aristotle and his disciples explicitly state that the argument for a first cause has nothing to do with whether an infinite number of concurrent intermediate causes is possible. Aristotle writes that "it makes no difference whether there is one intermediate or more, nor whether they are infinite or finite in number."[28] St. Thomas concurs, asserting that it does not "make any difference whether there are a finite or an infinite number of intermediates, because so long as they have the nature of intermediate they cannot be the first cause of motion."[29] Finally, we may record Scotus' claim that, "even if the group of beings caused were infinite, they would still depend on something outside the group."[30] I therefore conclude that the argument does not rest on the supposed simultaneity of causal series ordered *per se.* Hence it cannot be simply an application of the well-known

[28] See n. 1, *supra.*
[29] *Commentary on the Metaphysics of Aristotle* (Chicago, 1961), Bk. II, lec. 3, #303.
[30] Wolter, *op. cit.,* p. 42.

Aristotelian doctrine that an actualized infinity is impossible.[31]

An interesting recent proposal by G. E. M. Anscombe and P. T. Geach is that the argument involves a composition or grouping together of the members of the causal chain. Anscombe and Geach suggest the following as a paraphrase of the reasoning involved:

> If *B* is the cause of a process going on in *A*, or of *A*'s coming to be, then it may be that this happens because of a process in *B* that is caused by a further thing *C*; and *C* in turn may act because of a process in *C* caused by *D*; and so on. But now let us lump together the chain of things *B*, *C*, *D*, . . . , and call it *X*. We may predicate of each one of the causes *B*, *C*, *D*, . . . , *and also* of *X* as a whole, that it causes a process in *A* (or the coming-to-be of *A*) in virtue of being *itself* in process of change. But what is it that maintains this process of change in *X*? Something that cannot itself be in process of change: for if it were, it would just be one of the things in process of change that causes the process in *A* (or the coming-to-be of *A*).[32]

Our first reaction to this presentation of the proof might be to object that it commits the fallacy of composition, in that an inference is made from a common property of the parts *B*, *C*, *D*, . . . to *X*'s having that same attribute. It was this maneuver which Hume had in mind when he wrote: "But the whole [chain of causes and effects], you say, wants a cause. I answer that the uniting of these parts into a whole . . . is performed merely by an arbitrary act of the mind, and has no influence on the nature of things."[33] Ockham had raised a similar objection: "I reply that the whole multitude of both essentially and accidentally ordered

[31] See *Physics*, Bk. III, chs. iv–viii.
[32] *Three Philosophers* (Oxford, 1961), pp. 113–114.
[33] *Dialogues Concerning Natural Religion* (New York, 1948), Pt. IX.

causes is caused, but not by some one thing which is part of this multitude, or which is outside this multitude, but one part is caused by one thing which is part of this multitude, and another by another thing, and so on *ad infinitum.*"[34]

It is not at all certain, however, that the Ockhamist-Humean criticism is effective. For although inferences of the form "All the parts of X have the property P, so therefore X has the property P" are not formally valid, yet many are valid in virtue of the meanings of the arguments substituted for "X" and "P."[35] This is the case with, for example, "All the bricks in that wall are red, and so the wall itself is red," and similarly with "Every part of the United States is in the Northern Hemisphere, so therefore the whole U.S. is in the Northern Hemisphere." On the other hand, many such inferences are quite invalid—as, for example, "Every brick in that wall weighs one pound, and so the entire wall weighs one pound," and "Every part of the U.S. is either east or west of the Mississippi, so therefore the whole U.S. is either east or west of the Mississippi." Thus if the Aristotelian argument really is based on an inference of composition, it cannot be rejected out of hand; each such proof must be considered on its own merits.

It seems to me, however, that Anscombe and Geach have introduced a superfluous issue in making the argument appear to rest primarily on an inference of composition. The *working* parts of their version of the proof are merely the following: the whole world, or at least some substantial part of it, X, is "itself in process of change. But what is it that maintains this process of change in X? Something that cannot itself

[34] Boehner, *op. cit.,* p. 124.

[35] I am indebted to Geach for bringing this point to my attention. For recent discussion, see W. L. Rowe, "The Fallacy of Composition," *Mind,* LXXI (1962), 87; Y. Bar-Hillel, "More on the Fallacy of Composition," *Mind,* LXXIII (1964), 125; and R. Cole, "A Note on Informal Fallacies," *Mind,* LXXIV (1965), 432.

be in process of change." The grouping together of
B, C, D, . . . to form *X* is in fact a cog having no
important connection with the clockworks; it is
merely used to prove the truism that the whole *X* is
undergoing change. Now a mainspring composition
argument would be: each part *B, C, D,* . . . of *X* is
moved by another, so therefore *X* itself is moved by
another. But neither Aristotle nor his medieval disciples nor Anscombe and Geach even suggest such an
inference. The only grouping together employed by
the latter pair is the trivial: *B, C, D,* . . . are each
changing, and so *X* is changing. This is a sound composition inference, but hardly succeeds in demonstrating the existence of an unchanging cause of *X*'s
changing.

V

I want now to suggest a reading of the argument
against infinite causal regresses on the basis of our
earlier understanding of the contrast between *per se*
and *per accidens* ordering of causal series. I think that
the substance of the proof was as follows, again using
moving causation as our paradigmatic example. Parallel arguments could obviously be constructed regarding Aristotle's other types of cause, and also regarding
Avicennian efficient causes.

The Aristotelian scientific model stipulates that all
motions are to be given causal explanations, and that
such explanations are to be of the form "*x* moves *y*."
(Compare the analogous Newtonian stipulation that
all accelerations are to be explained in terms of equa-
tions of the form "$F = ma$.") Suppose then that we
observe something, *a*, to be moving, and we wish to
explain this phenomenon by means of the Aristotelian
physics. The explanation must be of the form "*x* moves
a." Suppose further that *a* is moved by *b*, *b* is in turn
moved by *c*, *c* in turn by *d*, and so on indefinitely.
The issue is whether this series can continue *ad in-*

finitum. We now ask, what moves a? Well, it has already been stated that b moves a; so it may be suggested that "b moves a" is the desired explanation of a's motion, the desired value of "x moves a." But this would be an inadequate account of the matter. For b is itself being moved by c, which—owing to the transitivity of "x moves y"—thus yields the implication that a is moved by c, with b serving merely as an instrument or intermediate. But in turn d moves c; and so d moves a. But e moves d; therefore e moves a. And so on indefinitely. Now, so long as this series continues, we have not found the real mover of a; that is to say, we have not found the *explaining* value of the function "x moves a." The regress is thus a vicious one, in that the required explanation of a's motion is deferred so long as the series continues. With regard to any x which moves a, if there is a y such that y moves x, then we must infer that y moves a. And if for any x such that x moves a there were a y such that y moved x (and therefore moved a as well), then no explanation of a's motion would be possible with the Aristotelian model. There would of course be any number of *true* statements of the form "x moves a"—namely, "b moves a," "c moves a," "d moves a," and so forth. But none of these is to count as the Aristotelian *explanation* of a's motion. Nor, it must be noted, is any such explanation given merely by asserting that there is an infinite regress of movers of a. "An infinite regress of movers move a" is not a possible value of the function "x moves a," for the variable in the latter ranges over individuals, not classes (and *a fortiori* not over series, finite or infinite). An uncaused motion, however, is no motion at all; in other words, an inexplicable motion would be an unintelligible motion. There must be, therefore, an unmoved mover of a.

The foregoing case is to be contrasted with giving an explanation of, for example, Jacob's birth. Such an account is to be of the form "x begat Jacob." The complete and unique explanation of that form is that Isaac begat Jacob. We do not get a new value for the function on the grounds that Abraham in turn begat Isaac, since this does not imply that Abraham begat Jacob; on the contrary, it implies that he did not do so. So a full explanation of Jacob's birth can be given regardless of whether his family tree extends back to infinity. An explanation of Isaac's copulation is still required, of course; but that will center on his actions with Rebecca, rather than on his having been sired by Abraham. (The Aristotelians would contend that Isaac's copulation, being a locomotion, must be the termination of an essentially ordered *moving* series. This means that there indeed is a *per se* series which terminates in Jacob's birth, but it does not ascend through Isaac, Abraham, Terah, and so on; rather, it goes back through Isaac's copulation and thence instantaneously back through a series of contiguous movers reaching up to the celestial spheres. Aquinas writes that "whatever generates here below, moves to the production of the species as the instrument of a heavenly body. Thus the Philosopher says that 'man and the sun generate man.'"[36] God is then in turn causally responsible for the locomotion of the heavenly spheres—though not of course by himself changing.[37] In this way each man is supposed to be efficiently caused by God via an essentially ordered series of movers, regardless of whether he has an infinite regress of ancestors in an accidentally ordered genealogy series.)

[36] *ST*, I, Q. 115, Art. 3, Reply Obj. 2; the quotation from Aristotle is from *Physics,* 194b13. See also *ST,* I, Q. 118, Art. 1, Reply Obj. 3, where Aquinas asserts that the act of begetting is "concurrent with the power of a heavenly body."

[37] Aristotle held that God is merely the final cause of the celestial rotations; cf. *Metaphysics,* 1072a19 ff. The medievals tended to abuse Avicenna's distinction (n. 2, *supra*) by saying that God is somehow the efficient cause of that locomotion, though perhaps with the intelligences (angels) as intermediates; see E. Gilson, *The Elements of Christian Philosophy* (New York, 1963), pp. 71–74.

VI

What are we to say of the foregoing argument, once so widely accepted? I want to suggest that its salient feature (aside, of course, from the transitivity of the relevant causal relations) is the quasi-*legalistic* connotation of "cause" which is employed. It is precisely the sense of a cause as *responsible* for its effect—as against its being merely a concomitant of its effect —which entails that *b*'s being moved by *c* renders the *true* statement "*b* moves *a*" unacceptable as the Aristotelian explanation of *a*'s motion. As it were, the *responsibility* for *a*'s motion is passed on back to *c*, and then on back to *d*, and so on back through the transitive series. Hence Aristotle's assertion: "It is clear that everything that is moved is moved by the movent that is further back in the series as well as by that which immediately moves it; in fact *the earlier movent is that which more strictly moves it.*"[38] This seems to be a way of saying that an unmoved mover has some sort of causal *responsibility* in a way that a moved mover has not.

Consider the following case. Mr. Alpha is in his automobile, stopped at an intersection. Immediately behind him sits Mr. Beta in his own car. Behind Mr. Beta is Mr. Gamma, behind whom is Mr. Delta, and so on indefinitely. Suddenly Alpha's car is rammed from the rear, damaging his bumper. So Alpha, desiring to recover the expense of repairing his automobile, accuses Beta of having caused the accident, and brings suit against him. Beta, however, successfully defends himself in court on the grounds that he had himself been rammed into Alpha by Gamma. So Alpha now sues Gamma. But the latter, it turns out, had in turn been rammed by Delta. So Alpha takes legal action against Delta. And so on indefinitely. Now, if this series of

---

[38] *Physics*, 257a10-13; my italics. See also n. 24, *supra*. The etymology of "αἰτί-α" supports my thesis, I think.

rammings extended *ad infinitum,* there would be no one whom Alpha could successfully sue as having caused the dent in his bumper; there would, in short, have been *no* cause for the accident at all. But if there were no cause, no mover, then there would be no effect, no moved, either—which is patently false, since Alpha's bumper *is* dented and his car *was* moved. Therefore there cannot be a regress to infinity of ramming automobiles, but rather someone was the first cause of the whole series of accidents; someone can properly be said to have moved Beta into Alpha, Gamma into Beta, Delta into Gamma, and so on. Therefore there is someone from whom Mr. Alpha can collect his expenses.

In this rather queer argument the legalistic sense of "cause" is manifest; the cause of the damage to Alpha's car will lie wherever legal responsibility lies, in this sense of "cause." It seems to me to be an allied (though not identical) notion of causation which is being employed in the Aristotelian argument against infinite regresses in all *per se* ordered causal series.

If my interpretation of the argument is correct, there arise two questions regarding its soundness: (1) whether it is *proper* in scientific explanation to employ a sense of "cause" as being responsible for its effect, or whether only concomitances may be mentioned; and even if the former be proper, (2) whether there could be any *a priori* guarantee that there will always be a *successful* employment of that sense of causation regarding observed phenomena. But answering these questions would obviously require giving a full analysis of the notions of causation and of explanation in natural science—a task far beyond the scope of this paper. I close the present discussion with the following remarks made in another context by J. L. Austin:

My general opinion about this doctrine is that it is a typically *scholastic* view, attributable, first, to an obsession with a few particular words, the uses of which are over-simplified, not really understood or carefully studied or correctly described; and second, to an obsession with a few (and nearly always the same) half-studied "facts." (I say "scholastic," but I might just as well have said "philosophical"; over-simplification, schematization, and constant obsessive repetition of the same small range of jejune "examples" are . . . far too common to be dismissed as an occasional weakness of philosophers.)[39]

[39] *Sense and Sensibilia* (Oxford, 1962), p. 3. See also the comment in Wittgenstein's *Philosophical Investigations* (Oxford, 1963), #593: "A main cause of philosophical disease—a one-sided diet: one nourishes one's thinking with only one kind of example." One wonders whether the lines of attack mentioned in my last paragraph could be forestalled by elaborating on the next-to-last paragraph of section III above—that is, by means of recently familiar talk about stipulations, conventions, theoretical entities, and the like. So, e.g.: is the Aristotelian God perhaps a theoretical entity in a way not unlike a Newtonian force? Cf. the succinct discussion of "The Nature of Scientific Theory, Illustrated by the Case of Mechanics" in M. Black, *A Companion to Wittgenstein's* Tractatus (Ithaca, 1964), ch. lxxxi.

ST. THOMAS AQUINAS

AND THE LANGUAGE

OF TOTAL DEPENDENCE

JOHN N. DECK

What are the implications of total dependence? What is involved in saying that one thing depends entirely upon another? What can be said in respect to cases of total dependence, and what can not be said?

Before these questions there is a prior one: *Is* there any total dependence, as a matter of fact? We readily observe that in the world one thing depends, or at least seems to depend, upon another. But total dependence, dependence such that everything that the dependent in any way is is due to that upon which it depends—this is not readily observable.

Historically, total dependence has been "seen" almost exclusively in the relation of other things to a first cause, of creatures to God. The relation of other things to a First has been described in this way by Plotinus and St. Thomas Aquinas, among many. Now if God does not exist, or if he exists in such a way that creatures do not totally depend on him there is, perhaps, no actual case of total dependence. Nevertheless, it seems interesting to work out the implications of total dependence, not only because it is the core of a persistently influential view of creatures and God, but because it is at least the limiting case, the abstract pole, of *dependence*, an inescapable feature of the world of which philosophy must take account.

I take total dependence to entail (1) that B is de-

Dialogue, Vol. VI, 1967, pp. 74–88. Reprinted with permission of the author and the editors of *Dialogue: Canadian Philosophical Review—Revue Canadienne de Philosophie*.

pendent upon A, but that A is independent of B (that there is no reciprocity, no reciprocal action), (2) that B is dependent on nothing else than A, and (3) that there is nothing in B which is independent of A.

Total dependence entails non-reciprocity. Some philosophers and theologians have regarded and do regard the relation between God and creatures as one in which there is give-and-take, perhaps "dialogue." Creatures are dependent upon God, but God is also—probably in another way—dependent on creatures. The fact that only dependence, and in some cases interdependence—never total dependence—is *prima facie* observable is an invitation to conceive the creature-God relation as reciprocal. Such treatments, whatever they may have to recommend them, cannot directly concern a discussion of the theoretical implications of total dependence. If, however, such accounts of creature and God proved to be true, they would be strong indications that the consideration of total dependence has no actual application.

Total dependence entails non-reciprocity, but not *vice versa*. Thus in Aristotle's philosophy, according to a plausible interpretation, the "first causes," the prime movents, cause material things to be in motion but are not themselves acted upon by material things—but the material things are based on a "matter" which is not due to the causality of the prime movents. That is to say, requirement (1) is satisfied here but not (2) and not (3).

At first glance, it might seem easy to speak the language of total dependence. If B is to be regarded as totally dependent on A, B can (it would appear) be described in a way that will satisfy the three requirements stated above. But in significant historical instances, I believe it can be shown that thinkers who "meant" to portray things as entirely dependent on a First were not ultimately successful. In Plotinus, for example, there is no reciprocity between the One and the Intelligence. The One is the father, the maker, of the Intelligence. There is not, according to Plotinus' apparent intention, any other cause for the Intelligence but the One. And yet I believe it can be found that there is something in the Intelligence which does not depend on the One.

In this paper I will concentrate upon St. Thomas Aquinas, taking his treatment of creatures as a paramount case of the attempt to speak the language of total dependence. For him, "Everything that in any way is, is from God."[1] For him, creatures are related to God, God is not related to creatures. Everything is dependent upon God, and upon nothing else, as an originative source of existence. But does St. Thomas, after all, have something in the creature which is independent of God? The discussion of this last, specific point will lead us into the technicalities of his doctrine, and into a criticism which can remain largely within the texture of his philosophic vocabulary (Part I). The investigation of St. Thomas's doctrine will reveal, I believe, something that can *not* be said if one wishes to speak the language of total dependence, and this will be developed more generally, and in a less specific idiom, in Part II.

I

For St. Thomas, creation can be taken to mean the "present" dependence of all other things upon God, without reference to a possible temporal beginning of the world. That is to say, it can be taken to mean the simple causal dependence of the creature upon the Creator. (This is the sense in which I will use the word in this paper.) The creature is dependent on God in the sense that the creature is receptive of existence from God. The creature is thus a recipient of existence, and in this way St. Thomas sees a "composition"

---

[1] *Summa Theologiae* I, 44, 1c.; *Contra Gentiles* II, 15. (*Summa Theologiae* will be abbreviated hereafter as *S.T.*; *Contra Gentiles* as *C.G.*)

within the creature in reference to its dependence upon God. The creature, or the substance or *essence* of the creature is a recipient, a potency; the existence of the creature is an act. This composition, the composition of essence and existence, is in the creature itself, and not only in someone's thoughts about the creature. The latter point is often expressed by saying that for St. Thomas there is a "real distinction" between existence and essence in a creature.[2] The creature's existence is a received existence, received from the creator who is unreceived existence, pure existence. This is expressed by saying that in God existence and essence are the same, "not distinct."

What I am interested in is the "picture" presented in St. Thomas's work: God as Existence, creatures as totally dependent on God and dual because of this dependence: composed of existence and essence. The method by which one can hope to see what is "right" or "wrong" with this picture cannot be the method which St. Thomas himself uses to present his doctrine. St. Thomas's statements about the identity of existence and essence in God, and their composition in creatures, occur in many contexts. It will be necessary to attend sufficiently to the context of a statement to ensure that no purely verbal mistake is made about the meaning of the statement. But then it may be necessary to take—not to "wrench"—the statement out of its context, subject it to philosophic analysis, see what it can or must imply, and confront it with other state-

[2] The doctrine of a real distinction between essence and existence in creatures is commonly held to be the kernel of St. Thomas's metaphysics. E.g.: Gilson speaks of "the central place of this thesis in Thomistic metaphysics." *The Christian Philosophy of St. Thomas Aquinas,* (New York) 1956, p. 11; "This doctrine, whose place in Thomism is central . . .", *ibid.,* p. 34. For Maritain, the "real distinction between essence and existence in all that is not God" is "The most fundamental and most characteristic metaphysical thesis of Aristotelianism as re-thought by Thomas Aquinas." *Existence and the Existent,* (New York) c. 1948, p. 35.

ments from other contexts and their implications. A less radical technique will yield something that is basically only a transcription of the doctrine—a collation of mutually supporting and reciprocally clarifying texts which may give the illusion of a basic consistency not actually present.

More specifically, St. Thomas's statements about existence and essence occur in proofs. The internal order of these proofs, what is being concluded to in them, or their interconnection are not necessarily of concern. The proofs will not necessarily be treated as proofs. Individual statements and at times connected statements in them will be taken as manifestations of St. Thomas's view of creatures vis-à-vis God.

Certain central texts in two of St. Thomas's major works, the *Summa Theologiae* and the *Summa Contra Gentiles,* bear upon the composition of existence and essence (substance) in creatures. In these texts there are statements and arguments which treat the existence-essence composition of creatures *in function of the causing of creatures by God.* The exegesis of such statements will lead directly to a confrontation between the existence-essence composition and creation.

(In St. Thomas's texts, these statements and arguments bearing on the causal relation of creatures to God are mingled freely with statements and arguments which treat the existence-essence composition as involved in the "diversification" or "limitation" of being. Although St. Thomas seems to see no difference between the two types of statement, the diversification-limitation perspective is considerably different from the causal. If essence is said to "diversify"[3] or to

---

[3] As in *C.G.* II, 52, 2: "But existence, insofar as it is existence, cannot be diverse: but it can be diversified through something which is in addition to existence; as the existence of a stone is other than the existence of a man."

"limit"[4] existence it would appear that existence is being taken as a logical universal. The relation of essence to existence becomes analogous to the "diversification" and "restriction" of a generic term, such as "animal" by a specific difference, such as "rational," in classical logic.)

Because of the theological nature of the two *Summas*, the existence-essence distinction in creatures occurs first in each of them as something to which allusion is made while treating explicitly the identity of existence and essence in God.

In the *Contra Gentiles* (I, 22, 6), St. Thomas states that if the existence of God is not identical with his essence, it cannot be a part of his essence either, since the divine essence is simple. So if it were not identical with his essence, it would have to be in addition to his essence. But "Everything which is not of the essence of something, and yet belongs to that thing, belongs to it through some cause." On this basis he argues that if God's existence were caused by his essence, then, since it is substantial existence which is in question, this would mean that God would be the cause of his own existence, while if his existence were caused by some other cause, God would not be the first cause.

"Everything which is not of the essence of something, and yet belongs to that thing, belongs to it through some cause." Does this statement reveal anything of St. Thomas's view of the essence-existence situation in creatures? It is true that the focus here is upon God. It is granted that both God's existence and

---

[4] As in *De Potentia* I, 1, 3c.: "The existence of man is limited to the species of man, because it is received in the nature of the species of man, and the same is the case with the existence of horse, or of any creature at all. But the existence of God, since it is not received in anything, is not limited to any mode of the perfection of existing, but has all existence in itself, and so, just as existence taken universally can extend to an infinite number of things, so the divine existence is infinite . . ." Cf. *S.T.* I, 50, 2 ad 4; *C.G.* I, 43, 8.

his essence are uncaused. It is granted that God's existence "belongs" to his essence. The reasoning, in brief, is that what belongs to an essence but is in addition to that essence is caused: God's existence is not caused; God's existence is not in addition to his essence.

But in the context, St. Thomas does not seem to have in mind only the theoretical possibility of existence belonging to something and yet not being of its essence, but the actual state of creatures—as he envisages them. "For those things which are not *per se* one, if they are joined, are necessarily united through some cause. Existence therefore belongs to that essence through some cause . . . Therefore, that essence which acquires existence from another, is not the essence of God." Apparently he refers here to creatures, to which existence belongs through their cause.

Is anything implied about the essence of a creature? The existence, which is not of the essence, belongs to the creature through some cause. What of that which is of the essence? Does that belong to the creature through some cause, or is it causeless?

It is obvious that to say that what is not of the essence is caused does not imply logically that what is of the essence is uncaused. But why single out that which is not of the essence and say precisely that *it* is caused unless a contrast is involved between the caused existence and that which is of the essence, which is just "there," so to speak, uncaused? There appears to be a contrast between what belongs to a thing through a cause and what just belongs—*without a cause*. Can there be anything causeless in a creature?

In the parallel passage in the *Summa Theologiae* (I, 3, 4c), the preliminaries are omitted; a statement that ". . . whatever is in anything in addition to the essence, must be caused . . ." is placed at the head of the argument.[5] This is used to show that "It is neces-

[5] Note that here the word "essence" is used directly, enabling us to avoid the cumbersome circumlocutions needed in dealing

sary that that, the existence of which is other than its essence, have existence caused by another." To possess caused existence and to possess existence in addition to essence, then, go together—and this is the meta-physical situation of a creature. The existence must be caused when it is in addition to the essence. Again, is that which is not in addition to the essence, but rather *is* the essence, uncaused?[6]

A caused existence for an uncaused essence? In *C.G.* II, 52, 6, we read:

> The substance of anything is to it through itself and not through something else; whence to be lucid in act is not of the substance of air, because it is to it through something else. But the existence of any created thing is to it through something else, other-wise it would not be caused. Therefore the existence of no created thing is its substance.

"The substance of anything is to it through itself and not through something else." The meaning here is un-mistakable. A created, caused thing has its existence through something else (its cause), but its substance is to it through itself.[7]

"To it through itself" contrasts with "to it through

---

with the argument from the *Contra Gentiles,* in which the phrase "that which is of the essence" has been employed.

[6] Against the suspicion that a causeless essence, or a causeless what-is-of-the-essence is involved here, it may be objected that St. Thomas's doctrine is that, for caused things, the existence makes the essence to be: the causing of the essence and of what-is-of-the-essence is precisely the causing of existence to accrue to the essence. It must be pointed out that this explana-tion assumes *some* basis for an essence-existence distinction (perhaps potency-act) while it destroys the basis implied in noting that the existence, precisely, belongs to the thing through a cause.

[7] Cf. the following expressions in another argument from this same chapter: "Existence itself pertains to all other things from the first agent by a certain participation. But that which pertains to something through participation, is not the substance of that thing." (*C.G.* II, 52, 9).

something else." Although in the latter expression the "through" expresses causality, St. Thomas probably does not mean that the substance, which is "through" the created thing, is caused by the created thing. The statement is intended to mean, rather, that a created thing "just has" or "just is" its substance.

And yet the whole force of the argument derives from the contrast between "through itself" and "through something else." If there is no distinction intended between the "through itself" and the "through something else," the argument could not begin to prove a distinction between substance and existence. The "through itself" expresses something about the substance which renders substance different from existence in terms of what substance is "through"— which means in terms of cause. Substance is "through" nothing else—that is the point of the contrast. Thus the uncausedness (or self-causedness!) of substance is not just a manner of speaking, but is functional in the argument.

It might be urged that to say that the substance of a created thing is from itself, which phrase would safeguard the thing as an entity distinct from its Creator, need not mean that its substance is uncaused. Perhaps the substance "of itself" is not such that it can be caused or uncaused, since "of itself" a created substance is nothing.[8] But to say that a created substance is in or of itself nothing has, ultimately, one of two meanings: (1) that some "nothing" enters into the composition of created things. This view is indefensible and, once one has moved above the level of imagination, incomprehensible; or (2) that there is no created substance which is not caused. This latter is an obverted way of saying that the created substance

[8] "Each and every created thing, just as it does not have existence, except from another, *and considered in itself is nothing,* in the same way needs to be conserved in the good appropriate to its nature by another." *S.T.* I-II, 109, 2, ad 2. (Italics mine)

is caused, which, in turn, contradicts the statement that the substance of a created thing is "to it through itself."

St. Thomas's account of the creature is thus inconsistent. For the substance or essence of a created thing to be "to it through itself" is incompatible with the total dependence of the creature upon the Creator. The essence-existence composition must be taken, in the light of the three texts discussed, as a composition of the causeless with the caused. As such, it cannot be the composition of a creature, which is meant to be entirely, totally caused.

But even in the face of "the substance of anything is to it through itself and not through something else," it may be objected that St. Thomas's position has nothing to do with causeless essences. Does he not repudiate the notion that there are eternal possibles, possible essences, to some of which God gives existence, enabling them fully to be?[9] Is he not far removed from the imaginational perspective in which essences are "there" (where?) waiting to receive existence? Is it not his position that the essence is nothing "before" it receives existence, that the essence "is" in any sense whatever only while it is receiving existence?[10] In the case of essence and existence there is no receptor prior to the receiving.[11] Existence actuates *now* a substance distinct from existence.

It should be noted that the mere removal of the notion of a temporal priority for essence does not remove the difficulty. The essence might not be "just

[9] Cf. *S.T.* I, 9, 2c; *S.T.* I, 46, 1, ad 1.

[10] *De Potentia* III, 5, ad 2: ". . . before it [the quiddity, the essence] has existence, it is nothing." It should be noted that such statements may tend to give the imaginational picture of a "nothing" which receives existence and so becomes a "something." The notion here would probably be better expressed by saying "there is no essence before it has existence."

[11] "Simultaneously with giving existence, God produces that which receives existence." *De Pot.* III, 1, ad 17.

there" when it is not receiving existence, and still be "just there" "to it through itself" when it is receiving existence.

But is it not plain that the reception of existence is exactly the *causing of essence?* Does not existence, in coming from the cause, constitute its own receptor for itself? Can a doctrine, in which the reception of existence is necessary for an essence to *be* in any sense, justly be charged with involving a notion of causeless essence? Is not Thomas's meaning that the very essentiality of essence is due to existence? As he says himself ". . . all other substances have existence from the first agent: and through this the substances themselves are caused, because they have existence from another." (*C.G.* II, 53, 3). This statement cannot stand with "the substance of anything is to it through itself" (from the immediately preceding chapter in the *Contra Gentiles!*). But is it not closer to what St. Thomas "really meant"?

What is basic here is the belief that the existence of creatures is "received" by the creatures. God creates creatures; creatures receive existence from God. Since the existence of created things is received, it is received by or into some receptor. The creatures "in themselves," then, seem to be recipients of existence. The essence or substance of the creature is a receptor of existence.

Put in the form that "possibles wait for existence," the fundamental belief is crudely expressed. Perhaps the phrase "The substance of a created thing is from itself; its existence is from its creator" is less crude. To say that the existence projects its own receptor appears sophisticated. But in each case the necessity for a receptor is recognized.

This notion is the fundamental metaphysical error in St. Thomas's account. Quite possibly the fact that the instances of causation with which we are familiar are, in St. Thomas's language, cases of a cause acting upon a potential principle, whether a substance or

matter, encourages one to construe creation after the
same fashion. But if to create is to cause *ex nihilo*,[12]
that is, with no matter upon which the cause works,
why is something strictly analogous to matter, a potential principle receptive of existence, being posited?
If it is seen to be absurd that a creator should work
upon a pre-"existent" matter, why is it not seen as
absurd that there should be a potency present to receive existence when existence is being given?

If the creature, or the essence or the substance of
the creature, is considered as a receptor of existence,
a semi-independent term of the creature-Creator relation has been posited. The creature, or its essence or
substance, is being considered as something which
has some shade of being in its own right and receives
existence from the Creator. Notice that it makes little
difference whether we say "and *then* receives" or
"concurrently receives." The assertion that it is constituted as a receptor only by receiving does not ne-
gate the semi-independence of its receptivity.

Therefore, for the same reason that a Creator cannot act on a pre-"existent" matter, he cannot act upon
any "matter," upon any potential principle. If there is
creation, it must be without qualification *ex nihilo*.

St. Thomas holds, however, that the act from the
agent—even when this agent is the Creator—must be
received into a potency:

What is in anything from the agent, must be act:
for it is the role of the agent to make something (to

[12] According to *S.T.* I, 45, 1 ad 3, "ex nihilo" can have two
legitimate meanings when applied to creation. It can refer to
the order of creation: there is no existence of creatures preceding creation. Or it can mean that there is no matter upon which
the creator works, no "material cause": "Something is made
from nothing, that is, it is not made from something." Our concern is with the latter meaning. ". . . creation is the production
of some thing according to its entire substance, presupposing
nothing which is either uncreated or created by anything."
S.T. I, 65, 3c.

be) in act. But it was shown above that all other substances have existence from the first agent: and through this the substances themselves are caused, because they have existence from another. Existence itself, therefore, is in caused substances as a certain act of theirs. That however which act is *in*, is potency: for act, insofar as it is act, is referred to potency. Therefore in any created substance whatever there is potency and act. (*C.G.* II, 53, 3).[13]

In this argument the initial phrase *"what is in anything* from the agent" predetermines the result. At the outset a distinction has been presupposed between "anything" and "what is in it from the agent." The effect of the agent is already being viewed as *in* something—a recipient, a subject, a "matter," and in this Aristotelian atmosphere it is no surprise that, as the effect of the agent is act, that which it is "in" is potency. Now when the agent in question is the first agent, the total cause, is it proper to say that the effect of this agent is *in* anything? The effect of the total cause must be the total caused. How is the total caused in anything?

But *still* it might seem that, according to the text just quoted, God is the total cause and the creature totally caused. ". . . all other substances have existence from the first agent: and through this the substances themselves are caused, because they have existence from another." Is he not saying clearly that *all* that is in the creature is caused by the Creator, since the act (existence) is from the agent (the Creator) and the potency (essence) is caused through the act? This appears also to be in line with a text in which St. Thomas says explicitly that the essence is created:

[13] "First agent" does not mean first in time, but first in order. God is called the first agent because there is no agent in order above him. He is the agent who does not have an agent acting upon *him*. The expression is equivalent to "first cause," which means "uncaused cause."

> Argument: Since therefore the essence of the thing is in addition to its existence, it seems that the essence of the thing is not from God. Reply: It must be said that from the fact that existence is attributed to the essence, not only existence but the essence itself is said to be created: because before it has existence, it is nothing. . . (*De Pot.* III, 5, arg. 2).

The notion of the essence as the recipient of existence is close to the surface here: this text accords perfectly with the picture of the essence as the recipient of the creative influx. Thus, while it affirms that the essence is created, it involves the notion that the essence, as the recipient of the creative influx, is simultaneously constituted by the influx it receives. In effect, this text affirms that the essence is both a recipient and is created.

This is all very well, but it hardly answers the question whether there can be any recipient at all—even a created recipient—of the creative influx. According to what was quoted just above from *C.G.* II, 53, the act, existence, is what is in the creature from the creator. The potency, essence, is the recipient of what "comes" from the agent, that is, *of the effect of the agent.* Now if the total effect of the agent is the act, *and* the potency through the act, how can the potency receive the effect—the total effect—of the agent?

If, on the other hand, the potency is not included in the effect of the agent, the essence is not included in the effect of God, then the essence must be uncaused, uncreated.

In short, it is inconsistent to hold that there is a created recipient of what is in creatures from God. If there must be a recipient, it would have to be the "substance" which is "to the creature through itself and not through another." But this view, in turn, as we have amply shown, is inconsistent with creation altogether. There cannot be a recipient—if we are to have creation, there cannot be an essence in creatures receiving existence from God.

In a widely different context, St. Thomas says something which tends to show that he himself recognizes that the creature cannot be a recipient subject:

> It must be said that not everything which is accepted, is received in some subject, otherwise it could not be said that the entire substance of a created thing is accepted from God, since there is no receptive subject of the entire substance. (*S.T.* I, 27, 2 ad 3)[14]

Exactly. The entire substance of the creature is the effect of the first agent. For the effect of this agent, "there is no receptive subject." Therefore (what is not said here, certainly), the creature can be, or have, *no essence*—since essence has been called, exactly, a receptive subject. Or—to save something at this point —the creature cannot be, or have, an essence distinct from its existence. There can be no essence-existence composition in the creature.

II

In one noteworthy instance, the composed creature has come to grief. If he is composed of essence and existence as St. Thomas explains them, he cannot be totally dependent. I should like to suggest that if he is "composed" at all—if there is any duality in him with respect to his relation to his Creator, he cannot be totally dependent.

A total-dependence theory of creature and God must make some sense of "God creates the creature."

[14] The quoted passage occurs in an article in which St. Thomas is arguing that in the Blessed Trinity the Son is "generated" by the Father. Encountering the objection that the existence of anything generated is received existence, he answers that the existence of the Son is not received in a subject, but is "accepted" from the Generator.

Now this phrase presents at once two terms, God and creature, and invites the notion that the creature is somehow "there," being acted upon by God, receiving something from him. What the creature is said to receive from the Creator—form, order, goodness, unity, existence—does not matter. "The creature receives X from the Creator"—this very phrase suggests a creature standing over against the Creator, receiving something from him, being acted upon by him. In this fashion the patent grammatical duality in the expression "God creates the creature," has become metamorphosed into a duality in the creature. The duality of God and creature has become reflected into the creature itself. Two "parts" have now shown up in the creature: One part is "his" or "him," the other part is "from the creator." By moves such as these (a) "God creates the creature" has not been explicated at all: the creature-God relation has been simply reproduced within the creature and (b) the presence, within the creature, of the "him" or "his" in contrast to the "from God" has compromised the total dependence of the creature.

What can be made of "the creature is related to the Creator" if the relation is total dependence? It cannot be that the creature is one and his relation to the Creator a second. If the creature is to be totally dependent, there can be nothing in him other than his relation to the Creator. Perhaps one should say that the creature cannot be a term of the relation (for then, cut it as you will, he will be in some fashion independent), he must *be* the relation.[15] If the notion of relation is relevant here, it would seem that "total dependence" cannot be said in any other way.

[15] For St. Thomas, characteristically, there is a duality here also: the creature cannot *be* the relation: ". . . according as creation is truly a relation, the creature is its subject, and is before it in existence, as a subject to an accident. But it has a certain *ratio* of priority on the part of the object towards which it is said, which object is the source of the creature." (*S.T.* I, 45, 3, ad 3.)

Those who wish to say that the creature is totally dependent must take account of "otherness." If the dependent is not other than that on which it depends, dependence itself disappears. So it might appear that the creature is composed of otherness and dependence. But, once again, dualizing the creature hurts rather than helps. The otherness between the creature and God, by being "explained" in this way, merely reappears at once as the contrast between two parts in the creature. Meanwhile, one part, the "otherness from God," by being contrasted to dependence, begins to escape from dependence.

The otherness of the dependent cannot be different from the dependence of the dependent. There can be no dependent which is not other. Conversely, otherness for a creature is itself totally dependent. Thus, for a creature, otherness and dependence cannot be two distinct parts or the cause, or effect, of two distinct parts.

In general, a two-part structuring of the dependent (for convenience, "the creature") is incompatible with total dependence. The two parts will be rendering some internal difference within the dependence of the creature upon the Creator. It would be pointless to regard the creature as double if the two parts are considered on a par, and no one in fact has done this. This would too obviously be a multiplication without necessity. If the two parts are unequal, what can make them unequal? Only their connections with the Creator. Perhaps one is "closer" to the Creator—another more remote? Is it a partial eluding, an escaping however humble from the Creator's agency? Or is the more remote a radically deficient being that "really needs" a boost from the Creator? Then what about the more proximate part? Can this, in this respect, be any different?

If the creature is taken as dual, there will be an uneasy shuffling between these two positions: the more remote part needs the Creator more, or the more remote part needs the Creator less. If it needs him more, the more proximate part needs him less—and here there will be a tendency to take the more proximate part of the creature as part of the Creator, to the detriment of the whole notion of creature. If the more remote part of the creature needs the Creator less, this can mean only that it has a trace of independence.

In short, a totally-dependent creature cannot be dual. If the creature as a creature is composed of two unequal parts (act-potency; form-matter; existence-essence; dependence-otherness; the "from God" and the "its own"), one part must escape from the divine causality and so from dependence. If there is any total dependence anywhere, either of creature upon God or of anything upon anything else, the dependent must be a *one* in respect to that upon which it depends.

DIVINE FOREKNOWLEDGE AND

HUMAN FREEDOM

ANTHONY KENNY

In this paper I intend to discuss whether belief in God's foreknowledge of the future is compatible with belief in the freedom of human actions. Before stating the problem in further detail, I must make clear which problems I do *not* intend to consider. I shall not discuss whether there is a God, nor whether it is the case that some human actions are free. I shall not try to show that an action which is causally determined is not free, nor that God knows the future free actions of men. It might be thought, indeed that this last at least needs no proving: surely, if there is a God at all, He knows all that is to come; a God who did not know the future would not be a real God. But this is not so. It is indeed the case that any God worthy of the name knows everything that there is to be known; but it does not follow from this alone that He knows the future free actions of men. For many philosophers have maintained, and some do maintain, that statements about as yet undecided free actions, such as the statement "The United States will declare war on China", are as yet neither true nor false. Since only what is true can be known, then if it is not yet true either that the U.S. will declare war on China nor that the U.S. will not declare war on China, then not even God can know whether the U.S. will do so or not. Again, as a matter of history there have been philosophers who have believed that God was omniscient without thereby believing that God knew the

Revised version of a paper read at Liverpool in 1960. In the original preparation of the paper I had the advantage of discussions with Miss G. E. M. Anscombe and Mr. A. N. Prior.

future free actions of men. Indeed, as we shall see, even a philosopher so orthodox as St. Thomas Aquinas denied, in one important sense, that God knows the future when the future is not already determined by causal necessity. Even to theists, therefore, it needs to be proved that God knows what is going to take place through the free action of his creature. As I have said, I do not intend to argue for this. I intend merely to investigate whether there is or is not compatibility between two statements, namely, "God knows beforehand everything that men will do" and "Some actions of men are free". Even in this restricted area I intend to examine only two arguments which have been brought up to show that the statements are incompatible. The question of incompatibility retains its interest for philosophers even if both statements are in fact false.

It is necessary, as a final preamble, to insist that the problem to be discussed concerns only foreknowledge and not foreordaining. Just as people have believed that God knows beforehand all that happens in the world, so also they have believed that He ordains beforehand all that happens in the world. Just as no human action escapes God's prescience, so no human action escapes His providence. Accordingly, just as there is a problem how God's foreknowledge may be reconciled with human freedom, so also there is a problem how human freedom may be reconciled with God's providence. In particular, since according to traditional Christian belief, no-one is saved who is not predestined by God to be saved, those who accept that belief have a special problem in reconciling it with the belief that those who are damned are damned through their own fault. These further problems are interesting, complicated and difficult; but they will not be our concern in this paper.

The problem may be stated as follows. God's foreknowledge appears to be incompatible with human freedom. It does not seem to be possible both that

God should know what I shall do in the future, and that I shall do freely whatever it is that I shall do. For in order for me to be able to do an action freely, it is necessary that it should be within my power not to do that action. But if God knows what my action is going to be before I do it, then it does not seem to be within my power not to do it. For it cannot be the case both that God knows that I shall do such and such an action, and that I shall not in fact do it. For what God knows must be true: and indeed what anybody knows must be true, since it is impossible to know what is false. But if what God knows is true, and God knows that I will do such and such an action, then it must be true that I will do it. And if it is true that I will do it, then it seems that nothing I can do can prevent it coming true that I am doing it. And if nothing I can do can prevent it coming true that I am doing it, then I cannot prevent myself doing it. And if I cannot prevent myself doing a certain action, then that action cannot be free. Therefore, either God cannot know what I shall do tomorrow, or else whatever I shall do tomorrow will not be done freely.

For example: if God knows now that I will tell a lie this time tomorrow, then it seems that I cannot be free not to tell a lie this time tomorrow. For it cannot be the case both that God knows that I will tell a lie tomorrow, and that I will not in fact tell a lie tomorrow. For what God knows must be true: so that if God knows that I will tell a lie tomorrow, it must be true that I will tell a lie tomorrow. But if it must be true that I will tell a lie tomorrow, then I cannot be free not to tell a lie tomorrow. But if I am not free not to tell a lie tomorrow, then when tomorrow I tell a lie, I shall not do so freely. A similar argument appears to hold, no matter what human action we consider instead of telling lies. Therefore it seems that if God foresees all human actions, no human action can be free.

This difficulty is a very old one. It is stated, for in-

stance, in St. Thomas Aquinas' *Summa Theologiae*, Ia
14, 3, 3. Aquinas' statement of the difficulty is as follows: "Whatever is known by God must be; for whatever is known by us must be, and God's knowledge is
more certain than ours. But nothing which is future
and contingent *must* be. Therefore, nothing which is
future and contingent is known by God." This difficulty is recognizably the same as the one which I have
just stated more verbosely. The only difference of importance is that while I spoke of future free actions,
St. Thomas speaks of future contingent events. St.
Thomas uses the word "contingent" as equivalent to
"not causally determined". Assuming that no causally
determined action is a free action, a free human action would be a contingent event within the meaning
of St. Thomas' phrase. Indeed St. Thomas expressly
states (ibid, *Sed contra*) that free human actions are
contingent events. He thought also that there were
other contingent events besides free human actions:
the budding of a tree, for instance. Whether he was
correct in thinking this is an interesting question, but
not to our purpose.

To the difficulty which he has set, St. Thomas provides a long answer. Part of his answer runs as follows. "The proposition 'whatever is known by God
must be' can be analysed in two ways. It may be taken
as a proposition *de dicto* or as a proposition *de re;* in
other words, it may be taken either *in sensu composito*
or *in sensu diviso*. As a *de re* proposition, it means:
Of everything which is known by God, it is true that
that thing must be.
So understood the proposition is false. As a proposition *de dicto* it means:
The proposition "whatever God knows is the case" is
necessarily true.
So understood, the proposition is true."

There is much more in St. Thomas' answer than this
paragraph, but this argument, as it stands, seems to me
an adequate answer to the difficulty. In order to un-

derstand it one must know something about the medieval distinction between propositions *de dicto* and propositions *de re*. Consider the following proposition.
(1) If there is a University at Oxford, then necessarily there is a University at Oxford.
Someone who asserts that proposition may be taken to assert
(2) "If there is a University at Oxford, then there is a University at Oxford" is a necessary truth.
Or he may be taken to assert
(3) If there is a University at Oxford, then "there is a University at Oxford" is a necessary truth.
The medievals would have called proposition (1), if interpreted in the sense of proposition (2), a proposition *de dicto;* if interpreted in the sense of proposition (3) they would call it a proposition *de re*. The difference between the two interpretations is obviously of crucial importance. For (2), which merely states that a certain conditional—whose consequent is a repetition of its antecedent—is necessarily true, is itself true. But (3) is false, since its antecedent is true (there is a University at Oxford), and its consequent is false (it is not a necessary truth that there is a University at Oxford, since there has not always been a University at Oxford).

It is not difficult to see how to apply this to the problem in hand. The proposition "Whatever is known by God is necessarily true" if taken *de dicto* means
(4) "Whatever is known by God is true" is a necessary truth.
Interpreted *de re*, however, it means
(5) Whatever is known by God is a necessary truth.
Proposition (4) is true, but it has no tendency to show that acts foreseen by God are not free. For, it is equally a necessary truth that if I will tell a lie this time tomorrow, then I will tell a lie this time tomorrow: but this necessary truth has no tendency to show that my telling of a lie tomorrow will not be free. On the other hand, (5) if true would rule out the possi-

bility of free action. If it is a necessary truth that I will
tell a lie tomorrow, then I have no choice in the matter. But this need not trouble us; for proposition (5)
is simply false. If God knows everything, then God
knows that I am now writing this paper; but "I am
writing this paper" is not a necessary truth, since it
was in fact false ten days ago. We might bring out the
difference between the two interpretations of "whatever is known by God is necessarily true" by punctua-
tion, as follows.

(4a) Whatever is known by God is, necessarily, true.

(5a) Whatever is known by God is necessarily-true.

It seems to me, therefore, that St. Thomas' answer
to this particular difficulty is entirely satisfactory. But
he puts to himself a further, and more persuasive, difficulty; and his answer to this second difficulty does
not appear satisfactory at all.

The further difficulty runs as follows. In any true
conditional proposition whose antecedent is necessarily true, the consequent is also necessarily true. That
is to say, whatever is implied by a necessary proposition is itself a necessary proposition. The following is
clearly a true conditional proposition: "If it has come
to God's knowledge that such and such a thing will
happen, then such and such a thing will happen." The
antecedent of the conditional, if it is true at all, appears to be necessarily true: for it is in the past tense,
and what is past cannot be changed. What has been
the case cannot now not have been the case. Therefore, the consequent is also necessarily true. Therefore, whatever is known by God is a necessary truth.

This is a powerful argument: it appears, at least at
first sight, impossible to deny any of its premises. St.
Thomas himself treated it with great respect: before
putting forward his own solution he considered and
rejected three attempts to deny one or other premise.
In the end, he could find no alternative to accepting
the argument, while trying to show that the conclu-

sion is not, as it appears to be, incompatible with the occurrence of contingent events.

His solution runs as follows. God, he says, is outside time: God's life is measured not by time, but by eternity. Eternity, which has no parts, overlaps the whole of time; consequently, the things which happen at different times are all present together to God. An event is known *as future* only when there is a relation of future to past between the knowledge of the knower and the happening of the event. But there is no such relation between God's knowledge and any contingent event: the relation between God's knowledge and any event in time is always one of simultaneity. Consequently, a contingent event, as it comes to God's knowledge, is not future but present; and as present it is necessary; for what is the case, is the case, and is beyond anyone's power to alter. Hence, we can admit that what is known to God is a necessary truth; for as known by God it is no longer future but present. But this necessity does not destroy contingency: for the fact that an event is necessary when it happens does not mean that it was predetermined by its causes.

St. Thomas adds plausibility to his solution with a famous illustration. "To us, because we know future contingent events as future, there can be no certainty about them; but only to God, whose knowing is in eternity, above time. A man who is walking along a road cannot see those who are coming after him; but a man who looks down from a hill upon the whole length of the road can see at the same time all those who are travelling along it. So it is with God . . . Future events which are in themselves contingent cannot be known to us. What is known to God is necessary in the way in which it lies open to God's knowledge (namely, in its presentness); it is not necessary in regard to its own causes."[1]

[1] *Summa Theologiae*, 14, 13 ad 3 (words in brackets from the body of the article). The preceding paragraph is a mosaic of translations from *De Veritate* 2, 12.

This explanation of St. Thomas has become the classic solution of the problem raised by God's foreknowledge. It is still sometimes presented in popular expositions of Christian theology, for instance in *Theology and Sanity* by F. J. Sheed. "If God knew last Tuesday what you were going to do next Tuesday, what becomes of your free will? . . . God did *not* know *last* Tuesday. Tuesday is a period of time and part of the duration in which I act. But God acts in eternity which has no Tuesdays. God acts in the space-lessness of his immensity and the timelessness of his eternity: we receive the effects of his acts in space and time" (p. 117).

Despite the authority of St. Thomas, the solution seems fundamentally misconceived. In the first place, it forces one to deny that it is true, in any strict sense, that God knows future free actions. St. Thomas insists repeatedly that no-one, not even God, can know contingent events *qua* future: he says of such events that we should rather say "if God knows something, then it *is*" than "if God knows something, then it *will be*" (*De Veritate* 2, 12 ad 7). Strictly speaking, then, God has no *fore*knowledge of contingent events: as He knows them, they are not still future but already present. A defender of St. Thomas might reply that this does not matter: when we say that God knows future events we mean merely that (a) God knows all events (b) some events are future *to us*. Of any event which is future to us it will be true to say that God knows it, though he will not know it *qua* future. Thus, let us suppose that at some future date a man will land on Mars. The event which is the landing on Mars is, so far as we are concerned, in the future; but to God it is already present. Thus, although we cannot say that God knows that a man *will* land on Mars (for this would be to make God know it *qua* future) we can say that God knows, timelessly, the event which is the landing on Mars. And this event is future to us, that is to say, it comes later in the time series than e.g. your reading this.

But this reply does not meet the objection. If "to know the future" means know more than "to know a fact which comes later in the time series than some other fact" then we, no less than God, can know the future. For we know about the Wars of the Roses which *were* future when Cleopatra was a girl. If we were to take St. Thomas' suggestion seriously, we should have to say that God knows that a man *is landing* on Mars; but we cannot say this, since the statement that a man is landing on Mars, being false, cannot be known, even by God, to be true.

St. Thomas' solution then, is not so much a defence as a denial of God's foreknowledge. But it forces us to deny not only God's foreknowledge, but also God's omniscience. For the statement that God's foreknowledge is outside time must mean, if anything, that no temporal qualifications can be attached to God's knowledge. Where God is the subject, verbs of knowing cannot have adverbs of time affixed to them. We cannot, therefore, say that God knows now that Brutus killed Caesar; nor that God will know tomorrow what time I went to bed tonight. But as A. N. Prior has remarked, it seems an extraordinary way of affirming God's omniscience if a person, when asked what God knows *now*, must say "Nothing", and when asked what he knew *yesterday*, must again say "Nothing", and must yet again say "Nothing" when asked what God will know *tomorrow*.

An argument *ad hominem* against St. Thomas' position may be drawn from the notion of prophecy. St. Thomas believed that God could foretell, and had foretold, future contingent events. He believed, for example, that God, as the principal author of the Epistle to the Romans, had foretold the conversion of the Jewish people to Christianity. On the view that God's knowledge is timeless, such prediction becomes inexplicable. For, if God's knowledge is timeless, then we cannot attach to statements about God's knowledge such adverbial clauses as "at the time when the Epistle to the Romans was written". We cannot, for example, say "At the time when the Epistle to the Romans was written God already knew that the Jews would finally be converted". But if God did not then know it, how could he then foretell it? To put it bluntly: if God did not then *know* that the Jews would be converted, he had no right then to *say* that they would.

Indeed, the whole concept of a timeless eternity, the whole of which is simultaneous with every part of time, seems to be radically incoherent. For simultaneity as ordinarily understood is a transitive relation. If A happens at the same time as B, and B happens at the same time as C, then A happens at the same time as C. If the BBC programme and the ITV programme both start when Big Ben strikes ten, then they both start at the same time. But, on St. Thomas' view, my typing of this paper is simultaneous with the whole of eternity. Again, on his view, the great fire of Rome is simultaneous with the whole of eternity. Therefore, while I type these very words, Nero fiddles heartlessly on.

If St. Thomas' solution to the difficulty is unacceptable, is it possible to give a different one? The objection ran thus. What is implied by a necessary proposition is itself necessarily true. But from "it has come to God's knowledge that such and such will be the case" it follows that "such and such will be the case". But "it has come to God's knowledge that such and such will be the case" is necessarily true; therefore "such and such will be the case" is necessarily true. Therefore, if God knows the future, the future is not contingent.[2]

---

[2] Using *"Lp"* for "Necessarily *p*", *"Gp"* for "It has come to God's knowledge that *p*", and *"Cpq"* for "If *p*, then *q*", we could symbolise the argument thus: *LCLCGppLCLGpLp; LCGpp; LGp;* ergo, *Lp.*

The premises of the argument appear difficult to deny; yet if its conclusion is true there is no freedom or else no foreknowledge. For if it must be the case that I will murder my grandfather, then I am not free not to murder my grandfather; and conversely, if I am free not to murder my grandfather, then God cannot know that I will murder him even if in fact I will do so.

Let us examine each premise in turn. It appears incontrovertible that what follows from a necessary proposition is itself necessary.[3] Moreover, it cannot be denied that "it is the case that *p*" follows from "It has come to God's knowledge that *p*": this is true *ex vi termini* "know". So, for any substitution for "*p*", if "It has come to God's knowledge that *p*" is necessarily true, then "it is the case that *p*" is also necessarily true.

But is it true, for all substitutions for "*p*", that it must be the case that it has come to God's knowledge that *p*? St. Thomas accepted it without question. "It has come to God's knowledge that *p*" is a proposition in the past tense, and for St. Thomas as for Aristotle all propositions in the past tense are necessary. Now let us first notice that even if this doctrine were true, there has occurred a significant change in the sense of "necessary". Hitherto, "necessarily" has been used in such a way that in every case it could have been replaced by "it is a logical truth that . . ." But if an Aristotelian claims that "Cesare Borgia was a bad man" is now necessarily true, he must be using "necessarily" in a different sense. For he cannot claim that it is a logical truth that Cesare Borgia was a bad man. Again, let us notice, that the necessity of past propositions, if they are necessary, is not something that is *eo ipso* incompatible with freedom. If it is now necessary that Cesare Borgia was a bad man, it does not follow from this alone that it was, when he was born, necessary that he *would* be a bad man. For, according to Aristotle, necessity applies only to true past and present

[3] *LCLCpqLCLpLq* is a law in every standard modal system.

propositions, not to future propositions of contingent fact. But, when Cesare Borgia was born, the proposition "Cesare Borgia will be a bad man" was a future-tensed proposition of contingent fact—as indeed it still is.

It is clear, then, that if present- and past-tensed propositions are, as Aristotle thought, necessary in a way in which future-tensed propositions are not, they are not necessary in the way in which logical truths are necessary; and they are not necessary in a way which excludes the freedom of the action they report, if they report an action at all.

But is there any sense at all in which past- and present-tensed propositions have a necessity which is not shared by future-tensed propositions? The very least which seems to be demanded of a proposition if it is to be called "necessary" is that it is, always has been, and always will be, true. In this sense of "necessary" the proposition "there is a God" is necessarily true if it is true at all; but of course the proposition "there is a God" is not a logical truth, as critics of the ontological argument, from Gaunilo to Russell, have frequently pointed out. Now the proposition "Queen Anne is dead", which is a true present-tensed proposition if ever there was one, is not a necessary truth in this sense at all, since before 1714 it was not true. The past-tensed proposition "Queen Anne has died" will indeed never cease to be true; but it *was* not true in King Alfred's day. So, even if "necessary" is given the weak interpretation of "true at all times", there seems no reason to believe the Aristotelian doctrine that past- and present-tensed propositions *in materia contingenti* are necessary.

Yet is it not true that what has happened cannot now not have happened, and that which is happening cannot now not be happening? We have a very strong inclination to think that there is some way in which we can change the future, in which we cannot change the past. But this inclination appears to be a delusion.

There appears to be no sense in which we can change the future in which we cannot change the past. As A. N. Prior has pointed out, whatever changes of plan we may make, the future is whatever takes place after all the changes are made; what we alter is *not* the future, but our plans; the real future can no more be altered than the past. The sort of case which we have in mind when we are tempted to say that we can change the future is this: suppose that I have no intention of typing "elephant" backwards; then I decide I will do so; and finally I do so. Does not my decision change the future, since without my decision the word would never have been typed backwards? No, for even when I had no intention of doing so, e.g. ten years ago, it *was* true that I would, ten years later, type "elephant" backwards; and so my decision altered nothing except my own intentions. There is, indeed, a sense in which we can change the future: we can change the truth-value of a future-tensed proposition. Suppose that it is true that I will commit suicide: then the proposition "A.K. will commit suicide" now has the truth-value "true". I can change this truth-value by committing suicide; for once I have committed suicide the proposition "A.K. will commit suicide" ceases to be true and the quite different proposition "A.K. has committed suicide" becomes true instead. But if "to change the future" means merely "to change the truth-value of a future-tensed proposition" then in a corresponding sense I can change the past no less than the future. Nothing is easier. Tnahpele. The past-tensed proposition "A.K. has typed 'elephant' backwards" which *was* false, is now true; and so I have changed the past.

It seems, then, that there is no sense in which we can change the future in which we cannot change the past. Still, it does seem true that we can bring about the future, but cannot bring about the past; our present activity may have a causal effect on the future but cannot have a causal effect on the past. Consequently deliberation about the future is sensible, deliberation about the past absurd; so if God's knowledge of what I will do tomorrow is already a thing of the past, deliberation about what I will do tomorrow appears already pointless, and once again there appears to be an incompatibility between foreknowledge and freedom.

However, in certain cases, it does seem that present actions can affect the past. By begetting a son, I make my grandfather, long dead, into a great-grandfather; by becoming Poet Laureate I make my late grandmother's belief that I would one day be Poet Laureate into a true belief. In such cases, of course, what we are doing is establishing new relations between past things and events and present or future things or events. But the truth of a belief, and the question of whether a certain belief does or does not constitute knowledge, involve relationships between those beliefs and the events they concern. So it is possible that it is precisely by telling a lie today that I bring it about that God knew yesterday that I would tell a lie today. Of course, I do not bring it about by today's lie that God yesterday *believed* that I would lie; but it is my current lie which makes his belief then true.

Even so, it might be retorted, this does not make it possible for God to have *known* yesterday without curtailment of my freedom; because knowledge is not true belief, but justified true belief; and the justification of a past belief would have to be past grounds for the belief; and nothing in the past could be adequate grounds for a belief about my current action unless it necessitated that action. To this the reply is open that even in non-theological contexts there seem to be cases where true belief, without grounds, constitutes knowledge. One such case is our knowledge of our own actions. Commonly, we know what we are doing with our hands, and we do not know this on the basis of any evidence or grounds. Of course, we can be mistaken: I may think I am typing "piece" and in fact be typing "peice". But when I am not mistaken, my belief about what I am doing constitutes knowledge. It does not seem unreasonable to suggest that in this respect a Creator's knowledge of his creature's actions might resemble a human agent's knowledge of his own actions.

There seems, then, no reason to maintain that "It has come to God's knowledge that p" is a necessary truth, in any of the senses we have suggested, merely because it is past-tensed. Might it not be argued, however, that it is a necessary truth for a different reason: namely, that it is a truth about God's knowledge, which is the knowledge of a necessarily omniscient necessary being? If God is omniscient, it might be argued, then whatever we substitute for "p", "it has come to God's knowledge that p" will be true. But "if it has come to God's knowledge that p" is true no matter what we substitute for "p", then it must be something like a logical truth, and so a necessary truth in the sense in which necessity is incompatible with freedom.

It does not take a moment to detect the fallacy in this argument. God's omniscience does not at all imply that whatever we substitute for "p" in "God knows that p" is true. For instance, if we substitute "$2 + 2 = 3$" we get not a necessary truth but the falsehood "God knows that $2 + 2 = 3$". It is indeed a logical truth that if p is true, then p is known by any omniscient being; but this is insufficient to provide the premise needed by St. Thomas' objector.[4] A sentence such as "God knows that I am sitting down" expresses not a necessary, but a contingent truth: it may be true now, but it was not true last night and it will cease to be true as soon as I stand up. In fact, God's knowledge will only be necessary where what He knows is necessary: "$2 + 2 = 4$" is a necessary truth, so "God knows that $2 + 2 = 4$" is a necessary truth.[5] But, by

[4] We have not LGp but $LCpGp$.
[5] We have not $LCpLGp$, but $LCLpLGp$.

definition, a contingent proposition—such as a proposition reporting or predicting a free action—is never a necessary truth. Hence, the argument that we have been considering has no tendency to show that human freedom and divine foreknowledge are incompatible.

There are other arguments to prove this incompatibility: Aquinas alone gives thirteen of which we have considered only two. None, however, are as initially plausible, or as complicated to unravel, as the two we have considered.

III

PHILOSOPHY OF MIND

INTELLECT AND IMAGINATION IN AQUINAS

In the first article of question 85 of the First Part of
the *Summa Theologiae* St. Thomas affirms that the
human intellect understands material things by abstracting from phantasms (*intellectus noster intelligit
materialia abstrahendo a phantasmatibus*). My purpose in this paper is to air certain problems in the
interpretation of this theory.

Every word in the formula quoted raises a difficulty, not excluding the preposition "from". The verb,
for instance, is traditionally translated "understands",
but this translation is not beyond question. "*Intelligere*" often does seem to correspond to "understand",
but sometimes it appears a more general verb, like the
English "think".

In some places Aquinas follows Aristotle in distinguishing two kinds of understanding, two types of intellectual operation. On the one hand there is the understanding of simples (*intelligentia indivisibilium*),
and on the other hand there is compounding and dividing (*compositio et divisio*). (See *De Veritate* I, 3;
IV, 2; *S.Th.* Ia, 17, 3).

To compound and to divide is to make affirmative
and negative judgements (*In I Perihermeneias*, 3).
Faced with the content of any proposition, one may
either make or withhold a judgement about it; if one
makes a judgement one may do so truly or falsely,
one may do so with or without hesitation, and one
may do so on the basis of argument or on grounds of
self-evidence. According to various combinations of

In writing this paper I have been influenced by the work of
Bernard Lonergan S.J. (*Verbum: Word and Idea in Aquinas*);
but I have not adopted the whole of his subtle reconstruction
of Aquinas' theory of abstraction.

these possibilities, one's state of mind in relation to the propositional content will be an instance of belief, opinion, doubt, knowledge, or understanding. Whereas forming a belief, accepting an opinion, entertaining a doubt, coming to a conclusion, and seeing a self-evident truth are all exercises of the intellectual faculty or understanding, the seeing of self-evident truths is understanding *par excellence* (*De Veritate* XIV, 1). Since Aquinas uses the same verb to refer to the specific activity of grasping self-evidence and as a generic term for various kinds of thought, we cannot tell from the occurrence of the verb alone whether his theory of abstraction is meant as an account of thought in general, or as an account of the grasp of self-evident truths in particular.

St. Thomas observes that any judgement which can be made can be expressed by a sentence (*De Veritate* II, 4). This does not mean that thought is impossible without verbalisation, for it does not follow that every judgement that *is* made *is* put into words, either orally or in imagination. It does mean, however, that compounding and dividing is the mental analogue of the utterance of affirmative and negative sentences.

The understanding of simples is related to the entertaining of judgements as the use of individual words is related to the construction of sentences. An example of the understanding of simples would be knowledge of what gold is—knowledge of the *quid est* of gold. Such knowledge can be exercised in judgements about gold, and without some such knowledge no judgement about gold would be possible. Some such judgements, such as "gold is valuable" or "gold is yellow" require no great understanding of the nature of gold; they presuppose little more than an awareness of what the word "gold" means. A chemist, on the other hand, knows in a much richer way what gold is. Not only can he list many more of the properties of gold, but he can relate and present those properties in a systematic way, linking them, for instance with gold's atomic number and its place in the periodic table of the elements. The chemist's account of gold would seem to approximate to the ideal described by St. Thomas as knowledge of the quiddity or essence of a material substance (e.g. Ia 3, 3 and 4; 17, 3). In many places St. Thomas observes that one can know what a word "A" means without knowing the quiddity or essence of A. We know, for instance, what the word "God" means, but we do not and cannot know God's essence (e.g. *S.Th.* Ia, 2, 2 ad 2). Learning the meaning of a word and acquiring a scientific mastery of the essence of a substance are both exercises of intelligence; but the grasp of essences is understanding *par excellence*. In the case of the understanding of simples, then, no less than in compounding and dividing, we meet a distinction between a broad and a narrow sense of "understand". In the broad sense, the acquisition and application of any concept, the formation and expression of any belief count as exercises of the understanding; in the narrow sense, understanding is restricted to insight into essences and the intuition of self-evident truths. Clearly, it is desirable to know whether St. Thomas' theory of abstraction is presented as an account of understanding in the broad sense or of understanding in the narrow sense. If the former, it is a general account of the operation of the intelligence by which language-using human beings surpass dumb animals; if the latter, it is an account of the methodology of *a priori* science. In what follows I shall try to keep both interpretations in mind.

The ambiguity we have noted carries over from the verb *"intelligere"* to the noun *"intellectus"*. The intellect is a capacity, and capacities, as Aquinas frequently observes, are specified by their exercises: to explain the nature of the capacity to ϕ you must explain what ϕing is (*S.Th.* Ia 77, 3; 87, 3). The intellect or understanding, being precisely the capacity to understand, cannot be explained without an explanation of what it is to understand. So if "understand" presents problems, "intellect" will present analogous problems too. But they are not the only problems presented by Aquinas' theory of abstraction by the intellect.

The intellect, according to St. Thomas, is not one faculty but two: or rather it is a single faculty with two powers: the agent intellect (*intellectus agens*) and the receptive intellect (*intellectus possibilis*). Ia, 79, 3 of the *Summa* explains why it is necessary to posit an agent intellect, taking a cue from Aristotle's cryptic dictum in the *De Anima* that there is in the soul one mind for becoming all things and one mind for making all things (III, 430a15).

Plato, St. Thomas says, had no need to posit an agent intellect to make the objects of understanding actually intelligible, because he believed that the forms of material things subsisted without matter and were thus fit objects of understanding, being immaterial *species* or Ideas. But according to Aristotle, there are no forms of things in nature subsisting without matter, and forms existing in matter are not actually intelligible. Consequently, says Aquinas, the natures or forms of perceptible things which we understand need to be made actually intelligible, fit objects of understanding, by some power on the side of the intellect. This is the agent intellect which makes actually intelligible objects of understanding by abstracting *species* from material conditions (*S.Th.* Ia 79, 3).

There is much in this that is difficult to understand: a crucial term is the word transliterated "*species*". In the passage just summarised it is first used as an expression for Platonic Forms, synonymous with the Latin word "Idea". Indeed no English word seems to correspond better to the Latin word "*species*" than the word "idea". If the English word is dangerously ambiguous, that is all to the good, since the Latin word is ambiguous in closelly parallel ways.

Ideas may be ideas *of* or ideas *that*: the idea of

gold, the idea that the world is about to end. Similarly, species may correspond either to the understanding of simples, or to affirmation and negation. (See, for example, *S.Th.* Ia IIae, 55, 1). For *species*, in one sense, are dispositions of the human intellect (Ia IIae, 50, 4), and to the two types of intellectual activity correspond two types of dispositional properties of the intellect. If the two types of activity are interpreted in the broad sense, as the acquisition and application of concepts, and as the formation and expression of beliefs, then the two types of dispositions, the two types of *species*, will be the concepts and beliefs themselves. To have the *species* corresponding to the proposition that p will be to have the belief that p; to have the *species* of A will be to have the concept of A, to have the ability to think of A.

In summary fashion, we might say that for Aquinas ideas include both concepts and beliefs. But here we meet a further ambiguity: for in contemporary philosophy "concept" has two contrasting uses. In one sense, which we might call the Wittgensteinian sense, a concept is something subjective: to possess a concept is to possess a certain skill, for instance to have mastered the use of a word (e.g. *Philosophical Investigations,* I, 384). It was in this sense that the word was used in the preceding paragraph. But in another sense, which we might call the Fregean, concepts are something objective. For Frege a concept is the reference of a predicate. In the sentence "Eclipse is a horse", according to Frege, just as the name "Eclipse" stands for a horse, so the predicate ". . . is a horse" stands for a concept—and a concept is not something in anyone's mind, but a particular type of function, a function whose value for every argument is a truth-value (*Philosophical Writings,* trs. Geach-Black, 43, 59). To this objective use of "concept" there corresponds an objective use of "*species*", to refer not only to Platonic ideas, which Aquinas rejected, but also to Aristotelian forms, which he accepted.[1] It is in this sense that Aquinas can say that *species* are the objects of the intellect's activity (Cf. *ScG*, II, 73).

More commonly, however, Aquinas says—as in the quotation from which we began—that what the intellect understands, the object of the intellect, is (the nature of) material things. A material thing, according to Aristotelian hylemorphism, is composed of matter and form; an individual man such as Peter is a parcel of matter bearing the form of humanity. Aquinas, in opposition to Plato, often insists that there is not in the world any humanity as such, or Ideal Man; there is only the humanity of Peter, the humanity of Paul, and so on (*S.Th.* Ia. 84, 4). The humanity, or human nature, of Peter would be an instance of what Aquinas calls "a form existing in matter"—something in his terminology "intelligible" (because a form), but not "actually intelligible" (because existing in matter). Humanity in the abstract is actually intelligible, but humanity in the abstract is nowhere to be found; humanity in matter is found wherever there are men, but humanity in matter is as such no fit object for the mind. It is to bridge this gap that the agent intellect is necessary. Presented with humanity in matter, the agent intellect creates the intellectual object, humanity as such. In what way is it presented with humanity in matter? "In phantasms" Aquinas replies; and for the moment we may paraphrase this as "in experience".

Let us try to present this doctrine in non-hylemorphic terms. In order to possess a concept of something which can be an object of an experience, it is not sufficient simply to have the appropriate experience. Young children see coloured objects before they painfully acquire colour-concepts; dumb animals can see and taste a substance such as salt but they cannot

---

[1] On the analogy between Fregean functions and forms, see Geach's paper *Form and Existence*, p. 29 above in this volume.

acquire the concepts which language-users can exercise in general judgements about salt. A special ability unshared by animals is necessary if human beings are to acquire concepts from the experience which they share with animals. Animals share with human beings the experience of pain, and human beings *feel* pains from birth if not before; but as Wittgenstein observed we acquire the *concept* "pain" when we learn language (*loc. cit.*). Again, rats can see, and discriminate between circles and triangles; but no amount of gazing at diagrams will make a rat a student of geometry. The specifically human ability to acquire complicated concepts from experience, and to grasp geometrical truths presented in diagrams, will perhaps be what Aquinas has in mind when he speaks of the agent intellect.

Contrasted with the agent intellect, there is the receptive intellect (*intellectus possibilis*). The receptive intellect is the power to exercise the dispositions acquired by the use of the agent intellect. "One and the same soul" we are told "in so far as it is actually immaterial, has a power called the agent intellect which is a power to make other things actually immaterial by abstracting from the conditions of individual matter, and another power to receive ideas of this kind, which is called the receptive intellect as having the power to receive such ideas" (*S.Th.* Ia 79, 4 ad 4). The receptive intellect is, St. Thomas says, the *locus* of *species*, the storehouse of ideas (*S.Th.* Ia 79, 6, esp. ad 1.). Varying the metaphor, the receptive intellect is the unwritten tablet, the *tabula rasa*, of which Aristotle wrote (*De Anima* III, 430a1). As concepts and beliefs are acquired through the operation of the agent intellect upon experience, the tablet becomes covered with writing, the empty storehouse fills up with ideas. To find out the contents of a man's receptive intellect at a given time you must find out what he understands, what he knows, what he believes at that moment. In fact the *intellectus possibilis* of a man may be thought of as the collection of concepts and beliefs that he possesses: it is his mind in the sense in which we speak of the contents of a mind.

Frequently Aquinas speaks of the receptive intellect in hylemorphic terms. As prime matter is to the forms of sense-perceptible objects, so the receptive intellect is to all ideas. Prime matter is matter which as such is not any particular kind of stuff; not that there is any matter which is stuff of no particular kind, but that matter, *qua* matter, is not stuff of any particular kind, and can be stuff of any kind whatever. Similarly, the receptive intellect does not, as such, contain any particular ideas, but can contain any idea whatever: "to begin with it is in potentiality to all such ideas" (*S.Th.* Ia 84, 3). True to his hylemorphism, Aquinas prefers the language of *informing* to that of *containing:* the intellect is *informed* with various *species* (*S.Th.* Ia 79, 6). We use the same metaphor, oblivious of its hylemorphic background, when we speak of being informed upon a topic, or acquiring information about it.

According to hylemorphic theory, to acquire the form of F-ness is to become F: thus, to acquire the form of redness is to become red, just as to possess the form of humanity is to be a man. If we treat an idea, then, as a form informing the intellect, it seems that we must say that the intellect becomes F when it is informed by the idea of F-ness. This, then, will be why Aristotle said that there was in the soul a mind for becoming everything, and that the mind when it understands becomes different things in turn (*De An.* III, 430a15; cf. *S.Th.* Ia 79, 6).

What can we make of this strange conclusion? St. Thomas says that as physical matter has potentialities which are realised by perceptible *esse,* so the receptive intellect has potentialities which are realised by mental *esse* (Ia IIae, 50, 4). Commenting on this passage, I once wrote as follows.

A leaf may be now green and now brown; when it was green it had a potentiality of being brown which is realised when it is brown; the "is" in "is brown" stands for an *esse* which is perceptible *esse*, the *esse* of *being brown*. Now it is clear that a man's capacity to think is realised when he thinks a particular thought; but it is not as if we could say that a man thinking of a horse *is* a horse, or even *is* intelligibly a horse, so why does St. Thomas speak of *esse* here? Perhaps the answer is to be sought on these lines. The history of a man's intellect is the history of the thoughts he has, and at any given moment there is nothing actual which makes a man a thinking being other than the thought he is thinking. In this sense, my intellect is my present thought of a horse, a thought which is capable of changing into a thought of anything else whatever. Now if we think of "a thought of a horse" as meaning the same as "a horse in thought" we can say that the intellect of a man, who is thinking of a horse, is a horse in thought. Generalizing, then, we can say that if a man is thinking of X, his intellect is X-in-thought; and further, that no matter what X may be, a human intellect *can* be X-in-thought. This last conclusion, reached in a roundabout fashion, I take to be a more or less literal translation of '*Intellectus habet potentiam ad esse intelligibile*' (*Summa Theologiae*, Blackfriars edition, XXII, 40–41).

I now think that this is misleading in several ways. In the first place, what St. Thomas means by the information of the receptive intellect by an idea is not the episodic exercise of a concept in the thinking of a particular, dated, thought; but rather the acquisition of the lifetime or at least long-term capacity to think thoughts of a certain kind. The exercise of such a capacity is not itself a form but is an activity proceeding from the form: to adapt St. Thomas' standard illustration, it is related to the form as the activity of

heating the kettle is related to the form of heat possessed by the stove. For a stove to be hot is, *inter alia,*
for it to be able to heat the kettle; for me to possess
the concept *round* is for me to be able, *inter alia,* to
reflect that the earth is round (Ia IIae, 50, 4; 51, 3).

Secondly, it is not part of St. Thomas' theory that
the intellect, when it acquires the concept *horse,* becomes a real horse, or even, strictly speaking, becomes
an immaterial horse. The concept *horse,* being applicable to any horse, is not the concept of any particular horse. It is not the concept of an immaterial
horse either, for it is part of the concept of a horse
that a horse should be a material object. A horse, being
a material object, must have a certain size and mass;
and this, too, is part of the concept *horse,* that a
horse should have a certain size and mass. But there
is no particular size or mass which a horse *qua* horse
must have, and so no particular size or mass belongs
to the concept. St. Thomas makes a similar point.

> There are two kinds of matter: common matter,
> on the one hand, and designated or individual mat-
> ter on the other. Common matter is e.g. flesh and
> bone; individual matter is e.g. this flesh and these
> bones. Now the intellect abstracts the idea of a nat-
> ural thing from individual perceptible matter, but
> not from common perceptible matter: it abstracts,
> for instance, the idea of *man* from this flesh and
> these bones, which do not belong to the concept
> but are parts of the individual . . . but the idea of
> *man* cannot be abstracted by the intellect from
> flesh and bone as such (*S.Th.* Ia 85, 1 ad 1).

If, then, the receptive intellect when informed by the
species of F-ness becomes F, the receptive intellect
does not become a real horse, but an abstract horse;
and an abstract horse is not something, on Aquinas'
theory, which exists anywhere outside the mind.

Thirdly, my observation that one thought may turn
into another thought was not to the point. For the

analogy between prime matter and the receptive intellect stands in need of a qualification which St. Thomas himself makes at Ia, 84, 3 ad 2. Prime matter, he says, has its substantial *esse* through form—for matter to exist is for it to be F—and there cannot be existent matter which has no form.

But the receptive intellect does not have its substantial *esse* through its ideas: the intellect of a newborn baby exists though it has no ideas; consequently the ideas which inform the intellect are accidental forms (like the form of heat in water) rather than substantial forms (like the form of horse or man). And when St. Thomas follows Aristotle in describing the mind as *becoming* its object, the becoming must be thought of as the acquisition of a new characteristic (like *becoming red*) rather than as the turning into a new kind of thing (like *becoming a butterfly*).

The restriction on the analogy between prime matter and the receptive intellect occurs in the course of an attack on the doctrine of innate ideas: and it is in contrast to that doctrine that Aquinas' own theory of abstraction is worked out. Plato had maintained, Aquinas says, that the human intellect naturally contained all intelligible ideas, but was prevented from using them because of its union with the body. Against this Aquinas marshals both empirical and metaphysical arguments.

> If the soul has a natural knowledge of all these things it does not seem possible that it should so far forget this natural knowledge as to be ignorant that it has it at all. For nobody forgets what he naturally knows, as that the whole is greater than its parts and so on. Plato's theory seems especially unacceptable if the soul is, as maintained above, naturally united to the body; for it is unacceptable that the natural operation of a thing should be altogether impeded by something else which is also natural to it. Secondly, the falsity of this theory ap-

pears obvious from the fact that when a certain sense is lacking, there is lacking also the scientific knowledge of things perceived by that sense. A blind man, for instance, cannot have any knowledge of colours. This would not be the case if the soul's intellect were naturally endowed with the concepts of all intelligible objects (*S.Th.* Ia, 84, 3).

Later, Aquinas praises Aristotle for taking a middle course between the innate idealism of Plato and the crude empiricism of Democritus.

Aristotle maintained that the intellect had an activity in which the body had no share. Now nothing corporeal can cause an impression on an incorporeal thing, and so, according to Aristotle, the mere stimulus of sensible bodies is not sufficient to cause intellectual activity. Something nobler and higher is needed, which he called the agent intellect: it makes the phantasms received from the senses to be actually intelligible by means of a certain abstraction (*S.Th.* Ia 84, 6).

In what sense, on Aquinas' account, are concepts *abstracted from* phantasms? Principally, there appear to be two separable doctrines united in the theory. The first is that concepts and experiences stand in a certain causal relation; the second is that they stand in a certain formal relation.

The causal relation is spelt out in the continuation of the passage just cited.

In this way, then, intellectual activity is caused by the senses on the side of the phantasm. But since phantasms are not sufficient to affect the receptive intellect unless they are made actually intelligible by the agent intellect, sense-knowledge cannot be said to be the total and complete cause of intellectual knowledge, but only the material element of its cause.

To say, then, that concepts are abstracted from experience is to say at least that experience is a necessary causal condition for the acquisition of concepts. How far this is true seems to be partly an empirical matter and partly a philosophical question. It is an empirical matter, for instance, to discover how much a blind man might learn of a textbook on optics. It is a philosophical question how far mastery of such a textbook could count as "possession of the science of colour" without e.g. the ability to match colours against colour samples.

Besides having a causal relation to experience, Aquinas' ideas have a formal relation to them: that is, concepts on his theory are abstract *in comparison with* experiences. Sense-experience, he believed, is always of a particular individual; intellectual knowledge is primarily of the universal (Ia, 86, 1). Consequently, intellectual concepts can be said to abstract from much that is included in sense-experience. This is the sense of "abstraction" that is spelt out in the passage from which this paper began (*S.Th.* Ia, 85, 1).

> It is peculiar to (the human intellect) to know form existing individually in corporeal matter but not *as* existing in such matter. But to know that which is in individual matter but not *as* in such matter is to abstract the form from the individual matter which the phantasms represent.

In answer to an objector, Thomas goes on to clarify.

> What belongs to the specific concept (*pertinet ad rationem speciei*) of any material thing such as a stone, or a man, or a horse, can be considered without the individual characteristics which are not part of the specific concept. This is what it is to abstract the universal from the particular, or the intelligible idea from the phantasms, namely, to consider the specific nature without considering the

individual characteristics which are represented by
the phantasm (*Ibid.* ad 1).

This formal relation is distinct from the causal relation, for what Aquinas says here would be true even
if universal concepts were not acquired from experience. Even innate ideas would still be more abstract
than representations of individuals, whether these latter were themselves acquired or innate. For to have
the concept of man is not to be able to recognise or
think of a particular man with particular characteristics. It is *inter alia* to be able to recognise any man no
matter what his particular characteristics, to think
about men without necessarily attributing particular
characteristics to them, and to know general truths
about man as such. And this is true no matter how
the concept has been acquired.

In modern philosophy there is a familiar, if no
longer popular, theory that the acquisition of universal concepts can be explained by selective attention
to features of particular experience. One version of
the theory was ridiculed by Berkeley in *The Principles of Human Knowledge* (8ff), another was treated
by Wittgenstein in *Philosophical Investigations*. Wittgenstein writes:

> When someone defines the names of colours for me
> by pointing to samples and saying 'This colour is
> called "blue", this "green" . . .' this case can be
> compared in many respects to putting a table in my
> hands, with the words written under the colour-
> samples.—Though this comparison may mislead in
> many ways.—One is now inclined to extend the
> comparison: to have understood the definition
> means to have in one's mind an idea of the thing
> defined, and that is a sample or picture. So if I am
> shewn various different leaves and told 'This is
> called a "leaf"', I get an idea of the shape of a leaf,
> a picture of it in my mind.—'But what does the pic-
> ture of a leaf look like when it does not shew us any

particular shape, but "what is common to all shapes of leaf"? Which shade is the "sample" in my "mind" of the colour green—the sample of what is common to all shades of green?

But might there not be such "general" samples? Say a schematic leaf, or a sample of pure green?' Certainly there might. But for such a schema to be understood as a *schema,* and not as the shape of a particular leaf, and for a slip of pure green to be understood as a sample of all that is greenish and not as a sample of pure green,—this in turn resides in the way the samples are used (I, 74).

Aquinas' language in his last quoted passage might make it look as if he held a theory such as Berkeley and Wittgenstein criticised. But in fact this appears unlikely. First of all, the theory described by Wittgenstein demands that an idea be treated quite seriously as a mental *picture.* St. Thomas speaks of ideas as being likenesses of the things which are thought of by their aid, and this has sometimes led people to think that he was talking of mental images. But according to his terminology mental images seem rather to be phantasms; and phantasms are sharply distinguished from ideas. Phantasms, he says, come and go from day to day, but ideas remain for life; the image of one man differs from the image of another, but both are recognised as men by one and the same idea or *species* (ScG, II, 73 and 78).

Moreover, the "mental sample" view of abstraction leaves no room for the task Aquinas assigns to the agent intellect. When Aquinas talks of the need for the agent intellect to make the phantasms actually intelligible, he seems to be making the same point as Wittgenstein is making when he says that even a schematic sample has to be understood *as a schema* if it is to help us to understand what a leaf is. Indeed Aquinas expressly rejects the idea that a concept is just a mental image shorn of inessential features.

Through the power of the agent intellect and through its attention (*conversio*) to the phantasms, there results in the receptive intellect a certain likeness which is a representation of the things whose phantasms they are, but only in respect of their specific nature. It is thus that the intelligible concept is said to be abstracted from the phantasms; it is not that numerically the same form, which was at one time in the phantasms, later comes into the receptive intellect, in the way in which a body may be taken from one place and transferred to another.

This is confirmed when Aquinas contrasts the abstraction made by the intellect with that made by the senses. For even the senses, he explains, do abstract in a way.

A sense-perceptible form is not in the same manner in the thing outside the soul as it is in the sense-faculty. The sense-faculty receives the forms of sense-perceptible things without their matter, as it receives the colour of gold without the gold; and similarly the intellect receives the ideas of bodies, which are material and changeable, in an immaterial and unchangeable fashion of its own (*S.Th.* Ia 84, 1).

The less materially a faculty possesses the form of the object it knows, Aquinas explains, the more perfectly it knows: thus the intellect, which abstracts the ideas not only from matter but also from material individuating characteristics, is a more perfect cognitive power than the senses, which receive the form of what they know without matter but not without material conditions (Ia, 84, 2). Perceptible qualities outside the soul are already actually perceptible; but since there are no Platonic ideas, there is nothing outside the soul actually intelligible corresponding to material objects (Ia 79, 3 ad 1).

Aquinas frequently insists that phantasms play a necessary part not only in the acquisition of concepts, but also in their application. During our mortal life, he says, "it is impossible for our intellect to perform any actual exercise of understanding (*aliquid intelligere in actu*) except by attending to phantasms." He offers two proofs of this thesis. First, although the intellect has no organ of its own, the exercise of the intellect may be impeded by injury to the organs of imagination (as in frenzy) or of memory (as in amnesia). Such brain damage prevents not only the acquisition of new knowledge, but also the utilization of previously acquired knowledge. This shows that the intellectual exercise of habitual knowledge requires the cooperation of imagination and other powers. Secondly, he says, "everyone can experience in his own case that when he tries to understand something, he forms some phantasms for himself by way of examples in which he can so to speak take a look at what he is trying to understand." Similarly "when we want to make someone understand something, we suggest examples to him from which he can form his own phantasms in order to understand" (Ia 84, 7).

A metaphysical reason is offered to explain this. The proper object of the human intellect in the human body is "the quiddity or nature existing in corporeal matter". The quiddities of corporeal things must exist in corporeal individuals.

Thus, it is part of the concept of a stone, that it should be instantiated in a particular stone, and part of the concept of a horse, that it should be instantiated in a particular horse, and so on; so the nature of a stone or of any material thing cannot be completely and truly known unless it is known as existing in the particular; but the particular is apprehended by the senses and the imagination. Consequently, in order to have actual understanding of its proper object, the intellect must turn to phantasms to study the universal nature existing in the particular (Ia, 84, 7).[2]

Several things are noteworthy about this whole argument. First, it starts from the premise that there is no bodily organ of the intellect. One might be inclined to ask: how does St. Thomas know that brain activity is not necessary for thought, even for the most abstract and intellectual thought? Second, these two possible lines of answers suggest themselves. The first is that St. Thomas would agree that there is not in fact, in this life, any thought, however exalted, which is not accompanied by brain activity. But he would say that this was precisely because there was no thought, however exalted, which is not accompanied by the activity of the imagination or the senses. The second is that even if brain activity is a necessary condition for thought, this does not make the brain an organ of thought in the way that the eyes are the organ of sight and the tongue and palate are organs of taste. An organ is, as its etymology suggests, something like a tool, a part of the body which can be voluntarily moved and used in characteristic ways which affect the efficiency of the discriminatory activity which it serves. The difficulty is that these two answers seem to cancel out. In the sense of "organ" in which there is no organ of thought, there is no organ of imagination either—I cannot move my brain in order to imagine better in the way that I can turn my eyes to see better—and in the sense in which the

[2] As it is more than usually difficult to provide an untendentious translation of this passage, I give the original. *De ratione naturae lapidis est, quod sit in hoc lapide; et de ratione naturae equi est, quod sit in hoc equo: et sic de aliis. Unde natura lapidis, vel cuiuscumque materialis rei cognosci non potest complete, et vere, nisi secundum quod cognoscitur ut in particulari existens: particulare autem apprehendimus per sensum et imaginationem. Et ideo, necesse est, ad hoc quod intellectus actu intelligat suum obiectum proprium, quod convertat se ad phantasmata, ut speculetur naturam universalem in particulari existentem.*

brain is an organ of the imagination there seems no good reason to deny that it is an organ also of the intellect.

Again, the second argument seems to concern rather the first acquisition of understanding than its later utilisation. This is so whether we think of St. Thomas as having in mind the production of diagrams (as when in the *Meno* Socrates taught the slave-boy geometry) or the construction of fictional illustrations (as when Wittgenstein imagines primitive language-games in order to throw light on the workings of language). It does not seem to be true that whenever concepts are exercised there must be something going on, even mentally, which is rather like the drawing of a diagram or the telling of a detailed story.

Despite all this, it does seem true in one sense that there must be some exercise of sense or imagination, some application to a sensory context, if one is to talk at all of the exercise of concepts or the application of the knowledge of necessary truths. For a man to be exercising the concept, say, of red, it seems that he must be either discriminating red from other colours around him, or having a mental image of redness, or a mental echo of the word "red", or be talking, reading, or writing about redness, or something of the kind. He may indeed be able to *possess* the concept *red* without this showing in his experience or behaviour on a given occasion, but it seems that without some vehicle of sensory activity there could be no *exercise* of the concept on that occasion. Similarly with the knowledge of a general truth, such as that two things that are equal to a third are equal to each other. For this knowledge to be exercised it seems that its possessor must either enunciate it, or apply it say in the measurement of objects, or utilise it in some other way even if only in the artful manipulation of symbols.

This seems both true and important, but the nature of Aquinas' arguments for his thesis makes it doubtful whether he understood it in this sense. It is true that he does say that the phantasm employed in the exercise of the concept of A need not be the phantasm of A itself. But when he says this he has in mind particular cases where A is something immaterial and to that extent unpictureable (*S.Th.* Ia 74, 7 ad 3). Whereas it seems that for it to be the case that every exercise of a concept involved attention to a phantasm, it would rarely be the case that the phantasm attended to was a representation of the object of the concept.

Attention to phantasms (*conversio ad phantasmata*) is, according to Aquinas, something which is necessary for every exercise of every concept, whether in general or particular judgements. But uses of general concepts in judgements about perceptible particulars presented him with a special problem: the judgement, for instance, that this tomato is red, that these particular objects matching a single standard match each other. Aquinas thought that it was the sensory context which gave the judgement its particular reference; and this view has recently been defended by Geach (*Mental Acts,* 65ff.). In expounding Aquinas, however, Geach appears to misrepresent his position. "Aquinas' expression", he writes, "for the relation of the 'intellectual' act of judgement to the context of sense-perception that gives it a particular reference was *conversio ad phantasmata*". But *conversio ad phantasmata,* as we have seen, is needed for all judgements, and not just for judgements about particulars; and for the special relation to sensory context involved in judgements about particulars Aquinas uses a different metaphor and speaks of reflection on sense-appearances, *reflexio supra phantasmata.*[3] This is introduced at *S.Th.* 86, 1, in answer to the question whether our intellect knows particulars. The answer reads as follows.

[3] On the distinction between *conversio* and *reflexio,* see Lonergan, *Verbum,* 159 ff.

Our intellect cannot directly and primarily know particular material things. The reason is that the principle of individuation in material things is individual matter: but as was said above, our intellect understands by abstracting intelligible ideas from such matter. What is abstracted from individual matter is universal, and so our intellect is directly capable of knowing only universals. But indirectly and by a kind of reflection it can know individuals, because as was said above even after it has abstracted intelligible ideas, it cannot exercise them in acts of understanding without turning to phantasms. . . . Thus, by means of its ideas it directly understands the universal, and indirectly the particulars of which the phantasms are phantasms; and thus it forms this proposition, *Socrates is a man* (Ia 86, 1).

Exactly what is meant by "reflection" is and remains obscure in Aquinas' writings, and I shall not attempt to investigate it here. But I must turn to the overdue task of interpreting the notion of *phantasm*. There are many passages in Aquinas, some of which have been quoted, where translations such as "sense-appearances" or "sense-impressions" suggest themselves (e.g. *S.Th.* Ia, 74, 6). But in other places it seems, as one would expect, that phantasms are produced by the *phantasia* or imagination. This, we are told, is the locus of forms which have been received from the senses as the receptive intellect is the locus of ideas (*S.Th.* Ia 78, 4). These forms, we are told, may be reshuffled at will to produce phantasms of anything we care to think about: we can for example combine the form which represents Jerusalem and the form which represents fire to make the phantasm of Jerusalem burning (*De Veritate*, XII, 7). This makes a phantasm appear to be something like a mental image. But if we accept this interpretation, then it seems that St. Thomas is wrong in saying that phan-

tasms are particular in the way sense-impressions are.
I cannot see a man who is no particular colour, but
I may have a mental image of a man without having
a mental image of a man of a particular colour, and
I may imagine a man without being able to answer
such questions as whether the man I am imagining is
dark or fair. Imagination differs from sensation in another way which makes it misleading to combine the
two under a single rubric such as "phantasm". It is
not possible to be mistaken about what one is imagining in the various ways in which it is possible to be
mistaken about what one is seeing: a man's description of what he imagines enjoys a privileged status
not shared by his description of what he sees. There
are some passages in which St. Thomas seems to suggest that whenever we see something we have at the
same time a phantasm of what we see; and sensory
illusions are explained by saying that the senses themselves are not deceived, but only the *phantasia* on
which they act (*In IV Met*, lect. 14). It seems implausible to suggest that whenever we see a horse we
have at the same time a mental image of a horse.
Perhaps the theory is that if we see accurately our
phantasm of a horse is a sense-impression; if we are
mistaken about what we see, and there is no horse
there at all, then our phantasm is a mental image. This
theory seems to be confused in several ways, but it is
hard to be sure whether St. Thomas held it or not.

Certainly St. Thomas is prepared to call the imagination a *sense*: sight, hearing, etc. are outer senses, the
memory and the imagination are inner senses. This
suggests an unacceptable assimilation. We can see
some reason for calling the imagination a sense if we
reflect that the power to have visual imagery depends
on the ability to see. But this was not St. Thomas'
reason for calling the imagination a sense, because he
thought that this dependence was not a matter of
logic but a contingent fact (*De Veritate*, XII, 7). In
fact he thought that the inner senses resembled the

outer senses in having particular objects and bodily organs. As we have seen, both these points of resemblance seem in fact to be lacking. Consequently it is difficult to accept Aquinas' theory of the inner senses, and in particular of the imagination, without modification.

This has important consequences not only for his theory of abstraction but also for the whole problem of the relations between mind and body. In the course of a polemic against Averroes, Aquinas had occasion to raise the question: what makes an individual's ideas *his* ideas (Ia, 76, 1 and 2)? Clearly, there need be nothing in the content of a belief held by one man to distinguish it from a belief held by others. Innumerable people besides myself believe that $2 + 2 = 4$: when I believe this, what makes the belief *my* belief? Aquinas' answer, in effect, is that my beliefs are beliefs of the soul which is individuated by my body, and because they are acquired and employed with the aid of phantasms generated by my brain (Ia IIae, 50, 4). This answer seems to lead to an account of the relationship between mind in body which is fundamentally as dualistic as that of Descartes. For it follows, and St. Thomas himself drew the conclusion, that the body is necessary for intellectual activity not in order to provide the mind with an instrument, but only to provide the mind with an object—phantasms being, in one sense of the word "object", the object of the intellect's activity. (See Aristotle, *De Anima* 1, 403a8ff, and St. Thomas' commentary). If this is a correct account then my body is no more essentially concerned in my thought than Leonardo is concerned in my looking at the Mona Lisa. This is what enables St. Thomas to say that thought is an activity of the soul alone, and thus that the soul, having an independent activity, is capable also of independent existence, as an incorruptible substance in its own right (*S.Th.* Ia 75, 6).

The question "What makes my thoughts *my*

thoughts?" has an oddly contemporary ring. It would perhaps be rash to think that contemporary studies have provided an answer to the question; but they have certainly shown one direction in which to look for an answer. My thoughts, surely, are the thoughts which find expression in the words and actions of *my body*. If we are to make progress with such perennial problems as "can my thoughts outlast my body?" it seems that we must investigate the relation between thought and its expression in linguistic and non-linguistic behaviour. It is a weakness of St. Thomas' philosophy of mind that he has very little to say about this relation.

THE IMMORTALITY OF THE SOUL

The Traditional Argument

HERBERT MC CABE

I have been asked to present once more the traditional thomist argument that the soul must be immortal because by the soul we think and understand.
I intend simply to restate the argument which St.
Thomas develops in *Q.D. de Anima* a.14, and in Ia,
75, 2 and 6.

First I should like to make it clear that the argument
with which I am dealing is intended to be a demonstration; that is, it is intended to make it quite certain
that the soul is immortal. I should not be surprised to
find that the argument is full of unsuspected flaws,
but I should be very surprised to find that it rendered
the immortality of the soul probable or highly likely.
A man of proper modesty might say, "I find this argument entirely convincing, but I have been wrong so
many times before; for this reason I only find it very
probable that the soul is immortal." My point is that
there cannot be an *argument* to show that it is probable that the soul is immortal. I shall not argue this
point: I only mention it because one sometimes hears
modern scholastics saying that no argument for the
immortality of the soul can be absolutely convincing.
I think that such an argument cannot claim to be
anything less.

First of all, then, why do we speak of a soul at all?
We say that Fido sees and barks and wags his tail
and so on. He sees with his eyes and without them he

A paper read to a Symposium at Spode House, Staffordshire,
and reprinted with permission of the author.

cannot see. Nevertheless, when we want to find out whether Fido sees or not we do not simply examine his eyes. We know that termites cannot see, not because we have examined their eyes but because they behave in exactly the same way in the dark as in the light, etc. To find out whether an animal sees we look at its whole behaviour, we look at what it does with its feet as well as what it does with its eyes. But Fido won't go blind if you injure his feet, whereas he may well go blind if you injure his eyes. The whole animal is concerned in seeing, but the eyes specially. The other parts of the body have no special task in seeing; there are all kinds of things that they might do to show that seeing is going on, but the eye has a special task. What the eye does is only seeing if this special task plays some part in the whole behaviour of the animal. An eye cannot see by itself, even if it goes through the motions, just as a leg cannot walk by itself. What sees is Fido with his eyes.

We say that Fido has a soul and is not simply a collection of instruments because we say that these instruments are doing certain jobs—seeing, swallowing, walking etc.—and what they are doing would not be these jobs unless the tasks they performed were parts of the behaviour of the whole animal. To talk about the activities of a thing as seeing, or eating etc., in fact to talk about its behaviour at all, is to talk about it as having a soul, or it is to talk of it as though it had a soul (e.g. we sometimes talk about machines as if they grasped and swallowed and detected and rejected, and this is to talk of them *as if* they had souls).

When Fido is dead he no longer *behaves*, things go on but they are no longer behaviour. Perhaps we could stimulate any of the organs of the body so that it did the same things as it did in life, but we would not call this seeing or sneezing or walking just because there is no general response of the whole animal. When Fido dies he is not *altered* in some way. It is not that something is true of him now which was not true of him before: but a whole way of talking about him has become inappropriate. He has been replaced by something or else some things which have to be spoken about in a different way. We cannot say that the group of chemicals which is Fido's corpse have stopped barking or are blind. It is true that until the chemical changes are well advanced we still do use animal language; we speak of his head and legs and tail, but this is simply to speak of the corpse as though it were an animal (cf. the machines) and the words are used, as Aristotle says, equivocally.

All this is to say that Fido's death is, in traditional terms, a *substantial change*. To lose the soul is to lose the substantial form and not just an accidental form, it is to perish and not just to be altered. The substantial form is that in virtue of which the thing is what it is (e.g. that in virtue of which Fido is a dog) and hence that in virtue of which the thing is at all. For Fido to cease to be a living dog is for him to cease to be at all.

Having buried Fido let us turn to George. George, like Fido, is an animal, and in his case, too, we speak of a soul. What makes his eyes genuine eyes that *see*, and makes his legs genuine legs that *walk*, is his soul. It is his soul that makes his body what it is. But the soul of George is not simply a matter of his having genuine bodily organs. Of course it is by his soul that George sees and walks, but it is also by his soul that he does some other things which are not bodily activities, notably understanding. I know it sounds scandalous to suggest that understanding is an operation that can be placed beside or alongside bodily activity, but this seems to me no more inevitably misleading than to say that George both sees and walks. Certainly seeing is not an operation in the sense that walking is and, of course, understanding is an operation in yet another sense. The general modern practice seems to be to restrict the word "operation" to bodily

or physical processes. I think this arises because of a
strong emphasis on the difference between what St.
Thomas would call transient and immanent activity.
This is all to the good, but while most philosophers
would agree in warning us not to be misled by treating
seeing or thinking as an operation in the sense that
running or pushing is an operation, there seems to be
no generally agreed advice on how we *are* to talk
about seeing and thinking. Until a new terminology
appears we shall have to be content with the old one.

The conclusion that George performs by his soul
activities which are not bodily activities will be taken
to show that the soul of George is subsistent. And this
will be taken to show that the doctrine that his soul
does not perish is not a trivial doctrine, as it might
appear at first sight. For as we shall see there is a
trivial sense in which the soul of Fido, or the number
2, cannot perish. To say that some things can and
others cannot perish is, of course, to lay claim to a
theory of perishing, and at the risk of being very
tedious I must say something briefly about this.

A thing cannot simply *be* in the vague. It has to be
something. For an elephant to be is not for it to have
a common property called being or existence; it is for
it to be an elephant. And if it is to cease to be, it
must be by its ceasing to be an elephant.

Each thing, says St. Thomas, has existence according to its own form, hence existence and form cannot
be separated.

Where there is form there is existence. Things cease
to be by ceasing to be this kind of thing; that is, they
cease to be by losing the form in virtue of which they
are what they are. The kind of change in which they
perish is a change in which their form is replaced by
another form, and for this to happen is for a new thing
to come into existence.

When we say that something, e.g. a dog, can perish,
we are saying both that it is (a dog) and that it is
capable of becoming an indefinite variety of other

things. That in virtue of which it is a dog we call its *form*. That in virtue of which it is capable of being something other than it is we call its *matter*. To have this capacity just is to be perishable.

Perhaps I ought to say here, to avoid misunderstanding, that there is a sense in which absolutely anything which is not God is capable of not being. Even a "necessary being", which is imperishable in the sense that it cannot substantially change into something else, is capable of not existing in the sense that its existence is *received* from God. I am here concerned simply to show that the soul cannot perish.

Now since matter and form are the terms in which we analyse perishing, it seems clear that we cannot sensibly talk of either matter or form themselves perishing. It is as though I should say "We shorten this pole by making it less than a yard long; now how do we shorten a yard itself?" The difficulty about shortening a yard is not that it is peculiarly tough, but that it has not got any length to decrease. A yard, unlike a yard-stick, is not 36 inches long, it is 36 inches. It is therefore trivial to say that a yard cannot be shortened: it is crazy to speak of a yard being 36 inches long and hence equally crazy to speak of its being or becoming less than 35 inches long. In the same way it seems trivial to say that a form cannot perish. It clearly is trivial in the case of a form which is simply that in virtue of which something is; but it would not be trivial in the case of a form which itself existed.

At first sight we might be inclined to think that to say a form exists is like saying that a yard is 36 inches long; it is one of the things we may not do with language.

Thus St. Thomas says: "Existence is not taken away from anything that has it except by taking its form from it; hence if what has existence is the form itself, it is impossible that existence should be taken from it."

And this certainly looks like saying: "Wetness is not taken from anything that has it except by taking water from it; hence if what has wetness is the water itself, it is impossible that wetness should be taken from it."

In this second case we do not say that whereas other things can be dried with phosphorus pentoxide or towels, water has a special logical resistance to such methods and remains immutably wet; we say that water can only be called wet in the special sense that it makes other things wet.

Similarly in the first case we do not say that whereas most things can be destroyed by massacre or fire or atomic fission, forms have a queer logical durability that resists all attack; we say that forms only exist in the pickwickian sense that they are that in virtue of which other things exist. Philosophers have often said that just as words like "wet" and "36 inches long" have a restricted field of application, so "exists" can only be used of certain kinds of things; some of them, for example, have thought that "God exists" can only mean "God is what makes sensible things exist".

Metaphysical objections can be dealt with as they are brought up; for the moment let me remind you of what St. Thomas is saying when he says that "this form exists". St. Thomas simply says that man has an operation by his soul which is not an operation of the body and that therefore his soul itself subsists. The subsistence of the soul has no more *content* than that. If St. Thomas had argued that the body has also operations which are not operations of the soul, he would have held, as e.g. Descartes seems to have done, that man is two substances, a soul and a body. This, of course, he constantly denies.

There are two points to be made clear here. The first is that St. Thomas did not think that the soul is immortal because it is immaterial. He held that the soul of Fido is immaterial and that the number 2 is immaterial. His argument is not simply that the soul is not material but that it subsists immaterially inasmuch as it operates immaterially. The second point is that he does not make what would ordinarily be called a psychological search to find this operation of the soul. We are not going to be presented by introspection with an activity of the mind which is commonly overlooked. We shall not in the end be able to see ourselves think, except in the sense that it is perfectly easy to see ourselves or other people thinking. We shall simply be concerned to see what is involved in saying that we understand something. We shall not be able to tease much out of this but we shall find that whatever understanding means, it *at least* means a non-bodily operation.

St. Thomas illustrates his argument with the aid of medieval physiology. The eye, he says, can see all colours just because the pupil of the eye has no colour itself. The same point can, I think, be made with coloured spectacles. A man who wears blue spectacles does not simply see things differently from a man with colourless spectacles; he sees *less* because he cannot distinguish between white and pale blue. If we are told that a man can distinguish all the colours then we can be sure that his spectacles are themselves colourless and invisible. Now St. Thomas says: by his mind a man can understand the natures of all corporeal things and therefore it cannot itself possess the nature of any corporeal thing. To understand, therefore, is not the function of any corporeal thing.

In St. Thomas' view one can possess a nature, say the nature of a dog, naturally—this would be *to be* a dog; or one can possess it intentionally or intelligibly—this would be *to know* the nature. He argues that one could not possess *every* bodily nature intentionally if one possessed *any* bodily nature naturally. The mind must be beyond any particular bodily nature because it stands over, transcends, them all.

Now it sounds arbitrary to say that understanding a nature means possessing it, even if we qualify the possessing by saying "only intentionally, of course". But here we ought to notice how little "possession" or "having" means here: it is just the word we use with "nature": George *possesses* or *has* the nature *of* George.

What is being said is that, for example, the nature which is the meaning of the word "cow" having *esse naturale* constitutes that cow a cow and not, e.g. a horse, and having *esse intentionale* in my mind constitutes my understanding the understanding of the meaning of "cow" rather than, say, of "horse".

This doctrine will be totally misunderstood if it is not recognized that it is intended to be *obvious*. It is not a description of a process by which we understand, if there is any such process. It is a platitude; it says "What I have in mind when I know the nature of a cow is the nature of a cow and nothing else". Now in case someone says "But if the nature you have in your mind is that of a cow, surely your mind must be a cow—for to have the nature of an X simply means to be an X", St. Thomas merely replies that to understand the nature of a cow is to have this nature precisely *without* being a cow, and this is what is made clear by saying that one has the nature *in mind*. To have it in mind doesn't mean anything except that you have the nature without being the thing whose nature it is. And this he calls "having the nature intentionally".

The mind, for St. Thomas, just is the locus of intentional being.

Suppose someone thought of the mind as a place or as an instrument, like the retina of the eye, or the nose. And suppose he said: I understand what a cow is because I have a representation or picture of a cow in my mind. This picture is what makes him able to distinguish between what a cow is and what a horse is. The picture by which he understands what a cow is differs from the picture by which he understands what a horse is in ways exactly corresponding to the differences between horses and cows. Now one of the characteristic things about a picture is that it is first of all something in its own right—a piece of canvas or wood —and then it resembles something. Now it is just the things that the picture has in its own right that must be forbidden to the picture in the mind. If it were a picture on wood, it would not serve to distinguish a cow from a cow painted on wood; if it were made of cast iron it would not help to tell a cow from a cast iron lawn-cow. There is no *mental stuff* that the picture could be made of—it must have everything the cow has and nothing else. It cannot *resemble* a cow because anything except the sheer resemblance will be an alien element like wood or cast iron. It must be simply everything that a cow has and nothing else. And what is this except to be the nature of the cow?

I have said a lot about the act of understanding, but this might seem a puzzling notion. Where is such an act to be found? What, for instance, connects a calculation on a bit of paper with an act of understanding, if there is such an act?

To answer this question we may digress for a moment. St. Thomas connects understanding with knowing what a thing is, with knowing the *quod quid est* of a thing. To know the *quod quid est* of a thing means knowing the kind of questions which can be asked and which cannot be asked about it.

This sense of the question "What is it?" is answered by trying to give a definition and the purpose of a definition is to give some account of the field of discourse to which the thing belongs, to know the definition is to know how to talk appropriately about the thing. It follows from this that the question "What is it?" is the one question which can never be inappropriate; there are indeed ways of answering the question which will be inappropriate—it would be wrong to expect an account of the ways in which we should talk about something of which we cannot talk because we do not understand it.

This sense of the question "What is it?" is not simply one important sense amongst others. There are innumerable ways in which the question may be asked, but in all these cases the question is asked because we have lost touch with the speaker. We have not understood something which we suppose him to understand. We may merely have lost touch physically as when we do not hear him and we say "What"— meaning "please repeat that", or we may fear that we may have not got the right nuance of meaning in one of his words, or we may be simply at a loss. Now I suggest that the fundamental sense of "What is it?" has to do with the fundamental way in which we lose touch with, or come to grips with, a speaker. We ask this question when there is danger of complete cross-purposes, when we are in danger of talking different languages. We need to know the answer to this sense of the question "What is it?" lest the things that the speaker says should sound like "The square root of aluminium is. . . ." To be told the answer is to be told how to talk about the thing under discussion and how not to talk about it.

Now to return to the question where the understanding comes in. The understanding comes into the calculation in so far as the calculation is an exercise of this knowing how to talk about something. It is this that characterises it as a *sum*. It is not an element in what goes on which makes the difference between a mechanical and a human calculation. To say that would be like saying that the one element which distinguished a man from a very life-like statue was his humanity. It is a queer thing to ask for the one important difference which will enable you to distinguish between a man thinking and a machine. You might not be able to distinguish between them under some circumstances and in some respects, but this is just because the calculating machine is intended to be an imitation man, just as a statue is an imitation man.

AQUINAS ON INTENTIONALITY

PETER SHEEHAN

If we regard a thought as a mental event, questions
arise of this form: what account are we to give of the
relation between the mental event which is the
thought and the object of the thought, particularly in
the cases in which the object of the thought is some
material thing other than the thinker? And relatedly:
what account are we to give of thinking of something
to explain satisfactorily the relation between the
thought and its object?[1]

There are several objections to some of the most obvious accounts of what the thought of X consists in,
and thus to some obvious answers to these questions.
Consider the following, which I offer as a general
argument directed against any view which maintains
that the thought of X consists in the mental occurrence of any entity or experience (A) which bears
some relation (natural, conventional or otherwise,
R) to the object of the thought X. It is thus directed
against the view that the thought of X is a matter of
the occurrence in the mind of the word 'X' (or other
appropriate words), the image, picture, etc. of X, or
the idea of X, where this is given some further rela-

I wish to express my thanks to Mr. Justin Gosling, Dr. A.
Kenny and Reverend P. Crittenden for discussions of the topics
of this paper and for help in preparing it, and also to the
trustees of the Dr. H. Nowland Travelling Scholarship for support of the research on which it is based.

[1] This paper will assume that the concept of a mental event
can be made sufficiently clear to be usable and that a workable
definition of "object of thought" can be given as follows: that
the object of thought is what is referred to by the phrase or
clause in object position in the answer to the question "what are
you thinking of?" i.e. whatever is referred to by X in "I am/was
thinking of X." The implications lying behind both of these
cannot be taken up here.

tional account. With the premise that one knows at
the time, and not through any observation, recognition or inference, what is the object of one's thought,
the argument is: On such an account, for the thought
to be of X, A must occur and the person concerned
must believe that A stands in the given relation to X
(ARX). But the belief that ARX must actually be entertained at that time, for he knows immediately at
the time what it is that he is thinking of. If the belief
were not actually entertained, but were still what
makes my thought of X, then it must be possible that
I am unable to recall it, or uncertain as to what A is
related to. This situation would then be one in which
I thought of something, or thought that I had thought
of something, and yet never knew what it was that I
was thinking of, a situation clearly excluded by the
above. But to entertain the belief that ARX requires
that it be possible to think of X other than through the
occurrence of A. Now applying the account consistently we might say that this thought of X consisted of
the occurrence of some B, and the entertaining of the
belief that BR_1X. It is clear at this point, however,
that this line of argument leads to a vicious regress
and hence that it must be possible to think of X other
than through the mental occurrence of something related to X. And not just in some cases—in all our cases
of thinking of X, there must be a thought of X other
than via some relation.

There are several remarks to be made in further exposition of this argument. Firstly, it may be worth
pointing out that the above argument turns essentially
on the supposed necessity of the entertaining of the
belief that ARX, although it might seem that it could
be mounted just from the fact that this belief must at
least be held if the thought is to be of X and known to
be of X. But this is false as one can say that holding
the belief ARX commits one only to at some stage
entertaining (or being in a position to entertain) ARX
in the form of A, R, and some uniquely specifying

description (e.g. the cow in the corner) of X. That is, holding the belief that ARX requires that one is able to think of X apart from the occurrence of A, but it at least needs another argument to show that this may not be through the occurrence, at some other time, of a uniquely specifying description of X. In other words, if only the *possession* of the belief were required, then the regress as described would not be set up, for the condition that the person concerned can think of X independently of the occurrence of A is not required at the time, to make sense of the original act of thinking of. But if to explain the peculiar knowledge we have of the object of our thought we must at that time entertain (on the account under discussion) the belief ARX, the whole argument remains.

Secondly, the premise that one knows at the time, and not through any observation, recognition or inference, what is the object of one's thought needs some discussion, for it may be challenged as hopelessly vague or charged with begging the question against the relation view. The cases which I have in mind are such as these: I am sitting thinking of X, a friend of mine, or it occurs to me that X might come, and I describe this by saying that I was thinking of, or thought of, X. Now it seems clear that one thing is not possible in such cases, viz. that I believe at the time that I was thinking of, or thought of, someone but that in fact I was not. I may of course be thinking of Y and call him X, or forget whom I was thinking of, or believe that I was thinking of a real person X who in fact does not exist. But it is not possible that I believe at the time that I was thinking of someone or something and not be able to say who it was[2], and my failure not be ascribable to my having forgotten: in other words,

[2] Finding myself confused and not being able to pick out a single actual person won't count as not being able to say who it was. As this last phrase is used here I can say who it was all right. The trouble is that what I say is confused or contradictory.

that my failure to be able to say whom or what I was thinking of should show that I falsely believed at the time that I was thinking of someone or something. This I take to be the cash value of the premise about knowing at the time, and it is all that the argument requires. If problems are felt about the class of cases of which this is claimed and to which the argument applies, this can be cleared up by saying that the argument applies only to the class of cases for which the premise holds.

Let us consider some more specific cases of the mental occurrence A and the relation R. For example, it might be said that thinking of X is having a picture or image of X, or of something one associates immediately with X, occur to one. That is, A here is a picture or image, and the relation R is the relation "being a picture of" or "being an image of". Now apart from the likely objection that one can think of X without any given picture occurring to one (and perhaps without any at all), the above objection comes to the fact that here knowing what one is thinking of would be a matter of recognizing or realizing or being aware of what the picture was a picture of, and that this involves both the possibility of misrecognition and the difficulty that to be able to recognize A as a picture of X at a given time (i.e. in a way which excludes the possibility that it may turn out that I did not know what it was a picture of) seems to involve thinking of X other than through the occurrence of A, and so on. And the same applies if we were to say that what occurred was the word "Peter", and the relation was "standing for" or "being the name of" (i.e. if we endeavour to give an account of this aspect of thought in terms of naming or standing for, linguistic relations). One would need to be aware that "Peter" was the name of *that* person, and this would seem to involve one again in the difficulties above. Thus consider Ayer's claim: "Thus we may define an object of thought as follows: 'A is thinking of X if and only if either (1) A is using certain symbols of which at least one designates X, or (2) there is a Y such that A is using certain symbols of which at least one designates Y and it is a fact that X is Y . . .' (2 further conditions)."[3] This clearly gives an account of thinking of something in terms of a given expression referring to that thing. Now the claim of the argument will be that if this account were correct it would follow that it could turn out that the person could not say, and did not know, who it was that the symbol designated, in which case it would have been true that he thought he was thinking of someone or something but was mistaken. But in the relevant use of "thinking of", this does not make sense. Further, this could be avoided only by requiring that he know at the time who it designated, but this implies thinking of X other than via the symbol, and on the current account leads to a regress.

There is a further simple objection to the sort of view expressed by Ayer's "A is using certain symbols of which at best one designates X",[4] at least when this is interpreted as A using a certain symbol to mean X, and generally to any view which explains what I am thinking of, and my knowledge of what I am thinking of in terms of what I mean or intend by the use of a given symbol. Namely: using a certain symbol and meaning or intending X by the use of it is essentially an intentional action (e.g. it would make sense to ask why I meant X rather than Y by the use of it, or to plan to, or decide to, use it to mean X on a given occasion), but most of our cases of thinking of something are not intentional actions, and so this could not be a correct account of these cases. Now one clearly could not unintentionally use a symbol and mean or intend X by the use of it—to establish that a given action was unintentional is sufficient to establish that

[3] A. J. Ayer, *Thinking and Meaning*, Inaugural Lecture, University College, London, 1947, p. 13.
[4] *Thinking and Meaning*, p. 13.

nothing was meant or intended either in it or by it, in any relevant sense of "meant".[5] And it also seems clear that if something could not be said to be either intentional or unintentional, then one could not be said to mean or intend something either in it or by it.

Another argument against the "relation" view of thinking of something can be mounted by considering the fact that at least very often, a person is unable to say what it was that his thought of X consisted in or even what, if anything, occurred in his mind when he thought of X. If I am trying to think of an unmarried professor of philosophy and suddenly think of Ryle and am then asked "Did thinking of Ryle involve the having of an image of him, did the word 'Ryle' occur, or something else?", I will very often not be able to answer this question. And this is a general fact—very often the mind flounders on such a question, and it cannot be certainly answered. In claiming this as a fact, I am not claiming that it is a fact that we can think of something without having any images of or symbols for that thing occur in the mind, for this latter claim could at least be disputed, and it be asserted e.g. that people could be trained so that they could always report what images or symbols they had. Be that as it may, it cannot be denied that *now* many people are often unable to say with certainty whether or not they had an image or a symbol, but those people still know perfectly well who or what they are thinking of. And from these juxtaposed facts it follows that knowing what one is thinking of cannot be, in these cases at least, a matter of knowing or recognizing what the image is an image of, or the symbol a symbol for, or of knowing who or what you are using the symbol to mean. But if thinking of something consists in the occurrence of an image or of a symbol for that thing in the mind, or of using a symbol to mean that thing,

[5] This last phrase is intended to exclude e.g. the sense in which a Freudian may claim that I meant something by un-intentionally knocking over the vase.

then this must be what knowing what one is thinking of amounts to. So it follows that those doctrines are false.

Now it must be noted concerning this argument that it presumes that a person's not being able to say what his thought of X consisted in is not to be ascribed in general to his having forgotten, but this seems reasonable. Although there could of course be cases in which I have forgotten, if I just think of Ryle and am immediately asked what that thought consisted in, word or image, the supposition that I knew but have forgotten is surely highly implausible, and this would apply to very many such cases. Not only would this supposition be implausible, but it would get very close to being vacuous. For if someone were to claim in this case that I have always forgotten, he has to provide some reason for believing that I ever knew, and such a reason could only be forthcoming from me, but I have explicably disavowed knowing. But, it may be objected, consider reading—people can often say what they read, or what a certain passage said, and yet have no chance of repeating what the exact words were, but reading certainly involves recognizing the words on the page. So could not this be an analogy for thinking of something? That is, to the extent to which this argument is that the fact that in general a person cannot say what his thought consisted in shows that he could not know what his thought was of by recognizing what it consisted in, then the case of reading seems to provide a counter-example.

The reply to this must be twofold. Firstly, reading a passage is surely a case in which forgetting is plausible, simply because of the number of words involved, and a person would normally know, unless he had forgotten, the words of a single sentence which he had just read. So the case is not quite as clear as the example might suggest. Secondly, it may be queried whether it is completely certain that we read by recognizing individual words. Indeed, if it were established

that even after reading a simple sentence a person
could say what it meant but not repeat the words, then
would not this be exactly what would show that he
does not read by recognizing the various words? For
surely recognizing this as a word for "cat" or a name
for my mother (or as an image of my mother) entails
being aware of some word, name or image.

"Image or symbol" views of thinking of break up
into two types, one claiming that thinking of consists
in just the occurrence of the image or symbol, the
other claiming that it consists in the image or symbol
being used to mean or intend a given thing. Against
both the arguments I have presented seem decisive.

What, then, is the relation between thinking of
something and the object of that thinking? Faced with
this seemingly intelligible and appropriate question,
but also with apparently sound reasons for rejecting
the only obvious forms of answer, we might turn for
illumination to some medieval doctrines, seeing that
medieval writers are so often said to have first introduced the term "intentionality" and that some such
doctrine is often presented as a solution to the problem. If the arguments so far are accepted literally as
showing the falsity of any view which maintains that
the thought of X consists in the occurrence in the mind
of anything related to X, or the use of any word or
symbol to mean X, then it might seem to follow that
the thought must somehow involve the occurrence of
X itself. But of course when I think of my cat, *it* does
not occur in my mind simpliciter, so we might suppose
that it occurs in my mind in another mode of being, a
mode of being which is nothing other than a thing's
being thought of. Such a mode of being would entail
that what so existed was being thought of, and so the
problem about our knowledge of what we are thinking
of would not arise—to have my cat occur to me in that
way *is* to think of my cat, and to think of my cat involves knowing that I am thinking of my cat, so having my cat occur in this way also essentially involves

knowing that I was thinking of my cat. That is, this mode of being is, in a way, essentially conscious of itself. Further, we might add, the mind is nothing apart from the possibility of reception of such thoughts, and so there is no question of a knowing subject being aware of the occurrence of my cat in this mode in the mind, no question of a subject recognizing or observing that occurrence.

Now this type of view, which is sometimes offered as Aquinas' position, would certainly resolve our problem, but at a very substantial cost. For to say that anything is my cat seems to entail that what is so described is material, possesses some matter—to say that this is a cat but is not material is surely a clear contradiction. But the doctrine sketched above seems committed to a non-material mode of being of my cat, and it now seems completely obscure what could be meant by saying that this, in any sense, *is* my cat. (Or, for even clearer examples, take my car or my chair.) Other objections might arise too (e.g. prima facie circularity, problems with the idea of modes of being or existence) and so if this is the view of Aquinas it seems to be in great difficulties.

But of course this is a far too simplified, and essentially misleading, statement of any view which could be represented as being that of Aquinas on this topic, and we need to go into the matter more carefully. In his article on Aquinas in "Three Philosophers,"[6] P. T. Geach expounds Aquinas' doctrine by saying:

> What makes a sensation or thought of an X to be *of an* X is that it is an individual occurrence of that very form or nature which occurs in an X—it is thus that our mind "reaches right up to the reality"; what makes it to be a *sensation* or *thought* of an X rather than an actual X or an actual X-ness is that X-ness here occurs in the special way called *esse inten-*

[6] *Three Philosophers*, G. E. M. Anscombe and P. T. Geach, Basil Blackwell, Oxford, 1961, p. 95.

tionale and not in the "ordinary" way called *esse naturale*. This solution resolves the difficulty. It shows how being of an X is not a relation in which the thought or sensation stands, but is simply what the thought or sensation *is*. . . .

Let us try to see if this view could be understood as a solution to the problems of this paper. In stating it, Geach seems to use the terms "form" and "nature" interchangeably, as they are often used in such discussions, but as they can also be used in somewhat different senses, I will treat them in their different interpretations.

Consider then the view that the thought of an X (i.e. a particular known X) consists in the occurrence of the nature of that X with *esse intentionale*. Now for Aquinas the nature of a thing is what is given by its definition, and is *this* form plus matter, but not *this* matter, for it is essential to what this thing (e.g. my chair) is only that it should have some matter, not that it should have this matter. But now if one were to allow sense to speaking of the nature of a thing in this sense occurring at all, then 1) surely to suppose that this form and matter (i.e. the nature of this chair or cat) occurred immaterially, with non-material *esse*, is to suppose a contradiction, and 2) it would be completely obscure how such a thought would be of *this* cat or chair rather than any other cat or chair, for all cats (or all chairs) presumably have the same nature, and what is held to individuate this cat from among other beings with this same nature is the possession of this matter.

So perhaps the sense in which "nature" is different from "form" is not relevant, and the suggestion becomes just that the thought of X consists in the occurrence in the mind of the (individualized) form of X. Now why it is asserted that two modes of *esse* are involved is obscure, for we are surely not to suppose that there are two modes of being of the *form* of X.

But, it might be suggested, the basic distinction here between *esse naturale* and *intentionale* is that between the occurrence of a form together with matter and its occurrence without matter. But at this point the problem above arises—what individuates *this* cat or chair among other cats or chairs is the occurrence of the form together with a particular parcel of matter, and so a form free of relation to any matter could not be regarded as the form of this cat rather than of any other cat. Further, even if this were somehow solved, there would still arise a problem concerning how I knew what my thought was of, parallel to the ones raised earlier—this individualized form is the form of this cat rather than that one by bearing some relation to the former, and so one could only know what particular cat one was thinking of by knowing that this relation held, and so on.

Some remarks need to be made concerning these possible interpretations and the arguments given. Firstly, concerning whether *intentionale* and *naturale* could be taken as denoting modes of *esse* of the form in question, it might be urged that there is evidence (e.g. 1a Q56 art 2 ad 3) for believing that Aquinas was prepared to allow forms to have two such modes of *esse*. This passage concerns the knowledge which one angel (a pure subsisting form) has of another, and Aquinas has to confront the difficulty that if angel A knows angel B by the occurrence of the form of angel B in his intellect, this will imply that angel B himself is in A's intellect, as B is simply a subsisting form. His solution of this problem is to invoke the distinction between *esse naturale* and *intentionale* of B, and he goes on to draw a parallel with the form of colour on the wall, which exists with *esse naturale,* but in the mind of someone knowing it has *esse intentionale.* But this seems to apply only when the form is of something without matter, such as an angel or a colour; I can find no reason for believing that

Aquinas could have allowed that the form of a material thing could have two such *esses*.

Secondly, I have followed Geach in the above by allowing a distinction between individualized and non-individualized forms in Aquinas, and if it is further allowed that individualized forms could differ from case to case within the limits laid down by the definition of the species, it may be objected that such differences could enable the "form" doctrine to handle our problem. Be this last point as it may, the characteristic direct textual evidence for the presence of this distinction in Aquinas (e.g. 1a Q75 art 5 ad 1) also shows clearly that it is not individualized forms which occur in the mind in thought or knowledge. In the passage just quoted, for example, a distinction between "individual" and "absolute"[7] forms is used to explain the difference between the way primary matter receives forms and the way the intellect receives forms, and how the intellect can be moved from potentiality to act by the occurrence of a form without itself being composed of matter and form. Compare also "For if the intellectual soul were composed of matter and form, the forms of things would be received into it as individuals, and so it would only know the individual"[8]. So it will clearly be mistaken to think of individualized forms as what occurs in the mind in thought—but now it is becoming obscure how St. Thomas' doctrine could be interpreted as a solution to the problems of this part.

Thirdly, it seems a characteristic doctrine of Aquinas that for a form of A to exist it is simply for there to be something which is A[9]—only the form of

[7] These are the terms used in the English Dominican translation, as given in *The Basic Writings of St. Thomas Aquinas*, ed. by A. C. Pegis, Random House, 1945, p. 695. All quotations and references will be to this translation and edition, unless otherwise stated.

[8] 1a Q75 art 5.

[9] Cf. 1a Q84 art 4.

the human body, the soul, is held to be capable of existing independently of its matter. How then can he say that the form occurs immaterially in the mind when something is thought of?[10] This can probably be resolved by the distinction between individual and absolute forms. The doctrine of 1a Q75 art 5 is that as matter is the principle of individuation of forms, if the intellect was composed of matter and form then forms would be received into it as individuals, but in fact the form of a stone absolutely is in the intellectual soul. So he would seem to be prepared to allow that absolute forms can exist independently of their matter.[11]

This suggests the fourth point, which in turn leads on to the most important considerations. For we must notice that the main objection raised above to construing the doctrine of the occurrence of the form in the mind as a solution to the current problems (that the same form is common to, e.g., many different cats, and what individuates them is their different matter) was known to Aquinas, and its consequences were accepted by him. At 1a Q86 art 1 the question is raised whether the intellect knows singulars, and Aquinas argues that only universals are directly known, for matter is the principle of individuation of singulars and the mind understands by abstracting the intelligible species from such matter. Yet singulars are indirectly known, via the phantasms in which the intellect understands the species. This is consistent with the many passages in the *Summa* which stress that the mind's knowledge is primarily through the universal, and makes clear that if the remarks of

10 Compare e.g. "A thing is known in as far as its form is in the knower" *S.T.* 1a Q75 art 5.

11 But this still leaves the problem as to why St. Thomas speaks of intentional or mental *esse* here, as e.g. at 1a 2ae Q50 art 4 ad 2, and the comment on this passage in A. Kenny (ed. *and translation*) *Summa Theologiae, Dispositions for Human Acts,* Eyre and Spottiswoode, 1964, pp. 40–41.

Geach quoted earlier are interpreted as an answer to our problems (as they may but need not be)[12] then they over-simplify and misconstrue Aquinas' doctrine. So we need to attempt to understand the role of the phantasms in this "indirect" knowledge or thought of singular.

Aquinas stresses that phantasms are necessary for thought or understanding in two ways, that the mind can only understand through intelligible species abstracted from the phantasms and that it can only understand its proper object, actual existing things, through the phantasms. "Our intellect both abstracts the intelligible species *from* the phantasms in as much as it considers the natures of things universally, and yet understands these natures *in* the phantasms, since it cannot understand the things of which it abstracts the species, without turning to phantasms . . ." (1a Q85 art 1 ad 5). The point which concerns us here is that on this view what makes a thought or judgement *of* a particular X is that it is an act of judgement or a thought turned towards a particular set of phantasms. Now this relation to phantasms which introduces particularity into the judgement is mentioned by Aquinas very often (e.g. 1a Q85 a 7, 2a 2ae Q175 a 4: "and it is in considering these phantasms that the intellect judges of and co-ordinates sensible objects",[13] 3a Q11 ad 2 ad 1) but as far as I can see is never clarified beyond the use of the metaphors already given.

But this hardly matters for our purposes, for it has become clear that if Aquinas' doctrine is applied to our problem, then what makes my thought one of this

[12] If one takes "thought of an X" as Geach uses it in the passage given as e.g. "thought of a dog" rather than "thought of some particular dog" then Geach's remarks do not relate directly to my problem. This may well be his intention, but it is not altogether clear to me.

[13] Translated in P. Hoenen S.J., *Reality and Judgement According to St. Thomas,* Charles Scribner's Sons, New York, p. 28.

X rather than some other X (of this man or horse rather than some other man or horse) is the fact that certain phantasms or images are somehow involved. This account, however it is more fully filled out, would seem to be susceptible to the arguments already brought forward against the image or symbol view. For if it is the character of the phantasms or images which determines, in the sort of cases we are considering, what particular man my thought is of, then both the "knowing at the time" argument and the argument from not knowing what occurs are applicable and decisive. As far as our problem is concerned, the principle involved here is no different from that of the views already discussed.

The fact of the matter seems to be that the current problem was not one which greatly occupied Aquinas' attention, and unless quite drastic revisions are made his doctrine could not provide a solution to it. And it may be doubted in view of the discussion of this paper whether even drastic revisions would be successful.

IV

MORAL PHILOSOPHY

THE SCHOLASTIC THEORY OF

MORAL LAW IN THE MODERN WORLD

ALAN DONAGAN

Although no more than one religion can be true, it is now generally accepted that there may be honest mistakes about whether a given religion is the true one. Yet neither scholastic philosophers nor most plain men have yet been brought to agree that there may be honest fundamental mistakes about morality. Differences about morality are socially divisive, because many plain men consider that the state ought to enforce morality by legislation, if it can do so without infringing its citizens' moral rights. I remember that the church in which I was brought up as a child in Australia provoked great hostility by supporting legislation to close all liquor bars, in order to make it difficult to commit the sin of drinking alcohol. Since there are more drinkers than would-be divorcers, that hostility was much greater than that aroused towards the Catholic Church in New York by the opposition of some Catholics to changes in the divorce laws. Such examples remind us that the question I propose to discuss: 'How can what belongs to common morality be distinguished from what belongs to the way of life of a particular religion?' is, if nothing else, a timely one.

Yet it is not merely timely. St. Thomas himself recognized that only some precepts of the divine law (the revealed positive law of God) are also precepts of the natural law (the law of reason 'whereby each one knows, and is conscious of, what is good and

Proceedings of the American Catholic Philosophical Association, 1966, pp. 29–40. Reprinted by permission of the author and of the Association.

what is evil'[1]). Those precepts of the divine law that
are not precepts of natural law are not binding on
non-Christians. Undoubtedly, when the Church has
been powerful, its members have been tempted to
impose religious duties on non-Christians in the name
of morality; and when it has been weak, to draw back
from denouncing moral wrongs on the plea that the
wrongdoers are outside the Church's jurisdiction. Yet
the scholastic theory of natural law provides a foundation for distinguishing the duty to obey the moral
law, which for Christians is both moral and religious,
from purely religious duties that fall outside common
morality. It is therefore worth inquiring whether the
scholastic theory may become common ground for
Christian and non-Christian philosophers. If St.
Thomas was right, there is no reason why it should
not.

1. The Natural Law and Contemporary Analytic Phi-losophy

My first thesis, then, is that the scholastic theory of
natural law, in particular, St. Thomas' version of it,
may have something to offer contemporary non-
Christian moral philosophy. There are two reasons for
dismissing this thesis as a fantastic absurdity. The first
is derived from a cardinal doctrine of modern ethical
theory, the second from a cardinal doctrine of scholasticism.

The vast majority of analytic philosophers would accept the doctrine of the autonomy of ethics as fundamental. Following A. N. Prior, that doctrine may be
formulated as follows: 'the claim to deduce ethical
propositions from ones which are admitted to be non-
ethical'[2] is fallacious. It is true that this doctrine has

[1] Gloss on *Romans* ii, p. 14, quoted by St. Thomas, *Summa Theologiae*, I–II, 91, 2.
[2] A. N. Prior, *Logic and the Basis of Ethics* (Oxford, 1949), p. 95.

recently been questioned;[3] but I do not think that it has been shaken. If the scholastic theory of natural law should imply that ethics is not autonomous, it could have no serious influence on analytic ethical theory. Yet St. Thomas himself appears to imply it, by deriving the first precept of the natural law, *bonum est faciendum et prosequendum, et malum vitandum*, from a non-ethical statement about the nature of good, *bonum est quod omnia appetunt.*[4]

Fortunately for my thesis, what St. Thomas said need not be interpreted as denying the autonomy of ethics. He certainly did not mean that we all ought to do and promote whatever we in fact seek; for he admitted that many of us seek what is evil. His statement that *good is that which all things seek* must be understood as meaning that good is that which all things *by nature* seek; and, since man is a rational animal, applied to man it means that human good is that which all men seek *by virtue of their nature as rational animals.* Evildoers choose to do and to promote what is opposed to what they seek by virtue of their rational nature; they affront their own reason. Now I do not think that any analytic philosopher would deny that the words '*quod omnia appetunt*', so understood, express an ethical concept. The objection to my thesis from the analytic side therefore fails: the scholastic theory of natural law is not incompatible with the autonomy of ethics, or at least is not obviously so.

The objection from the scholastic side goes deeper. The scholastic philosophers were theologians too, and

[3] E.g., by John Searle, 'How to Derive "Ought" from "Is",' *Philosophical Review*, LXXIII (1964), pp. 43–58; Max Black, 'The Gap Between "Is" and "Should",' *Ibid.*, 165–81. G. J. Warnock's verdict on the matter is of interest: 'the anti-naturalist thesis . . . while probably true, has really no great importance for moral philosophy. It is a thesis . . . about the "general theory" of evaluation . . .' (*Contemporary Moral Philosophy* [London, 1967], p. 68).

[4] *Summa Theologiae*, I–II, 94, 2.

every great scholastic system is Christian: that is, its purely philosophical part is presented as not merely incomplete and incompletable by philosophy alone, but as finding its completion in revealed theology. It is, therefore, legitimate to doubt whether the theory of natural law is intelligible to philosophy alone. Partly for this reason, Miss G. E. M. Anscombe has expressed the view that the scholastic theory of moral law is theological in essence, and that the part of scholastic moral theory that is philosophical in the Aristotelian theory of the cardinal virtues.[5] And it cannot be denied that St. Thomas defines natural law theologically: having explained that a rational creature is subject to divine providence in a higher way than a brute, in that it partakes of the divine reason, he lays it down that 'such participation of the eternal law in a rational creature is called natural law'.[6] The eternal law, being 'the very Idea of the government of things existing in God the ruler of the universe',[7] is studied by theology rather than by philosophy.

Yet from the fact that St. Thomas, in a theological work, defines natural law theologically, it follows neither that it cannot be defined philosophically, nor that a philosophical definition would be incomplete, as, according to St. Thomas, any account of the natural end of man that neglected divine revelation would be incomplete. Although this is not stated in terms by St. Thomas, it is implied by his assertion that 'all men know . . . the common principles of the natural law'.[8] It is also presupposed in his derivations of the various precepts of the natural law, in none of which does he make any appeal to revealed theology.

[5] 'Modern Moral Philosophy,' *Philosophy*, XXXIII (1958), pp. 1–19. In Miss Anscombe's position, I can find no place for natural law; she makes all law positive, i.e. either divine or human.

[6] *Summa Theologiae*, I–II, 91, 2.

[7] '[I]psa ratio gubernationis rerum in Deo sicut in principe universitatis existens' (*Summa Theologiae*, I–II, 91, 1).

[8] *Summa Theologiae*, I–II, 93, 2.

Nor does he explicitly draw upon natural theology, except in deriving precepts having to do with divine worship.

At this point, St. Thomas can be instructively contrasted with Kant. In an excellent Thomist textbook of Ethics I found the following:

> The distinctive thing about the rationally free agent is not, as Kant thought, that he is a law unto himself. Man is not the ultimate source or principle of the moral law. Rather, human reason is subject to the laws of reality, which come from the divine reason.

These remarks exhibit a misunderstanding precisely opposite to the misunderstanding that St. Thomas has no strictly philosophical conception of natural law. Kant defines the moral law philosophically. After defining an objective principle as 'valid for every rational being',[9] he goes on to say that if there is to be a moral law for men, i.e. a categorical imperative, 'it must be such that from the idea of something which is necessarily an end for everyone because it is an *end in itself*, it forms an *objective* principle of the will'.[10] I take it to be patent that Kant is not saying that a rational being is a law unto himself: such a being must indeed determine for himself what the law is, but he must do so according to *objective* principles. And those objective principles are valid for every rational being because they have an objective foundation in 'something which is necessarily an end for everyone because it is an end in itself'.

Writing as a philosopher, Kant defined the moral law without reference to God. Yet he held, as a theologian, that the moral law is derived from the divine reason. In the *Groundwork* he was at pains to

[9] *The Moral Law, or Kant's Groundwork of the Metaphysic of Morals*, tr. H. J. Paton (London, 1948), p. 88 (2nd German edn., p. 51n.).
[10] *Ibid.*, p. 96 (2nd German edn., p. 66).

point out that the divine will cannot be said to be subject to the objective principles of the moral law as to imperatives, because it is 'already of itself necessarily in harmony with [them]'.[11]

Kant and St. Thomas differ about what the fundamental principles of the moral law are, although not as much as many believe; but they do not differ in any significant way about the relation between what St. Thomas would call the 'natural law' and what he would call the 'eternal law'. From the point of view of moral philosophy, the natural law is a set of precepts the binding force of which can be ascertained by human reason; from the point of view of theology, it is that part of what God eternally and rationally wills that can be grasped by human reason as binding upon human beings (Kant would say, upon all rational beings). Just as in theology Kant may agree with St. Thomas that the moral law is a participation of the eternal law in a rational creature, so in moral philosophy St. Thomas may agree with Kant that in determining what the precepts of the natural law are, theological considerations are out of place.

On this point, what holds of Kant also holds of contemporary analytic philosophy.

2. *Scholastic Derivations of the Precepts of the Natural Law.*

If non-scholastic philosophers have much to learn from what scholastic philosophers have accomplished in the theory of natural law, why have they not done so? Prejudice and ignorance are part of the explanation. But they are not the whole of it. My second thesis is that, despite what has been accomplished, no adequate scholastic *philosophy* of natural law has yet been elaborated. That, too, must enter into any satisfactory explanation of why non-scholastic philosophers have neglected the scholastic achievement.

---

[11] *Ibid.*, p. 81 (2nd German edn., p. 39).

It should also be mentioned in any explanation of why explicit natural law arguments are rarely found convincing by non-Catholics.

I shall try to establish my second thesis by examining St. Thomas' derivation of a precept of the natural law that is not very controversial: the precept that lying (*mendacium*) is evil and to be avoided. St. Thomas defines a lie as speech contrary to the speaker's mind,[12] and he holds lying so defined to be prohibited by the natural law for the following reason:

> . . . since words are naturally signs of thoughts, it is unnatural and wrong for anyone by speech to signify something he does not have in his mind (*Summa Theologiae*, II–II, 110, 3).

This argument plainly presupposes an unstated principle, namely, that if an activity has a natural end, then it is unnatural and wrong voluntarily to engage in that activity in such a way as to prevent the attainment of its end. Both this presupposition, and St. Thomas' explicit premiss, that the natural end of speech is to signify what the speaker thinks, may be questioned.

What is meant by the 'natural end' of a process? The concept is Aristotelian, and it is too fundamental to be usefully defined. Natural processes go on of themselves, as natural substances come into being from other natural substances, without the help of any artificer. Living things, the best specimens of natural substances, are generated, grow, and decay in characteristic ways. It is usual to speak and think of them as tending to grow to maturity, and as resisting decay. In general, Aristotle would say of such things

---

[12] This is far more satisfactory than St. Augustine's 'a false statement uttered with intent to deceive', for reasons explained by St. Thomas (*Summa Theologiae*, II–II, 110, 1 *ad* 1, 3). Yet variants of St. Augustine's definition still turn up in contemporary analytic philosophy. E.g. C. D. Broad, *Five Types of Ethical Theory* (London, 1930), p. 209.

that their natural end is to achieve the state of maturity characteristic of their species. Similarly, of the parts of a thing which has a natural end, Aristotle would say that their natural end is to contribute to the efficient functioning of the whole: thus, the natural end of an eye is to enable its possessor to see. The same also holds of processes that go on in natural things: if they contribute to the efficient functioning of the thing in which they occur, as most of them do, then their natural end is to make that contribution. It makes no difference whether those processes are voluntary or involuntary. Thus the natural end of the involuntary process of breathing is (on Aristotelian principles, although Aristotle did not know it) to convey oxygen to the blood, and to expel carbon dioxide from the lungs; and the natural end of the voluntary process of eating is to convey food to the digestive organs.

It cannot be too strongly insisted upon that Aristotle neither personifies nature nor endows it with *conscious* purpose. Conscious purposes are found in nature, in intelligent beings; but most natural ends or purposes are not conscious. Art imitates nature, but nature is not an artificer.[13] '[T]hose things are natural which, by a continuous movement originated from an internal principle, arrive at some completion: the same completion is not reached from every principle; nor any chance completion; but always the tendency in each is towards the same end, if there is no impediment.'[14]

I will not question that there are, in Aristotle's sense, natural things and natural processes. However, the use in ethics to which Aristotle and St. Thomas put the concept of a natural end presupposes more than that. Above all, it presupposes that it is wrong to frustrate nature. This presupposition must, of course,

[13] Aristotle, *Physics*, II, 199 b 25–31.
[14] Aristotle, *Physics* (tr. R. P. Hardie and R. K. Gaye) II, 199 b 15–19.

be qualified. When a cow eats grass, it prevents that grass from completing its natural growth; and when a man slaughters and eats or sells the flesh of a cow, he prevents that cow from completing its natural growth. Hence, St. Thomas lays it down that the sub-rational part of nature is for the use of the rational part.[15] This, if I understand it correctly, is an ethical and not a physical principle. From the point of view of physics, the flesh of cattle is no more naturally food for man than is the blood of man food for mosquitoes. But, although he allows man's right to use non-rational natural things for his own purposes, St. Thomas denies that he may voluntarily engage in any natural activity, if he does so in such a way as to prevent that activity from arriving at its natural end. If you voluntarily engage in eating, you must not increase your capacity to eat by resorting, as some Romans did, to the vomitorium; for that would prevent the activity of eating from arriving at its natural end of digestion.

A second presupposition, which has important moral consequences, is that natural things and processes have only one end, or have one that is pre-eminent. Aristotle seems to have thought this obvious. 'Nature', he declared in the *Politics*, 'is not niggardly, like the smith who fashions the Delphian knife for many uses; she makes each thing for a single use'.[16] Eating both nourishes and gives pleasure; but Aristotle would consider it obvious that the pre-eminent natural end of eating is nourishment, not pleasure.

We are now in a position to decide upon the validity or otherwise of St. Thomas' demonstration that lying is wrong. In my opinion, neither its premiss, that the natural end of speech is to express what is in the speaker's mind, nor its presupposition, that it is wrong voluntarily to engage in a natural activity and to prevent that activity from arriving at its natural

---

[15] St. Thomas Aquinas, *Summa contra Gentiles*, III, 22, [8].
[16] Aristotle, *Politics* (tr. Benjamin Jowett) I, 1252 b 1–5.

end, is evident upon reflection. Let me take each in turn.

It is simply not true that speech is related to its alleged end of expressing what is in the speaker's mind in the way in which eating is related to nourishment, or the eye to seeing. If eating is not completed by digestion, the body has been interfered with in some way; and an eye in which there is no sight is either defective or damaged. But, from the point of view of natural science, a lying speech act is not, *per se*, either defective or interfered with. If speech acts have a natural end, in Aristotle's sense, it is to express whatever thought the speaker chooses to express.

It is, indeed, possible to argue that veracity must be the norm for speech acts. As Professor J. M. Cameron has observed in his Terry Lectures, 'Lying could not be the norm for purely logical reasons, since the point of telling a lie is that it should be taken to be the truth and this could not happen unless truth-telling were the norm'.[17] But it does not follow that the natural end of a speech act is to conform to that norm; for a thing tends towards its natural end provided there is no impediment, and a lying speech act does not in the least tend towards truth. Nor, conceding that veracity is the norm for speech, does it appear to follow that every speech act ought to conform to that norm. If people wish to communicate by speech, then logically they must normally tell the truth—but not always. And this logical necessity does not appear to me to be a moral obligation. It holds for liars and truth-tellers alike.

St. Thomas' presupposition that it is wrong voluntarily to engage in any natural activity in such a way as to prevent it from arriving at its natural end, is equally vulnerable. If St. Thomas considers that ra-

---

[17] J. M. Cameron, *Images of Authority* (New Haven, 1966), p. 27. Professor Cameron does not use this premiss in the way I object to. He argues only that mendacity could not count as a moral *virtue*.

tional beings have the right to interfere with and even destroy sub-rational natural things for their own purposes, why should he think it wrong *per se* for them to interfere, for their own purposes, with the natural activities in which they engage? I am aware that, in asking this, I shall appear to some to be frivolous and wanting in natural piety. But any philosopher who wishes to argue as St. Thomas does should take account of the fact that I am by no means alone. In the sagacious and lucid introduction to his translation of the third and fourth books of Aristotle's *Politics*, Richard Robinson has stated my objection more sharply than I:

> Once we have explicitly asked ourselves why we should do anything just because nature does it, or why we should aid nature in her purposes, we see that there is no reason why we should. Let nature look to her own purposes, if she has any. *We* will look to *ours*.[18]

3. *Strengths and Weaknesses in the Scholastic Theory of Natural Law.*

It does not follow from the objections I have urged against St. Thomas' discussion of lying that his theory of the natural law is false. St. Thomas' definition of the natural law, and his statement of its first precept, neither of which I desire to question, are logically separable from his derivation of further precepts from the first precept. Indeed, I make bold to say that one reason why the scholastic theory has had less influence outside Catholic circles than it merits, is that it is assumed to be a seamless unity, and that little is known of it but arguments like St. Thomas' against lying. It is widely believed that if you reject such arguments (that against artificial contraception is, of

[18] *Aristotle's* Politics *Books III and IV*, tr. with Introduction and Comments by Richard Robinson (Oxford, 1962), xxiii.

course, the best known) then you must deny that there is a natural law: that is, you must abandon the conception of the moral law as a matter of human reason.

If my objections to St. Thomas' discussion of lying are just, then St. Thomas was mistaken in looking to Aristotelian natural philosophy for a way of specifying the goods that the natural law bids us seek, and the evils it bids us avoid. But nothing in his definition of natural law obliged him to make that mistake. Nor did anything in Aristotle's *Ethics* do so. I am inclined to conjecture that he was led to make it by his belief in creation: accepting Aristotle's views about natural teleology, and believing that the natural world was created by God, it may have seemed reasonable to treat the ends of natural things and processes not only as divinely appointed, but as divinely sanctioned. Yet, as we have seen, St. Thomas himself invoked the doctrine of the subordination of the weaker and less perfect in nature to the stronger and more perfect,[19] to justify man's interference with *some* natural processes.

I do not wish to give the impression that the only part of the scholastic theory of the natural law that I think strong is its foundation, or that I wish to level the edifice erected by the scholastics on that foundation. The treatment in scholastic philosophy of specific moral questions is every whit as important as the treatment there of first principles. Indeed, if one looks for exact and detailed inquiry into the more notorious moral difficulties, there is almost nowhere to go in contemporary philosophy except to the writings of the neo-scholastics.

[19] '. . . quaedam etiam perfectiora et virtuosiora ex quibusdam imperfectioribus et infirmioribus [nutrimentum habent]' (*Summa contra Gentiles*, III, 22, [8]).

4. Prospect.

My final thesis is that in order to correct the weakness in the scholastic theory of natural law I believe myself to have detected, it is necessary to re-examine, without theological preconceptions, the philosophical problem of how to derive specific moral precepts from the first precept of the natural law. I venture to suggest a possible way of doing so.

St. Thomas' recognition of subordination in nature, and his doctrine that 'man is the end of the whole order of generation',[20] suggests that he might have accepted Kant's principle that 'man, and in general every rational being, exists as an end in himself, not merely as a means for arbitrary use by this or that will'.[21] The principle is, in my opinion, self-evident. It must not be interpreted as implying that man is not ordered towards anything higher, as St. Thomas held that he is ordered to God, but rather as implying that if he is so ordered, it must be in a way consistent with his nature as an end. This is, of course, amply acknowledged in Christian theology.

Kant's principle, which I take to be implicit in the work of St. Thomas, furnishes a way of specifying good and evil. Let me sketch how it might be applied to the case of lying. According to it, any act by the nature of which a rational being is used *merely* as a means is evil; and hence, by the first precept of the natural law, is to be avoided. But, in ordinary conditions of free communication, to tell another something that you do not believe is to use him merely as a means. By arrogating to yourself the right to misinform him merely because for some reason you so choose, you treat him merely as a means to your ends.

[20] *Summa contra Gentiles*, III, 22, [7].
[21] *The Moral Law, or Kant's Groundwork of the Metaphysic of Morals*, tr. H. J. Paton (London: 1948), p. 95 (2nd German edn., p. 64).

Hence in ordinary conditions of free communication, lying to others is unconditionally prohibited.

In conditions of violence, as for example in the classic case of a would-be murderer who demands with threats to be told in which direction somebody he is pursuing has made off, the situation is otherwise. By employing or threatening violence, the questioner has already treated the person questioned merely as a means. He has no right to be told anything, and the person questioned is entitled to protect himself, and the pursued quarry, by a lie. (It is a question whether the word 'lie' should be used in such a case. Perhaps the qualification, 'in conditions of free communication', should be added to St. Thomas' definition.)

In the cases I have considered, our principle yields results that conform to common-sense, and to the moral tradition generally, although in the latter case, under the influence of St. Thomas' argument, scholastic philosophers are apt either to be absurdly rigorous, or to explain away the justified lie by postulating improbable speech conventions (e.g. the so-called 'broad mental reservation'). But there are innumerable difficult cases. For example, what is it permissible to do when you are obliged to keep a secret, and find yourself in a situation, probably by your own fault, in which you will reveal the secret whether you answer a question truthfully or refuse to answer it? Any principle by which such cases are other than difficult might be dismissed on that ground alone. I submit that Kant's principle both exhibits their difficulty, and yet contains resources for dealing with them. It is instructive, armed with that principle, to work through the moral cases in a good manual of casuistry.

Lest I should appear to be recommending the absorption of scholastic moral philosophy into Kantianism, may I repeat that I am pleading for a fresh and purely philosophical approach to the problem of deriving the specific moral precepts of the natural law, and that one of my reasons for suggesting that

Kant's principle might be invoked in such derivations was that I took it to be implicit in St. Thomas' thought. Other suggestions ought also to be explored. Far from desiring that scholastic moral philosophy be absorbed in Kantianism, I hope that the influence of scholasticism may help us to free what is true in Kant's moral philosophy, which is a great deal, from the eccentric moral opinions Kant fallaciously drew from his principles.

That the existing scholastic theory of natural law has an important contribution to make to any rational theory of morality is beyond question. A thoroughly reconsidered and purely philosophical theory of natural law could do even more. It could provide the foundation of that rational moral consensus which is the necessary cement of a pluralist society.

THE FIRST PRINCIPLE OF

PRACTICAL REASON

A *Commentary on the* Summa theologiae, *1–2,*
Question 94, Article 2

GERMAIN G. GRISEZ

Many proponents and critics of Thomas Aquinas'
theory of natural law have understood it roughly as
follows. The first principle of practical reason is a command: *Do good and avoid evil.* Man discovers this
imperative in his conscience; it is like an inscription
written there by the hand of God. Having become
aware of this basic commandment, man consults his
nature to see what is good and what is evil. He ex-
amines an action in comparison with his essence to see
whether the action fits human nature or does not fit it.
If the action fits, it is seen to be good; if it does not
fit, it is seen to be bad. Once we know that a certain
kind of action—for instance, stealing—is bad, we have
two premises, "Avoid evil" and "Stealing is evil," from
whose conjunction is deduced: "Avoid stealing." All
specific commandments of natural law are derived in
this way.[1]

I propose to show how far this interpretation misses
Aquinas's real position. My main purpose is not to con-

Natural Law Forum, Vol. 10, 1965, 168–196. Reprinted in an
abridged version with the permission of the author and of the
editors. Copyright, 1965, *Natural Law Forum*.
[1] This summary is not intended to reflect the position of any
particular author. However, a full and accessible presentation
along these general lines may be found in Thomas J. Higgins,
S.J., *Man as Man: the Science and Art of Ethics* 49–69, 88–100,
120–126 (rev. ed., Milwaukee, 1958).

tribute to the history of natural law, but to clarify Aquinas's idea of it for current thinking. Instead of undertaking a general review of Aquinas's entire natural law theory, I shall focus on the first principle of practical reason, which also is the first precept of natural law. This principle, as Aquinas states it, is: *Good is to be done and pursued, and evil is to be avoided.*[2] Although verbally this formula is only slightly different from that of the command, *Do good and avoid evil,* I shall try to show that the two formulae differ considerably in meaning and that they belong in different theoretical contexts.

This paper has four parts. 1) Since I propose to show that the common interpretation is unsound, it will be necessary to explicate the text in which Aquinas states the first principle. 2) Since the mistaken interpretation restricts the meaning of "good" and "evil" in the first principle to the value of moral actions, the meaning of these key terms must be clarified in the light of Aquinas's theory of final causality. 3) Since the mistaken interpretation tends to oppose the commandments of natural law to positive action, it will help to notice the broad scope Aquinas attributes to the first principle, for he considers it to be a source, rather than a limit, of action. 4) Since according to the mistaken interpretation natural law is a set of imperatives, it is important to see why the first principle is not primarily an imperative, although it is a genuine precept.

I

Aquinas's statement of the first principle of practical reason occurs in *Summa theologiae,* 1-2, question 94, article 2. Question 90 is concerned with what law

---

[2] "Bonum est faciendum et prosequendum, et malum vitandum." *Summa theologiae* 1-2, q. 94, a. 2, c. (Leonine ed., Rome, 1882–1948). (*Summa theologiae* will hereafter be referred to as S.T.)

is, question 91 with the distinction among the various modes of law, and question 92 with the effects of law. Aquinas begins treating each mode of law in particular in question 93; in that question he treats eternal law. Thus he comes to the study of natural law in question 94. Questions 95 to 97 are concerned with man-made law. Questions 98 to 108 examine the divine law, Old and New.

Question 94 is divided into six articles, each of which presents a position on a single issue concerning the law of nature. The first article raises the issue: "Whether natural law is a habit." Aquinas holds that natural law consists of precepts of reason, which are analogous to propositions of theoretical knowledge. Hence he denies that it is a habit, although he grants that it can be possessed habitually, for one *has* these principles even when he is not thinking of them.

The second issue raised in question 94 logically follows. It is: "Does natural law contain many precepts, or only one?" Unlike the issue of the first article, which was a question considered by many previous authors, this second point was not a standard issue.[3] For this reason the arguments, which Aquinas sets out at the beginning of the article in order to construct the issue he wants to resolve, do not refer to authorities, as the opening arguments of his articles usually do. Three arguments are set out for the position that natural law contains only one precept, and a single op-

---

[3] Paul-M. van Overbeke, O.P., *La loi naturelle et le droit naturel selon S. Thomas,* 65 *Revue Thomiste* 73–75 (1957) puts q. 94, a. 1 into its proper perspective. Odon Lottin, O.S.B., *Le droit naturel chez Saint Thomas d'Aquin et ses prédécesseurs* 79 (2nd ed., Bruges, 1931) mentions that the issue of the second article had been posed by Albert the Great (cf. p. 118), but the question was not a commonplace. Obviously no one could ask it who did not hold that natural law consists of precepts, and even those who took this position would not ask about the unity or multiplicity of precepts unless they saw some significance in responding one way or the other.

posing argument is given to show that it contains many precepts.

The first argument concludes that natural law must contain only a single precept on the grounds that law itself is a precept[4] and that natural law has unity. The second argument reaches the same conclusion by reasoning that since natural law is based upon human nature, it could have many precepts only if the many parts of human nature were represented in it; but in this case even the demands of man's lower nature would have to be reflected in natural law. The third argument for the position that natural law has only one precept is drawn from the premises that human reason is one and that law belongs to reason.[5] The single argument Aquinas offers for the opposite conclusion is based on an analogy between the precepts of natural law and the axioms of demonstrations: as there is a multiplicity of indemonstrable principles of demonstrations, so there is a multiplicity of precepts of natural law. These four initial arguments serve only to clarify the issue to be resolved in the response which follows. Of themselves, they settle nothing. After the response Aquinas comments briefly on each of the first three arguments in the light of his resolution of the issue. The argument that there are many precepts of natural law Aquinas will not comment upon, since he takes this position himself.

Aquinas' response to the question is as follows:

1) As I said previously, the precepts of natural law are related to practical reason in the same way the basic principles of demonstrations are related to theoretical reason, since both are sets of self-evident principles.

2) But something is called "self-evident" in two

[4] A position Aquinas develops in q. 92, a. 2, and applies in rejecting the position that natural law is a habit in q. 94, a. 1.

[5] That law pertains to reason is a matter of definition for Aquinas; law is an *ordinance of reason*, according to the famous definition of q. 90, a. 4.

senses: in one way, objectively; in the other way, relative to us. Any proposition may be called "objectively self-evident" if its predicate belongs to the intelligibility of its subject. Yet to someone who does not know the intelligibility of the subject, such a proposition will not be self-evident. For example, the proposition, *Man is rational,* taken just in itself, is self-evident, for to say *man* is to say *rational;* yet to someone who did not know what man is, this proposition would not be self-evident. Consequently, as Boethius says in his *De hebdomadibus,*[6] there are certain axioms or propositions which are generally self-evident to everyone. In this class are propositions whose terms everyone understands —for example: *Every whole is greater than its parts,* and: *Two things equal to a third are equal to one another.* But there are other propositions which are self-evident only to the educated, who understand what the terms of such propositions mean. For example, to one who understands that angels are incorporeal, it is self-evident that they are not in a place by filling it up, but this is not evident to the uneducated, who do not comprehend this point.

3) Now among those things which fall within the grasp of everyone there is a certain order of precedence. For that which primarily falls within one's grasp is being, and the understanding of being is included in absolutely everything that anyone grasps. Hence the primary indemonstrable principle is: *To affirm and simultaneously to deny is excluded.* This principle is based on the intelligibility of being (and nonbeing), and all other principles are based on this one, as Aristotle says in the *Metaphysics.*[7]

4) But just as being is the first thing to fall within the unrestricted grasp of the mind, so good is the

[6] *Patrologia latina* vol. 64, col. 1311 (ed. J. Migne, Paris, 1844–1865).

[7] *Metaphysica* bk. iii, 1005^{b}29.

first thing to fall within the grasp of practical reason —that is, reason directed to a work—for every active principle acts on account of an end, and end includes the intelligibility of good.

5) It follows that the first principle of practical reason is one founded on the intelligibility of good— that is: *Good is what each thing tends toward.* Therefore this is the primary precept of law: *Good is to be done and pursued, and evil is to be avoided.* All other precepts of the law of nature are based on this one, in this way that under precepts of the law of nature come all those things-to-be-done or things-to-be-avoided which practical reason naturally grasps as human goods or their opposites.

6) Because good has the intelligibility of end, and evil has the intelligibility of contrary to end, it follows that reason naturally grasps as goods—in consequence, as things-to-be-pursued by work, and their opposites as evils and things-to-be-avoided—all the objects of man's natural inclinations. Hence the order of the precepts of the law of nature is according to the order of the natural inclinations.

7) First, there is in man an inclination based on the aspect of his nature which he has in common with all substances—that is, that everything tends according to its own nature to preserve its own being. In accordance with this inclination, those things by which human life is preserved and by which threats to life are met fall under natural law. Second, there is in man an inclination to certain more restricted goods based on the aspect of his nature which he has in common with other animals. In accordance with this inclination, those things are said to be of natural law "which nature teaches all animals," among which are the union of male and female, the raising of children, and the like. Third, there is in man an inclination to the good based on the rational aspect of his nature, which is peculiar to himself. For example, man has a natural inclination to

this, that he might know the truth concerning God, and to this, that he might live in society. In accordance with this inclination, those things relating to an inclination of this sort fall under natural law. For instance, that man should avoid ignorance, that he should not offend those among whom he must live, and other points relevant to this inclination.[8]

Aquinas's solution to the question is that there are many precepts of the natural law, but that this multitude is not a disorganized aggregation but an orderly whole. The precepts are many because the different inclinations' objects, viewed by reason as ends for rationally guided efforts, lead to distinct norms of action. The natural law, nevertheless, is one because each object of inclination obtains its role in practical reason's legislation only insofar as it is subject to practical reason's way of determining action—by prescribing how ends are to be attained.[9]

[8] S.T. 1-2, q. 94, a. 2, c. The translation is my own; the paragraphing is added. The two fullest commentaries on this article that I have found are J. B. Schuster, S.J., *Von den ethischen Prinzipien: Eine Thomasstudie zu S. Th.,* I-II, q. 94, a. 2, 57 *Zeitschrift für Katholische Theologie* 44-65 (1933) and Michael V. Murray, S.J., *Problems in Ethics* 220-235 (New York, 1960). See also Van Overbeke, *op. cit. supra* note 3, at 450-58; Gregory Stevens, O.S.B., *The Relations of Law and Obligation,* 29 *Proceedings of the American Catholic Philosophical Association* 195-205 (1955). Many useful points have been derived from each of these sources for the interpretation developed below.

[9] After giving this response to the issue, Aquinas answers briefly each of the three introductory arguments. All of them tended to show that natural law has but one precept. To the first argument, based on the premises that law itself is a precept and that natural law is one, Aquinas answers that the many precepts of the natural law are unified *in relation to* the primary principle. To the second argument, that man's lower nature must be represented if the precepts of the law of nature are diversified by the parts of human nature, Aquinas unhesitatingly answers that all parts of human nature are represented in natural law, for the inclination of each part of man belongs to natural law insofar as it falls under a precept of reason; in this respect all the inclinations also fall under the one first principle. To the

Now we must examine this response more carefully.

In the first paragraph Aquinas restates the analogy between precepts of natural law and first principles of theoretical reason. The latter are principles of demonstration in systematic sciences such as geometry. From the outset, Aquinas speaks of "precepts" in the plural. The first paragraph implies that only self-evident principles of practical reason belong to natural law; Aquinas is using "natural law" here in its least extensive sense.[10] It is clear already at this point that Aquinas counts many self-evident principles among the precepts of the law of nature, and there is a mistake in any interpretation of his theory which reduces all but one of the precepts to the status of conclusions.[11]

---

third argument, that law belongs to reason and that reason is one, Aquinas responds that reason indeed is one in itself, and yet that natural law contains many precepts because reason directs everything which concerns man, who is complex. Each of these three answers merely reiterates the response to the main question.

[10] In other texts he considers conclusions drawn from these principles also to be precepts of natural law—e.g., S.T. 1-2, q. 94, a. 4, c. This point is merely lexicographical, yet it has caused some confusion—for instance, concerning the relationship between natural law and the law of nations, for sometimes Aquinas contradistinguishes the two while sometimes he includes the law of nations in natural law. See Lottin, *op. cit. supra* note 3, at 61-73.

[11] A careful reading of this paragraph also excludes another interpretation of Aquinas's theory of natural law—that proposed by Jacques Maritain. *Man and the State* 84-94 (Chicago, 1951), is the most complete expression in English of Maritain's recent view. His position has undergone some development in its various presentations. Maritain suggests that natural law does not itself fall within the category of knowledge; he tries to give it a status independent of knowledge so that it can be the object of gradual discovery. He also claims that man's knowledge of natural law is not conceptual and rational, but instead is by inclination, connaturality, or congeniality. However, Aquinas does not present natural law as if it were an object known or to be known; rather, he considers the precepts of practical reason themselves to be natural law. Thus the principles of the law of

In the second paragraph of the response Aquinas clarifies the meaning of "self-evident." His purpose is not to postulate a peculiar meaning for "self-evident" in terms of which the basic precepts of natural law might be self-evident although no one in fact knew them.[12] That Aquinas did not have this in mind appears at the beginning of the third paragraph, where he begins to determine the priorities among those things "which fall within the grasp of everyone." No doubt there are some precepts not everyone knows although they are objectively self-evident—for instance, precepts concerning the relation of man to God: *God should be loved above all,* and: *God should be obeyed before all.* Man can be ignorant of these precepts because God does not fall within our grasp so that the grounds of his lovability and authority are evident to everybody.[13] However, basic principles of natural law on the whole, and particularly

---

nature cannot be *potential* objects of knowledge, unknown but waiting in hiding, fully formed and ready for discovery. Moreover, the fact that the precepts of natural law are viewed as self-evident principles of practical reason excludes Maritain's account of our knowledge of them. For Aquinas, there is no nonconceptual intellectual knowledge: *De veritate*, q. 4, a. 2, ad 5. How misleading Maritain's account of the knowledge of natural law is, so far as Aquinas's position is concerned, can be seen by examining some studies based on Maritain: Kai Nielsen, *An Examination of the Thomistic Theory of Natural Moral Law,* 4 *Natural Law Forum* 47-50 (1959); Paul Ramsey, *Nine Modern Moralists* 215-223 (Englewood Cliffs, N.J., 1962). Nielsen was not aware, as Ramsey was, that Maritain's theory of knowledge of natural law should not be ascribed to Aquinas.

[12] Nielsen, *op. cit. supra* note 11, at 50-52, apparently misled by Maritain, follows this interpretation. At any rate Nielsen's implicit supposition that the natural law for Aquinas must be formally identical with the eternal law is in conflict with Aquinas' notion of participation according to which the participation is *never* formally identical with that in which it participates.

[13] Thus Aquinas remarks (S.T. 1-2, q. 100, a. 3, ad 1) that the precept of charity is "self-evident to human reason, either by nature or by faith," since a knowledge of God sufficient to form the natural law precept of charity can come from either natural knowledge or divine revelation.

the precepts mentioned in this response, are self-evident to all men.

When Aquinas speaks of self-evident principles of natural law, he does not mean tautologies derived by mere conceptual analysis—for example: *Stealing is wrong*, where "stealing" means the *unjust* taking of another's property. Rather, he means the principles of practical inquiry which also are the limits of practical argument—a set of underivable principles for practical reason. To function as principles, their status as underivables must be recognized, and this recognition depends upon a sufficient understanding of their terms, i.e., of the intelligibilities signified by those terms.[14]

In the third paragraph Aquinas begins to apply the analogy between the precepts of the natural law and the first principles of demonstrations. *Being* is the basic intelligibility; it represents our first discovery about anything we are to know—that it *is something* to be known. The first principle, expressed here in the formula, "To affirm and simultaneously to deny is excluded," is the one sometimes called "the principle of contradiction" and sometimes called "the principle of noncontradiction": *The same cannot both be and not be at the same time and in the same respect.* In this more familiar formulation it is clearer that the principle is based upon being and nonbeing, for it is obvious that what the principle excludes is the identification of being with nonbeing. The objective dimension of the reality of beings that we know in knowing

[14] An intelligibility (*ratio*) is all that would be included in the meaning of a word that is used correctly if the things referred to in that use were fully known in all ways relevant to the aspect then signified by the word in question. Thus the intelligibility includes the meaning with which a word is used, but it also includes whatever increment of meaning the same word would have in a similar use if what is denoted by the word were more perfectly known. On "ratio" see Andre Hayen, S.J. *L'Intentionnel selon saint Thomas* 175-194 (2nd ed. Bruges, Bruxelles, Paris 1954).

this principle is simply the definiteness that is involved in their very objectivity, a definiteness that makes a demand on the intellect knowing them, the very least demand—to think consistently of them.[15]

To say that all other principles are based on this principle does not mean that all other principles are derived from it by deduction. In fact the principle of contradiction does not directly enter into arguments as a premise except in the case of arguments *ad absurdum.*[16] Rather, this principle is basic in that it is given to us by our most primitive understanding. All other knowledge of anything adds to this elementary appreciation of the definiteness involved in its very objectivity, for any further knowledge is a step toward giving some intelligible character to this definiteness, i.e., toward defining things and knowing them in their wholeness and their concrete interrelations. But the first principle all the while exercises its unobtrusive control, for it drives the mind on toward judgment, never permitting it to settle into inconsistent muddle.

In the fourth paragraph Aquinas states that *good* is the primary intelligibility to fall under practical reason, and he explains why this is so. On the analogy he is developing, he clearly means that nothing can be understood by practical reason without the intelligibility of *good* being included in it.

Now what is practical reason? Is it simply knowledge sought for practical purposes? No, Aquinas considers practical reason to be the mind playing a certain role, or functioning in a certain capacity, the capacity in which it is "directed to a work." Direction to work is intrinsic to the mind in this capacity; direction qualifies the very functioning of the mind. Practical reason is the mind working as a principle of action, not simply as a recipient of objective reality. It is the mind charting what is to be, not merely recording what al-

[15] *In libros Metaphysicorum Aristotelis* lib. 4, lect. 6.
[16] *In libros Posteriorum analyticorum Aristotelis* lib. 1, lect. 20.

ready is. In theory the world calls the turn, the mind must conform to the facts; in practice, the mind calls the turn. . . .

When I think that there should be more work done on the foundations of specific theories of natural law, such a judgment is practical knowledge, for the mind requires that the situation it is considering change to fit its demands rather than the other way about. Practical reason does not have its truth by conforming to what it knows, for what practical reason knows does not have the being and the definiteness it would need to be a standard for intelligence. Only after practical reason thinks does the object of its thought begin to be a reality. Practical reason has its truth by anticipating the point at which something that is possible through human action will come into conformity with reason, and by directing effort toward that point.[17]

Now if practical reason is the mind functioning as a principle of action, it is subject to all the conditions necessary for every active principle. One of these is that every active principle acts on account of an end. An active principle is going to bring about something or other, or else it would not be an active principle at all. It is necessary for the active principle to be oriented toward that something or other, whatever it is, if it is going to be brought about. This orientation means that at the very beginning an action must have definite direction and that it must imply a definite limit.[18]

There are two ways of misunderstanding this principle that make nonsense of it. One is to suppose that it means anthropomorphism, a view at home both in the primitive mind and in idealistic metaphysics. If every active principle acts *on account of an end,* so

[17] S.T. 1, q. 79, a. 11; 1-2, q. 57, aa. 4-5; 3, q. 78, a. 5, c.; *In libros Ethicorum Aristotelis* lib. 1, lect. 1. See John E. Naus, S.J., *The Nature of the Practical Intellect According to Saint Thomas Aquinas* (Roma, 1959).

[18] S.T. 1-2, q. 1, a. 2; *Summa contra Gentiles* 3, c. 2.

the anthropomorphic argument goes, then it must act *for the sake of a goal,* just as men do when they act with a purpose in view. But the generalization is illicit, for acting with a purpose in view is only one way, the specifically human way, in which an active principle can have the orientation it needs in order to begin to act. The other misunderstanding is common to mathematically minded rationalists, who project the timelessness and changelessness of formal system onto reality, and to empiricists, who react to rationalism without criticizing its fundamental assumptions. The rationalist, convinced that reality is unchangeable, imagines that the orientation present in an active principle must not refer to real change, and so he reduces this necessary condition of change to the status of something which stably is at a static moment in time. What is at a single moment, the rationalist thinks, is stopped in its flight, so he tries to treat every relationship of existing beings to their futures as comparisons of one *state* of affairs to another. It is the rationalistic assumptions in the back of his mind that make the empiricist try to reduce dispositional properties to predictions about future states.

Let us imagine a teaspoonful of sugar held over a cup of hot coffee. It is nonsense to claim that the solubility of the sugar merely means that it will dissolve. Solubility is true of the sugar *now,* and yet this property is unlike those which characterize the sugar as to what it actually is already, for solubility characterizes it with reference to a process in which it is *suited to be* involved. The orientation of an active principle toward an end is like that—it is a real aspect of dynamic reality. In the case of practical reason, acting on account of an end is acting for the sake of a goal, for practical reason is an active principle that is conscious and self-determining. Purpose in view, then, is a real aspect of the dynamic reality of practical reason, and a necessary condition of reason's being practical.

But must every end involve good? In some senses

of the word "good" it need not. Not all outcomes are ones we want or enjoy. But if "good" means that toward which each thing tends by its own intrinsic principle of orientation, then for each active principle the end on account of which it acts also is a good for it, since nothing can act with definite orientation except on account of something toward which, for its part, it tends. And, in fact, *tendency toward* is more basic than *action on account of,* for every active principle tends toward what its action will bring about, but not every tending ability goes into action on account of the object of its tendency.

Practical reason, therefore, presupposes good. In its role as active principle the mind must think in terms of what can be an object of tendency. In other terms the mind can think, but then it will not set out to cause what it thinks. If the mind is to work toward unity with what it knows by conforming the known to itself rather than by conforming itself to the known, then the mind must think the known under the intelligibility of the good, for it is only as an object of tendency and as a possible object of action that what is to be through practical reason has any reality at all. Thus it is that good first falls within the grasp of practical reason just as being first falls within the unrestricted grasp of the mind.

In the fifth paragraph Aquinas enunciates the first principle of practical reason and indicates the way in which other evident precepts of the law of nature are founded on it.

He points out, to begin with, that the first principle of practical reason must be based on the intelligibility of good, by analogy with the primary theoretical principle which is based on the intelligibility of being. The intelligibility of good is: *what each thing tends toward.* This formula is a classic expression of what the word "good" means.[19] Of course, we often mean more

---

[19] *Ethica Nicomachea* bk. 1, 1094^{b}3.

than this by "good," but any other meaning at least includes this notion. "Good is what each thing tends toward" is not the formula of the first principle of practical reason, then, but merely a formula expressing the intelligibility of good.[20] "First principle of practical reason" and "first precept of the law" here are practically synonyms; their denotation is the same, but the former connotes derived practical knowledge while the latter connotes rationally guided action.

Until the object of practical reason is realized, it exists only in reason and in the action toward it that reason directs. Now since any object of practical reason first must be understood as an object of tendency, practical reason's first step in effecting conformity with itself is to direct the doing of works in pursuit of an end. Just as the principle of contradiction expresses the definiteness which is the first condition of the objectivity of things and the consistency which is the first condition of theoretical reason's conformity to reality, so the first principle of practical reason expresses the imposition of tendency, which is the first condition of reason's objectification of itself, and directedness or intentionality, which is the first condition for conformity to mind on the part of works and ends. A sign that intentionality or directedness is the first con-

[20] D. O'Donoghue, *The Thomist Conception of Natural Law,* 22 *Irish Theological Quarterly* 101 (also, p. 107, n. 3) (1955), holds that Aquinas means that "Good is what all things tend toward" is the first principle of practical reason, and so Fr. O'Donoghue wishes to distinguish this from the first precept of natural law. However, Aquinas actually says: "Et ideo primum principium in ratione practica est quod fundatur supra rationem boni, quae est, *Bonum est quod omnia appetunt.*" S.T., 1-2, q. 94, a. 2, c. Fr. O'Donoghue must read "quae" as if it refers to "primum principium," whereas it can only refer to "rationem boni." The *primum principium* is identical with the first precept mentioned in the next line of text, while the *ratio boni* is not a principle of practical reason but a quasi definition of "good," and as such a principle of understanding. The principle of contradiction is likewise founded on the *ratio* of being, but no formula of this *ratio* is given here.

dition for conformity to practical reason is the expression of imputation: "He acted on purpose, intentionally."

In forming this first precept practical reason performs its most basic task, for it simply determines that whatever it shall think about must at least be set on the way *to something*—as it must be if reason is to be able to think of it practically. Any other precept will add to this first one; other precepts determine precisely what the direction is and what the starting point must be if that direction is to be followed out. The first principle of practical reason thus gives us a way of interpreting experience; it provides an outlook in terms of which subsequent precepts will be formed, for it lays down the requirement that every precept must prescribe, just as the first principle of theoretical reason is an awareness that every assent posits. Awareness of the principle of contradiction demands consistency henceforth; one must posit in assenting, and thought cannot avoid the position assenting puts it in. Similarly, the establishment of the first precept of practical reason determines that there shall be direction henceforth. In prescribing we must direct, and we cannot reasonably avoid carrying out in reality the intelligibility which reason has conceived.

Practical reason, equipped with the primary principle it has formed, does not spin the whole of natural law out of itself. It is true that if "natural law" refers to all the general practical judgments reason can form, much of natural law can be derived by reasoning. But reason needs starting points. And it is with these starting points that Aquinas is concerned at the end of the fifth paragraph. The primary precepts of practical reason, he says, concern the things-to-be-done that practical reason naturally grasps as human goods, and the things-to-be-avoided that are opposed to those goods.

Of course, we can be conditioned to enjoy perverse forms of indulgence, but we could not be conditioned if we did not have, not only at the beginning but also as an underlying constant throughout the entire learning process, an inclination toward pleasure. We can be taught the joys of geometry, but that would be impossible if we did not have natural curiosity that makes us appreciate the point of asking a question and getting an answer. Our personalities are largely shaped by acculturation in our particular society, but society would never affect us if we had no basic aptitude for living with others. The infant learns to feel guilty when mother frowns, because he *wants* to please.

Practical reason's task is to direct its object toward the point at which it will attain the fullness of realization that is conceived by the mind before it is delivered into the world. But in directing its object, practical reason presides over a development, and so it must use available material. Hence the basic precepts of practical reason accept the possibilities suggested by experience and direct the objects of reason's consideration toward the fulfillments taking shape in the mind.

In the sixth paragraph Aquinas explains how practical reason forms the basic principles of its direction. The primary precept provides a point of view from which experience is considered. Within experience we have tendencies which make themselves felt; they point their way toward appropriate objects. These inclinations are part of ourselves, and so their objects are human goods. Before intelligence enters, man acts by sense spontaneity and learns by sense experience. Thus in experience we have a basis upon which reason can form patterns of action that will further or frustrate the inclinations we feel.

We can reflect upon and interpret our experience in a purely theoretical frame of mind. In that case we simply observe that we have certain tendencies that are more or less satisfied by what we do. However, when the question concerns what we shall do, the first principle of practical reason assumes control and immediately puts us in a nontheoretical frame of mind. This principle provides us with an instrument for making another kind of sense of our experience. The object of a tendency becomes an objective which is to be imposed by the mind as we try to make the best of what faces us by bringing it into conformity with practical truth. Practical reason is mind directed to direct and it directs as it can. But it can direct only toward that for which man can be brought to act, and that is either toward the objects of his natural inclinations or toward objectives that derive from these. If practical reason ignored what is given in experience, it would have no power to direct, for what-is-to-be cannot come from nothing. The direction of practical reason presupposes possibilities on which reason can get leverage, and such possibilities arise only in reflection upon experience. The leverage reason gets on these possibilities is expressed in the basic substantive principles of natural law.

At the beginning of paragraph six Aquinas seems to have come full circle, for the opening phrase here, "good has the intelligibility of end," simply reverses the last phrase of paragraph four: "end includes the intelligibility of good." There is a circle here, but it is not vicious; Aquinas is clarifying, not demonstrating. In the fourth paragraph he is pointing out that the need for practical reason, as an active principle, to think in terms of end implies that its first grasp on its objects will be of them as good, since any objective of action must first be an object of tendency. Now in the sixth paragraph he is indicating the basis on which reason primarily prescribes as our natural inclinations suggest. Is reason merely an instrument in the service of nature, accepting what nature indicates as good by moving us toward it? No, the derivation is not direct, and the position of reason in relation to inclination is not merely passive. Using the primary principle, reason reflects on experience in which the natural inclinations are found pointing to goods appropriate to themselves. But why does reason take these goods as its own? Not because they are given, but because reason's good, which is intelligible, contains the aspect of end, and the goods to which the inclinations point are prospective ends. Reason prescribes according to the order of natural inclinations because reason directs to possible actions, and the possible patterns of human action are determined by the natural inclinations, for man cannot act on account of that toward which he has no basis for affinity in his inclinations.

The seventh and last paragraph of Aquinas' response is very rich and interesting, but the details of its content are outside the scope of this paper. Here Aquinas indicates how the complexity of human nature gives rise to a multiplicity of inclinations, and these to a multiplicity of precepts. It is noteworthy that in each of the three ranks he distinguishes among an aspect of nature, the inclination based upon it, and the precepts that are in accordance with it. Nature is not natural law; nature is the given from which man develops and from which arise tendencies of ranks corresponding to its distinct strata. These tendencies are not natural law; the tendencies indicate possible actions, and hence they provide reason with the point of departure it requires in order to propose ends. The precepts of reason which clothe the objects of inclinations in the intelligibility of ends-to-be-pursued-by-work—these precepts *are* the natural law. Thus natural law has many precepts which are unified in this, that all of these precepts are ordered to practical reason's achievement of its own end, the direction of action toward end.

II

There is one obvious difference between the two formulae, "Do good and avoid evil," and "Good is to be done and pursued, and evil is to be avoided." That difference is the omission of *pursuit* from the one, the inclusion of it in the other. The mistaken interpretation of Aquinas' theory of natural law overlooks the place of final causality in his position and restricts the meaning of "good" and "evil" in the first principle to the quality of moral actions. In this section I wish to clarify this point, and the lack of "prosequendum" in the non-Thomistic formula is directly relevant.

We have seen how important the conception of end, or final causality, is to Aquinas' understanding of natural law. Practical reason understands its objects in terms of good because, as an active principle, it necessarily acts on account of an end. Practical reason prescribes precisely in view of ends. The first precept is that all subsequent direction must be in terms of intelligible goods, i.e., ends toward which reason can direct.

Nevertheless, a theory of natural law, such as I sketched at the beginning of this paper, which omits even to mention final causality, sometimes has been attributed to Aquinas. Thus to insure this fundamental point, it will be useful to examine the rest of the treatise on law in which the present issue arises.

In defining law, Aquinas first asks whether law is something belonging to reason. His response, justly famous for showing that his approach to law is intellectualistic rather than voluntaristic, may be summarized as follows. The end is the first principle in matters of action; reason orders to the end; therefore, reason is the principle of action. The principle in action is the rule of action; therefore, reason is the rule of action. The rule of action binds; therefore, reason binds. But binding is characteristic of law; therefore, law pertains to reason.[21] From this argument we see that the notion of end is fundamental to Aquinas' conception of law, and the priority of end among principles of action is the most basic reason why law belongs to reason.

In the next article, Aquinas adds another element

[21] S.T. 1-2, q. 90, a. 1, c.

to his definition by asking whether law always is ordained to the common good. His response is that law,
as a rule and measure of human acts, belongs to their
principle, reason. But in reason itself there is a basic
principle, and the first principle of practical reason is
the ultimate end. Since the ultimate end is a common
good, law must be ordained to the common good.[22]
What is noteworthy here is Aquinas' assumption that
the first *principle* of practical reason is the last *end*.
The good of which practical reason prescribes the pursuit and performance, then, primarily is the last end,
for practical reason cannot direct the possible actions
which are its objects without directing them to an
end.

Thus we see that final causality underlies Aquinas'
conception of what law is. But it is central throughout
the whole treatise. In the treatise on the Old Law, for
example, Aquinas takes up the question whether this
law contains only a single precept. His response is that
since precepts oblige, they are concerned with duties,
and duties derive from the requirements of an end.
Hence it belongs to the very intelligibility of precept
that it direct to an end. Since the Old Law directs to a
single end, it is one in this respect; but since many
things are necessary or useful to this end, precepts are
multiplied by the distinction of matters that require
direction.[23] Again, what is to be noticed in this response is that Aquinas' whole understanding of law
clearly depends on final causality. Obligation is a
strictly derivative concept, with its origin in ends and
the requirements set by ends.[24] If natural law imposes
obligations that good acts are to be done, it is only
because it primarily imposes with rational necessity
that an end must be pursued.

In his youthful commentary on Lombard's *Books of
Sentences*, Aquinas goes so far as to consider the prin-

---

[22] S.T. 1-2, q. 90, a. 2, c.
[23] *Id.* at q. 99, a. 1, c.
[24] See Stevens, *op. cit. supra* note 8, at 202-205.

ciples of practical reason—which he already compares
to the principles of demonstrations—to be so many
innate natural ends.[25] He remarks that the habit of
these ends is synderesis, which is the habit of the principles of the natural law.[26] Hence in this early work
he is saying that the natural law is precisely the ends
to which man is naturally inclined insofar as these
ends are present in reason as principles for the rational
direction of action.

Later in the same work Aquinas explicitly formulates the notion of the law of nature for the first time
in his writings. Why are the principles of practical reason called "natural law"? Precisely because man knows
the intelligibility of end and the proportion of his
work to end. Suitability of action is not to a static nature, but to the ends toward which nature inclines.
Evil is not explained ultimately by opposition to law,
but opposition to law by unsuitability of action to end.
This early treatment of natural law is saturated with
the notion of end. . . .[27]

Thus it is clear that Aquinas emphasizes end as a
principle of natural law. But it is also clear that the
end in question cannot be identified with moral goodness itself.

To begin with, Aquinas specifically denies that the
ultimate end of man could consist in morally good action. Moral action, and that upon which it immediately bears, can be directed to ulterior goods, and for
this very reason moral action cannot be the absolutely
ultimate end.[28] Moreover, Aquinas expressly identifies the principles of practical reason with the ends
of the virtues preexisting in reason. Prudence is con-

[25] *Super Libros Sententiarum Petri Lombardi* bk. 3, d. 33,
q. 2, a. 4, q'la. 4, c. (ed. Mandonnet-Moos, Paris, 1929–1947).

[26] See Lottin, *op. cit. supra* note 3, at 68–73.

[27] *Super Libros Sententiarum Petri Lombardi* bk. 4, d. 33, q.
1, a. 1, c. (in St. Thomas, 7 *Opéra*, Parma ed., 1852–1873).

[28] *Summa contra Gentiles* 3, ch. 34 (ed. C. Pera, P. Murc,
P. Caramello, Turin, 1961).

cerned with moral actions which are in fact means to ends, and prudence directs the work of all the moral virtues.[29] Hence the principles of natural law, in their expression of ends, transcend moral good and evil as the end transcends means and obstacles.

This transcendence of the goodness of the end over the goodness of moral action has its ultimate metaphysical foundation in this, that the end of each creature's action can be an end for it only by being a participation in divine goodness. The goodness of God is the absolutely ultimate final cause, just as the power of God is the absolutely ultimate efficient cause.[30] This end, of course, does not depend for realization on human action, much less can it be identified with human action. But moral good and evil are precisely the inner perfection or privation of human action. Hence the end transcends morality and provides an extrinsic foundation for it. This point is of the greatest importance in Aquinas' treatise on the end of man. Aristotle identifies the end of man with virtuous activity,[31] but Aquinas, despite his debt to Aristotle, sees the end of man as the *attainment* of a good. The good in question is God, who altogether transcends human activity. Hence an end for Aquinas has two inseparable aspects—what is attained and the attainment of it. But if these must be distinguished, the end is rather in what is attained than in its attainment.[32]

Nor should it be supposed that the end's transcendence over moral virtue is a peculiarity of the supernatural end. Natural law does not direct man to his supernatural end; in fact, it is precisely because it is inadequate to do so that divine law is needed as a supplement.[33] Or, to put the same thing in another way, not everything contained in the Law and the

[29] S.T. 2-2, q. 47, a. 6, c.
[30] *Summa contra Gentiles* 3, chs. 18-19.
[31] *Ethica Nicomachea* bk. 1, 1098ª17.
[32] S.T. 1-2, qq. 1-5, esp. q. 2, a. 7.
[33] S.T. 1-2, q. 91, a. 4.

Gospel pertains to natural law, because many of these points concern matters supernatural.[34] And yet, as we have seen, the principles of natural law are given the status of ends of the moral virtues.

An attentive reading of the last two paragraphs of the response examined above would be by itself sufficient for our present point. The goods in question are objects of man's natural inclinations. These goods are not primarily works that are to be done. Rather, the works are means to ulterior ends: reason grasps the objects of the natural inclinations as goods and so as things-to-be-pursued by work. The works obviously are means to the goods. And what are the objects of the natural inclinations? Not merely morally good acts, but such substantive goods as self-preservation, the life and education of children, and knowledge.

Some interpreters mistakenly ask whether the word "good" in the first principle has a transcendental or an ethical sense.[35] The issue is a false one, for there is no question of extending the meaning of "good" to the amplitude of the transcendentals convertible with "being." The very text clearly indicates that Aquinas is concerned with good as the object of practical reason; hence the goods signified by the "good" of the first principle will be *human* goods. It must be so, since the good pursued by practical reason is an objective of *human* action. But to grant this point is not at all to identify the good in question with moral value, for this particular category of value by no means exhausts human goods. The preservation of human life is certainly a human good. The act which preserves life is not the life preserved; in fact, they are so distinct that it is possible for the act that preserves life to be morally bad while the life preserved remains a human good.

The failure to keep this distinction in mind can lead

[34] *Id.* at q. 94, a. 4, ad 1.
[35] E.g., Schuster, *op. cit. supra* note 8, at 54-55.

to chaos in normative ethics. But more important for our present purpose is that this distinction indicates that the good which is to be done and pursued should not be thought of as exclusively the good of moral action. The pursuit of the good which is the end is primary; the doing of the good which is the means is subordinate. The good which is the end is the principle of moral value, and at least in some respects this principle transcends its consequence, just as *being* in a certain respect is a principle (of beings) that transcends even the most fundamental category of being.[36]

Aquinas, of course, never takes a utilitarian view of the value of moral action. But his alternative is not the deontologism that assigns to moral value and the perfection of intention the status of absolutes. Utilitarianism is an inadequate ethical theory partly because it overly restricts natural inclination, for it assumes that man's sole determinate inclination is in regard to pleasure and pain. Aquinas recognizes a variety of natural inclinations, including one to act in a rational way.[37] Among the *ends* toward which the precepts of the natural law direct, then, moral value has a place. Hence good human action has intrinsic worth, not merely instrumental value as utilitarianism supposes. Moreover, because the end proposed by the utilitarians is only a psychic state and because utilitarians also hold a mechanistic theory of causality, utilitarianism denies that any kind of action is intrinsically good or bad. Thus actions are considered good or bad only by virtue of extrinsic consequences. Aquinas, on the contrary, understands human action not merely as a piece of behavior but as an object of

[36] Although too long a task to be undertaken here, a full comparison of Aquinas' position to that of Suarez would help to clarify the present point. See Walter Farrell, O.P., *The Natural Moral Law according to St. Thomas and Suarez* 103-155 (Ditchling, 1930). . . .

[37] S.T. 1-2, q. 94, a. 3, c.

choice. He considers a whole range of nonpsychic realities to be human goods. His theory of causality does not preclude an intrinsic relationship between acts and ends. Hence he holds that some species of acts are bad in themselves, so that they cannot become good under any circumstances.[38]

In sum, the mistaken interpretation of Aquinas' theory of natural law supposes that the word "good" in the primary precept refers solely to moral good. In fact, it refers primarily to the end which is not limited to moral value. The mistaken interpretation inevitably falls into circularity; Aquinas' real position shows where moral reasoning can begin, for it works from transmoral principles of moral action. The mistaken interpretation offers as a principle: *Do good.* It subsumes actions under this imperative, which limits the meaning of "good" to the good of action. Aquinas suggests as a principle: *Work in pursuit of the end.* This principle enables the good that is an end not only to illuminate but also to enrich with value the action by which it is attained.

III

The mistaken interpretation of Aquinas' theory suggests that law is essentially a curb upon action. Law is imagined as a command set over against even those actions performed in obedience to it. And of course it is much more opposed to wrong actions. In this section, I propose three respects in which the primary principle of practical reason as Aquinas understands it is broader in scope than this false interpretation suggests. A clearer understanding of the scope of natural law will further unfold the implications of the point treated in the last section; at the same time, it will be a basis for the fourth section.

[38] *Id.* at q. 18, aa. 6-7; *Super Libros Sententiarum Petri Lombardi* bk. 2, d. 40, q. 1, aa. 1-2.

The mistaken interpretation suggests that natural law is a set of imperatives whose form leaves no room to discriminate among degrees of force to be attached to various precepts. All precepts seem equally absolute; violation of any one of them is equally a violation of the law.

For Aquinas, however, natural law includes counsels as well as precepts. In other words, the first principle refers not only to the good which must be done, but also to the nonobligatory good it would be well to do.

In the article next after the one commented upon above, Aquinas asks whether the acts of all the virtues are of the law of nature. In his response he does not exclude virtuous acts which are beyond the call of duty. He does make a distinction: all virtuous acts as such belong to the law of nature, but particular virtuous acts may not, for they may depend upon human inquiry.[39]

Later, in treating the Old Law, Aquinas maintains that all the moral precepts of the Old Law belong to the law of nature, and then he proceeds to distinguish those moral precepts which carry the obligation of strict precept from those which convey only the warning of counsel.[40] Indeed, in treating natural law in his commentary on the *Sentences*, Aquinas carefully distinguishes between actions fully prohibited because they totally obstruct the attainment of an end and actions restricted because they are obstacles to its attainment. Lottin notices this point. Today, he says, we restrict the notion of law to strict obligations. But Aquinas took a broader view of it, for he understood law as a principle of order which embraces the whole range of objects to which man has a natural inclination. Consequently, when Aquinas wishes to

[39] S.T. 1-2, q. 94, a. 3, c.
[40] *Id.* at q. 100, aa. 1-2.

indicate strict obligation he often uses a special mode of expression to make this idea explicit.[41]

Suarez refers to the passages where Aquinas discusses the scope of the natural law. Although aware that Aquinas includes counsels as well as precepts in natural law, Suarez prefers to limit his concern to matters of strict obligation: "But we properly inquire concerning precepts."[42] It never occurs to Suarez to wonder why he himself narrows the scope Aquinas attributed to law.

The difference between the two points of view is no mystery. Aquinas thinks in terms of the end, and obligation is merely one result of the influence of an intelligible end on reasonable action. "Good" in the first principle, since it refers primarily to the end, includes within its scope not only what is absolutely necessary but also what is helpful, and the opposed evil includes more than the perfect contrary of the good. Like most later interpreters, Suarez thinks that what is morally good or bad depends simply upon the agreement or disagreement of action with nature, and he holds that the obligation to do the one and to avoid the other arises from an imposition of the will of God.[43] Hence "evil" in the first principle of natural law denotes only the actions which definitely disagree with nature, the doing of which is forbidden, and "good" denotes only the actions whose omission definitely disagrees with nature, the doing of which is commanded. An act which falls in neither of these categories is simply of no interest to a legalistic moralist who does not see that moral value and obligation have their source in the end.

Perhaps even more surprising is another respect in

[41] Lottin, *op. cit. supra* note 3, at 75, points out that Aquinas will add to the expression "law of nature" a further word—e.g., "precept"—to express strict obligation.

[42] De legibus II, 7, 11.

[43] *Id.* at II, 7.

which the first practical principle as Aquinas sees it
has a broader scope than is usually realized. "Every
judgment of practical reason proceeds from naturally
known principles."[44] The derivative is from the underived, the underivable principles. In practical reason it is self-evident precepts that are underivable,
natural law. Not only virtuous and self-restrained
men, but also vicious men and backsliders make practical judgments. Indeed, if evildoers lacked practical
judgment they could not engage in human action at
all.[45] It follows that practical judgments made in evil
action nevertheless fall under the scope of the first
principle of the natural law, and the word "good" in
this principle must refer somehow to deceptive and
inadequate human goods as well as to adequate and
genuine ones.

It is important, however, to see the precise manner
in which the principle, *Good is to be done and pursued,* still rules practical reason when it goes astray.
"Good" is not merely a generic expression for whatever anyone may happen to want,[46] for if this were
the case there would not be a single first principle but
as many first principles as there are basic commit-
ments, and each first principle would provide the major premise for a different system of rules. Still, if
"good" denoted only moral goods, either wrong practical judgments could in no way issue from practical
reason or the formula we are examining would not in
reality express the first principle of practical reason.

Aquinas mentions this point in at least two places.
In one he explains that for practical reason, as for
theoretical reason, it is true that false judgments occur. Yet even though such judgments originate in first
principles, their falsity is not due to the principles so

---

[44] S.T. 1-2, q. 100, a. 1, c.

[45] See *De malo* q. 3, a. 9, ad 7.

[46] A. G. Sertillanges, O.P., *La philosophie morale de Saint
Thomas d'Aquin* 109 (Paris, 1946), seems to fall into this mistaken interpretation.

much as to the bad use of the principles.[47] Similarly he explains in another place that the power of first principles is present in practical misjudgment, yet the defect of the judgment arises not from the principles but from the reasoning through which the judgment is formed.[48]

Just as the principle of contradiction is operative even in false judgments, so the first principle of practical reason is operative in wrong evaluations and decisions. First principles do not sanction error, but of themselves they set only limited requirements. As a disregard of the principle of contradiction makes discourse disintegrate into nonsense, so a disregard of the first principle of practical reason would make action dissolve into chaotic behavior. The insane sometimes commit violations of both principles within otherwise rational contexts, but erroneous judgment and wrong decision need not always conflict with first principles. Hence first principles must be supplemented by other principles and by a sound reasoning process if correct conclusions are to be reached. The first practical principle, as we have seen, requires only that what it directs have intentionality toward an intelligible purpose. The possible underived ends are indicated by the fundamental inclinations which ground appropriate precepts. "Good" in the first principle refers with priority to these underived ends, yet by itself the first principle cannot exclude ends presented in other practical judgments even if their derivation is unsound.

Assumption of a group of principles inadequate to a problem, failure to observe the facts, or error in reasoning can lead to results within the scope of first principles but not sanctioned by them. The first precept directs us to direct our action toward ends within human power, and even immoral action in part fulfills

[47] *De veritate* q. 16, a. 2, ad 6.
[48] *Super Libros Sententiarum Petri Lombardi* bk. 2, d. 39, q. 3, a. 1, ad 1.

this precept, for even vicious men act for a human good while accepting the violation of more adequate human good. The good which is the object of pursuit can be the principle of the rational aspects of defective and inadequate efforts, but the good which characterizes morally right acts completely excludes wrong ones.

After observing these two respects in which the mistaken interpretation unduly restricts the scope of the first principle of practical reason, we may note also that this principle as Aquinas understands it is not merely a principle of imperative judgments. Rather, it is primarily a principle of actions. Aquinas thinks of law as a set of principles of practical reason related to *actions themselves* just as the principles of theoretical reason are related to *conclusions.*[49] Law is not a constraint upon actions which originate elsewhere and which would flourish better if they were not confined by reason. Law, rather, is a source of actions. Law makes human life possible. Animals behave without law, for they live by instinct without thought and without freedom. Man cannot begin to act as man without law.

The first precept does not say what we *ought* to do in contradistinction to what we *will* do. Opposition between the direction of reason and the response of will can arise only subsequent to the orientation toward end expressed in the first principle. One whose practical premise is, "Pleasure is to be pursued," might reach the conclusion, "Adultery ought to be avoided," without this prohibition becoming a principle of his action. But the first principle of practical reason cannot be set aside in this manner, as we have seen, and so it cannot represent an imposition contrary to the judgment that actually informs our choice.[50] The first principles of practical reason are a source not only for

[49] S.T. 1-2, q. 90, a. 1, ad 2.
[50] For the notion of judgment forming choice see *id.* at q. 13, a. 3.

judgments of conscience but even for judgments of prudence; while the former can remain merely speculative and ineffectual, the latter are the very structure of virtuous action.[51]

Throughout history man has been tempted to suppose that wrong action is wholly outside the field of rational control, that it has no principle in practical reason. Naturalism frequently has explained away evildoing, just as some psychological and sociological theories based on determinism now do. No less subversive of human responsibility, which is based on purposive—and, therefore, rational—agency, is the existentialist notion that morally good and morally bad action are equally reasonable, and that a choice of one or the other is equally a matter of arational arbitrariness. Aquinas' understanding of the first principle of practical reason avoids the dilemma of these contrary positions. The first principle of morally good action is the principle of all human action, but bad action fulfills the requirement of the first principle less perfectly than good action does. If the first principle of practical reason were *Do morally good acts,* then morally bad acts would fall outside the order of practical reason; if *Do morally good acts* nevertheless were the first precept of natural law, and morally bad acts fell within the order of practical reason, then there would be a domain of reason outside natural law. However, since the first principle is *Good is to be done and pursued,* morally bad acts fall within the order of practical reason, yet the principles of practical reason remain identically the principles of natural law. More than correct principles are required, however, if reason is to reach its appropriate conclusion in action toward the good.

[51] *De veritate* q. 17, a. 2; S.T. 2-2, q. 47, a. 6. For a comparison between judgments of prudence and those of conscience see my paper, *The Logic of Moral Judgment,* 26 *Proceedings of the American Catholic Philosophical Association* 67-76, esp. p. 70, n. 7 (1962).

The mistaken interpretation of Aquinas' theory of natural law, with its restrictive understanding of the scope of the first practical principle, suggests that before reason comes upon the scene, the whole broad field of action lies open before man, offering no obstacles to his enjoyment of an endlessly rich and satisfying life, but that cold reason with its abstract precepts successively marks section after section of the field out of bounds, progressively enclosing the submissive subject in an ever-shrinking pen, while those who act at the promptings of uninhibited spontaneity range freely over all the possibilities of life. The true understanding of the first principle of practical reason suggests on the contrary that the alternative to moral goodness is an arbitrary restriction upon the human goods which can be attained by reasonable direction of life. The first principle of practical reason directs toward ends which make human action possible; by virtue of the first principle are formed precepts that represent every aspect of human nature. Together these principles open to man all the fields in which he can act; rational direction insures that action will be fruitful and that life will be as productive and satisfying as possible. Whatever man may achieve, his action requires at least a remote basis in the tendencies that arise from human nature. Similarly, actual being does not eliminate unrealized possibilities by demanding that they be not only self-consistent but also consistent with what already is; rather, it is partly by this demand that actual being grounds possibility.

IV

The mistaken interpretation of Aquinas' theory of natural law considers natural law precepts to be a set of imperatives. In this section I wish to show both that the first principle does not have primarily imperative force and that it is really prescriptive. The distinction between these two modes of practical discourse often is ignored, and so it may seem that to deny imperative force to the primary precept is to remove it from practical discourse altogether and to transform it into a merely theoretical principle. Hence I shall begin by emphasizing the practical character of the principle, and then I shall proceed to clarify its lack of imperative force.[52]

The good which is the subject matter of practical reason is an objective possibility, and it could be contemplated. But in that case the principle that will govern the consideration will be that agents necessarily act for ends, not that good is to be done and pursued. For Aquinas, practical reason not only has a peculiar subject matter, but it is related to its subject matter in a peculiar way, for practical reason introduces the order it knows, while theoretical reason adopts the order it finds.[53] The object of the practical intellect is not merely the actions men perform, but the *good which can be directed to realization, pre-*

[52] Even those interpreters who usually can be trusted tend to fall into the mistake of considering the first principle of practical reason as if it were fundamentally theoretical. Lottin, for instance, suggests that the first assent to the primary principle is an act of theoretical reason. At first it appears, he says, simply as a truth, a translation into moral language of the principle of identity. A formula of the first judgment of practical reason might be "That which is good, is good—*i.e.*, desirable," or "The good is that which is to be done, the evil is that which is to be avoided." Odon Lottin, O.S.B., 1 *Principes de Morale* 22, 122 (Louvain, 1946).

Significant in these formulations are the "that which (ce qui)" and the double "is," for these expressions mark the removal of gerundive force from the principal verb of the sentence. Thus Lottin makes the precept appear as much as possible like a theoretical statement expressing a peculiar aspect of the good—namely, that it is the sort of thing that demands doing. Sertillanges also tries to understand the principle as if it were a theoretical truth equivalent to an identity statement. Among his formulations are: "That which is to be done is to be done," and: "The good is an end worth pursuing." Sertillanges, *op. cit. supra* note 46, at 102, 109. . . .

[53] *In libros ethicorum ad Nichomachum*, lib. 1, lect. 1.

cisely insofar as that is a mode of truth.[54] Practical reason is related to the movement of action as a principle, not as a consequence.[55]

Laws are formed by practical reason as principles of the actions it guides just as definitions and premises are formed by theoretical reason as principles of the conclusions it reaches.[56] A law is an expression of reason just as truly as a statement is, but a statement is an expression of reason asserting, whereas a law is an expression of reason prescribing.[57] The primary principle of practical reason, as we have seen, eminently fulfills these characterizations of law. The principle is formed because the intellect, assuming the office of active principle, accepts the requirements of that role, and demands of itself that in directing action it must really direct. The precept that good is to be sought is genuinely a principle of action, not merely a point of departure for speculation about human life.

The principles of practical reason belong to a logical category quite different from that of theoretical statements: precepts do not inform us of requirements; they express requirements as directions for action. The point of saying that good is to be pursued is not that good is the sort of thing that has or is this peculiar property, obligatoriness—a subtle mistake with which G. E. Moore launched contemporary Anglo-American ethical theory. The point rather is to issue the fundamental directive of practical reason. "Is to be" is the copula of the first practical principle, not its predicate; the gerundive is the mode rather than the matter of law. To know the first principle of practical reason is not to reflect upon the way in which goodness affects action, but to know a good in

[54] S.T. 1, q. 79, a. 11, ad 2: *"Objectum intellectus practici est bonum ordinabile ad opus, sub ratione veri."*
[55] *Id.* at ad 1.
[56] S.T. 1-2, q. 90, a. 1, ad 2.
[57] *Id.* at q. 92, a. 2, c.

such a way that in virtue of that very knowledge the known good is ordained toward realization.

But if it is significant that the first principle of practical reason is really a precept and not merely a theoretical statement, it is less clear but equally important that this principle is not an imperative, as the mistaken interpretation of Aquinas' theory considers it to be.

Of course, so far as grammar alone is concerned, the gerundive form can be employed to express an imperative. However, Aquinas explicitly distinguishes between an imperative and a precept expressed in gerundive form. The imperative not only provides rational direction for action, but it also contains motive force derived from an antecedent act of the will bearing upon the object of the action. The prescription expressed in gerundive form, on the contrary, merely offers rational direction without promoting the execution of the work to which reason directs.[58]

To recognize this distinction is not to deny that law can be expressed in imperative form. At the beginning of his treatise on law, Aquinas refers to his previous discussion of the imperative.[59] Human and divine law are in fact not merely prescriptive but also imperative, and when precepts of the law of nature were incorporated into the divine law they became imperatives whose violation is contrary to the divine will as well as to right reason.

Nevertheless, the first principle of practical reason hardly can be understood in the first instance as an imperative. As we have seen, it is a self-evident prin-

[58] *Id.* at q. 17, a. 1.

[59] *Id.* at q. 90, a. 1, *sed contra,* ad 3; q. 91, a. 2, ad 2. But these references should not be given too much weight, since they refer to the article previously cited in which the distinction is made explicitly. Although arguments based on what the text does not say are dangerous, it is worth noticing that Aquinas does not define law as *an imperative for the common good,* as he easily could have done if that were his notion, but as *an ordinance of reason for the common good etc. Id.* at q. 90, a. 4, c.

ciple in which reason prescribes the first condition of its own practical office. On the one hand, the causality of God is not a principle evident to us. On the other hand, the operation of our own will is not a condition for the prescription of practical reason; the opposite rather is the case.

Aquinas' theological approach to natural law primarily presents it as a participation in the eternal law. This fact has helped to mislead many into supposing that natural law must be understood as a divine imperative. Of course, Aquinas holds that God's will is prior to the natural law, since the natural law is an aspect of human existence and man is a free creation of God. But Aquinas does not describe natural law as eternal law passively received in man; he describes it rather as a participation in the eternal law. This participation is necessary precisely insofar as man shares the grand office of providence in directing his own life and that of his fellows.[60] Every participation is really distinct from that in which it participates—a principle evidently applicable in this case, for the eternal law *is* God while the law of nature is a set of precepts.

From man's point of view, the principles of natural law are neither received from without nor posited by his own choice; they are naturally and necessarily known, and a knowledge of God is by no means a condition for forming self-evident principles, unless those principles happen to be ones that especially

[60] O'Donoghue (*op. cit. supra* note 20) tries to clarify this point, and does in fact help considerably toward the removal of misinterpretations. Still, his work is marked by a misunderstanding of practical reason, so that precept is equated with imperative (p. 95) and will is introduced in the explanation of the transition from theory to practice. (p. 101) Farrell (*op. cit. supra* note 36), by a full and careful comparison of Aquinas' and Suarez's theories of natural law, clarifies the essential point very well, without suggesting that natural law is human legislation, as O'Donoghue seems to think.

concern God.[61] Moreover, Aquinas simply does not understand the eternal law itself as if it were an imposition of the divine will upon creation;[62] and even if he did understand it in this way, no such imposition would count for human judgment except in virtue of a practical principle to the effect that the divine will deserves to be followed. Without such a foundation God might *compel behavior* but he could never *direct human action.*

Nor is any operation of our own will presupposed by the first principles of practical reason. Of course we do make judgments concerning means in accordance with the orientation of our intention toward the end. But our willing of ends requires knowledge of them, and the directive knowledge *prior to* the natural movements of our will is precisely the basic principles of practical reason. At any rate this is Aquinas' theory. He maintains that there is no willing without prior apprehension.[63] Moreover, the basic principle of desire, natural inclination in the appetitive part of the soul, is consequent upon prior apprehension, natural knowledge.[64] For the will, this natural knowledge

[61] The point has been much debated despite the clarity of Aquinas' position that natural law principles are self-evident; Stevens, *op. cit. supra* note 8, at 201, n. 23, provides some bibliography.

[62] Eternal law is "the exemplar of divine wisdom, as directing all actions and movements" of created things in their progress toward their end. S.T. 1-2, q. 93, a. 1, c. Those who misunderstand Aquinas' theory often seem to assume, as if it were obvious, that law is a transient action of an efficient cause physically moving passive objects; for Aquinas, law always belongs to reason, is never considered an efficient cause, and cannot possibly terminate in motion. By their motion and rest, moved objects participate in the perfection of agents, but a caused order participates in the exemplar of its perfection by form and the consequences of form—consequences such as inclination, reason, and the precepts of practical reason. See Farrell, *op. cit. supra* note 36, at ch. 4, esp. pp. 98–103.

[63] S.T. 1, q. 82, a. 4, ad 3.

[64] *Super Libros Sententiarum Petri Lombardi* bk. 4, d. 33, q. 1, a. 1, ad 9.

is nothing else than the first principles of practical reason.[65] The precepts of natural law, at least the first principle of practical reason, must be antecedent to all acts of our will. There is nothing surprising about this conclusion so long as we understand law as intelligence ordering (directing) human action toward an end rather than as a superior ordering (commanding) a subject's performance.

The theory of law is permanently in danger of falling into the illusion that practical knowledge is merely theoretical knowledge plus force of will. This is exactly the mistake Suarez makes when he explains natural law as the natural goodness or badness of actions plus preceptive divine law.[66]

The way to avoid these difficulties is to understand that practical reason really does not know in the same way that theoretical reason knows. For practical reason, to know is to prescribe. This is why I insisted so strongly that the first practical principle is not a theoretical truth. Once its real character as a precept is seen, there is less temptation to bolster the practical principle with will, and so to transform it into an imperative, in order to make it relevant to practice. Indeed, the addition of will to theoretical knowledge cannot make it practical. This point is precisely what

[65] *Id.* at bk. 2, d. 39, q. 2, a. 2, ad 2.

[66] De legibus, II, 7; Farrell, *op. cit. supra* note 36, at 147-155. Even excellent recent interpreters of Aquinas tend to compensate for the speculative character they attribute to the first principle of practical reason by introducing an act of our will as a factor in our assent to it. Lottin, for example, balances his notion that we first assent to the primary principle as to a theoretical truth with the notion that we finally assent to it with a consent of the will. Only free acceptance makes the precept fully operative. (*Op. cit supra* note 52, at 24.) Even so accurate a commentator as Stevens introduces the inclination of the will as a ground for the prescriptive force of the first principle. (*Op. cit. supra* note 8, at 202-203: "The intellect manifests this truth formally, and commands it as true, for its own goodness is seen to consist in a conformity to the natural object and inclination of the will.")

Hume saw when he denied the possibility of deriving *ought* from *is*.

In an interesting passage in an article attacking what he mistakenly considered to be Aquinas' theory of natural law, Kai Nielsen discussed this point at some length.[67] He begins by arguing that normative statements cannot be derived from statements of fact, not even from a set of factual statements which comprise a true metaphysical theory of reality. He points out that from "God wills x," one cannot derive "x is obligatory," without assuming the non-factual statement: "What God wills is obligatory." He proceeds to criticize what he takes to be a confusion in Thomism between fact and value, a merging of disparate categories which Nielsen considers unintelligible. But over and above this objection, he insists that normative discourse, insofar as it is practical, simply cannot be derived from a mere consideration of facts. In this part of the argument, Nielsen clearly recognizes the distinction between theoretical and practical reason on which I have been insisting. He concludes his argument by maintaining that the factor which differentiates practical discourse is the presence of decision within it.

To such criticism it is no answer to argue that empiricism makes an unnatural cleavage between facts and values.[68] I have tried above to explain how Aquinas understands *tendency toward good* and *orientation toward end* as a dimension of all action. If every active principle acts on account of an end, then at a certain time in spring from the weather and our knowledge of nature we can conclude that the

[67] *Op. cit. supra* note 11, at 63-68.

[68] Vernon Bourke, *Natural Law, Thomism—and Professor Nielsen*, 5 *Natural Law Forum* 118-119 (1960), in part has recourse to this kind of argument in his response to Nielsen. Although Bourke is right in noticing that Nielsen's difficulties partly arise from his positivism, I think Bourke is mistaken in supposing that a more adequate metaphysics could bridge the gap between theory and practice.

roses ought to be blooming soon. Similarly, from the
truth of the premises and the validity of the reasoning
we can say that the conclusion ought to be true. And
from the unique properties of the material and the
peculiar engineering requirements we can deduce that
titanium ought to be useful in the construction of
supersonic aircraft. But to get moral principles from
metaphysics, it is not from the *is* of nature to the *ought*
of nature that one must go. This illation is intelligible
to anyone except a positivist, but it is of no help in
explaining the origin of moral judgments. Moreover,
it is no solution to argue that one can derive the
"ought" of moral judgment from the "is" of ethical
evaluation: "This act is virtuous; therefore, it ought to
be done." Not even Hume could object to such a deduction. Precisely the point at issue is this, that from
the agreement of actions with human nature or with
a decree of the divine will, one cannot derive the
prescriptive sentence: "They ought to be done."

Aquinas knew this, and his theory of natural law
takes it for granted. *Good is to be done and pursued,
and evil is to be avoided,* together with the other self-
evident principles of natural law, are not derived from
any statements of fact. They are principles. They are
not derived from any statements at all. They are not
derived from prior principles. They are underivable.

The intellect is not theoretical by nature and practical only by education. To be practical is natural to
human reason. Reason is doing its own work when
it prescribes just as when it affirms or denies. The
basic precepts of natural law are no less part of the
mind's original equipment than are the evident principles of theoretical knowledge. *Ought* requires no
special act legitimatizing it; *ought* rules its own domain by its own authority, an authority legitimate as
that of any *is*. Of course, one cannot form these principles if he has no grasp upon what is involved in
them, and such understanding presupposes experience. However, one does not derive these principles

from experience or from any previous understanding. Aquinas' position is not: we conclude that certain kinds of acts should be done because they would satisfy our inclinations or fulfill divine commands. His position is: we are capable of thinking for ourselves in the practical domain because we naturally form a set of principles that make possible all of our actions. Practical principles do not become practical, although they do become more significant for us, if we believe that God wills them. Nonprescriptive statements believed to express the divine will also gain added meaning for the believer but do not thereby become practical. For instance, that the universe is huge is given added meaning for one who believes in creation, but it does not on that account become a matter of obligation for him, since it remains a theoretical truth.

Of course, I must disagree with Nielsen's position that decision makes discourse practical. This view implies that human action ultimately is irrational, and it is at odds with the distinction between theoretical and practical reason. If practical reason were simply a conditional theoretical judgment together with verification of the antecedent by an act of appetite, then this position could be defended, but the first act of appetite would lack any rational principle.[69] However, the primary principle of practical reason is by no means hypothetical. It directs that good is to be done and pursued, and it allows no alternative within the field of action.[70] In fact, the practical acceptance

[69] Bourke does not call Nielsen to task on this point, and in fact (*id.* at 117) even seems to concur in considering practical reason hypothetical apart from an act of will, but Bourke places the will act in God rather than in our own decision as Nielsen does.

[70] The mere fact of decision, or the mere fact of feeling one of the sentiments invoked by Hume, is no more a basis for "ought" than is any other "is." Hume misses his own point—that "ought" *cannot* be derived—and Nielsen follows his master. If some practical principle is hypothetical because there is an alternative to it, only a practical principle (and ultimately a non-

of the antecedent of any conditional formulation directing toward action is itself an action that presupposes the direction of practical reason toward the good and the end. The prescription "Happiness should be pursued" is presupposed by the acceptance of the antecedent "If you wish to be happy," when this motive is proposed as a rational ground of moral action.

But while I disagree with Nielsen's positive position on this point, I think that his essential criticism is altogether effective against the position he is attacking. If one supposes that principles of natural law are formed by examining kinds of action in comparison with human nature and noting their agreement or disagreement, then one must respond to the objection that it is impossible to derive normative judgments from metaphysical speculations. The invocation of a metaphysics of divine causality and providence at this point is no help, since such a metaphysics also consists exclusively of theoretical truths from which reason can derive no practical consequences. Of course, if man can know that God will punish him if he does not act in approved ways, then it does follow that an effective threat can be deduced from the facts. But no such threat, whether coming from God or society or nature, is prescriptive unless one applies to it the precept that horrible consequences should be avoided. I do not deny that the naked threat might become effective on behavior without reference to any practical principle. A threat can be effective by circumventing choice and moving to nonrational impulse. Such a derivation, however, is not at all concerned with the "ought"; it moves from beginning to end within the realm of "is."

hypothetical practical principle) can foreclose the rational alternative.

CHRONOLOGY OF AQUINAS' LIFE

AND WRITINGS

1225   Born at Roccasecca near Aquino, Italy.

1230   Schooled as an oblate at Monte Cassino Abbey.

1239   Attended University of Naples.

1244   Became Dominican despite family hostility.

1245   Studied at Paris under Albertus Magnus.

1248   Studied at Cologne under Albertus Magnus.

1252   Returned to Paris. Lectured on Scripture.

1254   Licentiate in Theology. Lectured on Sentences and wrote commentary on them. About this time wrote *De Ente et Essentia.*

1256   Became Professor of Theology at Paris. About this time wrote *De Veritate, In Librum Boethii de Trinitate,* and began *Summa contra Gentiles.*

1259   Went to Anagni. Continued *S.c.G.* About this time wrote *Q.D. de Potentia.*

1261   Went to Orvieto. Completed *S.c.G.*

1265   Went to Rome. Began writing commentaries on Aristotle.

1267   Went to Viterbo. About this time began writing *Summa Theologiae.* Wrote *Q.D. de Spiritualibus Creaturis.*

1269   Returned to Paris. Continued writing *S.Th.* About this time wrote *QQ.DD. de Malo, de Anima; de Aeternitate Mundi, de Unitate Intellectus, de Substantiis Separatis.*

1272   Went to Naples.

1273   Suspended work on the *Summa* after a mystical experience.

1274   Died while journeying to the Council of Lyons.

BIBLIOGRAPHY

1. Works of Aquinas and English Translations

Summa Theologiae (Summa Theologica). The most accessible Latin edition is the Marietti one (Turin, 1934 etc.) (The Leonine edition of St. Thomas' works [Rome, 1882–] is standard, incomplete, and inconvenient.) There is a complete translation by the Fathers of the English Dominican Province (2nd rev. ed. London 1920; reissued in 3 vols. New York, 1947) and a new translation in sixty volumes, begun in 1964 and shortly to be completed, published by Blackfriars in conjunction with Eyre and Spottiswoode (London) and McGraw-Hill (New York), each volume of which contains an introduction, the relevant Latin text with English translation, notes, explanatory appendices, a glossary and indices, under the general editorship of Thomas Gilby and T. C. O'Brien. References are often made to the *Summa* without title, or after the abbreviation *S.Th.*, by citing the Part, question, article (reply); thus: "Ia IIae, (q.) 3, (art.) 2, (ad. 2)" means: the reply to the second objection in the second article of the third question of the First Part of the Second Part.

Summa contra Gentiles, Turin and Rome, 1934. Translated by A. C. Pegis and others as *On the Truth of the Catholic Faith,* New York, 1955. It is cited as *S.c.G.* or *CG* by giving book and chapter number: e.g., *CG* I, 30.

Scriptum in IV Libros Sententiarum (Commentary on the Sentences of Peter Lombard), ed. P. Mandonnet and M. F. Moos, 4 vols., Paris, 1929–47. No English version. Reference is made to it by citing the book, distinction, question, article, solution or *quaestiuncula,* and reply: e.g. III *Sent.* 25, 2, 3, ii ad 3.

PHILOSOPHICAL COMMENTARIES

In Libros Posteriorum Analyticorum. Vol. I of the Leonine edition, Rome, 1882. Translated as *Exposition of the Posterior Analytics of Aristotle*, P. Conway, Quebec, 1956.

In Libros de Anima, ed. R. M. Spiazzi, Turin, 1949. Translated as *Aristotle's De Anima with the Commentary of St. Thomas*, K. Foster and S. Humphries, London and New Haven, 1951.

In Libros de Caelo et Mundo, ed. R. M. Spiazzi, Turin, 1952. No English version.

In X Libros Ethicorum, ed. R. M. Spiazzi, Turin, 1949. Translated as *Commentary on the Nicomachean Ethics*, C. I. Litzinger, Chicago, 1964.

In Libros Peri Hermeneias, ed. R. M. Spiazzi, Turin, 1955. Translated as *Aristotle on Interpretation—Commentary by St. Thomas and Cajetan*, J. Oesterle, Milwaukee, 1962.

In XII Libros Metaphysicorum, ed. R. M. Spiazzi, Turin, 1950. Translated as *Commentary on the Metaphysics of Aristotle*, Chicago, 1961.

In VIII Libros Physicorum, ed. P. Maggiolo, Turin, 1954. Translated as *Commentary on Aristotle's Physics*, R. L. Blackwell and others, London and New Haven, 1963.

DISPUTED QUESTIONS

Quaestiones Disputatae de Veritate, ed. R. M. Spiazzi, Turin, 1949. Translated as *Truth*, R. W. Mulligan and others, Chicago, 1952–54.

Quaestiones Disputatae de Potentia Dei, ed. R. M. Spiazzi, Turin, 1949. Translated as *On the Power of*

God, L. Shapcote and others, Westminster, Maryland, 1952.

Quaestiones Disputatae de Spiritualibus Creaturis, ed. L. W. Keeler, Rome, 1938. Translated as *On Spiritual Creatures,* M. C. Fitzpatrick and J. J. Wellmuth, Milwaukee, 1949.

Quaestio Disputata de Anima, ed. R. M. Spiazzi, Turin, 1947. Translated as *The Soul,* J. P. Rowan, St. Louis, 1949.

Quaestiones Disputatae de Malo, ed. R. M. Spiazzi, Turin, 1949. Partially translated as *On Free Choice,* A. C. Pegis, New York, 1945.

BRIEF WORKS

De Ente et Essentia, ed. L. Baur, Münster, 1933. Translated as *Being and Essence,* A. Maurer, Toronto, 1949.

In Librum Boethii de Trinitate Expositio, ed. B. Leiden, 1959. Partially translated by A. Maurer in *Division and Methods of the Sciences,* Toronto, 1953.

De Regno, ed. J. Perrier, Paris, 1949; translated as *On Kingship,* G. B. Phelan and T. Eschmann, Toronto, 1949.

De Unitate Intellectus, ed. L. W. Keeler, Rome, 1936. Translated as *The Unicity of the Intellect,* R. Brennan, St. Louis, 1946.

De Substantiis Separatis, ed. F. J. Lescoe, West Hartford, Conn., 1962. Translated as *Treatise on Separate Substances,* F. J. Lescoe, West Hartford, Conn., 1959.

De Aeternitate Mundi, ed. R. M. Spiazzi, Turin, 1954. Translated as *On the Eternity of the World,* C. Vollert, Milwaukee, 1965.

ANTHOLOGIES

Basic Writings of St. Thomas Aquinas, 2 vols., ed. A. Pegis, New York, 1945.

St. Thomas Aquinas: Philosophical Texts, Selected and translated with notes and an introduction by T. Gilby, London, 1951.

The Pocket Aquinas, ed. V. J. Bourke, New York, 1960.

St. Thomas Aquinas, Selected Writings, ed. M. C. D'Arcy, London: Everyman's Library, 1964.

Thomas Aquinas; Selected Writings, ed. Robert P. Goodwin, Indianapolis, 1965.

2. *Some Books about Aquinas in English*

Anscombe, G. E. M. and Geach, P. T. *Three Philosophers,* Oxford, 1961.

Bourke, V. J. *Aquinas' Search for Wisdom,* Milwaukee, 1965.

Chenu, M. D. *A Guide to the Study of Thomas Aquinas,* New York, 1965.

Chesterton, G. K. *St. Thomas Aquinas,* London, 1933.

Copleston, F. C. *Aquinas,* London, 1955.

Edwards, Paul, ed., *Encyclopedia of Philosophy,* London and New York, 1967, article "Thomas Aquinas, St." by V. J. Bourke.

Foster, K. *The Life of St. Thomas Aquinas,* London and Baltimore, 1959.

Garrigou-Lagrange, R. *Reality: A Synthesis of Thomistic Thought,* St. Louis, 1950.

Gilson, E. *The Christian Philosophy of St. Thomas Aquinas,* New York, 1956.

Grabmann, M. *Thomas Aquinas,* New York, 1928.

Grenet, Paul. *Thomism, an Introduction,* New York, 1967.

Henle, R. J. *St. Thomas and Platonism,* The Hague, 1956.

Jaffa, H. V. *Thomism and Aristotelianism,* Chicago, 1952.

Kenny, A. *The Five Ways,* London, 1969.

Klubertanz, G. P. *St. Thomas Aquinas on Analogy,* Chicago, 1960.

Lonergan, B. *Verbum: Word and Idea in Aquinas,* Notre Dame, 1967.

McInerny, R. M. *The Logic of Analogy, an Interpretation of St. Thomas,* The Hague, 1961.

Maritain, J. *The Angelic Doctor,* New York, 1958.

Owens, J. *St. Thomas and the Future of Metaphysics,* Milwaukee, 1957.

Pegis, A. C. *Introduction to St. Thomas Aquinas,* New York, 1965.

—— *St. Thomas and the Greeks,* Milwaukee, 1939.

Pieper, J. *Guide to Thomas Aquinas,* New York, 1962.

—— *The Silence of St. Thomas,* London, 1953.

Regis, L. *St. Thomas and Epistemology,* Milwaukee, 1946.

Rousselot, P. *The Intellectualism of St. Thomas,* New York, 1935.

Sertillanges, A. G. *St. Thomas Aquinas and his Work,* London, 1951.

Sillem, E. *Ways of Thinking about God,* London, 1961.

Weinberg, Julius R. *A Short History of Medieval Philosophy*, Princeton, 1964.

3. Periodicals

A list of articles about Aquinas in English alone would be enormously long. The following periodicals are specially devoted to the publication of articles about Aquinas and scholasticism.

Mediaeval Studies. Toronto.

Modern Schoolman. St. Louis.

New Scholasticism. Washington.

Proceedings of the American Catholic Philosophical Association. Washington.

The Thomist. Washington.

The *Bulletin Thomiste* (Le Saulchoir, Belgium) since 1921 has reported on all books and articles on Aquinas.

The standard bibliography is Mandonnet, P. and Destrez, J. *Bibliographie Thomiste*, rev. ed. M. D. Chenu, Paris, 1960. See also Bourke, V. J. *Thomistic Bibliography*, 1920–40, St. Louis, 1945.